FIGHTING TO LOSE

FIGHTING TO LOSE

HOW THE GERMAN SECRET INTELLIGENCE SERVICE
HELPED THE ALLIES WIN THE SECOND WORLD WAR

JOHN BRYDEN

DUNDURN
TORONTO

Editor: Allison Hirst
Copy-Editor: Dominic Farrell
Design: Courtney Horner
Printer: Webcom

Library and Archives Canada Cataloguing in Publication

Bryden, John, 1943-, author
          Fighting to lose : how the German secret intelligence service helped the
Allies win the Second World War / John Bryden.

Includes bibliographical references.

Issued in print and electronic formats.
ISBN 978-1-4597-1959-0

          1. World War, 1939-1945--Military intelligence--Germany. 2. World
War, 1939-1945--Secret service--Germany. 3. Intelligence service--History--
20th century. I. Title.

D810.S7B794 2014   940.54'8743   C2013-907437-6
                                                                    C2013-907438-4

1   2   3   4   5   18   17   16   15   14

We acknowledge the support of the **Canada Council for the Arts** and the **Ontario Arts Council** for our publishing program. We also acknowledge the financial support of the **Government of Canada** through the **Canada Book Fund** and **Livres Canada Books**, and the **Government of Ontario** through the **Ontario Book Publishing Tax Credit** and the **Ontario Media Development Corporation**.

Care has been taken to trace the ownership of copyright material used in this book. The author and the publisher welcome any information enabling them to rectify any references or credits in subsequent editions.

J. Kirk Howard, President

The publisher is not responsible for websites or their content unless they are owned by the publisher.

Printed and bound in Canada.

Cover design by Laura Boyle

VISIT US AT
Dundurn.com
@dundurnpress
Facebook.com/dundurnpress
Pinterest.com/dundurnpress

Dundurn	Gazelle Book Services Limited	Dundurn
3 Church Street, Suite 500	White Cross Mills	2250 Military Road
Toronto, Ontario, Canada	High Town, Lancaster, England	Tonawanda, NY
M5E 1M2	LA1 4XS	U.S.A. 14150

To Cathy:
Wife and editor-in-chief

CONTENTS

NOTE TO THE READER

Human nature does not change much over time, but politics and technology do. Books dealing with specific periods in the past often crash for the general reader if the context in which events took place is unfamiliar, or if the terminology is outdated and strange. Before beginning, the reader might like to glance through "Appendix: The Historical Context."

INTRODUCTION

In his book *Chief of Intelligence* (1951), British journalist Ian Colvin wrote that he was having lunch with a senior official in one of the ministries a few years after the Second World War and in conversation asked him how he thought British intelligence had done. The man replied with some emphasis: "Well, our intelligence was not badly equipped. As you know, we had Admiral Canaris, and that was a considerable thing."

Colvin did not know. The civil servant had made the mistake of assuming that because Colvin had been in Berlin before the war, and had sent back valuable information on the activities of those opposed to Hitler, he had been an agent of British intelligence himself. He had not been.

The official left it at that, but the incident set Colvin on a quest. He knew from his own experiences that Admiral Canaris, the wartime head of the Abwehr, the German intelligence service, had worked against Hitler. But a British agent?

"As I walked away from lunch that day it seemed that this must be the best-kept secret of the war." From then on, however, it was a brick wall with the exception of one veteran of the War Office who said: "Ah, yes, he helped us all he could." He said no more.

Colvin had no access to secret documents, especially those of the Foreign Office and War Office, much less those of MI5 and MI6 — Britain's Security

Service and Secret Intelligence Service respectively — but some of the officers close to Canaris had survived the war and he went to Germany and talked with them. Each had his own fragment of the Canaris story, and Colvin pieced together their memories. Apparently, Canaris did tip the British off to Hitler's moves against Czechoslovakia in 1938, and did foil his attempt to bring Spain into the war in 1940. He also forewarned the British of Operation Barbarossa, the 1941 invasion of Russia, and had been party to two attempts to kill Hitler.

It may have been a little too much to describe Canaris as a "British agent," Colvin concluded, but from what he was told, "his omissions in the intelligence field helped the Allies to achieve surprise and brought their certain victory mercifully closer."[1] He also found that Canaris was a passive player in the conspiracies against Hitler, rather than a principal actor.

Colvin had to rely on hearsay. Thus, the debate has gone back and forth over the ensuing decades, between those writers who portrayed Canaris as an unsung hero of the German opposition against the Nazis and those — mainly British — who have presented him as the ineffectual chief of a corrupt and inefficient secret service. By the end of the 1970s, the latter view had won out.

Documents released in Britain and the United States since the 1990s, however, combined with captured German records that have been available all along, show Canaris to have been a central figure in the German army conspiracies against Hitler and, even more remarkable, that the Abwehr under his direction had decisively intervened on the side of Germany's enemies in some of the major events of the war, most notably the 1941 Japanese surprise attack on Pearl Harbor and the 1944 Battle of Normandy.

This is much more than Colvin, or most of the contemporaries of Canaris, could ever have dreamed of.

The newly opened MI5 files are very incomplete. They have been extensively censored and "weeded," both officially and apparently surreptitiously — the damage being so enormous that the British security and intelligence services themselves may have lost sight of much of their wartime past. It can be recovered at least partially, however, by matching the newly released material to corresponding intelligence documents held abroad, and the surviving records of the Abwehr.

The situation is better in the United States, the relevant archives being those of the Federal Bureau of Investigation (FBI) and the Office for Strategic Services (OSS) — the wartime forerunner of the Central Intelligence Agency (CIA). The number of available files is enormous, for the Americans spared no expense in trying to determine how the German secret services, both army and Nazi, conducted operations. Many of the FBI/OSS files complement those of the British, and what is apparently missing on one side of the Atlantic can sometimes be found on the other.

What are consistently absent, because withheld by both, are the records that directly link the respective secret services with the wartime president, Franklin Delano Roosevelt, and the wartime British prime minister, Winston Churchill. There are no minutes of meetings or correspondence at hand between Roosevelt and William Donovan, or Churchill and Stewart Menzies, even though the OSS and MI6 chiefs reported almost daily. The Second World War can never be reasonably understood, however, without considering the effect secret intelligence had on the decisions of the four top protagonists: Churchill, Roosevelt, Hitler, and Stalin.

This book specifically addresses that challenge for the period 1939–1941. It has often meant weighing incomplete evidence and inferring conclusions rather than settling only for proof. It has also meant assuming at the outset that the secret services — British, American, and German — sometimes manipulated their own records.

The following, then, is a fresh perspective on the Second World War.

PROLOGUE

Corrupt? Inefficient? Stupid?

The FBI did not like the idea, but what could it do? Supreme meant supreme, and if the intelligence chief of the supreme commander of the Allied armies poised to invade Europe decided that the British should get first crack at interrogating captured German spies and spymasters, then that was that.

"With the understanding that G-2 [an army term for military intelligence chief] has agreed that the British shall have priority on all captured prisoners and records," the internal FBI memo lamented, "it will be seen that the British will be in a position to give the Americans only such intelligence data as they wish us to have."

It was early in January 1944. The Second World War was in its fifth year. Although the armies of Nazi Germany still occupied much of Europe, they were about to be crushed between the mainly American military machine gathering in the south of England and the Soviet colossus in the east. Barring a miracle of German secret-weapon technology, the end of the war seemed imminent.

"From our experiences in South America and ... the Ostrich source, we have seen the continual reluctance and refusal of the British to furnish us all pertinent information which we should normally have," continued the note to FBI heads of departments. "The British would be in a position to squeeze us out from the intelligence field in the Western Hemisphere; and if they are co-operating along those lines with G-2, it may result in the FBI being squeezed out of the intelligence field in the United States...."

Two years of working together against a common enemy had created an abyss of distrust between the FBI and the British secret services, MI5 and MI6.

The Anglo-American Allies were just then in the final stages of preparation for the cross-Channel invasion of German-occupied France. SHAEF, or Supreme Headquarters Allied Expeditionary Force — the command organization led by the American general (and later president) Dwight D. Eisenhower — was charged with leading the American, Canadian, and British armies being assembled in England; and if the landings were successful, the Allies expected to capture plenty of prisoners, including those from the German secret services. In anticipation of this, SHAEF G-2, British brigadier-general Kenneth Strong, had asked the FBI to supply a list of individuals the combat forces should be on the lookout for. Unfortunately, from the FBI's point of view, Strong had also agreed that such prisoners should be offered for interrogation first to the British.

"The possibility exists," the FBI memo continued, "that the British may have prompted this request on the part of G-2 and that this may be another move on the part of the British to gain as complete control as possible over the intelligence field. If the request is purely a G-2 request, to say the least it is naive...."[1]

Such bad feeling was somewhat like that of a child rebelling against its parents. The two secret services of the British — MI6, the Secret Intelligence Service, and MI5, the Security Service — tended to think that everything of value the FBI knew of counter-espionage it had learned from them, but that the FBI was not a good pupil. Unfortunately, the officers of both services had been a little too loose with their criticisms, and the FBI had caught on.

The fact was that the two British services had been in the business since the First World War, the "MI" in both standing for "military intelligence," although both had evolved into essentially civilian agencies. MI6 was responsible for covert intelligence-gathering abroad and MI5 looked after counter-espionage and counter-subversion at home.

The FBI had been essentially a police investigative organization until war broke out in Europe in 1939 and it found itself suddenly having to deal with German spies on U.S. territory. Informal co-operation with the British followed, with quite pleasant relations, until the United States entered the war at the end of 1941 after the Japanese attack on Pearl Harbor. Relations were not so rosy after that, for a variety of reasons. The Americans had too much money to spend on technology, for starters, and seemed to have a mania for arrests. The British were unnecessarily devious, and not nearly as smart as they seemed to think. By late 1944, neither side much liked the other.

The British were quick to act on General Strong's generosity. In February, they proposed that SHAEF set up a special joint agency whose particular task would be to identify and interrogate German intelligence personnel as they were captured. The so-named CI (counter-intelligence) War Room came into being in March 1945. Its steering committee was comprised of representatives from MI5 and MI6 for the British, and a British chairman, Lieutenant-Colonel T. A. "TAR" Robertson, the MI5 officer who had been directly in charge of Britain's double-agent program. The Americans were represented by individuals from U.S. Army G-2, and from X-2, the counter-intelligence division of the Office of Strategic Services,[2] the American overseas espionage agency more familiarly known as the OSS, created by presidential order in 1942.

As feared, so it happened. The FBI was excluded from this new committee. It had no grounds for protest. Its wartime mandate had been confined to the Western Hemisphere, and even though it had maintained a "European desk" in London, the counter-espionage war in Europe was not formally within the FBI's jurisdiction. Informally, however, the Bureau had tried to maintain close liaison with both MI5 and MI6, particularly where it had involved tracking and catching German agents operating in North and South America.

It did not matter. SHAEF went by the book. That meant putting the less-experienced OSS on the committee instead of the savvy FBI. The best the Bureau could do was persuade General Strong to direct that the FBI be informed when individuals on a list it provided were interrogated so the Bureau could suggest questions and receive a copy of the subsequent reports. FBI director J. Edgar Hoover himself wrote a letter outlining the topics he wanted covered.[3]

An internal memo of this period from Hoover's office — marked *not* to be shown to any of the other Allied counter-intelligence agencies — gives a good idea of the FBI's interests. It outlined what FBI personnel in Europe were to watch for as the Allied armies pressed the Germans back. Of top priority were enemy spies and their controllers, list attached. Next was any "cipher paraphernalia," such as slide rules, grilles, mechanical devices, instruction manuals, and code books. And finally, anything new on padlocks, combination locks, foreign locks, and luggage locks, with particular emphasis on "special precautionary methods added to insure against the picking of the lock when the owner is away." [4]

The War Room setup was simple enough. Based on a master list compiled by MI5, with contributions from the FBI, G-2, and the OSS, the British, American, and Canadian army units in Europe would screen prisoners of war and suspicious civilians for the particular individuals. Those so identified would first be interrogated in regional centres, then, if deemed important enough, passed on to Camp 020 in England for closer questioning.

Camp 020 was Latchmere House, a Victorian mansion near Richmond in south London that had served as a hospital in the First World War and had been converted into a high-security prison for the Second World War. Most of the spies so far captured by Britain had been interrogated there.

Camp 020 had a more formal title: the Combined Services Detailed Interrogation Centre, or CSDIC for short. The name captures the purpose. It was where suspected enemy spies were questioned in fine detail, where hidden microphones listened in on inmate conversations, where long periods of solitary confinement were used to soften up resolve. Short of using physical torture, it was a no-holds-barred institution whose sole aim was to pry secrets from those of the enemy especially enjoined to keep them.

The Americans forces fighting in Europe did as instructed. When German secret service individuals of interest were picked up during the fighting across France and into Germany, they were superficially questioned in the field and then forwarded with a preliminary report to Camp 020. A significant snag was volume. Both the German army's secret intelligence service, usually referred to simply as the Abwehr, and its Nazi security service counterpart — the Reichssicherheitshauptamt

(RSHA) — had been headquartered in Berlin, with sub-offices in many of the major cities in Germany and in the countries Germany occupied. Both also had offices in the capitals of neutral nations like Spain, Portugal, and Switzerland. One contemporary British document calculated that the wartime strength of the Abwehr in staff alone amounted to about twenty thousand individuals.[5] Add to that the personnel of the RSHA's foreign espionage and counter-espionage agencies and the number increases by about five thousand.

All this created a surfeit of plenty, especially after Germany surrendered in early May 1945. Allied army counter-intelligence officers, with MI5's list tucked under their elbows, still had to question everyone who was found to have had a connection with a German police or espionage service. Did they know this person or that person? How long? When was he last seen? Who did he report to? Who reported to him? These were the questions asked of the secretaries and chauffeurs, of the petty officials and hangers-on who had worked in the offices of the Abwehr and RSHA. For every fish caught, the Allied dragnet swept up innumerable small fry.

The immediate consequence was the overloading of Camp 020, plus the inconvenience of transporting prisoners to England. In September 1945, MI5 set up a satellite interrogation centre in the spa town of Bad Nenndorf in Germany. It became the Combined Services Detailed Interrogation Centre for the Western Europe Area or CSDIC(WEA). The Americans did likewise with a centre at Oberursel, near Frankfurt. Prisoners flowed in and reports flowed out. The total number of German security and intelligence personnel processed is unknown. The CSDIC(WEA) alone handled more than 350 up to the end of 1946. Several hundred more would have been processed at Camp 020 in London and at its other subordinate establishments. The Americans separately dealt with at least as many.[6]

These interrogation reports were generally only available to historians by chance or deliberate leakage prior to 1999, at which time they were released as part of MI5's ongoing program to transfer many of its wartime files to the Public Record Office, Britain's national archives. Similar (and sometimes the same) files became available in the United States after 1998, following the passing of the Nazi Wartime Crimes Disclosure Act, which required the public release of OSS, CIA, FBI, and army G-2 files relevant to the Holocaust. In both countries, the responsible authorities took a fairly liberal view of what files should be opened, with the result that it became possible to derive a much better insight into the secret-services war between the Western Allies and Germany.

The FBI's worry that SHAEF G-2 was giving too much opportunity to British intelligence proved well-founded. The CI War Room was conceived as a kind of clearing house for interrogation reports, each Allied intelligence service contributing those it collected in exchange for those of the others. In theory, it meant that participants would equally be able to build up a comprehensive picture of the German espionage and counter-espionage effort. It was not to be. At the February 1945 founding meeting, the British won agreement whereby the services would retain "ultimate control over their own sources of intelligence."[7] In other words, both the Americans and the British had the option of withholding information or entire reports. Given that the British were to have first choice on whom to interrogate, and be the first to receive captured Abwehr records, the Americans — G-2, the OSS, and, indirectly, the FBI — were put at an enormous disadvantage. Their understanding of the German secret services, the Abwehr and the RSHA, was in danger of only being as good as the British allowed it to be.

Trying to assess the German intelligence effort was going to be challenging in any case. The Abwehr's chief, Admiral Wilhelm Canaris — he who had taken it over in 1935, built it up under Hitler, and guided it through the war years to early 1944 — was dead, supposedly killed in an Allied air attack after his arrest, according to Ernst Kaltenbrunner, the former head of the RSHA. Some of Canaris's closest aides and confidantes and his immediate successor, Georg Hansen, were gone also, executed for their parts in the 1944 attempt to kill Hitler. The Abwehr's heads of espionage (Abteilung I) and counter-espionage (Abteilung III), Hans Pieckenbrock and Franz von Bentivegni, were prisoners of the Russians. The consequence of all this was that while most of the body, arms, and legs of the Abwehr had survived the war, its controlling minds in Berlin had not. As far as the British and American intelligence officers of the War Room knew, the Abwehr's headquarters leadership had ceased to exist.

On the other hand, most of the top leaders of the Nazi security service had been captured. The RSHA — and its Nazi-party predecessor, the Sicherheitsdienst (SD) — never did develop much of a foreign espionage operation. Before the war, they had been primarily focused on spying on Germans at home to safeguard the Nazi grip on political power and on identifying those elements of the population — Jews, Freemasons, and Communists — that should be persecuted in the interests of racial and social purity.[8] There was also an agreement, made under Hitler's eye, that the Abwehr would have sole responsibility for military and economic espionage abroad while Amt VI of the RSHA was to confine itself to gathering foreign political intelligence.

As for the second-tier senior Abwehr officers — the section heads in the various branch offices in Germany and throughout Europe — there was cogent reason for them to tell as little as possible. The Soviet Union had been given custody of the eastern third of Germany, and its secret services, the NKVD and GRU, were on the prowl for their former adversaries. Any Abwehr officer who had been in a position of responsibility risked being chloroformed and whisked away to the Russian zone if he hinted at the true extent of his knowledge. The Americans and British were receiving reports of kidnappings, which they must have assumed represented only a portion of the total.[9]

Many of the captured German intelligence officers were also looking beyond the present catastrophe. It was clear who Germany's next major adversary would be — the Soviet Union. It was in anticipation of this that the German army intelligence agency for Eastern Europe, Fremde Heere Ost, disbanded on its own, its records going into caves and its staff into hiding to await the day when Britain and the United States woke up to the fact they had defeated one enemy only to be faced with another.[10]

There was also concern that what was revealed to the British or Americans might get back to the Soviets. In the middle of the war, in a tour-de-force of counter-espionage, the Abwehr had discovered and rooted out a ring of Soviet-controlled spies that had penetrated the German army and foreign service at the highest levels. Dubbed the "Red Orchestra," these spies were mainly German idealists of good backgrounds who had been seduced by the noble promises of communism. It was only logical that senior Abwehr officers, aware of the Red Orchestra, would surmise that the Soviets had cultivated individuals of similar sentiment inside the British and American secret establishments. This fear was justified, as later events were to prove.

Possible war crime charges were a worry too. The Allies had advertised loudly and widely their intention to bring the perpetrators of the Second World War to justice. The Nuremberg War Crime Trials, which the Americans vigorously supported, advanced the principle that political and military leaders should be held accountable for atrocities committed in their names. The torture and execution of prisoners, the extermination of the Jews — these were crimes against humanity, and declaring that one was only "obeying orders" or that what was done was only done "by the leader's decree" was to be neither justification nor acceptable defence. The trouble was, even officers of the Abwehr who had been under the strictest orders to fight a fair war could not be sure what the Allies would deem a crime. Until the definition of war crime was sorted out, senior Abwehr officers had to be cautious on certain topics.[11]

Last, and most important, was the desire to protect operational techniques for the sake of the new German secret services that would inevitably be restarted as the country rebuilt. If the British and Americans apparently did not realize that some of their double agents were deliberately planted on them, why tell them? If Allied deception schemes had been allowed to go ahead in order to deceive the deceivers, why reveal it? The tricks of counter-intelligence are the most precious articles in a secret service's tool kit.

The job of a good interrogator, however, is to get information out of a person no matter how reluctant he might be to reveal it. Theoretically, the British were the most practised at this art. For them, the struggle with Germany began in September 1939, more than two years before the Americans got involved. When war was declared, MI5 had to deal with known Nazi sympathizers at home and foreign nationals who might be tempted to spy. Next came thousands of refugees — up to 150,000 of them — when Germany overran Western Europe in 1940. All ought to be screened. At the same time, there was a flurry of enemy agents dropped by parachute or brought in by boat as vanguard to Operation Sealion, Hitler's aborted cross-Channel attack. And there was also a modest but steady stream of miscellaneous minor spies and suspects taken off boats or arrested in the colonies. It was entirely logical that SHAEF G-2 should defer to British expertise and give Camp 020 in London and its subsidiaries first pickings among German intelligence service prisoners.

Unfortunately, Camp 020 was run from the start by a man who was more bully than brains. During the First World War, MI5 was teamed up with the Special Branch of Scotland Yard, and it was the latter, led by the redoubtable Sir Basil Thomson, that did the interrogations of espionage suspects. This entirely successful arrangement was abandoned prior to the Second World War in favour of MI5 doing everything itself. For the first year of the war, this meant that the interrogation of refugees and suspect persons was done ad hoc by MI5 officers who were sometimes recent recruits with minimal police or secret service experience.[12] Lieutenant-Colonel R.W.G. Stephens, later the commandant of Camp 020, was one such person.

Born in Egypt in 1900 to British parents, Stephens was educated in England from the age of twelve, first at Dulwich College and then at the Royal Military Academy, Woolwich. He served in the Indian Army for a time before returning to England in 1933; he then knocked about in odd jobs until joining MI5 in 1939. His name was put forward by his former commander in India, Sir William Birdwood (who failed famously at Gallipoli in 1915), in conformity with the practice of personal referrals by which the British secret services then normally acquired recruits. Indian Army veterans were well-represented in British intelligence, so Stephens's lack of police experience did not stand in his way. He did know something about courts martial, however, for he had helped write a book on the subject.

By complaining to higher authority in mid-1940 about the lack of proper facilities to question detainees, Stephens appears to have contributed to MI5's decision to set up an institution dedicated to hard-case interrogations. Latchmere House fitted the purpose because it was easily converted to a high-security prison and stood isolated in an open space called Ham Common in Richmond, a southern suburb of London. "Ham" became how staff informally referred to it. Stephens was made commandant.

In 1946, Stephens produced a memoir entitled "A Digest of Ham" as his contribution to the series of after-action reports that MI5 chief David Petrie had ordered be prepared. The idea was for each department to sketch out its wartime experiences; these would be used as the basis for an in-house history of MI5 from 1908 to 1945. Stephens's memoir was not finished in time, so an earlier Camp 020 report was used. It is too bad; it would have been interesting to see whether MI5's official historian still would have condoned Stephens's technique of "apparent severity" if he had had a chance to read in detail how he treated his prisoners.[13]

According to Stephens, a good interrogator must begin with "an implacable hatred of the enemy" and "above all a relentless determination to break down the spy." These attitudes translated into a routine procedure for first-time prisoners at Camp 020 that is best described in Stephens's own words:

> A board of officers is appointed. The atmosphere is that of a General Court Martial.
>
> One officer interrogates. In no circumstances whatever may he be interrupted....
>
> The prisoner is marched in and remains standing to attention throughout the proceedings. No liberties, no interruptions, no gesticulations. He speaks when he is spoken to. He answers the questions; no more, no less.
>
> Studious politeness, the courtesy of a chair, the friendliness of a cigarette, these things bring familiarity and confidence in a spy. Figuratively, a spy in war should be at the point of a bayonet....
>
> What should be the attitude of the interrogator? The bitter uncompromising approach is as effective as any. And as with a man, so with a woman — no quarter.... Pressure must be maintained.... The requirement is a driving attack in the nature of a blast which will scare a man out of his wits....[14]

This was not the way Scotland Yard did it in those days — probably ever. Stephens developed his own techniques as he went along, devising novel forms of intimidation that included all-night questioning and the threat of solitary confinement until insanity or death. He appears to have been making up his own version of interrogations to the "third degree," romanticized in the detective novels of the 1920s and '30s.[15]

By way of contrast, it is instructive to read the views of someone who actually was experienced. Lieutenant-Colonel Oreste Pinto was one of the security experts loaned to the British by the Dutch government-in-exile to help screen the huge influx of refugees that followed the 1940 German victories in Europe. He had trained and served in the First World War with the Deuxième Bureau, the French equivalent of MI5. He became the chief examiner at the London Reception Centre for refugees. Here is how he did it:

- The first interrogation of any arrival should be not so much an interrogation as the taking of a complete statement in detail by the examiner;
- This interrogation should in all cases be conducted with complete courtesy; at no time should the examiner express by word or mien, any doubt, surprise, or any other human emotion, except perhaps admiration;
- Obvious lying or bragging should be encouraged, not squashed. Contradictions should not be pointed out….;
- The more doubtful or suspicious a story is, the more the examiner should appear to accept it without hesitation. No questions or remarks of any kind whatsoever should be made by the examiner which might put the examinee on his guard and lead him to realize his story is disbelieved.[16]

The advantage of this soft approach, Pinto explained in his postwar book *Spycatcher* (1952), was that if the suspects were first put at ease it was easier to discern the likely innocent from the possibly guilty. The second interview was when to move in for the kill.

The idea behind both techniques was ultimately to "break" the prisoner, to get him or her to tell everything and sign a confession. The British judicial system was still functioning normally, so even spies caught red-handed were entitled to a fair trial and the courts still adhered to the principle of presumption of innocence. Consequently, the most egregious of spies could tell a good story and get off. One of the best tactics was for an accused to claim he or she only agreed to work for the Germans in order to escape to England. Or he was blackmailed into doing it. Or she didn't know the suitcase contained a wireless set. And so on. English juries were not in a hurry to send people to the hangman; consequently, even the best evidence was unpredictable as to result. A confession guaranteed conviction.[17]

Physical torture was not used because Camp 020 and the London Reception Centre were held to be civilian facilities and the Home Office strictly forbade it. The vicious mental methods Stephens used, however, were not much better. When the satellite interrogation centre opened in Bad Nenndorf in 1945, Stephens transferred there as commandant. There he gave his vicious streak full expression, and prisoners, many of them former Abwehr officers with German army commissions, were cruelly abused. Other British officers, appalled by what was going on, complained, and the subsequent investigation by Scotland Yard led to the start of court martial proceedings against Stephens. The charges against him included,

- Providing insufficient clothing;
- Intimidation by the guards;
- Mental and physical torture during interrogations;
- Solitary confinement for long periods with no exercise;
- Commitment to punishment cells, not for any offence, but because the interrogators were not satisfied with their answers....

Stephens was cleared, and it is not surprising. Had he been prosecuted, the harsh light of inquiry would have turned on what he might have being doing during the war. There had been little oversight. "The Home Secretary and his nominees took an ever-decreasing interest," Stephens wrote, "and visits from officials became increasingly rare with time."

During the last year of the war, Camp 020's busiest time, it was not inspected at all. The investigation by Scotland Yard, however, revealed that there probably had been torture. For example, there had been a "cage" that Stephens had put out of bounds to visits by the Red Cross. It was hushed up and the court martial charges dropped.[18]

Stephens also comes across as a bigot. In "A Digest of Ham," he frequently, perhaps always, notes when a suspect had a connection with someone Jewish. MI5's counter-intelligence chief, Guy Liddell, recounts in his diary a particularly ugly scene at a staff party in 1944 where a "fairly tight" Stephens made rude remarks to Victor Rothschild, MI5's staff scientist. Rothschild was the younger man and others had to intervene to prevent a "standup fight." The slur had to do with Rothschild not being a soldier but wearing an officer's uniform. Instant officers in wartime Britain were a common phenomenon; however, Rothschild was one of the most prominent Jewish names in England.[19]

Other ethnic groups and nationalities were not spared Stephens's disparaging generalities in his description of Camp 020. These attitudes appear to have sprung partially from a lack of general knowledge of the world beyond India and England. Any Canadian would be bemused to read Stephens's explanation of how the German spy Werner Janowski gave himself away after being landed from a submarine in mid-winter on the coast in the Gulf of St. Lawrence. Stephens wrote, "He attracted immediate attention by ordering a bath in his hotel, for in those northern regions no one bathed at that time of year." Janowski, who was as tough a customer as any spy could be, told his Camp 020 interrogators this silly fiction. Stephens believed it.

Stephens occasionally found something to admire in a prisoner. He was impressed by the 1941 parachute spy Josef Jakobs, who never admitted anything and told the British firing squad to shoot straight; he also relished the deviousness of the British safecracker Eddie Chapman, who claimed he had fooled the Germans into releasing him from prison in Jersey (one of the Channel Islands) by offering to spy against England. Ernst Kaltenbrunner, head of the Nazi security service, also came in for praise. Stephens acknowledged that the man was a "genius of evil," but he liked the way he stuck to his story ("everybody below me did it") and showed no fear. Kaltenbrunner was tried at Nuremberg, found guilty of multiple mass murders, and hanged. Stephens wrote that he was a "worthy" enemy and regretted that he did not get the opportunity to interrogate him.

The character and competence of Stephens is important historically. Any assessment of German intelligence efforts during the Second World War must rely heavily, now as then, on the quality of the interrogations Stephens oversaw and how truthfully the results of those interrogations were conveyed to other branches of the British secret services and through the War Room to the Americans. For starters, was Stephens able to persuade the senior Abwehr officers who passed through Camp 020 and Bad Nenndorf to talk freely about their accomplishments and failures? The Abwehr chiefs of station at Hamburg, Brussels, Bremen, Paris, Oslo, and so on were the real spymasters. Did Stephens get them to talk candidly?

More than three-quarters of the spies Stephens describes in "A Digest of Ham" were minor. Up until D-Day, the June 6, 1944, invasion of France, they comprised mainly neutral-nation suspects taken off ships or arrested at Gibraltar or Trinidad, the easily captured parachute spies of 1940, and a surprisingly high number of individuals who had turned themselves in and offered to be double agents. Many were poorly trained, ill-equipped, and many of their assignments were advertised beforehand by intercepted Abwehr wireless chat.[20] This was the human material that Stephens scorned and on which he practised his "uncompromising" tactics.

A hint of the very different kind of prisoners that were to come occurred in early 1944 when a real Abwehr officer arrived at Camp 020. Otto Mayer had been captured in an ambush by Communist partisans in Yugoslavia, and in a gesture of good will for the help they were then getting from the British, the Communists turned him over. Although in uniform and entitled to be treated as a prisoner of war, he was sent to Camp 020. Stephens gave him the works, but to no avail. Stephens wrote, "… the root trouble from an investigation point of view, the fact that he was a German patriot, remained. He was courageous enough to be indifferent to his fate."

After "months of interrogation," Mayer still gave away nothing.[21]

Stephens's methods were not suited to men of Mayer's calibre. They had the courage of their convictions and were honour-bound as German army officers. Many had been successful businessmen between the wars and they were generally mature, experienced, well-educated, and intelligent. Having only psychological pressure as a weapon, Stephens found himself dealing with Abwehr officers who were perfectly capable of facing him down. Rather than admit to failure, however, he was inclined to put reluctance down to having nothing worthwhile to tell.

Friedrich Rudolf was a close personal friend of Abwehr chief Admiral Canaris and headed up the Abwehr presence in France. Some of the fiercest and most desperate espionage and counter-espionage battles between the British and German secret services took place under his watch. In 1942, the following message from Abwehrleitstelle Frankreich to Berlin was intercepted and deciphered by the British:

> Detailed report regarding capture between 23rd and 28
> March of 13 secret transmitters working for the English

Intelligence Service and 18 agents (including 8 W/T operators). 38 enemy transmitters have been rendered harmless and there are now only 3 enemy transmitters still working in the Occupied Territory. *ALST* has at its disposal 3 W/T connections with the English Intelligence Service.[22]

The last sentence means that Abwehr headquarters in France had "turned" three captured British wireless operators and were using them as double agents to transmit German-controlled messages back to the British. Nevertheless, all Rudolf could remember of that period was that a woman agent named Katze had been captured by *Funkspiel* ("radio game"), but she had revealed nothing of value. The only thing true about this statement was the name of the German double agent — Mathilde Carré, alias LA CHAT, alias KATZE.

While the report on Rudolf does not indicate who interrogated him, Stephens would surely have been involved given that Rudolf was a very senior Abwehr officer. In any case, Stephens approved the finding that "the prisoner is co-operative, but the infm [information] obtained from him is fragmentary and vague" because he had "devoted himself mainly to social duties ... keeping himself in the picture only in a very general manner." And further: "Domestic worries appear to have affected his memory and robbed him of the power to concentrate."[23]

Either Rudolf was putting on an act, or he had been questioned only superficially. There is reason to suspect the latter. The first report on him was extremely sketchy, only four pages, with CSDIC(WEA) then asking the CI-War Room for a "show of interest" or the case would be closed. The OSS promptly replied that it would like Rudolf to be asked about the July 20 plot to kill Hitler, about the Stockholm spy Karl-Heinz Kramer, and about the Abwehr black-market organization "Otto" that operated in Paris. The immediate CSDIC(WEA) response was dismissive and the final report on Rudolf makes no mention of these entirely legitimate questions.[24]

In "A Digest of Ham," Stephens shows many signs of being partisan, of not wanting to disclose Abwehr successes that could embarrass MI5 or MI6. In contrast, he is almost gleeful in noting that the interrogation of Colonel Hermann Giskes revealed in fine detail how Abwehr counter-intelligence in Holland trounced the wartime British secret-service upstart, Special Operations Executive (SOE).

When France, Holland, Belgium, and Denmark fell to the Germans in 1940, Prime Minister Winston Churchill proposed "setting Europe ablaze" by splitting off MI6's sabotage division as a self-standing agency that would concentrate on sending agents into German-occupied Europe to organize sabotage and resistance cells. This was SOE, disliked generally in MI6 because sabotage incidents made intelligence-gathering harder since they put the Germans on their guard. Over a period of twenty months, Giskes captured every one of SOE's agents as they landed by boat or airplane in Holland, and played back their captured radios, asking for and receiving nearly two hundred parachute drops of weapons and sabotage material.[25] "Through and through, he riddled the Allied espionage organizations in that country," Stephens wrote, "and many indeed were the SOE agents he successfully turned and played back...."

This praise, however, was to have limited circulation. The Giskes interrogation report was to be handled "with a certain discretion as to publication and distribution." When Giskes was sent back to Germany from Latchmere House, he spent several months at Bad Nenndorf under "an enforced vow of silence." This was undoubtedly Stephens's code for some kind of isolation.

Trying to suppress discovery of this British catastrophe was never going to succeed. Giskes could not be kept at Bad Nenndorf forever. Three years after being set free, his story was published in Germany as *Spione uberspielen Spione* (1949). An English-language edition, *London Calling North Pole* (1953), soon followed. Until then, the British officers who had been in charge of SOE had basked in some of the postwar victory glow. No longer. Former SOE agents who had lost comrades to the German concentration camps and firing squads suddenly realized the incompetence they had noted in SOE during the war had been pervasive. They began to speak out. To make matters worse, in 1953 a former SOE agent published a memoir, *Inside North Pole*, recounting how he had been captured by Giskes's team, saw that the whole SOE effort in Holland was compromised, made a daring escape from prison, struggled for five months through occupied Belgium and France to get to Spain, Gibraltar, and back to England — only to be disbelieved by British intelligence and arrested as a spy.[26]

Stephens had first view of all of this. The Camp 020 interrogation of Hugo Bleicher — arguably the most adroit counter-intelligence agent of the war — is another sorry tale of SOE initiatives emasculated by the Germans, this time in France. Like Giskes in Holland, Bleicher and his colleagues, posing as French Resistance fighters, helpfully manned the lights that guided agent-laden British aircraft in, collected parachute canisters filled with weapons, and arranged that the weapons be stored in safe places where they could be accidentally destroyed. Whenever SOE-led Resistance groups got a little too strong, Bleicher arranged for their culling.[27]

These SOE disasters are candidly stated in Bleicher's Camp 020 interrogation report. However, Bleicher was also the key player in the breakup of the Interallie spy ring set up in France in late 1941 by refugee Polish soldiers under Roman Garby-Czerniawski. He did this by seducing Czerniawski's mistress, Mathilde Carré, alias LA CHAT. When all were arrested, he had Carré play back the network's wireless set to London, learning thereby that the British intended some kind of strike against the French port of St. Nazaire. Berlin was alerted. The attack turned out to be a commando raid aimed at knocking out the port's battleship-sized dry dock. It was a qualified success only because the forewarned defenders were not expecting an explosives-laden destroyer to lead the charge. The British commandos themselves were wiped out.[28]

This was as perfect an example as one could wish of a successful "double-cross" — the British term for continuing the transmissions of a captured spy in order to obtain intelligence from the enemy secret service. The German terms were *Funkspiel*, literally "radio game," or, more generally, *Gegenspiel*, literally "contrary game" but equivalent in meaning to "double-cross." Bleicher was drawing British blood by the method when MI5's famed "Double-Cross System" was still in its infancy. His British secret service victim, however, was not SOE, nor MI6. It was, in fact, MI5.[29]

The Camp 020 report on Bleicher as received by the Americans through the CI-War Room makes no mention of St. Nazaire. It merely acknowledges that the Interallie radio was taken over and messages were exchanged with London. This, combined with the failure to pursue Rudolf on the same subject, is an example of the Camp 020 output being manipulated. If a prisoner seemed likely to have information that exposed MI5 mistakes, Stephens was not anxious to extract it, nor likely to report it.

Conversely, Stephens was quick to accept what he wanted to hear. In the one paragraph he devoted to the interrogation of Major Nikolaus Ritter, the Abt I Luft (air espionage) officer who had been spymaster to most of the double agents run by MI5 during the war, Stephens wrote without blush that "in all frankness he admitted his failure as an intelligence officer, but adduced it [was] in part to the superiority of the British Security Service."[30] Ritter did disclose, however, that in mid-1941 he had figured out that two of his most important agents, Arthur Owens and Wulf Schmidt (A-3504 and A-3725), had been reporting back by wireless under British control. He did not inform Berlin of this, he added — hardly likely for a man hand-picked by Canaris and who had the right to speak directly to him.[31]

Ritter operated from Ast Hamburg, the largest Abwehr espionage centre outside Berlin, and his chief, Herbert Wichmann, also landed up at Camp 020. Of him, Stephens noted:

> Wichmann was willing enough to talk, but the trouble was that he had no memory. His many friends at Ham confirmed it; his few enemies admitted it. Under patient handling such facts as he could be made to remember were gradually drawn from him.
>
> His espionage activities against Britain had not been markedly successful: "All attempts to spy on England," he said, "were disappointing; in spite of much effort, nothing of value was ever achieved."[32]

The trouble with this statement is that Wulf Schmidt had been dispatched to England as a parachute spy in 1940 and reported back to Hamburg by wireless until early 1945. If all the spies Ast Hamburg sent to England were failures, then that must have included Schmidt. That means the hundreds of messages TATE (Schmidt) sent were not believed. It would seem that the spy Stephens described as "the most remarkable double agent of the war" had not fooled the Germans after all. Stephens, however, was impervious to this logic.

Stephens did not want to hear of any failures by MI5, and was ready to ensure that the files did not disclose them. At its most extreme, this involved withholding embarrassing interrogation reports. The interrogation report on Major Ritter, for example, is missing from his file and there is no indication in what remains that he was ever asked a single question about Arthur Owens, a.k.a. SNOW, the first wireless spy MI5 supposedly doubled back on the Germans and the one most credited for the much-vaunted wartime victory of British intelligence over German intelligence. Indeed, all but one of the spies who were "turned" to become double agents between September 1939 and December 1940 were known by Stephens to have been dispatched by Major Ritter — SNOW, CHARLIE, RAINBOW, DRAGONFLY, GANDER, SUMMER, and TATE. There is nothing to indicate Ritter was asked about any of them.

Fortunately, Stephens could not control the interrogations done by the various American intelligence agencies. They went about their work with equanimity, and a genuine desire to discover where the Abwehr did succeed. The quality of the postwar interrogations in the National Archives in Washington is as day is to night compared to what survives in Britain's National Archives (the PRO).

While Stephens is surely not solely to blame, the evidence is every-where that he became obsessed with demonstrating that British intelligence had overwhelmingly dominated its Abwehr adversary, because of British superiority on the one hand and German incompetence on the other. It was probably Stephens who wrote the article in the September 1945 issue of *Interim: British Army of the Rhine Intelligence Review* that concluded, "Results of interrogations have shown that the view which has been held during the war is justified; the German Intelligence Service was almost uniformly corrupt, inefficient and stupid."[33]

The writer attributed these deficiencies to "the most naive conceptions of British and American policy and method" and to the fact that "except in the most rare cases, the GIS had to recruit its agents not from idealists, but from the fearful, the avaricious and the opportunists."

He was absolutely wrong on all counts. What it meant was he could not imagine how someone like Major Ritter, surely destined for some role or other in the secret intelligence services of postwar Germany, would be quite happy to see British intelligence continue to deceive itself.

PART I

A SPYMASTER'S INCREDIBLE STORY
1945

It was three months after Germany's surrender and still there had been little progress in getting a handle on how decisions were made at the top of Germany's secret intelligence service, the Abwehr. Its chief, Admiral Wilhelm Canaris, was dead, although how he had died was still uncertain, and his top aides were either still missing or out of reach as prisoners of the Russians.

Enter General Erwin von Lahousen. The U.S. Army intelligence officers who first interrogated him must have been delighted. Here before them — tall, slightly stooped, aristocratic in bearing, every inch an officer — was the Abwehr's head of Abteilung II (Sabotage). It was he who had been charged with sowing confusion behind enemy lines. It was he who knew what explosions on what roads and railways, in what factories and military installations, aboard what ships, were to be credited, not to dive-bombers and submarines, but to the invisible army of saboteurs he must have led. Little was known. Eight saboteurs landed by submarine in the United States in 1943 had been captured, tried, and executed, but how many more had entered unnoticed? What damage had they done that had been assigned to other causes? This was the man who knew.

What he said was totally unexpected.

Lahousen revealed that he had actually discouraged sabotage against the Americans and British. Instead, he had been a member of an inner circle around Admiral Canaris whose members conspired against Hitler and did everything they could to undermine the Nazis. The story he told was incredible.[1]

Lahousen was Austrian. He came from an aristocratic family with a long tradition of military service. At the time of the *Anschluss* — Germany's annexation of Austria in early 1938 — he was a forty-one-year-old senior intelligence officer with the Austrian General Staff, specializing in Czechoslovakia. To his surprise, shortly after the takeover he was invited to join the German intelligence service, known universally by its short title, the Abwehr. This did not make much sense, since he was an Austrian patriot, without much sympathy for the Nazis, and the Abwehr was Germany's most secret of secret organizations. He was soon to learn, however, that it was precisely because of his dislike of the Nazis that he had been sought out.[2]

Admiral Wilhelm Canaris did not fit the picture of a secret service chief. On arriving at Abwehr headquarters in Berlin, in one of the several stately homes that had been converted to army offices on tree-lined Tirpitzuferstrasse, Lahousen faced a small man, standing five-foot-four, with white hair and bright blue eyes, dressed in the dark blue uniform of a naval officer.

The office at 74–76 Tirpitzuferstrasse was modest — simple furniture, a small safe, a sofa, and an iron bedstead so that its occupant could take a nap in the afternoon, perhaps, or for sleeping over in times of crisis. Instead of the usual portrait of Hitler on the wall, there was a signed picture of the Spanish dictator General Francisco Franco, a Japanese woodblock print, and a picture of Colonel Walter Nicolai, Germany's spymaster of the First World War. A map of the world over the sofa completed the decor.[3] The rest of the room was plain, almost tawdry, yet here Lahousen was, at the command centre of what he knew to be the largest and most sophisticated secret intelligence organization in Europe, and possibly the world.

At that very first interview — as Lahousen told his American interrogators — the Abwehr chief took him deeply into his confidence. Czechoslovakia was next on Hitler's list, Canaris said. The Nazi leader was going to use the excuse of the Sudeten Germans to invade. As the

Western powers and the Soviet Union would never stand for it, it would mean a European war. Lahousen was being drafted to help dampen Hitler's enthusiasm for the venture. The Austrian officer was suddenly faced with the proposition that Germany's chief of secret intelligence was planning to act against his own government.[4]

Canaris explained his strategy. He had in mind that the Abwehr should overvalue the intelligence reports coming out of Czechoslovakia. The strength of its fortifications and army, the will to resist of its people, the determination of its government — all this was to be deliberately exaggerated. The likelihood of British, French, or Russian intervention was to be emphasized. Lahousen's role was to endorse the reports as an intelligence specialist on Czechoslovakia. This would give them tremendous credibility and might put Hitler off his plan.

Lahousen was taken aback. Canaris was sharing a mortally dangerous scheme with a stranger and non-German. Only someone with great confidence in his own judgment would dare such a thing. If the Nazis ever got hint of what Canaris was saying, he was a dead man.

They shook hands. Lahousen would do it. Thereafter a bond of absolute trust sprang up between the two men. Lahousen stuck by Canaris for the next five years, through plot after plot against the Nazis, until Canaris's arrest and execution separated them forever.

General Lahousen's opening remarks must have been riveting to his American listeners. And there was more, much more.

First of all, Canaris's plan was all for nought. Hitler won what he wanted from Czechoslovakia without invasion. The Western powers, England and France, caved in to his demands with the infamous Munich Agreement of 1938 whereby the western edge of Czechoslovakia was shaved off and attached to Germany without the consent of the Czechs. The British prime minister, Neville Chamberlain, came home from his meeting with Hitler waving a piece of paper and declaring "Peace in Our Time." The generals opposed to Hitler were poised to oust him the moment he gave the invasion order. However, Hitler won what he wanted without having to give it and the rebellion melted away.

Hitler's success over Czechoslovakia emboldened him and he next made territorial demands of Poland. Lahousen recalled Canaris's very words at the time:

> I am convinced that the other [G]reat Powers will not be caught this time by the "political sleight-of-hand tricks of this pathological liar." War means a catastrophe far greater and beyond comprehension for Germany and all mankind [should there] be the victory of this Nazi system. This must be prevented under all circumstances.[5]

When Hitler invaded Poland in September 1939, Britain and France did indeed stand their ground and the general war that Canaris feared followed. It made him all the more determined to topple Hitler.

What Canaris next had in mind, now that the war had actually started, was a coup d'état. On formally naming Lahousen the new chief of Abwehr II (Sabotage), he assigned him his share of the enterprise. He was to devise a plan for seizing key members of Hitler's entourage and of the Nazi security service. He was also to be prepared to take over the broadcast radio stations. Canaris was to look after forming a special Abwehr commando unit to carry out any gunplay. The necessary small arms and explosives were already on hand, hidden next door at 80 Tirpitzuferstrasse, headquarters of OKW/Chi, the German army's cipher branch.[6]

What went wrong, Lahousen explained, was that success came too early to the commandos. Later to gain fame as the Brandenburg Regiment, the recruits were mainly Germans who had grown up outside the fatherland and who were fluent in the languages of their adopted countries. High standards of resourcefulness and physical fitness were demanded. Their first great test came during the 1940 invasion of Belgium and Holland when small bands of Brandenburgers donned enemy uniforms and by ruse seized key bridges and other objectives in advance of the German armies. They were so proud of their small role in Germany's victorious conquest of France and the Low Countries, Lahousen explained, that if they had been given any cause even to suspect their commanders of disloyalty, "they would have shot them out of hand."

And so it went. Lahousen was invited to put his thoughts on paper and it made gripping reading. He said all of the Abwehr's division heads — Oster, Pieckenbrock, Bentivegni, Bürkner, and himself — were party to the conspiracy to undermine the Nazis. He told of two bomb plots against Hitler before the disastrous attempt of July 20, 1944; of repeated efforts to persuade senior army generals to arrest Hitler; of alerting Germany's Axis partners and neutral countries to Germany's military intentions; of only pretending to undertake missions; of secretly working with resistance movements in Austria and Czechoslovakia.

One of the most significant items was the revelation that in 1940 Canaris had personally blocked Hitler's effort to seize Gibraltar, the British fortress colony overlooking the narrow western entrance to the Mediterranean. This was decisive. The sweeping victories of Erwin Rommel in the Western Desert were recent memory. So, too, was his final expulsion from North Africa in 1943 due primarily to his not being able to keep his lines of supply from Italy open. They were straddled by Malta with its air bases, and the sea between Italy and Tunisia became a graveyard of Italian freighters. Malta had been supplied and sustained by British convoys from Gibraltar. Had that not been possible, Rommel would have reached Cairo. No one in Lahousen's audience would have thought otherwise.

Lahousen told how Canaris was sent to Spain several times by Hitler because he had made many friends there during the First World War, and because of the help he had given the dictator, Franco, during the Spanish Civil War. Instead of promoting Hitler's proposal that Spain join the war, or at least allow German troops to cross Spanish territory, Canaris spoke against it. He needed to be persuasive because Spain had long lusted for return of "The Rock," which the British had occupied in the eighteenth century and used as a naval base ever since. The outcome of his talks with the Spanish foreign minister, General Gomez Jordana, was never in doubt. As Lahousen explained:

> The report to the Foreign Office (through Amt Ausland, OKW) which I made up according to a directive from CANARIS, before his meeting with JORDANA went approximately as follows:

"Spain will continue to support, as heretofore, the Axis powers, but retains her status as "Non-belligerent," and will defend herself against *every* attack on her territory, even, if the case should arise, against Germany."

JORDANA actually expressed himself far more carefully and hesitantly in the attendant conversation when it did take place ...[7]

In other words, on this occasion Canaris replied for Spain before meeting with its government. As the Spanish were notoriously savage guerrilla fighters and the civil war had just concluded, Hitler dropped the initiative.

The "secret tasks" assigned to Lahousen as head of Abwehr II also included

- *Passive* conduct of Abwehr II work with external show of great activity;
- Failure to carry out enterprises whose execution can be avoided in any way;
- Extensive alleviations of the hardships created by the brutalities of the Nazi regime .

Examples of the first two included the supplying of false reports on vessels sabotaged in the Mediterranean, the covert disobeying of an order to sabotage the French fleet at Toulon, contriving not to carry out Hitler's order to murder the French general, Henri Giraud, and tipping off the Italian secret service to a Nazi plan to kill the Pope. The Abwehr II War Diary, Lahousen said, was largely composed of "puffery" and information faked by his trusted aide, the former German journalist Karl-Heinz Abshagen.

As to the third task, Lahousen's American audience must have been surprised at the extent of the Abwehr's aid to the victims of the Nazis, especially Jews. Canaris himself sheltered Hans von Dohnányi, a distinguished German jurist dismissed from the civil service because of his part-Jewish parentage, putting him to work in the office of his chief of staff, Hans Oster. These two, in turn, Lahousen said, used the Abwehr as cover to help Jews get out of Germany, sending them abroad as spies and then fabricating reports from them. Jewish "V men" were also used by Canaris in "counter-activity" exploits. This must really have raised the eyebrows of Lahousen's American listeners. They would have had fresh in their minds the horrors of the recently discovered death camps, grim witnesses to Nazi extermination policies. Yet here they were, being told that the Abwehr — the German army's secret service — had absorbed what Jews it could in order to save them.[8]

Lahousen revealed that the conspiracy against the Nazi dictator extended well beyond the Abwehr. He named as involved several high-ranking army officers, including Field Marshal Erwin von Witzleben, the first commander in the West after the fall of France, as well as two chiefs of the general staff, General Ludwig Beck and General Franz Halder. There were others outside the army, as well: some in the Ministry of Justice, the Reich Foreign Office, and even a few senior officials in the Nazi security services.

Canaris's secret channels of influence extended nearly everywhere in the army, and especially to the military intelligence officers attached to the armies and army groups, and to Fremde Heere, the military intelligence-collating agency of the German army high command. For a time, from January 1941 to November 1942, he even had a fellow-conspirator in the top job at Fremde Heere, the former military attaché to Japan, General Gerhard Matzky, whom Lahousen described as being in the inner circle of Canaris's "counter-activity."[9]

Another item Lahousen disclosed must have been disappointing to British intelligence, especially to MI5's Lieutenant Colonel T.A. "TAR" Robertson, who chaired the Allied committee that oversaw the collection and distribution of espionage-related interrogation reports.[10] In describing how Canaris wanted quietly to discourage sabotage against Britain and the United States, Lahousen told of replacing an efficient Abt II officer in Paris with an ineffective one who never did anything other than send one agent code-named FRITZSCHEN to England. Lahousen said he was convinced from the start that the man was a British double agent, and so he was: FRITZSCHEN was the British double agent ZIGZAG, the English felon and con man, Eddie Chapman. In January, 1943, MI5 staged an elaborate deception, complete with phony photographs and phony reports in the press, aimed at convincing the Germans that FRITZSCHEN had successfully set off an explosion at an aircraft factory. Lahousen revealed he had paid no attention.[11]

Lahousen also said he only sent a handful of sabotage agents to England and Ireland, and only in token response to Hitler's orders that the Abwehr do so. It was intended that they fail.

"It would seem that our views on the causes of the Abwehr's ineffectiveness and inertia should be revised," an American noted in sending along the Lahousen reports to Colonel Robertson, adding that the descriptions of the Abwehr working against Hitler were backed up by two other interrogations.[12] The words must have made the Englishman wince. Robertson had been in charge of MI5's double-agent operations during the war. Lahousen's remarks about not running saboteurs indicated the captured saboteurs he had "turned" into double agents had been phonies in the first place. Indeed, all those enemy agents landed with sabotage assignments in 1940–41 must not have been genuine.

This was not something the architect of MI5's already celebrated "double-cross system" would have wanted to hear. It suggested his first and star double agent, Arthur Owens, had really been working for the other side.

Most spectacular of all, Lahousen said he believed Canaris had been personally in touch with the Allied intelligence services, and specifically with MI6, through intermediaries in Switzerland. And he named names.

> Frau SZYMANSKA — Wife of the last Polish attaché to Berlin. A very wise, also politically highly educated woman, whom CANARIS looked up regularly in Switzerland, and whose family in Warsaw was protected and especially looked after by the Abwehr. Her husband, Colonel or General SZYMANSKA, fought at that time with MONTGOMERY's Army in Africa.
>
> I have various indications that she was one of the most active supporters of CANARIS' "counteractivity" just as, in general, I, and other like-minded persons, calculated that CANARIS maintained direct contacts via Switzerland to the Allied intelligence services.
>
> Countess THEOTOKIS — a very clever Greek, Jewish or half-Jewish, perfectly clear in her political

attitude, was along with her family supported strongly by CANARIS. She lived at that time 1941–42 in Corfu. CANARIS met her often in Rome or Venice. I believe she was connected with the British IS (Intelligence Service). The KO-Leiter Italy, Oberst HEIFFERICH, should know more about her.[13]

The Americans already had a dossier on the countess. A June 1944 OSS report on the Abwehr in Italy forwarded to the FBI mentioned that she had "received great assistance from the Germans in connection with her frequent trips from Greece to Italy, and from Italy to Switzerland and Germany. It was thought that the head of the German service, Admiral CANARIS, was particularly interested in her."[14]

Anyone who read that report and then the one on Lahousen would know why.

Lahousen's story about Canaris and his campaign to undermine Hitler's Reich was stamped *SECRET* and filed away for the next half century. Some of what he disclosed came out at the Nuremberg Trials, where he was a star witness against the leading Nazis accused of war crimes, but his testimony then was dependent upon the questions asked of him. Consequently, only a limited picture of Canaris as an opponent of the Nazis emerged, leading most historians to conclude that he supported those who plotted against Hitler, but rarely got involved himself. Lahousen's 1945 interrogation portrays him as the prime mover.[15]

HITLER'S ENEMY WITHIN
1933–1939

Wilhelm Canaris was born in 1887 in a village in the Ruhr near Dortmond. His father was an engineer and both parents were decidedly middle class — well-educated, moderately patriotic, and moderately religious. Normally a son in such a family would go into business but the young Canaris joined the navy and the beginning of the First World War found him serving in the South Atlantic as a junior officer on the cruiser *Dresden*.

It was a dramatic voyage for the twenty-seven-year-old. The *Dresden* took part in the 1914 Battle of Coronel, where a German squadron under Admiral Graf von Spee sank two British heavy cruisers, HMS *Monmouth* and HMS *Good Hope*, only to be ambushed by a superior British force a few months later, with the loss of all of Graf von Spee's ships save the *Dresden*. She was eventually cornered in a Chilean harbour and scuttled, her crew going into internment. Canaris, however, showed his resourcefulness by learning Spanish, disguising himself as a Chilean, and making his way back to Germany. He served out the rest of the war first in Spain, as a spymaster and agent recruiter, and then as a successful U-boat commander. Few could match his war record for bravery, cunning, versatility, and determination.

Canaris continued in the navy after the war, visited Japan in 1925, and then was named to the naval staff of the Defence Ministry, which involved him in secret shipbuilding and rearmament talks in Spain and Greece. In 1929 he got to know Count Theotokis, and visited him several times on the island of Corfu. He returned to a sea command aboard the battleship *Schlesian*, and in 1934 was appointed chief of the Abwehr, then still a modest-sized organization attached to the War Ministry. His reputation must have been a key factor in his getting the job; he was seen as astute, a good administrator, and a subtle manager of men. He was also known to be politically savvy and brave. This last quality was especially needed. He was being put at the focus of three of the most dangerous men of the century. Lahousen called them the three H's: Hitler, Himmler, and Heydrich.

To appreciate the delicate game Admiral Canaris was to play over the next decade, the story of Hitler's murder of Ernst Röhm must be told.

Röhm was the head of the Sturmabteilung — usually simply the SA — a civilian army of malcontents, sociopaths, and labour radicals born from the street protests that became a daily feature of German life following the 1929 stock market crash. Germany under the Weimar Republic was then one of the most liberal democracies in Europe, but its elected politicians were blamed for the soaring unemployment and rampant inflation occasioned by the worldwide Depression. While still just a fringe political party, the Nazis organized the violent side of the protests along military lines and by 1931 the "Brownshirts" — the name given them for the quasi-uniforms the SA took to wearing — numbered some four hundred thousand, four times greater than the actual German army.

When Hitler finally won power, Röhm made the mistake of bragging publicly that he was the Nazi leader with the real clout, and that the new German chancellor would do well to pay him close attention. That Hitler most certainly did.

By all accounts, Röhm was an ugly character. He was a huge hulk of a man, encased in layers of flesh, with a red face and puffy cheeks divided by a domino moustache teetering on his upper lip. He was given to creature excesses — sex, food, alcohol, preferably all at once — and reports of his binges, sometimes involving hundreds of his SA followers, were graphic and gruesome. Such behaviour was perhaps not surprising for someone who ordered phalanxes of like-minded louts into innocent neighbourhoods to smash windows, kick in doors, and randomly beat up people.

They were, as one commentator of the period noted, "beefsteak Nazis" — brown on the outside but red inside. They were the German "Bolsheviks" of the Depression and Hitler harnessed their communist sentiments as a means to his political ends. He promised them a "revolution" that would transfer power from the corporate elites and bosses to the workers. The word *Nazi*, indeed, is a contraction of the first word of the party's full German title, Nationalsozialistische Deutsche Arbeiterpartei — in English, National Socialist German Workers' Party. Röhm expected Hitler to live up to this name.[1]

(It is one of the great fictions of the post–Second World War era that the Nazis were right-wing fanatics. In fact, they were zealous left-wingers imbued with a strong sense of nationalism.)

In the beginning, Hitler needed Röhm. His strategy was to take over government legally by manipulating the social instability fuelled by his followers. Elections in Germany were by proportional representation, leading to chronic minority governments that were short-lived and indecisive. The constitution stipulated that the Reich chancellor (prime minister) could rule by decree in a national emergency if given this power by the Reich president — at that time the eighty-five-year-old First World War–hero Field Marshal Paul von Hindenburg.[2] The role of the SA was to create so much violence and chaos in the streets throughout Germany that all sectors of society — big business, small business, landowners, merchants, churches — would long for the stability Hitler promised should the Nazi party win government, and be amenable to one-man rule when it did.

In the lead-up to the election of 1933, Röhm served Hitler well. There were window breakings, street fires, and beatings in abundance. The theme song of the Brownshirts as they marched by torchlight ran like this:

> *String up the old monarchists on lamp-posts*
> *Let dogs bite at their bodies 'til they fall*
> *Hang black pigs in all the synagogues*
> *Let the churches have it with grenades.*[3]

A year later, after the Nazis won a majority in the Reichstag and a desperate and confused Hindenberg gave Hitler emergency powers, such sentiments were no longer needed, and not wanted. A stable one-leader, one-party Germany required the co-operation of the corporate and social establishments and Hitler immediately set about building these alliances. Röhm, however, publicly insisted that Hitler fulfil Nazi promises to nationalize the big industries and break up the holdings of large landowners. "Honour the Revolution," he proclaimed. Röhm had to go.

Getting rid of the commander of one's own private army is a tricky business, but Hitler had an enthusiastic helper. The minister in charge of Germany's police, Heinrich Himmler, former chicken farmer turned top Nazi, also had assembled a private army for Hitler, the Schutzstaffel, better known simply as the SS. It numbered two hundred thousand in 1933, half that of the SA, but its members were a cut above, drawn to it for reason of personal prestige, rather than politics. The designer-created black uniforms of the SS were smart, gave a sense of elitism, and were popular with the girls.

Himmler's army called for good, manly specimens, and an SS man needed only to look in the mirror to see confirmation of Himmler's quack theories of Aryan superiority: blond, high cheeks, strong chin and noble nose, set off by a peaked hat with glamorous badges, and a black tunic with silver highlights. Good looks, at least in the eyes of the beholder, masked every other inferiority, and for this gift of self-esteem the SS man offered Himmler his absolute loyalty. If Himmler and Röhm had been driven to open battle it would have been a bloody affair.

Hitler opted for murder, with Himmler supplying the killers. In the early morning of June 30, 1934, Hitler arrived at a hotel in the spa town of Bad-Wiesee at the head of a truck convoy of SS troops. Röhm was there with some of his key subordinates for a weekend of partying. Hitler burst in on him in his bedroom, yelling curses as pistol shots sounded in the room next door. Röhm's deputy and the chauffeur he was sleeping with were killed in their blankets. The rest of the SA in the hotel, including Röhm, were seized, manacled, loaded into the trucks and taken away. Simultaneously, elsewhere in the country, SS troops rounded up other leaders of the SA.

Röhm himself was flown to Berlin where he was taken to the fortress of Lichterfelde, stood against the courtyard wall, and shot by firing squad. The shootings continued all that Saturday and much of Sunday. People in the neighbourhood could hear the repeated volleys, accompanied by muffled cries of "Heil Hitler! It is the will of the Führer!" *Bam! Bam!* It was said that the wall in the courtyard remained stained with blood for months.[4]

It became a general purge. The Nazis used the opportunity to kill former political rivals and prominent critics of the new regime. The prisons filled. Hitler proudly called it the "Night of the Long Knives" and people understood it to mean that no longer was anyone free from arbitrary arrest, and execution without trial. This was the new Germany, the stable Germany everyone had longed for, and it turned a blood-streaked face to the world.

Historians have sometimes criticized the German army for not intervening. Hitler called it putting down a revolt, but plainly it was a blood purge. The army, however, was but a feeble leftover of the Treaty of Versailles at the time, and there was no guarantee that it could win against the SS. Its soldiers were scattered in depots across the country, and it must be admitted that there was no certainty as to how they might view the recent political developments. Would they even obey their commanders? Calling out the army would not have worked.

Instead, the army leadership chose to co-operate. Hitler had destroyed the SA, which had been a threat to the army as well as to Hitler, so that was a good thing. Hitler promised to build up the armed forces, and that was good also. When Hitler demanded that army officers swear an oath of fealty directly to him, rather than to the constitution, there really was no alternative. A "no" would mean dismissal and that gained nothing. On the other hand, when Hitler proposed arming and organizing the SS along army lines, that was going too far; the SS might someday supplant the army. The first line of defence for those senior officers who saw the peril was to retain control of the army's secret intelligence service: the Abwehr.[5]

There was urgent need to act. After Hitler consolidated his power by eliminating Röhm and destroying the SA, Himmler tried to secure control of all major police and security organizations, including the Abwehr. An internal political fight followed, which pitted Himmler against the army's chief of the general staff and the navy's grand admiral, Erich Raeder. One solution, as they saw it, was to put in a new Abwehr chief, one who had the kind of war record that would impress the Nazis, and who possessed the personal skills to work successfully with them while retaining his personal and professional qualities as a soldier. They proposed Canaris.[6]

It was a highly calculated choice. The primary pressure for bringing the Abwehr under Nazi control was coming from Reinhard Heydrich, the brilliant thirty-year-old chief of the Nazi party's security service, the Sicherheitsdienst, or SD.

The SD had been set up under Himmler to spy out political opponents of the Nazis and Heydrich quickly achieved a reputation for ruthlessness, sharpened by his part in Hitler's bloody purges. Canaris, however, had been the thirty-six-year-old commander of the training ship *Berlin* when Heydrich was on board as an impressionable nineteen-year-old cadet. The younger man naturally still deferred to his elder, even though politically he was his superior. Canaris was to manage their relationship with great skill.[7]

Hitler made few mistakes in these early days. He seems to have had an uncanny political intuition, and despite the riot and mayhem fomented by the SA, his advance to absolute power was by legal means, not force. He made promises — full employment, respect for the churches, peaceful rearmament, the redistribution of wealth, a dignified treatment of Jews, and so on — everything the masses of people wanted to hear, and he promoted his messages by radio broadcasts, advertising, and orchestrated rallies. He was received enthusiastically, garnered the votes he needed over several elections, and took over. Then, out of reach of the ballot box, he broke his promises.[8]

He made one crucial error, however. He permitted a secret service to exist and flourish outside Nazi control. He decreed that the Abwehr would look after all foreign intelligence-gathering related to the economic and military war-making capacity of potential enemy states, while Heydrich's Sicherheitsdienst would be responsible for homeland intelligence-gathering aimed at ferreting out critics of the regime, with the secondary assignment of collecting foreign *political* intelligence. Canaris ensured that this demarcation of responsibilities was strictly adhered to.

Thus it came to be that Canaris, from the start a potential opponent of the regime, stood at Hitler's side. As Germany's senior secret intelligence chief he reported to him personally. The "Night of the Long Knives," however, had made him into a secret enemy. As an early member of Canaris's inner circle of conspirators told American interrogators:

> For a long time the Abwehr had been the center of gravity for all anti-Hitler activities within the armed forces. This feeling of rebellion existed for many years before the war; it actually began in 1934, when Admiral Canaris was put in charge of the Abwehr.
>
> The events of June 30, 1934, proved to Canaris that Hitler was and would remain a confirmed revolutionary to whom the exploitation of trust, decency, and truth was a mere instrument of policy. Hitler was ready to deny today what he swore yesterday, provided that his plans and aims were thus served.[9]

And so began a ten-year campaign of intrigue and treachery against the regime, at all times requiring infinite finesse. Against such opponents, the smallest misstep could be fatal.[10]

First and foremost, it was necessary to obtain and retain Hitler's confidence. That required putting together the best possible intelligence service. There was no time to learn on the job, so Canaris did the next best thing. He picked up a book. His First World War predecessor, Colonel Walter Nicolai, actually wrote two books recounting his experiences, *Nachrichtendienst* (1920) and *Geheime Mächte* (1925), and one only need read the second of those two to see that there was good reason why Canaris had Nicolai's picture on his wall; it was the blueprint for the intelligence service he put together in time for the Second World War.

Geheime Mächte, oddly enough, was first published in English as *The German Secret Service* (London, 1924), so the Abwehr's British adversaries always had at hand Canaris's espionage "bible," as it were. It would turn out, however, that few in British intelligence would actually read it.[11]

Nicolai was secret service chief from 1914 to 18 and although he felt his organization did well enough, he also found great fault. The trouble, he wrote, was the German government did not appreciate that gathering intelligence should go far beyond just meeting the needs of the armies in the field. He complained that Germany's leadership disastrously failed to demand the economic and political information on its enemies it needed for strategic decision-making

Propaganda was also a potent weapon the Germans failed to exploit. The smarter British, he wrote, succeeded in labelling German soldiers as barbarians — the "Huns" — which generated images of rape and pillage, alienating people in the neutral countries and stiffening the resolve of the enemy's armed forces. Worse still, the enemy, well-informed of political events and opinion in Germany, sowed dissent on the home front, causing Germany to succumb in 1918 to mutiny at home while still undefeated on the battlefield.

The propaganda criticism was not lost on Hitler, especially in terms of ensuring German popular support for the Nazi regime. One of the first things he did on coming to power in 1933 was to put one of his most loyal followers, Joseph Goebbels, in charge of manipulating public opinion through the then still novel mass media outlets, radio and film. He was hugely successful, selling ultra-nationalistic ideas at home and abroad with great skill. The huge rallies of the Nazi faithful and the broadcasts of Hitler's speeches deeply impressed ordinary Germans, listening to radio in their parlours or watching the newsreels at their local cinemas. Indeed, Nazi propaganda pervaded German life, promoting everywhere the idea that Germans were special, that they were superior to other nationalities, and that destiny called upon them to take a dominant place in Europe and the world. Patriotism blossomed.

Then there were the Jews. Goebbels fostered hatred of them as a means to Hitler's political ends. It is an ancient trick, based on the principle that hate unites, and is especially effective when people are suffering.[12] The collapse of the stock market in 1929 triggered the Great Depression and no country was hit so hard as Germany, already staggering under the burden of First World War reparations. People lost their savings, lost their jobs, saw the factories idled, and looked for someone to blame. Jews were an ideal target because they traced back to cultural roots decidedly different from other Germans, making them seem outsiders. This, combined with Nazi claims that real Germans were descendants of some vague Nordic race — Aryans — created the proper chemistry of hate, which was easily kept simmering because Jews seemed to be successful in every social niche: business, science, the arts, cinema, the civil service, and so on. They also had much representation at the bottom of the social and economic ladders, but it served the Nazis to ignore that.

Hitler's systematic attack against the Jews, it should be added, had nothing to do with Christianity. Hitler was against all sects of Christianity. He was a champion of a totally secular society, alike in principle to what the Communists were then imposing in the Soviet Union.

Having blamed Jews for just about every national ill on the road to power, Hitler had to act against them when he achieved it. Starting immediately, in 1933, the Nazi government launched public campaigns for the boycott of Jewish businesses and products. This rather unfocused attack was followed by legislation in 1935 that defined a "Jew" by ancestry — three or more grandparents of the Jewish faith, or, for a *Mischling* ("half-breed" in English; "Métis" in French), one or two Jewish grandparents — and imposed special restrictions on all so deemed a Jew. The actual religion of the individual was not a factor; under the Nuremberg Laws a person could be a practising Catholic and still be deemed a Jew, with all the consequential restrictions on marriage, voting, and the holding of public office.

Even more ominous, statutory Jews were required by law to identify themselves on census returns, thus putting the names and addresses of every one of them on record with the government. This greatly facilitated the roundups and mass exterminations that came a few years later.[13]

Public persecution and humiliation of the Jews notched up to a deadly level on November 10, 1938, with *Kristallnacht* (Crystal Night), so-named because of the Nazi-orchestrated rampage that saw the windows of 7,500 Jewish-owned stores smashed and four hundred synagogues torched. Ninety-one Jews were killed, marking the beginning of the murders that would eventually run into the millions. Ordinary Germans saw little of the actual violence, but what they did see the next day was swaths of sidewalk and roadway flashing and sparkling in the sun, below gaping store fronts where once there had been glass. Perhaps some felt shivers of premonition; broken glass everywhere would be a common sight when Germany's cities were mass-bombed just a handful of years further on.

Canaris apparently tried to help mitigate the violence of *Kristallnacht*, for afterward he received the private thanks of Jewish community leaders. From then on, throughout the war, he secretly helped what Jews he could.[14]

In the meantime, Canaris's best tactic against the Nazi regime was to build up as effective a secret service as he could. He took his cues from Nicolai's books and reorganized the Abwehr so that one of its main tasks was to build up as complete a picture as possible of the economic and social fabric of potential enemy states, collecting the information covertly and from open sources. He staffed the Abwehr's offices with mature and worldly veterans of the First World War who had gone into business and had acquired skills in management and administration. He also tapped into the intelligence-gathering potential of business and commercial enterprises with operations abroad, and systematically recruited informants from among the sailors and officers manning German merchant vessels calling at foreign ports.

Indeed, Abwehr files captured toward the end of the war show that a huge pre-war effort had been made to collect economic, social, and industrial information, especially on the United States. Colonel Nicolai had observed that Germany had been badly surprised by the tremendous war-making capacity of the Americans when they entered the war in 1917, and it resulted in crucial setbacks on the battlefield. Although the Nazi leadership hoped that the Americans would not be drawn into a second European conflict, Canaris ensured that Germany would be well-informed if they were. Reports by Abwehr spies in the United States ran into the thousands by late 1941.[15]

Canaris read Nicolai's books cover to cover. He responded to his complaint that collecting intelligence at the fighting front had been ineffective by creating the Aufklarungkommandos, special mobile units of military intelligence personnel that were to follow immediately behind the advancing troops and search for documents left behind when enemy positions were overrun. He met Nicolai's suggestion that full advantage be taken of advances in aircraft and wireless development by doing clandestine aerial surveys of England's south coast and Germany's border areas with France and the Low Countries, developing portable wireless transmitters, and generally modernizing the paraphernalia of espionage.[16] Hitler supported all these measures; Canaris needed spare no expense.

By 1939, the Abwehr was the most advanced and effective secret intelligence service in the world.

THE GERMAN INTELLIGENCE SERVICE

In contrast to the British, where the various secret services were fragmented into separate organizations, each answering to the appropriate civilian or military department, the Abwehr dealt with most of the major security and intelligence tasks. It answered solely to the army high command — Oberkommando des Heeres or OKH — before the war, and then, after it started, to Hitler's headquarters, the armed forces high command — Oberkommando der Wehrmacht or OKW. It consisted of three main departments: Abteilung I: Espionage; Abteilung II: Sabotage; and Abteilung III: Counter-espionage.

Smaller departments had specialized responsibilities — Abteilung Wirtschaft focused on economic intelligence, for example. These names were almost always abbreviated by the Germans themselves as Abt I, Abt II, Abt III, Abt Wi — or, if the reference was to the headquarters department in Berlin, Abwehr I, Abwehr II, Abwehr III, and so on.

The Abw/Ausland (Foreign Affairs) department collected open intelligence, largely obtained from the Abwehr-appointed military attachés posted to the German embassies abroad. The Zentrale — Abwehr Z — was the administration, finance, and records department, the latter an archive containing the names and personal files of thousands of spies, informers, enemy agents, and persons of interest. The equivalent in Britain was the Central Registry administered by MI5 but serving the same function for both the Security Service and the Secret Intelligence Service (MI6). Zentrale was headed by Hans Oster, a dedicated foe of the Nazi regime.

Abw I was subdivided into Eins Heer (IH: Army Espionage), Eins Marine (IM: Naval Espionage) and Eins Luft (IL: Air Espionage).

Abw III also had a number of subdivisions, the most important being IIIF (Counter-espionage agents bureau). Its main task was to compromise and destroy enemy clandestine organizations by infiltrating them with its own spies and informers. The ultimate prize was to get an IIIF agent into the enemy's intelligence service.[17]

The main departments were usually mirrored in the Abwehr's sub-offices, called Abwehrstellen or "Asts" for short. Thus there was an Ast Hamburg, an Ast Wilhelmshaven, an Ast Weisbaden, and so on, each usually with IH, IM, and IL desks as well as an IIIF section. The pattern was repeated as Nazi Germany conquered its neighbours, with the establishment of Ast Brussels,

Ast Dijon, Ast Bordeaux, and so forth. Abwehr offices in neutral countries were called Kriegsorganisationen, or KOs for short, the two most important being KO Portugal in Lisbon and KO Spain in Madrid. These Abwehr stations worked under the cover of the German embassies.

Each Ast or KO was encouraged to recruit and run its own secret agents, coordination being effected by keeping Berlin informed. Thus, Ast Hamburg and Ast Cologne both could have spies in Britain, France, or wherever. This had the advantage of insulating agent networks one from the other, so that if one was penetrated or blown, the others would not be. Also, since individuals with the right temperament and skills for espionage were hard to come by, the chances of finding persons suitable for specific tasks, in terms of language ability, background, and motivation were immensely increased if every Abwehr office and its sub-offices — called Nebenstellen, or "Nests" — were on the lookout. The really successful spies, the many that the British and the Americans did not catch, were obtained in this way.

Ast Hamburg and its satellite, Nest Bremen, were the two principal overseas intelligence-gathering centres, for both were great ports with a large number of companies engaged in shipping and overseas commercial enterprises. Businessmen travelling abroad were persuaded to informally share their observations with Abwehr representatives on their return, while seamen were recruited to act more directly by taking pictures, collecting postcards, and gathering information and documents on the harbours and railways at their ports of call. They were also useful as couriers for Abwehr spies resident in the target countries.[18]

Nest Bremen ended the war with some four hundred secret agents in its card index. It was the only Abwehr office whose files were recovered at the end of the war, so, counting the others, the number of spies and informers on file at Zentrale in Berlin must have run well into the thousands.[19]

THE NAZI SECRET SERVICES

The Nazi security and intelligence services were also fairly simply structured. Before the war they comprised: (1) the security service (Sicherheitsdienst, or SD) under Heydrich; and, separately under Himmler, (2) the security police (or Sipo); (3) the criminal investigation police (Krimminelpolizei, or Kripo); and (4) the Secret State Police (Geheimestaatspolizei, notoriously better known by its abbreviation, the Gestapo). The first was set up originally to gather intelligence on the Nazi party's political rivals and expanded as time went on to surveillance of just about every aspect of German national life. The second and third had the normal police tasks, while the fourth was an organization deliberately designed for abduction, torture, and murder.

The Gestapo's primary mandate was to arrest and eliminate the "internal enemies" identified by the SD. These typically included politicians, Jews, Freemasons, church leaders, and generally anyone critical of the regime. As time went on, the Gestapo increasingly acted on its own in defining and liquidating "undesirables." When dealing with German citizens, there was some token deference to an individual's legal rights, but in the occupied countries, no such rights were recognized.

The SD and the three police services were consolidated under Heydrich at the start of the war as the Reichssicherheitshauptamt (RSHA), the Reich Security Head Office. It became a bureaucracy like any other government department, except that its mandate was the wholesale suppression of human rights, and murder.

The functions of the RSHA were grouped into numbered offices. Thus Amt IIIB was engaged in promulgating "public health," which in Nazi parlance meant compulsory abortions on female slave-labourers, denying education to children in conquered territories, and the "resettlement" of ethnic minorities. Amt IIIC was charged with controlling education and undermining organized religion. It named university professors and manipulated scientific research while promoting neo-pagan festivals and cultural events as alternatives to Christian festivals. Amt IV was the Gestapo, with Amt IVA being responsible for suppressing every form of political dissent, Amt IVB for the persecution of Jews and other minorities, and Amt IVC for the administration of concentration camps. Amt VI collected foreign political intelligence.[20]

What made all this madness possible was Amt I, the personnel office. It undertook to find the right people for the various departments and tasks: psychopaths and sadists for the Gestapo and for the murder squads of the Einsatzkommandos in Russia, bigots and criminals for Amt III, and others with a wide range of character flaws and emotional defects that could be put to good use bullying their fellow human beings. As one RSHA insider described it, the model Gestapo man was "without any moral scruple, even without any conception of moral values, cunning to the point of brilliance, with sadistic leanings and definite pathological tendencies."[21] It was Amt I's task to obtain such "raw material."

At the top of this pyramid of terror was Heydrich, now thirty-five and now with the title "Chief of the Security Police and SD." He was unusual for an ardent Nazi in that he was an intellectual, cultured, and a gifted musician, playing the violin with skill and sensitivity. Yet with a pen stroke he routinely ordered the deportation, even the murder, of hundreds, thousands, or millions of individuals. He was one of the prime architects of the Holocaust, the systematic extermination of European Jews that formally began in 1942. It was as though his mind and his conscience were separated by a pane of frosted glass; what he did not see, he could not feel, and what he could not feel, he did not care about.

There were normal human feelings in Heydrich, however. Canaris quickly befriended him and even bought a house in the same street when he and his family moved to Berlin in 1935. The two families socialized, playing croquet in the afternoons and having dinners together. Heydrich often expressed his suspicion of Canaris to his subordinates, but he could never shake the deference felt by a former cadet for his former commander.[22]

Canaris was Germany's spymaster-in-chief. His fundamental business was deceit. He well appreciated the ancient axiom: The most dangerous enemy is he who poses as your friend. He was just such a friend to Heydrich.

Canaris was to use this, and use it well.

THE BRITISH SECRET SERVICES

Like old wine cellared too long, Britain's secret services, MI5 and MI6, had become somewhat musty over the economically parched years of the 1920s and '30s. There were no fresh brooms to sweep their porches of entrenched ideas firmly rooted in past experiences.

The double agent, for instance, was still a novel concept to Britain's handful of counter-espionage officers in the late 1930s. During the First

World War, it was government policy that spies captured in the United Kingdom were invariably to be either imprisoned or executed; there was little incentive for Vernon Kell's Security Service — first MO5g and then MI5 — to experiment with having them continue to report back to their spymasters as if still free, and so be used to feed the enemy disinformation. Twenty years later, little had changed.

In 1938, however, following talks with the French Deuxième Bureau, MI5 decided to give it a try. A Major Sinclair was assigned the task, but progress was modest, given that before the Second World War the resources for finding spies in the first place were meagre. Britain in peacetime largely respected the customary rules for freedom of movement and individual privacy.[23]

The predecessor of the Secret Intelligence Service, on the other hand — Mansfield Cumming's MI1(c) and then afterward MI6 — had used double agents extensively during the First World War, especially against the German secret service operating in France and neutral Holland.[24] MI6 continued to use them in the interwar years against a new adversary, the intelligence services of Soviet Russia operating in the countries of Western Europe. MI6 officers were posted as passport control officers (PCOs) in the embassies abroad, where they screened for possible spies using the simple but ingenious principle that it would be necessary for all foreigners heading for British territory to check in first with British passport control.

Not much is known of the codes and ciphers used by the PCOs and their sub-agents during the 1930s, but apparently they were not of a very high order. For the most part, intelligence collected from spies in foreign lands could be sent back to England by diplomatic bag or mailed, and it was assumed that other countries did the same. As for MI5, it relegated "ciphers" to its female support staff, so it can be safely assumed that when the war began in 1939, MI5 officers were largely ignorant on the subject.[25]

MI6 had had an advantage. Unlike the United States, which dismantled its wartime code- and cipher-breaking agency in the late 1920s, Britain's Foreign Office saw to it that the Admiralty's similar and spectacularly successful "Room 40," and the code-breaking unit of the War Office, MI1(b), were retained with their original staffs largely intact. Reorganized as the Government Code & Cipher School — a cover implying only oversight of government ciphers — its real mission was peacetime espionage, the primary target being the intercepted enciphered telegrams of foreign diplomats. This properly put its twenty-five cryptographers under MI6 and its chief (after 1923), Admiral Hugh Sinclair.[26]

British intelligence — the term encompassing all government organizations with an active or potential role in foreign intelligence gathering — extended its reach to all international communications. By 1939, through government carrot-and-stick policies toward private corporations, all but a handful of the world's undersea telegraph cables passed at some point through British or Commonwealth territory. It was the same with the international mails. Most letters posted from one continent to another had to go through a British choke point. This enabled MI6 to have almost anyone's overseas letter or telegram intercepted and looked at. It was a remarkable achievement.[27]

MI5, of course, could have letters and cables intercepted at home, but, with the onset of war, its requirements took firm second place to those of MI6 and the intelligence departments of the armed forces. MC1 (Military Censorship 1) was under the War Office and headquartered along with MC4 (Telegraph Censorship) in the former Wormwood Scrubs Prison along with the MI5's archive and library, the Registry. The chief military censor was rebuked at the beginning of 1940 for MC1 spending too much effort examining letters and telegrams for security reasons rather than for intelligence gathering.[28] The fact was, MI5 was the weak sister of Britain's secret services. From the 1917 Russian Revolution on, it had focused mainly on domestic labour discontent, first in the armament industries during the war, and then, afterward, more broadly in the working classes. The Bolsheviks in Russia had seized estates, destroyed the nobility, and had executed the British king's cousin, Czar Nicolas II. Visions of similar phalanxes of grimy workers spilling out of the industrial ghettos of England armed with shovels and coal rakes haunted the Establishment in Britain. This led Vernon Kell, MI5's director from its pre–First World War beginnings, to sideline the task of countering foreign espionage in favour of deploying most of his resources in the 1920s and '30s against communist subversion in Britain's labour movement.[29]

Indeed, even in the mid-1930s, when Nazi Germany and fascist Italy became ever more clearly threats to Britain's interests, MI5's response was anti-subversion rather than counter-espionage, the principal effort being to infiltrate homegrown German- and Italian-leaning fascist organizations. Up to the outbreak of war, only one officer, Colonel W.E. Hinchley-Cooke, was working full-time on German counter-espionage, while Italy did not even rate attention. "There was a natural tendency not to take the military threat from Italy very seriously," noted one MI5 officer looking back at those early days.[30]

The tools MI5's two dozen or so officers had to work with were basic: a plainclothes team of six to shadow suspects; Home Office warrants (HOWs) giving permission to open mail and listen in on telephone conversations; paid and unpaid informers; and a huge collection of files on individuals who had come to notice, generally for something they had done or said that was "Bolshi." This latter was the Registry, and accounted for eighty of the 103 mainly female, mainly clerical staff who backed up the officers who led the various sections. It kept thousands of names and the "person files" (PFs) that went with them. It served as memory bank to both MI5 and MI6.[31]

MI5 did get a chance to move forward with the times. In mid-1938, with tensions mounting over Hitler's threats to Czechoslovakia, Lieutenant-Colonel Adrian Simpson was appointed adviser to MI5 on matters to do with wireless interception. He had been chief of MI1(b), the code- and cipher-breaking agency of the army (the War Office) during the previous war, and a senior executive with the Marconi Telegraph Company since.[32] Advances in technology had made the wireless transmitter a practical and available alternative to the mails for spies reporting to their home countries, and Simpson proposed that MI5 set up a wireless listening section capable of detecting their transmissions. It was to consist of fixed stations and mobile units to close in locally.

MI5 rejected the idea, however, being firmly of the view that German agents would only be using the mails or couriers to send in their reports. The matter was turned back to the War Office, which responded by creating MI1(g), a new military intelligence section consisting of a veteran First World War signals officer and two or three staff who were given space in Wormwood Scrubs along with MI5 and the Telegraph Censorship Department. There they received reports from three fixed Post Office wireless receiving stations with direction-finding capability and twenty-seven "volunteer interceptors" — amateur radio operators scattered across the country. MI5's role was to make the appropriate inquiries when suspicious transmissions were located, and to call in the police where warranted.[33] This was the responsibility of B3, a one-man section of MI5 that also looked after reports of suspicious lights and carrier-pigeon sightings.

In contrast, when prodded by the Foreign Office, MI6 undertook to develop its own secret wireless service. The task was given in 1938 to a former First World War signals officer, Captain Richard Gambier-Parry, whose first priority was to develop quick and secure communications for key diplomatic posts abroad. He began by recruiting experienced wireless operators from the merchant marine. He put them through additional training with Scotland Yard's wireless section and outfitted them with the best available sending and receiving sets, mostly of American manufacture. He had operators in the embassies in Prague, Paris, and The Hague in time to wireless back to London the reaction in those capitals to Prime Minister Neville Chamberlain's deal with Hitler to carve up Czechoslovakia.[34]

The different ways in which MI5 and MI6 reacted to suggestions regarding wireless would turn out to be a fair indication of the mentalities of the two services on the eve of war.

PART II

THAT "STUPID LITTLE MAN"

September 1939–April 1940

Arthur Owens was a weasel. No doubt about it. The forty-year-old Welsh-man with Canadian citizenship elicited instant dislike on first encounters. He was bony-faced, scrawny, and small, with nicotine-stained fingers and transparent, irregular, mismatched ears. "A typical Welsh underfed Cardiff type," the police description concluded.[1]

British intelligence was reminded that Owens was not so savoury by the arrival at Scotland Yard of Mrs. Owens in mid-August 1939, there to denounce her husband as a genuine German agent. Yes, she told her interviewers, she knew all about him working for the British while pretending to spy for the Germans, except, she said, he really was spying for the Germans. Now, according to his wife, he had gone off to Hamburg again, this time with a girlfriend, but no, that was not why she had decided to report him. He had been trying to get their son into his spy ring, and when she protested, he had threatened to shoot her. So here she was, doing her duty by disclosing that he was now in Germany with the most recent RAF code book.[2]

Everything Mrs. Owens said was true. MI6 had originally acquired Owens as a secret agent in 1936. He had first presented himself to Naval Intelligence Division of the British Admiralty as an electrical engineer who often visited Germany and who might be able to bring back the occasional tidbit of military interest. The navy sent him along to MI6, which took him up on the offer.

All seemed well for some months, until a letter from Owens to a known German secret service cover address was intercepted. It was written in open code and appeared to be talking about "toothpaste" (torpedoes) and "shaving cream" (submarines). A Major Vivian of MI6 discussed it earnestly with his superiors and it was thought that perhaps Owens was playing the Germans along and that he would reveal all shortly.[3] Six months later he did.

Owens claimed that one of his informants in Germany, a man named Pieper,[4] had turned out to be working for the German secret intelligence service (the Abwehr) and had proposed that he do so too. After several cloak-and-dagger meetings, he agreed, figuring it would enable him to better help the British by reporting what was asked of him. The Germans, he assured his listeners, only wanted him to work as a "straight" spy; there was no thought of using him as a double agent.

Owens, of course, was offering to be a double agent for the British, and while MI6 officially turned him down, it used him in that capacity anyway. For the next two years, he was allowed to collect information for the Germans so long as he occasionally reported his activities and contacts to Scotland Yard's counter-intelligence division, Special Branch. His letters continued to be intercepted, but they never contained anything of importance.[5]

In January 1939, Owens reported that he had received a transmitter from the Germans. It had been deposited for him in a left-luggage locker at Victoria Station in London, and he brought it in to Scotland Yard, where it was examined. It was given back to him; however, his intercepted letters indicated that he could not get it to work. It was probably disabled at MI5's request, for this was the Security Service's first "concrete" indication that Germany intended to have its spies communicate by wireless, and it was not set up to handle the eventuality.[6]

Nothing much happened for the next six months. Owens continued to report occasionally to Special Branch and his correspondence continued to be monitored, but nothing harmful was found. Much later, however, it was discovered that the Germans had given him a second cover address and that Owens's son had used it to send them sketch maps of the aerodromes at Biggin Hill and Kenley. Owens could have been secretly using this channel, too.[7]

Mrs. Owens then made her appearance at Scotland Yard. Among other things, she indicated that her husband really did have a working transmitter and that he drove out into the countryside to use it. She said his secret cipher was based on the word *congratulations*, each letter being assigned a number. He had since disposed of the transmitter, she added, and the last time she saw him, he had been drinking heavily, depressed by the growing certainty of war. He was thinking of coming over to the British once and for all.[8]

Arrangements were made to arrest Owens whenever he showed up again.

On September 4, the day after Britain declared war over Germany's invasion of Poland, Owens telephoned his usual contact at Scotland Yard to say that he wanted to cut his ties with the Germans. They arranged to meet at Waterloo Station, but this time there was no going off for a private chat. Instead of one inspector, there were two policemen and a bus ride to Wandsworth Prison. As the doors of that venerable institution opened to receive him, Owens offered as proof of his loyalty the address of his girlfriend's flat. His wireless set, he said, would be found in the bathroom.

Colonel Simpson and B3's Captain Thomas Robertson (thirty years old and probably MI5's youngest officer) accompanied police to the flat that evening. The wireless set was duly found, but it was a receiver only, apparently put together by Owens himself. The landlord, however, reported that he had earlier buried a package in the garden at the request of Owens's girlfriend. He had assumed it contained belongings related to the breakup of Owens's marriage. When it was dug up, it contained a transmitter.[9]

The next day, Robertson and a Colonel J.S. Yule turned up at Wandsworth Prison and tested Owens on his Morse Code–sending ability. He was not very good. A few days later, Robertson returned with a Mr. Meakin, a civilian wireless operator from MI1(g)., and with his transmitter. As Owens had left it with Scotland Yard, it was understood not to be working, but working it was. He had been using it to send messages to Hamburg as recently as two weeks earlier.[10] Now, here it was, being set up in the prison with hopes of him being able to contact Germany. Owens must have thought he was lost. As the set was warming up, his hand went out to it, felt at the base, and it died.

The risk of electrocution was worth it. Captain Robertson and Mr. Meakin were not wireless technicians. They took it away to be fixed, returning the next day to try again.[11]

Having yanked himself back from the abyss, Owens set about bridging it. He told Captain Robertson that his first message should be: "All ready. Have repaired radio. Send instructions now. Awaiting reply." This was sent at intervals over the next two days, but with Mr. Meakin rather than Owens on the telegraph key. On September 11, the Germans finally answered.[12]

Reception was too poor to develop the contact, so the next morning Owens was removed to the police jail at Kingston-on-Thames and the transmitter was set up in an unfurnished top-floor flat in town where the aerial could be strung in the attic. Owens had said the next message should be "Must see you Holland at once. Bring weather code. Radio town and hotel. Wales ready." He explained that at his last meeting with the Germans in Hamburg, it was arranged that as soon as the war started he was to send daily weather reports, as well as go to Wales to see if he could recruit some willing saboteurs from among the Welsh nationalists.

The second message was repeated morning and afternoon, with Mr. Meakin again on the telegraph key. The German reply, when it came, was too garbled to understand, and when the Hamburg station kept signalling for acknowledgement, Meakin broke off. Nevertheless, real contact with the enemy had been achieved. It must have been a huge thrill for young Captain Robertson.[13]

The triumph was illusory. Every Morse operator's natural sending rhythm — or "fist" as it was called — is unique and hard to imitate. The German army signals personnel who trained Owens would have known instantly that it was not he who was on the telegraph key, especially as they had just recently received several of his messages. Mr. Meakin should have been alert to this problem, but he was only a civilian volunteer on assignment to the then very mysterious "secret service." He was probably not inclined to press upon Robertson an opinion about anything.[14]

The *congratulations* code used would also have alerted the Germans. The cipher actually given to Owens was based on the best-selling novel *Oil for the Lamps of China* by Alice Hobart, the keyword being derived from

THAT "STUPID LITTLE MAN" · 71

the page that matched the date of a message.[15] The delays in replying to Meakin's first transmissions were probably due to the Germans debating whether to answer when it was so obvious it was the enemy sending.

The next day (September 13), Robertson proposed to his superiors that Owens be allowed to go to Holland to meet the Germans as arranged. They agreed.[16]

The decision must have astonished Owens. When war was declared, he really had no choice but to turn himself in, as he was certain to be arrested anyway. Yet, he could hardly have dreamed that he would succeed so well in pitching himself as a double agent as to be permitted to go back across the Channel to the enemy, alone. Nevertheless, he was immediately released from jail and allowed to move into the flat with his girlfriend, Lily. On September 15, two "watchers" shadowed him down to the docks and to the ferry terminal. That was as far as the surveillance went; MI5's mandate did not extend beyond British territory.[17] (It must be remembered that in 1939, only Germany, France, and Britain were at war in Europe. Belgium, Holland, and Denmark were neutral, so the regular cross-Channel ferry services were still running.)

It seemed to work like a charm. Owens returned a few days later and told of meeting his spy chief, DR. RANTZAU, and giving him a yarn about having found a Welsh separatist who would be only too happy to plant bombs for Hitler. RANTZAU, who looked like an American, and whose smile, Owens said, was illuminated by a gold tooth, was enthusiastic and wanted the man brought over to the Continent at once so that he could be trained in Germany for raising Cain in Wales. Owens displayed the coin RANTZAU had given him that would be the Welsh traitor's secret sign. Weapons would be shipped by submarine. From MI5's perspective, Owens's test mission as a double agent had been a brilliant success.[18]

At this point in the war, MI5 knew next to nothing about the German secret services. Admiral Canaris was little more than a name, and MI5 did not know that his organization had three distinct divisions and that each ran its own agents.[19] And, had the MI5 officers read the espionage literature generated by the previous war, they would have realized that no responsible spymaster would risk a valuable spy successfully in place by having him engage in penny-ante fireworks.

DR. RANTZAU — whose real identity was Major Nikolaus Ritter — was the Abt I Luft (Air Espionage) chief at Ast Hamburg, and three days after he met Owens, supposedly at a hotel in Rotterdam, the following teletype message was sent by Hamburg to Berlin (A-3504 is Owens):

> To: OKW Abw I Luft/E and Ii
> 3504 reports on 18.9.39
> [Translation]
> Liaison engineer of the War Ministry with Philips in Holland told me the following: A new ultrashortwave receiver has been built which is being set up along the whole east coast of England. With this one can flawlessly pick up the shortwave radio transmissions that are produced by the sparking between the spark plugs and magnets of aircraft motors. With this one can with reasonable certainty fix the distance and the number of the [aircraft] motors....
> Ast Hamburg B Nr. 1252/39 I Luft geh[20]

Owens did not get it quite right, but right enough. At the meeting with the Germans, he tipped them off to what was then Britain's most vital military secret: the development of a radio device that was being installed along the coast to give early warning of approaching aircraft. The device was later to become most famously known by its acronym — radar (from radio detection and ranging).

It was a huge espionage coup.[21] Radar works by bouncing radio waves off a distant target and determining its range by measuring the return time of the reflections. The message suggests it involved picking up radio emissions from aircraft motors, but the Abwehr's technology section (Abw Ii) would have recognized the mistake. What was important was that Owens's information indicated that the British were building a coastal radio-beam system that would enable aircraft to be detected and tracked at long range. The Germans were working on radar themselves, but this told them that the British were dangerously farther ahead. An operational system would be of tremendous advantage to the British should it come to a clash in the sky between the Luftwaffe and the Royal Air Force. This report and seventeen others from Owens were sent to Berlin the same day.

Robertson was not alone to blame for this security catastrophe. He had sought and obtained advice and approvals from Maxwell Knight, of MI5's Section B2 (Counter-subversion), which included the fledgling double-agent section, as well as from the B Division chief, Brigadier Jasper Harker, and his deputy, Captain Guy Liddell. While it is likely Owens picked up the radar information himself, it is also possible it was given to him with some of the other messages for passing along to the Germans. MI5 at the time had no staff of its own "with any technical or scientific knowledge or training." Robertson's bosses, if unaware that an electronic air-defence system was actually being built, may have thought the item harmless fodder.[22]

For their part, despite the quantity of intelligence they garnered, the Germans must have been suspicious. There is a mocking ring to the report Owens made on his return. He spoke of DR. RANTZAU's dark plan to undermine the morale of British troops by having secret agents talk down Britain's chances in pubs, of a "general meeting of German spies from all over the world" to take place in Spain, and of submarines being gathered to attack the troop transports and other vessels concentrating in the Thames Estuary and between Folkestone and Dover — suicidal in those shallow waters. All this Robertson passed on by telephone, followed by letter to MI6, Naval Intelligence, and other interested parties.

Owens also reported being told that the Germans were massing troops at the rate of six hundred thousand a day on the Dutch frontier with the intention of striking through Holland and Belgium. This was a significant deception. Most of the German forces were still in Poland and the German army general staff was terrified lest the French and British perceive the weakness and attack.[23]

Because DR. RANTZAU insisted that Owens begin wireless transmissions immediately, Captain Robertson was given the lead in developing the case. He had the transmitter installed in a lockable room in Owens's flat and arranged for Mr. Meakin to operate it as before. The idea was for Owens to be on hand so that replies could be put in his words.

Owens said DR. RANTZAU wanted him to begin immediately with local weather observations. Robertson sought the necessary clearances.

This meant going to the deputy director of intelligence in the Air Ministry, Major A.R. Boyle, who said that it was a decision that would probably have to come from the War Cabinet. While waiting, on September 23 Robertson had a first weather report transmitted anyway, but it was deliberately inaccurate. Abwehr records show that it was spotted as false immediately.[24]

The code Owens said the Germans gave him for his weather reports is another indication that they were suspicious and were not taking him all that seriously:

WEATHER REPORTS

Visibility: Code letter "V"
That will comprise V1, V2, V3, V4, etc.
Height Clouds: Code letter "H"
This will be transmitted in 500 yds, e.g.,
1 = 500 yds
2 = 1,000 yds
Speed of wind: Code letter "W"
From 0–9 represents approximately 0–50 m.p.h.
Rain: Code letters "RN"
Fog: Code letters "FG"
Snow: Code letter "SN"
For safety, all codes going out will be prefixed by the
letter "X," e.g.,
Partly cloudy will be X.P.C.
Half cloud "X.H.C."
Total cloud "X.T.C."
Temperature: Transmit every night
Code letter "F"
(Fahrenheit not centigrade)
Code word for numbers: HAPPY CHRISTMAS[25]

Two months later, when it was clear that MI5 knew virtually nothing about codes and ciphers, the Germans gave these codes the dignity of a little more complexity by adding extra letters (nulls) and eliminating some of the "X" prefixes.[26]

The "code" Owens said he was to use for his espionage reports was not much better. It was a single-transposition cipher whereby the message was written letter by letter horizontally in a rectangular crossword-type box, and then taken off by the vertical columns. The keyword was *congratulations* — just as Mrs. Owens had said. It could be broken by anagramming and was rated by cryptanalysts of the day as more puzzle than cryptogram. This suggests that Owens made it up from a library book or the Germans gave it to him as the code he would say he was using if caught.[27]

Surprisingly, Robertson did get the okay to send the weather observations. On September 26, he was told that the chief of the Air Staff and the deputy chief had "no problem" with the proposal. This seems odd because knowing what cloud cover to expect was useful information for enemy aircraft wanting to venture over the Channel. Germany's slow-moving Stuka dive-bombers were especially easy prey to roving British fighters. But these were the very early days of the war and the skies over England and the Channel were still mostly empty and serene. Yet it seems odd that the agreement of the navy was obtained, much less that of the War Cabinet. Winston Churchill was then First Lord of the Admiralty.[28] He should have objected, surely.

Three weeks later, Owens made a second trip to the Continent, this time with some answers to a list of questions the Germans had given him, and accompanied by a former MI5 informant, Gwyllem Williams, posing as a rebellious Welsh nationalist.[29]

Three days later, on October 22, Ast Hamburg informed Berlin by teletype that, according to A-3504 (a spy's real name was not given in such messages for security reasons), the new barrage balloons the Germans had asked about involved nothing more than the addition of stabilizer fins so that they would ride easier in the wind. This was given to Owens to pass along.[30]

Owens offered another item that may have been his own. He suggested that a large "Blue Diamond Line" vessel lying between Pembroke and Swansea was vulnerable to sabotage. This could only be a reference to one of the transatlantic liners operated by the Blue Star Line, perhaps even the *Arandora Star*, which was sunk by a German U-boat with great loss of life the following July. Liners, because of their troop-carrying capacity, were the equivalent of capital ships in time of war. If Owens was not making this up, it was delectable information. Major Ritter now really began to play the game.

Owens had a great story to tell MI5 on his return. He and Williams had been contacted at their hotel in Brussels and had travelled to Antwerp by train. The secret rendezvous was in the offices of a shipping firm in the city's dockyard area. Present were three men: DR. RANTZAU; a man introduced as "the Commander"; and another man, who was not introduced, but who only watched and said nothing. There was also a woman — "tall, thin, fair hair — wearing a dark green dress and coat, aged thirty-eight to forty, height five foot six." Owens could have had in mind Mata Hari, the famous femme fatale spy of the First World War popularized in the 1920s in both books and film. The meeting might have been a scene from the movie *Mata Hari* (1931), starring Greta Garbo and Lionel Barrymore.

He told them that Williams had been interviewed in an adjacent room by "the Commander," and that Owens had stayed with the others. When put together, the two men's stories tallied, Robertson noted in his report. Their main impression was that DR. RANTZAU and the Commander were grateful for the excellent answers to the questions Owens had been given, and now wanted to move quickly to foment mutiny and mayhem in Wales. The Commander, Owens judged, was in charge of all sabotage activities in Britain and knew the south coast of Wales intimately, leading him to believe there should be no problem getting explosives ashore by submarine. There were hints that the Germans were already co-operating in Ireland with the Irish rebels, the IRA, prompting Robertson to write in parentheses, "This is extremely interesting as it is a fairly concrete example that the IRA are being run by the Germans."

DR. RANTZAU also said there was a spy in the Air Ministry and another in the Admiralty, and for Owens to expect payment in England for his services, potentially putting another two enemy agents in MI5's sights. The Germans were anxious to learn more about aerodromes near Gloucester, what was going on at the Avonmouth Docks (Bristol), and hoped that Owens could soon arrange to go back to Canada to organize "a similar show" there.[31]

Furthermore, the Germans were pleased with the weather observations now coming in, and provided Owens with another list of questions. DR. RANTZAU also gave him a miniature photograph the size of a postage stamp bearing a message to a German agent in Britain. MI5 joyfully seized upon this as an example of German espionage technology, not realizing that the memoir of Germany's First World War spy chief, Colonel Walter Nicolai, published in England in 1924, reported that German intelligence had been using photographic microdots as small as one millimetre square.[32] As for the German agent, he was a fifty-year-old Britain-born businessman of German parents named Charles Eschborn, and he had surrendered to police the day after Owens.

Eschborn had told a compelling story. He admitted he had done a little spying for the Hamburg Abwehr during the previous months, but that it had been at the urging of one of his much younger twin brothers, one of whom was living with him in Manchester, the other of whom was in Germany. When war was declared, Eschborn was gripped by remorse, and so threw himself on the mercies of the British authorities. It worked, especially because Eschborn had served in the British Army in the First World War. His brother was interned while he was allowed to go free.

RANTZAU's message to Eschborn presented an opportunity that had not been thought of: he could be another double agent. He was approached, and, after some arm-twisting, agreed to reply to RANTZAU. MI5 was especially keen to develop the contact because Eschborn was an amateur photographer and the Germans were proposing that he help them develop the technique for making miniature photographs. MI5 saw this as a means of staying on top of this enemy initiative, oblivious to the fact that any commercial photographic studio, either in England or Germany, would be better equipped for the task.[33]

At about this time, MI5 began applying code names to its double agents: Owens was assigned SNOW, a jumbling of the letters of his surname; Gwyllem Williams became GW; and Charles Eschborn became simply CHARLIE. These code names seem an accurate indication of MI5's level of sophistication.[34]

Now things really sped up. Robertson vigorously petitioned his intelligence contacts in the army, navy, air force, and MI6 to come up with convincing material to feed the Germans. Owens was released from all supervision and encouraged to roam around the country looking for items of interest, as he would if he were a real spy. Robertson told him to try to penetrate into restricted areas to give eyewitness credibility to the stories he would tell DR. RANTZAU. He gave him thirty gallons' worth of petrol coupons and told him to visit as many aerodromes as he could; and when in Newcastle, urged him to see whether he could, by himself, locate the headquarters of 13 Fighter Group. He also suggested that Owens snoop around Harrogate, the spa town that had been taken over by the Air Ministry in anticipation of the bombing of London.[35]

These were wonderful opportunities for Owens as A-3504. An ordinary spy approaching even one aerodrome in wartime Britain risked execution if caught, and so would go cautiously. Owens could visit as many aerodromes as he could manage with absolutely no fear should he trigger base security. It emboldened Owens to gather information with an aggressiveness no ordinary spy could match. In one case, he talked his way past the entrance gate and drove around an airfield counting the parked aircraft. In the pubs of Harrogate, he cozied up to airmen and asked questions delicate enough to get him shot. Captain Robertson could not have made it easier for Major Ritter's A-3504.

To better assess the accuracy of the information Owens was collecting, Robertson again enlisted the help of Major Boyle over at the Air Ministry. Between them, they compiled much of the RAF's order of battle in England, supplementing "the complete list" of squadrons supplied by Boyle with contributions from MI5's newly created local security control officers (SCOs).[36] Neither man seems to have been concerned that by centrally collecting this data they increased the risk that the whole package could be leaked to the enemy.

As for whether Owens was telling the enemy more on his trips to the Continent than he should, Robertson put on record his conviction that Owens was entirely trustworthy: "He is a stupid little man who is given to doing silly things at odd moments, but I am perfectly convinced he is straightforward in the things that he gives me and the answers to my questions."[37]

Throughout this period, according to the Hamburg–Berlin teletype messages that Robertson never saw, this "stupid little man" steadily provided the Germans with high-grade intelligence on his trips across the Channel, some of it supplied by Major Boyle and some of it apparently gathered by Owens himself.

A LITTLE TOO EASY, PERHAPS?

January–April 1940

By the beginning of 1940, it would have been patently obvious to Ast Hamburg's Major Ritter that his British opponents had little clue about how to run a wireless spy. He must have shook his head when Owens told him that the MI5 wireless operator who sent A-3504's reports was a civilian, not a qualified military person, and that the people trying to run him as a double agent had little knowledge of codes and ciphers. It was the perfect circumstance for *Funkspiel* — the epitome of the spymaster's art.

It was initially not as ideal as Ritter might have imagined. Britain's War Office wireless listening service — formerly MI8(c) but now renamed the Radio Security Service (RSS) — was not looking for spies, but only for illicit signals that might be used as radio beacons to guide in German bombers. Only suspicious transmissions in Britain were being sought, and they were not being monitored at all for their content.

This changed in December with the arrival at the War Office of a Canadian army signals officer who was looking for advice on how to handle the obviously clandestine wireless traffic being intercepted by a Canadian signals intelligence unit in Ottawa. Within two weeks, E.W.B. Gill, an Oxford professor and former wireless intelligence officer of the First World War, was dispatched to the Radio Security Service, then still based at Wormwood Scrubs (London) along with MI5, to have it abandon the radio-beacon searches and listen instead for what might be German enemy-agent transmissions. As the Canadians had discovered, there was plenty of suspicious stuff out there, but neither MI6 nor the Government Code & Cipher School had shown much interest.[1]

On learning that an RSS volunteer operator was handling the wireless communications of a double agent code-named SNOW that MI5 was running, Major Gill undertook to have the German side of the traffic studied. It was soon found that Hamburg, SNOW's control station in Germany, was exchanging messages with another station, whose signal was moving along the coast of Norway — a ship. The cipher used was similar to the *congratulations* code that had been given to Owens, and Major Gill, with the help of Lieutenant Hugh Trevor-Roper, a twenty-six-year-old German-speaking Oxford scholar who had arrived with him, managed to puzzle it out.

The name of the ship was the *Theseus*, and it was reporting on neutral ships headed for British ports. On January 29, Gill forwarded this information to the Government Code & Cipher School, but instead of a thank-you, its chief, Commander Alastair Denniston, fired back that Gill should stick to listening and leave the cipher-breaking to the experts. Undaunted, Gill continued to have the *Theseus* traffic monitored, and extended the listening to other stations across the Channel that appeared to be exchanging transmissions of a similar type.[2]

The *Theseus* was a "spy ship," as the term was applied during the Cold War to vessels that roamed the high seas listening in on foreign radio communications using sophisticated wireless receiving equipment. Ships could be positioned precisely where the signals of a distant transmitter could best be heard.

In the case of spies, once their signals were picked up and copied, the ship could be moved to where it could best retransmit them to the mainland station. In the case of the *Theseus*, this would have been Hamburg. It worked the other way, too. The wireless operator for SNOW could be made to hear the *Theseus*, depending on where the vessel was transmitting from.[3]

The choice of wireless operator for the *Theseus* must have been deliberate. He was twenty-four-year-old Friedrich Kaulen, son of a German merchant. Fair-haired and good-looking, he was R-2220, an agent of Nest Bremen. His Abwehr assignment immediately before the *Theseus* had been two years as a spy in England for Abt I Luft, and he had received kudos for his excellent photographs of British secret air fields, anti-aircraft batteries, and searchlight emplacements.

Ordinarily, the wireless operator on a military vessel would be a naval rating or, in the case of a spy ship, perhaps an army signals specialist. Kaulen, however, was an amateur civilian radio hobbyist, much like the volunteer operators who did much of the listening for the RSS, and like the operator who transmitted for Owens. Kaulen's only second languages were English and French, an odd choice for a wireless operator who was to remain for months in Norwegian waters. On the other hand, if the Germans wanted to do a wireless deception — a *Funkspiel* — on the operator of Owens's transmitter, should they have figured out that it was under British control, it would make sense that they would use a person just like Kaulen, and do it from a ship.[4]

Kaulen's ability to understand English would be handy for confirming that he had Owens's signal, since he only spoke English. As for getting the correct frequency, that would not have been a problem: as a Nest Bremen spy, Kaulen's commanding officer would have been the Abt I Luft chief at Ast Hamburg — Major Ritter.

At Major Gill's urging, the Radio Security Service in London began avidly collecting the new traffic and, because he and Trevor-Roper shared a flat, they would work on the material in the evenings. By simple anagramming, they found they could break other messages, and these revealed that Hamburg was in contact with spies in Belgium, Holland, and Luxembourg.[5]

On March 20, at a meeting with Gill and Captain Robertson of MI5, Commander Denniston of the Government Code & Cipher School agreed to assign one of his codebreakers to the traffic.[6] This was to be sixty-six-year-old Oliver Strachey, who had briefly held a job with the India railway system before marrying the suffragette Rachel Conn Costelloe and enjoying a reversal of household roles until his First World War stint with MI1(b), the War Office code-breaking agency that Colonel Simpson had headed. He stayed on after the war when MI1(b) merged with the navy's Room 40 to form the Government Code & Cipher School (GC&CS). He was then with a GC&CS team working on German naval traffic.

Gill and Trevor-Roper were convinced they had found the Radio Security Service's noble purpose. They saw it as opening a window on the operations of the German secret services. Denniston remained cool. Strachey did not produce a decrypt from the new intercepts until April 14, a week after the German invasion of Norway.[7]

Denniston's dismissiveness is indicated by the fact that Strachey was no more than one senior citizen with a pencil and paper, whose output was assigned the lofty and surely sardonic title, Intelligence Service (Oliver Strachey) — ISOS. Denniston had good reason to be skeptical. The ciphers used for the messages Gill and Trevor-Roper were so excited about were of a First World War vintage that, thanks to the indiscretion of a former director of Naval Intelligence, the Germans had to know the British could easily break. Denniston could be sure they would not be using them for messages of any real value.

The former Naval Intelligence head in question was the famous Admiral Reginald Hall, who had presided over the codebreakers of the Admiralty's Room 40 during the First World War. He is widely credited with covertly releasing the intercepted "Zimmerman Telegram," which in 1917 helped bring the United States into the war. In 1919, the war over, he left the navy in a swirl of ill-feeling, probably having to do with how difficult he had been to work with while serving in his positions of high responsibility. He tended to be arrogant and autocratic, and there were some in senior government circles who probably were not sad to see him go, shoved a little, perhaps, by not giving him certain honours that he might have felt he deserved. He took with him some ten thousand decrypts of German navy, Foreign Office, and espionage messages, and stashed them at home.

In 1925, an American civilian lawyer approached Hall on the off chance he could help him with a case he was working on aimed at getting Germany to pay for damages for the "Black Tom" explosion that shook New York Harbor in 1916. What he needed was hard evidence linking the destruction of a munitions depot to German agents. Hall led Amos Peaslee to the stacks of decrypts, gave him the run of the house, including servants, for as long as he wanted, and went off to Scotland on a shooting holiday. Three days later, Peaslee had found and copied 264 cables and radiograms pertinent to German First World War covert operations in America.

The decrypts ignited a blaze of publicity when the case was heard in The Hague in 1927. The German government may have had its suspicions, but it had no idea of the extent to which the British had been reading its secret communications, and probably still were. The immediate and lasting consequence was the Government Code & Cipher School was locked out of all German Foreign Office and German army traffic, the Foreign Office switching to unbreakable one-time pads (single-use sheets of random letters whose numerical equivalents are added to those of the letters in a message to encipher it) and the army to high-security plug board ciphering machines (akin to early telephone switchboards, they allow for the creation of thousands of unique electronic circuits).[8] It stood to reason that the Abwehr, the German army's secret intelligence service, would have taken similar measures.

To make the breach in secrecy even worse — and it could hardly have been — the types of German ciphers compromised were subsequently described by the American cryptologist Herbert Yardley in the popular book *The American Black Chamber* (1931) and in detail by Helen Fouché Gaines in her *Elementary Cryptanalysis* (1939). The most vulnerable had been transposition ciphers, which at their weakest were solvable by anagramming.

Commander Denniston could have told all this to Gill and Trevor-Roper, but he did not. Colonel Simpson, as the former head of the British Army's wartime equivalent of Room 40, could certainly have explained it to Captain Robertson, except that the previous month he had been transferred out of MI5 to General Wavell's army in the Middle East.[9] Neither the Radio Security Service nor MI5 — as far as available documents show — were ever directly told that the ciphers of the type used by the Abwehr messages being intercepted had been compromised for years.

Probably to Denniston's complete surprise, with Hitler's invasion of Norway it was found that the *Theseus* was using these same simple ciphers to relay back to Germany the reports of spies on shore. Some of these deciphered messages were given to Churchill, again head of the Admiralty, and it undoubtedly caused him to remember the glory days of Room 40 when the signals of the German High Sea Fleet were being read. He ordered that the *Theseus* not be disturbed. When it was all over, and Norway lost, Gill again urged Strachey to get busy on the traffic that still was coming in from spies across the Channel, evidently in France, Belgium, and Holland. Strachey's output was so meagre, however, that Gill offered him one of his own staff to help move things along.[10]

Meanwhile, MI6's clandestine wireless service was coming of age. Its chief, Gambier-Parry, had been the marketing manager in Britain for the American radio and appliance maker Philco, and had recruited from the company a wireless engineer by the name of Harold Robin who developed a portable transmitter that weighed less than ten pounds. This, plus the introduction of super-secure one-time pads for enciphering messages, enabled MI6 to begin to deploy its own clandestine wireless observers in the field, rather than just in embassies, one such team reporting from a mountainside during the Norway crisis. This was a milestone in the modernization of MI6.[11]

Gambier-Parry's operational headquarters was in Bletchley Park, a stately property MI6 acquired near the start of the war to house the expanding Government Code & Cipher School. He hired experienced signals personnel co-opted from the army and navy, and growth was so rapid that before long the team had to be moved to new premises five miles away at Whaddon Hall. Its official designation was MI6 (Section VIII).[12]

Having a more professional wireless operation than the Radio Security Service, with its handful of signals personnel relying on Post Office and amateur radio listeners, MI6 (VIII) was capable of doing a far better job of tracking the clandestine wireless activity coming from the countries bordering Germany.[13] It may be that one reason that Strachey was breaking so little for Gill was that his decrypts were going first to MI6.

MI5, by contrast, remained slow to grasp the technical aspects of wireless technology. When someone wondered why the Germans were not worried about the British locating their agent's transmitter by taking bearings on its signal, Owens was told to raise the matter during his meeting with DR. RANTZAU in Antwerp at the beginning of April, and to ask whether he should be sending on different frequencies. Not necessary, DR. RANTZAU replied; it was very difficult to pinpoint the locations of illicit wireless sources. There had been one transmitting in the Wilhelmshaven area, he said, but despite all efforts it had been impossible to run it down.[14]

This was nonsense. A radio signal is strongest along the line of sight, a fact that enables a transmitter to be located simply by turning the aerials of two or more receivers toward where the signal is strongest and then drawing lines on a map to where they intersect. This was called direction finding (DF), the ancestor of the twenty-first century's Global Positioning System (GPS), and could be done over long distances or from close up by mobile receivers. The technique had been known during the First World War and was still being used by both sides to locate enemy warships at sea and enemy army and air force units on land. It was also used by government agencies like Britain's Post Office, Canada's Department of Transport, and the U.S. Federal Communications Commission to pinpoint the location of unlicensed wireless sets.

Obviously, in order to survive in enemy territory, it is helpful for a spy to change frequencies and call signs as often as practical, but the most important necessity is to send from different locations. DR. RANTZAU was not asked the most crucial question: Was it safe for JOHNNY — the name Ritter preferred to use for Owens — to always be sending from the same place? The Germans themselves were soon to provide the answer when Britain's sabotage agency, Special Operations Executive, began landing its agents into occupied Europe. Their wireless transmissions were DF'd and they were caught by the score.[15]

The only MI5 officer with the technical clout to challenge DR. RANTZAU's advice — Colonel Simpson — had left.[16] In his absence, Robertson chose to believe his German opponent. This is all the more ironic in that just at this time Denniston forwarded to him a report from the French direction-finding service, which had picked up the SNOW transmitter's signal and had identified it as coming from around London. "I shall be very glad," Robertson wrote Major Cowgill of MI6, "if you will reply to the French telling them that we know all about the station, and that they need worry no further."[17]

Yet, if the French could hear the SNOW transmitter and get bearings on it, surely Robertson should have thought the Germans would assume the British could, too. It appears he was blind to this logic. If he asked for Gill's opinion, it is not on the record.[18]

DR. RANTZAU did concede that it might be a good idea if JOHNNY changed his call sign from time to time. According to Owens, Ritter went out and bought two copies of the book *The Dead Don't Care* by Jonathan

Latimer, one for him to keep and the other for Owens. He then explained how every day they could both use them to derive a new call sign to locate the page and line where the letters could be found.[19]

In fact, Major Ritter was providing Owens with the means to secretly encipher his own messages, and in a way that was unlikely to be discovered. An agreed-upon published text — book, magazine, newspaper — enables spy and spymaster to construct an enormous number of fresh cipher keys. All they need to do is decide on which pages to find the key letters or key words on particular days. Provided the messages are then enciphered by the substitution method, rather than by transposition, they can be very difficult to break.

Owens may have been playing games here. When leaving Germany for Britain just before the war, he had been assigned the novel *Oil for the Lamps of China* by Alice Hobart for his cipher keys.[20] It could be he never used it because it was not consistent with his reading tastes, and would have stood out in his possession. The invasion of Holland and Belgium was impending, however, and he was going to really need his own secret cipher, especially if he had access to a transmitter through another spy, or he had his own hidden away.

One of the advantages to using a recently published popular novel to provide enciphering keys is that a spy can get his copy from a library or book store in the target country, sparing him the danger of triggering suspicions by having it in his possession crossing the border. By telling MI5 that he had brought his copy of *The Dead Don't Care* into England instead of getting it there, and by having it out in the open in his flat, Owens was waving his actual secret cipher under British noses.

ROBERTSON VERSUS RITTER

At this point it is pertinent to examine the backgrounds of the two protagonists in this MI5-Abwehr confrontation, beginning with Robertson.

He was a Scot, apparently so proud of his heritage that he was partial to wearing tartan "trews" (tight-fitting pants) to the office, and he was usually referred to by his initials — T.A.R. — standing for Thomas Argyle

Robertson. According to a biographical note in the Liddell Hart Centre for Military Studies, he was a graduate of Sandhurst (Churchill's military alma mater) and commissioned into the Seaforth Highlanders. He joined MI5 in 1931 and "took part in intelligence activities in both military and political spheres," which probably means he was used to infiltrate left-wing organizations. At the start of the war, he was in charge of the one-man section B3, responsible for investigating reports of suspicious wireless activity and lights and pigeon sightings.[21]

Robertson's German opponent, Owens's spymaster in Hamburg, was very different. In his early forties, a veteran of the trenches of 1914–18, Major Nikolaus Ritter, a.k.a. DR. RANTZAU, spent over a decade in the United States as a businessman in the textile industry before returning to Germany in 1936. He spoke, read, and wrote English fluently, liked the Americans, and was well-educated, well-travelled, and savvy. He had been assigned to Ast Hamburg by Admiral Canaris personally, and in 1937 returned to the United States to organize the Abwehr's espionage assets there. This put him into contact with Frederick Joubert Duquesne, a South African with a deep hatred of the British. Duquesne's mother had died in a British concentration camp during the Boer War (1899–1902), and he had made getting revenge his life's work. He had been a most successful spy and saboteur in England during the First World War, so Major Ritter was not lacking for a good tutor.[22]

Supplementing whatever advice Duquesne had to offer was a sensational book just then released in New York that claimed to tell the full story of Germany's espionage and sabotage activities in the United States from 1915 to 1918. Written by Captain Henry Landau, Britain's former spy chief for Belgium and Holland, *The Enemy Within* went into great detail about the personalities and the techniques of the German secret service in America, with lurid descriptions of such spectacular events as the 1916 Black Tom explosions in New York Harbor in which over one thousand tons of munitions were set alight. Naming some of the more notorious German agents of the period — Kurt Jahnke, Franz von Papen, Franz von Rintelen, and so on — it was billed as the book "that will cause reverberations in Washington, London, Paris and Berlin." It must have felt decidedly odd to Ritter to be reading it while on a mission to America to set up spy rings for the next war.

Captain Landau would also have been of particular interest to Ritter because his wartime mandate had covered the same two countries Ritter was to operate in, Belgium and Holland, and he had written another excellent book about these adventures, entitled *All's Fair: The Story of the British Secret Service Behind German Lines.* It is a classic, for Landau operated from neutral Holland and ran hundreds of spies in occupied Belgium whose lives absolutely depended on his good judgment and knowledge of spycraft.

If Ritter added Colonel Walter Nicolai's *Geheime Mächte* and Herbert Yardley's 1934 memoir on U.S. wartime code-breaking, *The American Black Chamber*, to his background reading — as he surely did — then he would have been well-prepared for the task Canaris had given him. Indeed, when he returned to Germany in the fall of 1937, he left behind a fully functioning espionage organization with agents in two of America's most sensitive defence industries — the Norden Company and Sperry Corporation. Others were similarly well-placed and by 1939 were producing excellent results.

Given this background, Ritter must have found it hard to believe that Owens had penetrated British intelligence so easily. It might have been reasonable for the British to allow an agent of impeccable background to make personal, private visits across the Channel to the enemy, but surely not someone they knew so little about. The diminutive Welshman — whom Ritter code-named JOHNNY but nicknamed DER KLEINER ("Little Guy") — had spent much of his life in Canada, and that is all, even by late 1943, that MI5 knew.[23]

Robertson appears to have been unconcerned by this. When objections to sending weather observations to the Germans gathered momentum in the Air Ministry, propelled by the misgivings of the director of Air Intelligence, Commodore K.C. Buss, he discounted the concerns. There was no need to worry, he wrote in one of his many notes to file, because the Germans were only getting "details of temperature, velocity, direction of the wind, height of cloud and visibility," but not the actual state of affairs — that is, whether it was snowing or raining. This suggests a rather implausible level of ignorance with respect to weather forecasting.[24]

In mid-February 1940, Commodore Buss was suddenly demoted and replaced by Major A.R. Boyle, now given the rank of air commodore. This settled the weather issue. Boyle had always supported Robertson's contention that Owens had to be given high-quality intelligence in order to maintain credibility with the Germans. The concerns raised by Commodore Buss faded.[25]

The fifty-three-year-old "Archie" Boyle seemed to be a proper successor to Buss. During the First World War he had done some flying, and in the late 1930s was attached to the intelligence branch of the Air Ministry. He had been under-secretary for the Royal Air Force when war was declared, and when Robertson first approached him, he had just been "put into uniform" and made deputy to the director of RAF Intelligence. Yet, for all this, he was sometimes surprisingly deficient in good judgment. At one meeting, when Robertson showed him some aerial photographs he was proposing Eschborn send the Germans, Boyle approved them, despite an aide pointing out that the buildings shown had their skylights painted over, a sure sign that the pictures had been taken from the air after the start of the war, and hence Eschborn could not have obtained them. Boyle and Robertson sent them anyway.[26]

To Robertson, at least according to his many notes to file, the real aim was to use Owens to catch other German spies. The two agents besides Owens so far identified through contact with DR. RANTZAU did not count. Eschborn had given himself up beforehand, and the other, Mathilde Krafft, was nothing more than a middle-aged woman with German sympathies who had been asked by Hamburg to mail Owens small sums of money. This was a thin return on running Owens as a double agent, and Robertson accused him of falling down on the job since no other spies in England had contacted him.[27] Ritter must have been surprised by this complaint when Owens told him of it, for it is a basic principle of good spycraft that agents sent into enemy territory are not to know each other, so that one arrest does not lead to others. But by now there had been many examples of MI5 not knowing the basics.[28]

MI5's perceived ineptitude was a valuable item of intelligence in its own right. The way MI5 handled Owens showed that its counterespionage expertise was very, very slight. Only absolute neophytes would let a freelance pre-war agent like Owens, whose background was unauthenticated, roam the countryside unsupervised in wartime. Robertson was to write this to file:

> I taxed him [Owens] on the subject of getting information for himself and not relying on us to give it to him. I naturally made the proviso that any information he obtained should be immediately sent to us. He has apparently started getting around a bit because he told me he paid a visit to Croydon Aerodrome and to Kenley. He said he was glad he had been to Kenley because the place had changed considerably since he was last there. He saw no machines out on the field and was proposing at a later date to make a good story and send it over.[29]

And again, incredibly:

> On Monday he went to Harrogate and thence to Grantham.... The following day he went to Newcastle and thence to West Hartlepool.... On that day he paid a visit to Wattisham aerodrome.... He said he had been able to obtain a little information about an aerodrome at Dishford, near Thirsk, Grantham and Wallisham aerodromes.... He did not find out anything about the 13th Fighter Group at Newcastle....[30]

It seems never to have occurred to Robertson that Owens might be giving him less than a full account of what he was seeing, that he might have another transmitter hidden away, that he might be in contact with an undiscovered spy, or he might be sending secret letters to a cover address outside the country that MI6 was unaware of. These possible scenarios seem never to have occurred to Liddell, Robertson's direct boss, either.

On the other hand, Owens had little need of these devices so long as he was able to take what he saw personally back to his German controllers across the Channel.[31] This recklessness, plus the infantile codenames — CHARLIE for Charles Eschborn and GW for Gwyllem Williams — could only have led the Germans, and Major Ritter in particular, to seriously doubt MI5's competence.

THE ABWEHR SPREADS ITS NET

February—April 1940

One of the reasons why Admiral Canaris had been so opposed to Hitler's military adventures and sabre-rattling in the 1930s was fear that Great Britain would be drawn into any war he started, with the United States inevitably following. He did not think Germany could win if that happened because the U.S. economy was the biggest in the world, giving it enormous military capacity. Hitler being Hitler, however, a confrontation with the Anglo-Americans was likely sooner or later. Canaris's task was to figure out how to deal with it.

The "sooner" arrived in the spring of 1940. A twenty-nine-year-old cipher clerk in the U.S. embassy in London, Tyler Kent, outraged by what he saw as Roosevelt's disregard for the will of Congress, took to stealing copies of the secret correspondence between the president and Winston Churchill, then head of the Admiralty. These messages were of the most sensitive nature, for they showed the president was keen to help Britain, under the table if necessary, despite America's official policy of neutrality. Kent amassed some 1,500 documents with the vague idea of someday releasing them to the public as proof of the president's perfidy. He kept them in his apartment.

Nothing much would have happened except that Kent divulged his secret to a White Russian named Anna Wolkoff who had strong fascist sympathies. The information and documents she pried out of him she passed to the Italian embassy — Italy was then still neutral — which passed them in turn on to Berlin, where they inevitably reached Canaris. It was one of the top espionage successes of the war in that the security shields of the United States and Britain were breached at the highest level.[1] Canaris now could be sure that Roosevelt was on side with Britain and would go to war against Germany if the opportunity presented itself.

MI5, it should be said, did catch on to Kent through some exceptional counter-espionage work by Maxwell Knight's B2 section, but too late. Kent and Wolkoff were arrested, but the intelligence bird had flown. Canaris had gained valuable knowledge that he probably shared with Hitler in the hope of dampening his ambitions. More important to the war, however, was what he himself eventually did with the information.

That was in the future. His current and ongoing problem was how to contain the Nazis in the face of Hitler's determination to expand Germany's frontiers in Europe, by war if necessary. Something of the Abwehr chief's thinking is evident from how he organized and staffed the outlying Abwehr offices, especially those in Spain and Portugal — the usual espionage battleground when Britain was at odds with a European power. His main consideration appears to have been to make sure the key positions were filled by anti-Nazi officers who were personally loyal to him.

The head of KO Portugal (Lisbon) was Kremer von Aünrode, alias Albrecht von Karsthof, a former intelligence officer with the Austrian General Staff. He was from Trieste, a city that was lopped off from Austria and given to Italy with the breakup of the Austro-Hungarian Empire after the First World War. This made him definitely not a Nazi, and likely no friend of Italy either. He was especially close to Canaris.

KO Spain (Madrid) was the largest and unquestionably the most important of the Abwehr branches in neutral countries and its chief was an old naval comrade from Canaris's First World War days, Captain Wilhelm Leissner, alias Gustav Lenz. Canaris brought Leissner out of retirement in 1935 to help manage the Abwehr's covert assistance to the Nationalists during the Spanish Civil War and kept him on as Germany slid to war itself. On Leissner's staff was Canaris's nephew, Joachim Canaris, responsible for evaluating espionage reports from Britain, and a little later, Karl-Erich Kuhlenthal, who had worked for Canaris during the Spanish Civil War and whose father had been military attaché to Paris and Rome before being dismissed by the Nazis.[2]

It can be safely assumed that all the key officers at KO Spain and KO Portugal were Canaris loyalists, and the same held true for Holland, where Traugott (Richard) Protze, another friend from his naval days, ran a separate intelligence office in The Hague that reported directly to Berlin. Alexander Waag, leader of KO Switzerland until July 1940, was connected to Canaris through his wife.[3]

These postings in countries where the English-speaking secret services would mount most of their operations ensured that Canaris could deal with them as he saw fit, and perhaps in ways that would never be accepted by the Nazis. It made possible informal talks with enemy opposite-numbers with less fear of being discovered by the Nazis, and quid pro quo exchanges of favours and information in order to satisfy political bosses impatient for results. The espionage struggle in Spain and Portugal was a polite game of billiards in comparison to the slashing and hacking that had gone on between the Soviets and the White Russians in Paris in the 1920s and '30s.

Add the KOs in Norway, Sweden, and Greece to the aforementioned and Canaris had Germany surrounded by an anti-Nazi espionage and intelligence-gathering network that could control the flow of overseas intelligence being fed to Abwehr headquarters in Berlin, and through it to the client intelligence agencies of the army, navy, and air force, the army high command (the Oberkommando des Heeres [OKH]), and Hitler's headquarters (the Oberkommando der Wehrmacht [OKW]).

This was a necessary tactic, so long as the intelligence chief of the army, with the misleading title Oberquartiermeister IV, remained outside the circle of general staff officers opposed to Hitler. The chief, General Kurt von Tippelskirch, was a no-nonsense officer of the old school who had spent four years of the First World War in a French prisoner-of-war camp. He was not a Nazi, but he could not be relied upon to work against the regime.

Similarly, there was the delicate problem that while the heads of the main departments of the Abwehr were all loyal to Canaris and committed anti-Nazis, this was not necessarily the case with the Berlin section heads. For instance, the officer in charge of Abw I Luft/E (E = England), Major Friedrich Busch, was a fervent Nazi,[4] and the German air force, the Luftwaffe, was generally pro-Hitler. Once Major Busch, who was no fool, received an intelligence report of genuine value, Canaris could try stopping him from forwarding it only at his own peril. This was especially awkward in that air intelligence was at a premium.

It was the development of the bomber that had made the difference. It had seen only limited use during the First World War, but its effect in 1937, during the Spanish Civil War, on the town of Guernica was enough to make those in the 1930s concerned about such things think that it might more quickly and cheaply subdue an enemy country than victories on the battlefield; it appeared to be the perfect terror weapon.

The raid on Guernica was conducted by an assortment of German and Italian bombers on loan to the Nationalist forces and was intended to assist a ground attack. The bombers missed their proper targets and destroyed three quarters of the town of five thousand instead. Resistance collapsed and the world was horrified. Guernica, thanks to the brush of Pablo Picasso, became the subject of one of the most powerful and famous war paintings of the twentieth century. All the experts agreed. In the next war, cities and civilians would be the primary targets.

Indeed, such was the alarm that the League of Nations followed up by unanimously passing a resolution declaring the "intentional bombing of civilian populations" to be illegal, and that, in time of war, the targets of air attacks "must be legitimate military targets and identifiable." The European powers, plus Japan and the United States, urgently looked to develop their own air defences and bombing capability. This created a huge market for espionage, particularly in the areas of bomb aiming, aircraft detection, armament, fighter aircraft, and ground-to-air defence. The Abwehr's response was to switch its military intelligence-gathering emphasis from naval to air, beginning with the establishment in 1937 of an AbtI/Luft (air espionage) section at Ast Hamburg manned by Nikolaus Ritter. His first spy was Arthur Owens, turned over to him from the naval section, and in July he received orders directly from Canaris to expand his espionage effort to the United States, with particular emphasis on stealing plans for the bombsight being developed by the Norden Company. Apparently, the Luftwaffe wanted to improve its aim.[5]

In 1939, Ritter received as his deputy a civilian lawyer, Dr. Karl-Heinz Kramer, who was to do seemingly good work for Ast Hamburg by developing spies in England through then neutral Hungary. These spies may never have existed, however, because later in the war Kramer became spymaster in Stockholm to the JOSEPHINE and HEKTOR networks in England, which supplied much intelligence to Hitler's headquarters, most of it misleading since the networks did not exist. Kramer's spies were his own invention and he wrote their messages himself. Kramer was to become very much a part of the "counter-activity" that was the mark of the anti-Nazi conspiracy in the Abwehr.[6]

One can see Canaris's reasoning. Air intelligence could be key to winning or losing the next war. He had to be the best-informed in Germany of advances in military aviation and air defence by Germany's neighbours, both to better assess the foreign danger but also to keep control over the flow of this intelligence to the Luftwaffe and to Hitler's headquarters should it become necessary to choke it off occasionally. To ensure he could do the latter if the time came, he needed like-minded anti-Nazis in charge at Abt1/Luft at Ast Hamburg. In Ritter and Kramer he had them.

Preparing for a ground war was more straightforward. France was the traditional enemy, and Hitler's foreign policy promised a clash sooner or later. The likelihood was that the initial battleground would again include Belgium and Holland, so Canaris flooded the three countries with spies well before the war, with more to come after it started. Some of them had the most ingenious covers.

Georges Delfanne — to give an example — was a twenty-seven-year-old former Belgian soldier who had knocked about in various odd jobs until recruited by the Abwehr. He was given the task of discovering what he could about the deployment of the Belgian army and set about it in classic spy style. Posing as a travelling salesman for special ink blotters, he toured Belgium on his bicycle, systematically visiting all military installations and encampments. His blotters were of a design especially useful to the military; sales were brisk and numerous, with Delfanne jotting down in his invoice book the names of the buyers and the location of their units. Before long, he was able to build up a complete picture of the Belgian army's order of battle, which was supplemented by pencil sketches of fortifications, bridges, ditches, gun emplacements, and anything else of military interest. On the eve of Hitler's invasion of France and the Low Countries in May 1940, the defences of Belgium had been laid bare.

What made Delfanne a living legend in the Abwehr, however, was his penetration of the great fortress of Eban-Emael, located near the Belgian-Dutch border. This massive structure, a small mountain riddled with tunnels connecting armoured cupolas, loomed over the Albert Canal. Completed in 1935, and garrisoned by 1,200 men, it was the key to the defences of Belgium and was considered impregnable. It was, however, to become forever associated with German military ingenuity, for it was famously captured by German troops landing gliders on its top and fanning out to blow up its big-gun emplacements with hollow charges. It surrendered in twenty-eight hours. Delfanne's contribution was to sketch with his coloured pencils vital details of the fortress that could not be seen from the air.[7]

One can imagine Delfanne at work: Spring, the grass green and bright before the entrance blockhouse, the sentries enjoying the warmth of the sun, a young man leaning on his bicycle nearby, smoking a cigarette. Over his shoulder there would be a cloth satchel containing a refilled bottle of the local wine, a half baguette of bread, some cheese, and his pencils. His sample blotters would be in a leatherette portfolio strapped to a frame on one side of the bicycle. Somewhere, perhaps also in the satchel, he would have a schoolboy's drawing kit comprising ruler, triangle, and protractor — everything he needed for triangulating the heights and depths of structures. In his back pocket would be his invoices with its names and locations....

The scene changes to May 10, gliders in the sky spiralling down like vultures, sweeping in to alight on the great back of the fortress, the little figures of men scurrying here and there, puffs of smoke, and panic within....

One can appreciate why it became the practice in wartime to shoot spies.

A SPY FOR THE FBI

The idea of selling himself to the British as a double agent seems to have been Owens's own idea, and it apparently took time for Major Ritter to believe that he had actually gotten away with it. Yet he had, and the results were very encouraging. It also showed that the Abwehr's MI5 adversary was but a parody of the omnipotent, all-seeing British Security Service of myth and movies. Alfred Hitchcock's *Sabotage* (1936) had depicted an organization of flint-eyed Englishmen in suits stalking a swarthy Bolshevik evildoer with relentless but noble professionalism. A German spy of superb cunning and method succumbed to the calculations and courage of British investigators in *The Thirty-Nine Steps* (1935). Real life, Ritter must have thought, surely could not have fallen this far short of fiction, but it had.

Ritter decided to try the double-agent trick on the Americans, the nearest thing to a U.S. security service being the Federal Bureau of Investigation. On February 7, 1940, an American of German extraction named William Sebold arrived by ship in New York City from Germany. Agents of the FBI awaited him; he was expected. Before departing, he had used the excuse of having lost his passport to call in at the American consular office in Cologne, where he warned officials that he had information of tremendous importance to impart to the appropriate authorities in the United States. It was arranged that he be met on arrival.

The story Sebold told the FBI had echoes of that told to Scotland Yard by Charles Eschborn. He had a brother in Germany, he said, and their grandfather had been a Jew, so he had no choice but to agree to spy when asked. He had come from the United States to visit his mother, and on arrival was approached by an agent of the German secret service. He took his spy training in Hamburg, but was determined from the outset to turn against the Germans as soon as he arrived back in America. And here he was.

When he said that he was to build his own transmitter and find his own radio operator, the FBI obligingly built it for him, establishing it at Centerport, Long Island, and manning it with its own operators. The Federal Communications Commission (FCC) was warned of the illegal transmitter so that it would not take action when its signal was picked up. His messages were to be in a transposition cipher, a new key being derived every day from the popular novel by Rachel Field, *All This and Heaven Too*. Radio contact with Germany was made on May 20, 1940.

Again, as with MI5, the FBI did not take some of the precautions elementary to operating a clandestine wireless transmitter. It always sent from the same location, apparently forgetting that the Germans would know the FCC would detect the signal and have it raided. Indeed, the radio direction-finding stations of the Canadian Navy and of Canada's Department of Transport quickly zeroed in on it.[8] The Germans would have known that the only way that Sebold's transmitter could stay alive was if it was under American control.

The Radio Security Service also missed this point. The Canadians sent their DF results to England and this led the RSS to inform the FBI that a suspicious transmitter had been detected on Long Island. The FBI replied that it knew this, and had its "exact location." The British encouraged the Americans to allow the clandestine station to continue to operate until fully investigated and the "extent of the organization behind it ascertained." In the meantime, the RSS copied the traffic and Strachey's ISOS section occasionally broke it, coming up with FBI-concocted gems like this:

> 13 Nov. 1940
> DUNN says U.S. Intelligence sends messages out of Germany by engraving them on silverware and camera parts, etc. Then they may spray them with a metal which is removed when the parts arrive here.

The FBI did not let on to MI5 that it was writing the messages until the following January.[9]

As for Sebold's story of feared persecution, it was a lie. Canaris despised the Nazi security and intelligence services, and he was opposed to the persecution of the Jews, helping them whenever he could. Indeed, one of the spies Major Ritter sent ahead of Sebold was Lily Stein, also Jewish, and when, a year later, she was arrested, she too claimed she had feared for family members. If this were really so, she could have safely contacted the appropriate authorities the moment she set foot in America.

What was particularly remarkable about the Sebold case was the questionnaire he brought to show Lily and the other agents he was to contact. It asked for detailed information on bombers locating targets by means of intersecting radio beams, on "electric eye" proximity fuses, on protective clothing for mustard gas, on airborne bacteriological warfare, and on self-sealing aircraft fuel tanks. In terms of identifying some of the current preoccupations of German war science, it was as revealing as the "Oslo Report," which disclosed German interest in pilotless aircraft and long-range gyroscope-guided rocketry. It had been surreptitiously delivered to the British embassy in Oslo four months earlier.[10]

The item in the Sebold questionnaire on navigating bombers onto their targets by radio beams is especially noteworthy.

> 1. Find out if International Telephone and Telegraph Co. have offered to French and English Governments a new procedure of bombing which works as follows: The airplane is directed by some sort of ray against the target and crosses a second ray shortly before reaching the target by which the bombs will be released. Try to get particulars pertaining to the construction of the device, and find out how it has worked in tests and whether there have been negotiations in the French and English Governments, with the view of selling it to them.[11]

What was being described was the *Knickebein* system already installed in German bombers but the existence of which the British only puzzled out the following June from prisoner-of-war eavesdropping, mysterious equipment in downed German aircraft, and wireless decrypts. Once this technology was discovered, Churchill ordered "absolute priority" for the development of countermeasures.[12]

As for the other items on the questionnaire, the British were not yet seriously considering germ warfare, work on gas-proof clothing had only just begun, and scientists in Britain were only in the very early stages of developing proximity fuses.[13] The latter was a major advance in tactical weaponry that the Allies managed to deploy later in the war. The idea was to have a miniature radio transmitter/receiver in the nose of a shell that would cause it to explode when near an aircraft or at a specified height from the ground. It was a war-winning weapon, in that it detonated anti-aircraft shells as they approached or passed by aircraft without having to actually hit them.

Had there been an information-sharing agreement between the Americans and British, the FBI could have been very helpful. Along with everything else, the Bureau could have told its MI5 counterparts that Sebold's questionnaire was in the form of four microphotographs no bigger than "pencil points" stuck to the back of his watch. But instead, it would take MI5 another year to learn about microdots.

The really curious thing about the Sebold questions, however, which perhaps some of the FBI men might have wondered about, was why he had them written out on microdots in the first place? They could have been memorized.

TOUCHÉ

The meeting with Major Ritter at the beginning of April 1940 was to be Owens's last Channel-crossing, and the most devastating for Britain's safety. Again the teletype machine Hamburg–Berlin clattered out the latest from Owens. The first message comprised a lengthy description of all the RAF repair and maintenance facilities in England, including those of the St. Athan air base, later to be bombed twelve times. Robertson, according to one of his notes to file, had obtained permission to send this information from Commodore Boyle, by then the new director of Air Intelligence.[14]

The second message was a follow-up on Owens's earlier report about the British developing a device to detect aircraft at a distance:

> Reference: Ast Hamburg 1252/39 I Luft 21.9.39
> [Translation]
> Agent 3504 reports 5.4.40 at a meeting in Antwerp:
> The equipment in the above report is now installed along the entire eastern coast and has been tested for the first time in March, allegedly with success. Aircraft were perfectly detected from a distance of 400 km and more, and it is hoped to be secure from surprise attacks in the future.
> The equipment is mounted on wooden towers, 20–30 feet high, 10–12 feet in diameter, some round, some square, some hexagon. On April 2, I counted six towers between Grimsby and Southbend, one of them stood directly on the coast at Lowestoft, the others placed at equal distances over this section. I cannot give you pre-

cise positions because the areas are strongly guarded. One can only drive by at high speed. To get close to the towers is impossible. I still hope to get further details some other way....[15]

It seems Owens had taken good advantage of his freedom and mobility. This time his information on radar was almost exactly right. He was describing the Chain Home radar system and correctly specified the range at which it could detect aircraft.

This was war-winning intelligence. If it came to a fight in the skies over England, the Luftwaffe had the numerical advantage. Electronic early warning would help the British even the odds. German scientists had been working on the idea themselves, but Owens's report showed that the British had already got there. It would have been obvious to most German airmen that if the Luftwaffe were to do battle over England, the towers should be the first targets to be destroyed.

This typed entry appears in Liddell's diary at the beginning of May: "He [Owens] has not been in a position to give the Germans very much from this country, except information we have planted on him."[16]

If someone in MI5 had given Owens the Chain Home radar item to plant on the Germans, then something surely was desperately wrong somewhere in that organization.

CANARIS BETRAYS THE CAUSE

November 1939–June 1940

Canaris earned high marks from Hitler for his part in the invasion and defeat of France, and rightly so. It probably would not have happened without him.

With the exception of Hitler, who was forever the optimist, things had looked pretty bleak to Germany's military leadership when the British and French declared war at the beginning of September 1939. France alone had a larger army, and when her troops and tanks, backed up by the British Expeditionary Force, moved up to the Belgium frontier, Hitler's generals were worried. A prompt attack while most of Germany's air and ground forces were still in Poland would have brought a quick defeat, and none of them wanted that.[1] No matter how much they despised Hitler, they could not forget that the French had gone out of their way to humiliate Germany after the Armistice of 1918, and it was not something they wanted repeated.

Fortunately for Germany, the French and British simply sat on their arms in the weeks needed to get the troops back from Poland. The two sides then lined up along the German and French frontiers, each waiting for the other to move. Hitler became restless and started pushing his generals to attack. It made them amenable to rebellion.

General Ludwig Beck, the former chief of the general staff who resigned in 1938 over Hitler's plan to invade Czechoslovakia, began circulating secret memos disparaging Germany's chances of winning against France and Britain, and predicting a war of attrition similar to that of the First World War. His fears were shared by many of the army's leaders, including Beck's successor, General Franz Halder, but when he began suggesting Hitler be deposed, there was reluctance. This changed when Hitler insisted that Germany take the offensive. Halder began talking of arranging an "accident" for the Führer.

The sixty-year-old Beck was a Prussian general of the old school, where the honour of the army and the Reich were intimately intertwined. He was appalled by the prospect of Germany once again violating the neutrality of Belgium, and worried about the damage this would do to Germany's image before the world. He also argued that the United States would surely come on side with the British and French as it had in the First World War, making Germany's defeat inevitable.[2]

Working with the Abwehr's Colonel Hans Oster and his aide, Hans von Dohnányi, Beck came up with a plan reminiscent of the aborted coup attempt of 1938. It called for the troops stationed in Berlin under General Erwin von Witzleben to surround the government quarter the moment Hitler ordered the offensive against France. Beck would then become temporary head of state until a caretaker government was formed. Along with Witzleben and Halder, General Walther von Brauchitsch, the army's commander-in-chief, and the quartermaster-general, Karl-Heinrich von Stülpnagel, were on side. There were important civilians, as well, including the former Reich minister of economics, Dr. Hjalmar Schacht. Canaris was on board, too.

The Abwehr's role — as Colonel Lahousen described it after the war — was to use its own specially trained commandos to rush in to seize and arrest the members of Hitler's entourage and Hitler himself, if possible. Meanwhile, in anticipation of the coup, Canaris was to put out peace feelers. This at first involved trying to set up the Pope as an intermediary between the conspirators and the British and French. Dr. Joseph Müller, a prominent Bavarian Catholic and lawyer, was given the task of making the approaches to the Vatican under the direction of Oster and von Dohnányi. Müller arrived in Rome in mid-September, and by mid-October had the Pope's commitment to help.[3]

The tactic Canaris used in Holland was more direct. On October 17, the MI6 office in The Hague received a telephone call from a Colonel

Teichmann on behalf of generals Gerd von Rundstedt and Gustav von Wietersheim, both just then finishing up their command assignments in Poland. An army-led coup d'état was in the works, Teichmann explained, and the two generals wanted to know what terms Germany could expect from Britain and France for a cessation of hostilities. Chamberlain's government was delighted when told of the overture, and shot back that a withdrawal from Poland and respect for Czechoslovakia's autonomy would be the principal conditions.[4]

The involvement of von Rundstedt was important. He was then Germany's highest-profile commander, having served in senior posts with the Reichswehr — the peacetime army — throughout the 1920s and '30s, and the British would certainly have known of him. He had been approached by the conspirators in 1938 but had turned them down. This time, however, in the wake of the SS carrying out Hitler's policy of subduing Polish resistance by executing the civilian leadership classes, he had changed his mind. Both he and von Wietersheim had protested the killings, but Himmler's and Heydrich's Einsatzgruppen carried them out anyway.[5]

With the blessings of Chamberlain, and at the direction of his War Cabinet, the two MI6 officers at The Hague had several preliminary meetings with representatives of the two generals, giving them a wireless set and a secret cipher so that they could maintain contact inside Germany. On November 3, the Germans wirelessed that the generals agreed in principle to the British terms and wanted to know what kind of negotiators would be acceptable.[6]

On November 4 all seemed well. Halder issued a secret alert to the conspirators to make ready. Then, the next day, everything fell apart. General von Brauchitsch had taken it upon himself to give Hitler one last chance by trying personally to persuade him to give up launching the attack. Hitler turned on him like an angry dog.

Brauchitsch was not a strong personality. Hitler threw one of his famous tantrums, which usually involved stomping about the room, slamming his fist on the furniture, and pounding on the walls, then alternating between raging at the top of his voice and holding his breath until his face went purple. The performance peaked with a slur about the defeatist "spirit of Zossen," a direct allusion to the general staff then headquartered near the village of Zossen. Brauchitsch wilted. Then Hitler paused. His voice dropped and his eyes bore into those of the army chief: "What are you planning?" Brauchitsch left the room, shaking.

Halder panicked when Brauchitsch told him what happened. He called off the plot forthwith and ordered all involved immediately to destroy any incriminating evidence. If Hitler wanted an offensive in the West, he was to get it. The conspirators had no choice but to set their plotting aside and bend their energies toward beating the French.[7]

It was not going to be easy. An assault on the string of forts the French dubbed the Maginot Line between Luxembourg and Switzerland seemed unlikely to succeed, while a straight thrust through Belgium was bound to be halted sooner or later, just as Beck predicted, with the familiar war in the trenches following. What this meant in blood and misery was still a current memory from the First World War. Nevertheless, the army's general staff dutifully resumed working on plans to attack through Belgium, as done in 1914, this time with Holland thrown in.

Hitler was aware of the army's misgivings, and it irked him. He regarded France as a rotten apple to be knocked down with a tap, but he, too, could see that the formula of 1914 was problematic. At the end of October, this had led him to propose using armoured forces to try to punch a hole through the right wing of the Anglo/French armies where they rested on Luxembourg, the idea being to go through the forested area known as the Ardennes and break out into the open country in France around Sedan.[8] The army general staff had been cool to the idea while it looked like the Nazis were to be overthrown; when the plot was shelved, they considered it more seriously. This, again, was where Canaris came in.

By late 1939, certainly thanks to Ast Hamburg's spy A-3504 — Arthur Owens in England — and thanks to the network of Abwehr spies in France strung out along its northern frontier,[9] Canaris was able to assure Hitler with great confidence that the British and French were grouping their forces along the western frontier of Belgium in expectation of a German attack through the Low Countries, and that they intended immediately to advance to meet it. Opposite the Forest of the Ardennes, however, the enemy was thinly spread. A blow there, Hitler was told, and the enemy front could split. By swinging to the west from the penetration, and driving toward the Channel, "the entire northern enemy group could be encircled and eliminated."[10]

On November 12, Hitler unilaterally ordered two panzer divisions and a motorized infantry division to army Group A, then commanded by von Rundstedt and holding the line facing the Ardennes. Von Rundstedt and his chief of staff, Erich von Manstein, had been badgering OKH for more forces for some time, but unsuccessfully. Now they were told they were to undertake what was to be a second major thrust into France — an armoured strike out of the Ardennes and across the Meuse River at Sedan.[11]

The idea quickly gained traction. That previous summer, the British military theorist B.H. Liddell Hart had come out with a new book that seemed to state the obvious: if the Germans should attack France, their best bet was to go through Belgium. The Forest of the Ardennes was least best, Liddell Hart wrote, because its narrow roads and deep gullies were easily defended. Hart was considered the leading theorist in armoured warfare, a still-novel concept, and his writings during the 1920s and '30s had made a deep impression on the German general staff, as well as with the staffs of other European armies. If Liddell Hart said the Ardennes was impractical for motorized forces, then the Germans could assume that the British and French thought so too. It was the perfect recipe for surprise.[12]

When Germany's most respected mobile warfare strategist, General Heinz Guderian, declared that the Ardennes could be crossed, and the attack should be as powerful as possible, planning began in earnest. Even General Halder was won over. A really strong blow in the solar plexus of the French defence just might knock the enemy off its feet. The three divisions allocated to von Rundstedt by Hitler were upped to a corps, and then to three, two-thirds of the available armoured formations. Instead of the attack through Holland and northern Belgium being the main thrust, it was to be diversionary, and this is where Canaris again came in. It was the Abwehr's job to ensure that the attackers had the best and latest information on the dispositions of the enemy. It was also the Abwehr's job to hide the real plan. Canaris succeeded brilliantly on both counts.[13]

First, however, Canaris had an urgent problem to solve. Halder's abrupt cancellation of the coup attempt had left the talks with the British in Holland dangling. They had got to the point where the two MI6 officers involved, Major Richard Stevens and Captain S. Payne Best, were poised to wrap things up whenever General Wietersheim became available in person. Now the whole thing had to be aborted. It could be many months before another coup attempt, and the longer it took, the more certain it was that something of the generals' peace overtures would leak back to the Nazis. Von Rundstedt and von Wietersheim were in deadly danger.

Canaris was famous among those close to him for his creativity in pulling hot irons from hot fires, and he demonstrated it this time. He and Germany's most dangerous man, Nazi security service chief Reinhardt Heydrich, were close, like cobra and mongoose, both socially and in their work, the younger man treating the older with wary respect. It seems that Canaris now told Heydrich that he had a sting operation underway that could lead to the kidnapping of two British intelligence officers. Heydrich's SD was just then in the process of amalgamating with the German police forces, including the Gestapo, to form the Reichssicherheitshauptamt (RSHA) — the Office for National Security. Canaris offered the new Nazi police and intelligence supremo-to-be an early chance to show his spurs.[14] Naturally, there is no written record of their plan, but it can be seen through the sequence of events that followed.

Halder called the plot off on November 5. Nevertheless, two days later Stevens reported to London that General Wietersheim was prepared to meet with him shortly. Then, on November 8, at 9:20 p.m., a bomb exploded at a reunion of Nazi party faithful at the Bürgerbräukeller, a famous beer hall in Munich, killing eight people and injuring sixty-three. Hitler had been the evening's speaker and had just left.

The Führer was shaken by the near miss. His train had just pulled into Nuremberg station when a pair of grim-faced officers boarded. Hitler met them in the corridor.

"What's happened?" he asked.

"Mein Führer, I have just received a report from Munich that an attempt has been made on your life. Roughly an hour after you left the Bürgerbräukeller there was a powerful explosion. The people who were still there in the hall were buried under the falling ceiling."

Hitler went pale. Gasping for breath, he asked for Himmler. He was told the SS chief was still in Munich. Hitler became excited. He ordered that Himmler stay until the criminals were caught: "Tell him that he should proceed ruthlessly and exterminate the whole pack of them, root and branch."[15]

The next day, on November 9, Stevens telephoned London to say that he and Best were on their way to meet the "Big Man." They never returned.

Best and Stevens arrived that afternoon at Venlo, a town on the border between Holland and Germany, enthused and full of hope, accompanied by a Dutch intelligence officer and a driver. The encounter with von Wietersheim was to take place in the patch of road between the crossing barriers. The Germans were waiting when the car carrying the English and Dutchmen pulled up. The parties got out.

Suddenly, the Germans sprang at Best and Stevens. They were manhandled into the German vehicles. Shots were fired. The Dutch officer fell. The German cars sped back over the border.

The kidnappings made headlines in Germany. Photographs of Stevens and Best were splashed across the newspapers next to that of Johann Georg Elser, an unemployed carpenter and sometime Communist who had been caught the same day. He had been held at the Swiss border a few hours before the explosion when found to be carrying some notes on making explosives, a postcard of the Bürgerbräukeller, and some suspicious metal parts. When news of the Munich bombing reached the frontier post, the officials there knew they had the man. In the newspapers, Best and Stevens were labelled the evil geniuses behind Elser's cowardly act, nabbed by the new amalgamated Nazi police and intelligence service.[16]

Heydrich was delighted and basked in the glow. The British government was mortified. German broadcast radio blared, claiming that Best and Stevens had been suckered into capture by means of a phony tale of treacherous generals plotting a coup. At the round table in Whitehall, Stewart Menzies, speaking for MI6, insisted that the offer from von Rundstedt and von Wietersheim had been genuine. A Foreign Office post-mortem intoned: "We must therefore conclude that the balance of evidence shows that the 'feelers' we received were not, originally at any rate, part of a plot organized by Herr Himmler."[17]

In other words, Chamberlain and his government — which included Churchill as head of the navy — actually did figure out the truth. They could only guess at what had gone wrong, however, and still held out hope that the generals might yet pull off their coup.

During the hullabaloo, the Nazi police and intelligence personnel involved never identified who the generals were supposed to have been. The British did not make public the names either.

As for Elser, despite the enormity of his crime and all the publicity, he was never brought to trial. According to exclusively Nazi sources, he was secretly shot at the Dachau concentration camp in April 1945 on Hitler's order. There is no way to prove this; just as there is no way to find hard evidence that he had been a stooge of Heydrich and Canaris all along.[18]

DECEIVING THE ALLIES

Air reconnaissance, the reports of spies, and the interception of the enemy's wireless traffic were important sources of intelligence on the disposition of the Anglo-French forces facing Germany, and by the end of April, Fremde Heere, the army headquarters agency responsible for collating intelligence from all sources, had a comprehensive picture of the location and strengths of the opposition armies along France's northern border. This it displayed at Zossen on a large terrain map of Western Europe, which was updated constantly. General Halder, now committed to the upcoming struggle, is said to have looked down on the map and pointed to the area of the Forest of the Ardennes: "Here is where they are weakest. Here we must go through!" [19]

The man responsible for maintaining the map was forty-year-old Captain Alexis Baron von Rönne, later to die for his role in denying Hitler victory in Normandy in 1944.

For his part, aside from the spies he already had in place, Canaris planted agents with wireless transmitters just over the borders of the target countries. Their specific task was to report any last-minute troop movements or other developments. Andreas Folmer was probably typical of these Abwehr infiltration agents.

Folmer was a thirty-two-year-old Luxembourger who had served fourteen years in the Belgian army before going off to the Belgian Congo to seek his fortune. Finding only heat and disease, he came back to Belgium and dabbled in illegal currency activities that soon landed him in jail. In 1938, the Belgian Deuxième Bureau recruited him for a secret photographic survey of the German fortifications along the border with Luxembourg, a mission he carried out with great success. Then, early the next year, he secretly went over to the Germans. His new spymaster, Captain Oscar Reile of Abt IIIF (Counter-espionage) at Ast Wiesbaden, gave him a transmitter and sent him back to Brussels as an "E-Mann" — the Abwehr term for a spy who has penetrated a foreign intelligence service. Folmer wirelessed numerous reports on the Belgian Deuxième Bureau's activities right up to May 9, when Reile told him to cross into Germany immediately. The invasion began the next day.[20]

The Abwehr's other task, one that was even more important, was to devise a deceptive cover for the invasion plan. Surprise was essential because the Forest of the Ardennes was a nightmare maze of narrow roads tight to the trees. Infantry and panzer units would be slow making their way through, and if the French caught on to what was happening too early, the German forces could be trapped there, densely packed, easy victims to air and artillery bombardment.

In solving this problem, Canaris decisively contributed to the success of the campaign. He made two moves: First, during the fall of 1939, MI5's star double agent, Arthur Owens — A-3504 to the Germans — repeatedly returned from his visits to his Abwehr controller across the Channel with reports that the Germans were planning to attack France through Belgium. These reports were true, but for the first two months of the war that did not matter since Canaris was expecting Hitler to be overthrown. With the collapse of the plot and the decision to go with the Ardennes, it then became simply a matter of cementing in the minds of the British and French the intelligence they had already been given.[21] This was achieved by allowing MI8(c), the wireless listening agency that Major Gill and Lieutenant Trevor-Roper put such store in, to pick the reports of Abwehr spies operating in France and the Low Countries who just happened to be using easy-to-break ciphers. This gave the impression that was where Germany's attention was directed.[22]

Second, Canaris allowed the peace overtures through the Pope to continue. By the New Year, this had led to the Pope privately informing the British envoy to the Vatican that a "violent" attack through Belgium was impending and that several highly placed generals were prepared to prevent it by overthrowing Hitler if they could expect reasonable peace terms. The Foreign Office, still unsure of what exactly had happened at Venlo, showed cautious interest.

Meanwhile, Oster had been warning the Dutch military attaché in Berlin, Major Gijsbertus Sas, that Holland was in the path of the coming offensive, tipping him off throughout the fall and winter to each tentative start date. He continued to do so into the spring, not knowing that the focus of the attack had shifted to the Ardennes. The Dutch government was skeptical, for Germany during the First World War had respected Holland's neutrality, but the British and the French heard about the warnings and took heed.[23]

At the beginning of May, when it seemed to Oster and Beck that the attack in the West was going to take place before their efforts through the Vatican matured, they sought to absolve "decent Germans" of blame. They authorized Müller to deliver this note to His Holiness:

> To the regret of my principal, I must inform you that our negotiations cannot continue because we have been unable to persuade the generals to act in the wake of the successful operation in Norway. The offensive is imminent. Hitler will probably violate the neutrality of Belgium and Holland.[24]

They asked that the message be transmitted to the Belgians, Dutch, British, and French. The Pope complied.

Two days later, on May 9, on the eve of the offensive, the Nazi wireless intercept service, the Forschungsamt, listened in on a late-evening telephone call from Sas to the duty officer at the Dutch Ministry of Defence. "Tomorrow at dawn," he said. "Hold tight. Will you please repeat? You understand what I mean, of course."[25] There could be no doubt what he meant. In Rome, the Belgian envoy was also alerted and his cable to his government intercepted; copies went to Canaris, Himmler, and Hitler. The latter is said to have been furious.

German forces invaded Belgium and Holland the following morning and the French and British leaped forward to meet them. As they did so, German panzers burst out of the Forest of the Ardennes, crossed the Meuse, passed Sedan, and then cut behind in a sprint for the Channel. It worked perfectly. The Allied armies had used up much of their fuel and fell back with difficulty. The British reached the coast at Dunkirk in disarray, there to be encircled. On May 20–21, the greater part of the British force was evacuated to England, but without its arms and transport. The Germans then turned toward Paris. France surrendered on June 22.

The world was astonished. Hitler crowed that it was the biggest victory in history. The issue of the leaked warnings was only feebly pursued. This suggests that Canaris told Hitler that the leaks were deception.[26] And so they had been. One can imagine Hitler clapping him on the shoulder and beaming: "Well done!"

DARKNESS OVER EUROPE

Britain's Secret Intelligence Service — MI6 — was devastated. In the interwar years it had invested primarily in communications intelligence, which had served it very well in the First World War. The Government Code & Cipher School had endeavoured to remain up-to-date on all the latest advances in cryptology, so that it could read the cable and wireless traffic of foreign diplomats and, hopefully, the wireless traffic of Germany's armed forces in the event of war. Conventional espionage was carried on much as always.

Such overseas networks of spies and informers as MI6 did have were mostly built around field staff stationed in the British embassies and consulates, usually under the nominal cover of passport control officers but also including a handful of independent spy networks. Little provision had been made for what would happen if the embassies and consulates were forced suddenly to close and the staffs to flee. Even MI6's secret wireless network collapsed after the German offensive, its teams having to pack up their transmitters and make for the coast.[27] As Hitler's armies drew up along the Channel opposite Dover, the British were faced with a virtual blackout on German activities in Western Europe.

This sorry situation is testimony to how completely MI6 had allowed the art of espionage to lapse. Spy-running was a passive activity dependant on Britons travelling abroad or locally recruited agents reporting to the MI6 officer at the British embassy. Little thought had been given to organizing stay-behind networks that could continue to report to Britain by clandestine wireless, by secret courier, or by letters in invisible ink if a country were overrun.[28] The defeat of Holland, Belgium, and France obliterated the main British foreign intelligence sources. With England facing invasion and the government and service chiefs clamouring for intelligence on German intentions, MI6 had nothing to offer.

An MI6 officer arriving back home after being ousted from his overseas posting was shocked by how desperate he found things:

> I could hardly believe my ears when I heard that crystal-gazing had become the rage in certain circles. It was true though. An enterprising fortune-teller had managed to convince some highly-placed officials that his glass ball could forecast events in the future and advise on current affairs. For a short time he had enjoyed a monopoly in the field of Western European intelligence and was even patronized by the Service Intelligence chiefs. It was argued that since no information was coming in, any sort was better than none; and consequently crystal-gazing was worth a try. I only hope none of our operations suffered from this naive outlook...."[29]

The "crystal gazer" was, in fact, a stargazer, the Hungarian astrologer Louis de Wohl. He had been in Britain since 1935 and had acquired a modest following in some of the more exalted female social circles. This he parlayed — in Britain's hour of crisis — into a dinner party that included Britain's foreign secretary, Lord Halifax.

In fairness to Halifax, and to those in British intelligence who gave de Wohl hearings over the months that followed, he sold himself by a basic lie. He claimed that at the very least he would be able to indicate what Hitler's astrologer was probably telling him, and that this would give some hint as to when the Nazi leader was likely or unlikely to undertake a major action.[30] This suggestion had a certain appeal, except that in reality Hitler hated astrologers, regarded the practice as dangerous quackery, and put its proponents into concentration camps. He was a hard-nosed pragmatist who had no time for organized religion much less astrological hocus-pocus. It is surprising that Britain's Foreign Office had not picked up on this.

De Wohl was made a captain in the army, given an office at Grosvenor House, one of London's fashionable hotels, and allowed to set up shop as the War Office's one-man Psychological Warfare Department. He then proceeded to issue pamphlets describing the stellar aspects of the leading Nazis, with special emphasis on those who were born under lucky stars. On the subject of Germany following up its victory with an attack across the Channel, he had this to say:

> The first good aspect favouring a combined operation that I could find was in the last ten days in May, when Jupiter would be in conjunction with the position of Neptune at Hitler's birth....[31]

By way of explanation, he wrote:

> As you will see, each heavenly body in our solar system is "linked up" with a certain realm of things. Mars is linked up with "all that is pointed," "all that is sharp and cutting," with iron, steel, weapons, war, aggression and so on. Neptune is linked up with or has a bearing on "all that is hidden" and "all that is un-ordered," with the chaotic, the intuitive, the secret. And, as Mars has a bearing on iron, Neptune has a bearing on dyes, chemicals, and oil, and also on the sea....

One of the recipients of these perambulations was the director of Naval Intelligence, Admiral John Godfrey. He was a celebrated no-nonsense officer, and it is amusing to imagine what he must have thought of it.[32]

Still, the nonsense aside, it was not hopeless. Britain did stand astride the world's postal and telegraph communications like no other country, and most of the world's letters and telegrams went through choke points it controlled. Moreover, the old chief, Admiral Sinclair, who had died of cancer the previous November, had been replaced by the talented, canny, and German-speaking Stewart Menzies, who had been with the service since 1923. He and Denniston, the Government Code and Cipher chief, had been Sinclair's key deputies, the latter in charge of the covert assault on foreign codes and ciphers, and Menzies in charge of foreign espionage and counter-espionage, most of it throughout the 1920s and '30s directed against the Bolshevik menace.

Menzies was fifty, a clubman, an enthusiast of the hunt, and a "somebody" in the highest social circles, ones that included the king and queen. During the First World War he had been liaison officer between army intelligence and Mansfield Cumming's fledgling secret intelligence service MI1(c). In the interwar years, he proved to be calculating and imaginative in his covert backing of the expatriate White Russians in their deadly struggles with the Soviets. He was an Etonian, an Establishment man; Communists were far more natural an enemy for him than Germans.[33]

However, Hitler was the enemy now, and he had just conquered most of Western Europe. The only card of real consequence in Menzies's hand was the gift bestowed some months before by Polish cryptologists of the theoretical solution to the enciphering machine used by the German armed forces, appropriately called Enigma. Denniston's team had frantically applied themselves to the insights and had begun to read some of the traffic of the Luftwaffe, but this source had dried up with the collapse of France. Menzies's best hope for the time being was to try to enlist the help of the refugee secret services whose countries had been conquered, and have his agents furrow the social circles, hotels, and bars of the remaining neutral countries, especially Portugal and Spain.

The intelligence situation must have deeply annoyed Winston Churchill. On the very day that Hitler launched his attacks in Western Europe, Churchill took over leadership of Britain's coalition government and became prime minister. A veteran of the War Cabinet of 1914–18, he had always pressed for a robust and aggressive secret service, having supported from the outset the covert interception of private mail, the pioneering code-breaking efforts of Room 40, and the pursuit of espionage generally. He was on record as believing that "the British Intelligence Service before and during the Great War was more skilfully organized, more daringly pursued, and achieved more important results than that of any other country, friend or foe."[34] This was not what he found in 1940.

Difficult as it was at MI6, at MI5 it was infinitely worse. Two decades of concentrating primarily on fighting Bolshevik subversion at home had left it without either the tools or the mentality to fight a sophisticated foreign espionage organization. In the first eight months of the war, when Britain had been wide open to the Continent with the ferry services running normally from Norway to Portugal, all MI5 had to show for its spy-catching efforts was one middle-aged woman caught sending a five-pound note to a known pre-war German agent. Any other spies in hand had turned themselves in.

Indeed, MI5 by its own admission still had no "practical working knowledge" of the Abwehr, other than what had been reported by Owens after his cross-Channel trips, a state of affairs that continued throughout the year.[35]

As prime minister, Churchill was entitled to see MI5's score card, and it would have been one of the first things he asked for. He was a war leader who counted scalps, but there were none to count.[36] He also had read *The German Secret Service* (1924), written by Germany's First World War spy chief, Colonel Walter Nicolai, and would have deduced from the book that Hitler had launched a massive espionage effort against Great Britain.[37]

Churchill fired Vernon Kell, MI5's chief since before the First World War, and his deputy, Eric Holt-Wilson. The service was shocked. The pair had been a team for three decades. Now here was sixty-eight-year-old Kell, grey-faced, clearing out his desk. "I get the sack from Horace Wilson," he bitterly noted in his diary June 10. Wilson was head of the civil service.[38]

Kell, who had been at the centre of so many national secrets for so long, resented being abruptly terminated like any ordinary bureaucrat. He died suddenly in March 1942.[39]

Churchill turned over ultimate control of MI5 to a high-level panel he set up within a week of taking power. The Home Defence (Security) Executive was tasked with coordinating the security activities of the War Office, the Home Office, and the Commander-in Chief, Home Forces, the latter's job being to prepare England for invasion. For chairman, Churchill chose Lord Swinton, formerly Philip Cunliffe-Lister, MP, who had been made secretary of state for air in 1935 to oversee the secret buildup of Britain's air defences, leaving the post in 1938. He interpreted his new mandate as being directly responsible for MI5 and proceeded to overhaul it by putting in his own people. Administrative chaos ensued.

A Mr. Crocker became joint head of B Division with Guy Liddell, who took over from Brigadier Harker when the latter moved up to replace Kell as chief. Robertson became the assistant to a Mr. Frost in the new "W Branch," the *w* standing for "wireless." The new section's mandate, building on the experience gained from running the SNOW transmitter, was to detect enemy agents by their intercepted communications, with illicit letters, lights, signals, and pigeons thrown in on top of wireless. Non-wireless double agents remained in a separate section under Major Sinclair.

Expansion of the service went out of control. New people were brought in merely because they were a friend of a friend, sometimes without the administrative staff being consulted beforehand, or even told after. There was no training, no corporate memory to be shared, no required reading list. Every officer got his own department. Co-operation up the chain of command or laterally was token or nil.

MI5 did recover eventually, with the 1941 reorganization carried out by veteran Indian Police officer David Petrie, but throughout the remainder of 1940 and into the early months of the following year, it was a dysfunctional Humpty-Dumpty organization whose pieces made no sum. It is against this background that MI5's further actions should be viewed.[40]

On the German side, it was the complete opposite. The Abwehr had performed superbly. Based on the recommendations of his First World War predecessor, Colonel Walter Nicolai, Canaris had built up an organization that had outfoxed, outmatched, and outplayed all its secret service adversaries: Belgian, Dutch, French, and British. The triumph was complete, down to the detail of deploying special Abwehr reconnaissance units behind the advancing German armies to sweep up the documents left behind by enemy headquarters units that had been overrun. It was magnificent, and tragic; Canaris had betrayed his own cause.

Canaris had delivered Hitler his victory; there is no getting around it. He did not have to tell Hitler the enemy was weak in front of the Ardennes; he could have said they were strong. He had given Hitler good intelligence, and the Führer had acted upon it.

One can imagine the Abwehr chief's discomfort as he watched Hitler basking in the glory. The German people now adored him. He was cheered whenever he appeared in public; young girls pelted him with flowers and swooned before him. Most of the doubting generals now allowed that he might be a military genius, or at least credited him with that superior intuition that the Prussian military caste believed was the mark of a great commander. The likes of Italian dictator Benito Mussolini, and the war party in Japan, saw their own ambitions mirrored in his success, with Mussolini declaring war on France mere days before its surrender. All this had been made possible because Canaris had decided to help Hitler.

Most devastating of all, the common soldiers and young officers of the German armed forces now worshipped Hitler. They would willingly and blindly lay down their lives for him. No chance now of Canaris using the Brandenburg Regiment in a coup attempt. The elite Abwehr commandos, trained to the teeth by the Nazi-hating Colonel Heinz, were proud of their exploits behind enemy lines and of their seizure of key bridges over Holland's canals. An order to act against Hitler would not be obeyed. Overthrowing a criminal regime had suddenly become infinitely more difficult.

Canaris, with Halder and the other dissident generals, undoubtedly felt he had had no choice. Hitler was still legally head of state and head of government. They could arrest him, or even kill him, but so long as he was Führer and chancellor, by right of majority vote in the Reichstag, they had a soldier's moral obligation to obey him. Once General Halder backed away from the planned coup, there was nothing for it but to try to make the attack against France succeed. At the very least, the army leadership owed it to the ordinary German soldier. Victory saves lives; defeat loses them.

Canaris was a man of normal sensitivity. It must have plucked at his conscience when it sank in that in order to give Hitler victory he had exploited the loyal Oster and the honest Beck. The latter had been seized with wonderment and disbelief as he followed the sweep of the German army through northern France. His whole argument had hung on the premise that the offensive would be quickly halted. He was totally mystified. "Beck stands before the carelessness and bad leadership of the English and French as before a riddle," one of his co-conspirators wrote.[41]

The answer to the riddle was Canaris. He had made it happen.

For now, Canaris could only hope that Hitler would be content to consolidate his gains while the conspirators reorganized to deal with him afresh. Assassination perhaps? There was no shortage of volunteers. Eliminate Hitler, eliminate the Nazis, and a responsible Germany would return, stronger than ever. The British could again be brought to the table.

Or could they?

Venlo and the Vatican. They would be remembered by the British. They would be seen as two very good reasons why German offers to stop the fighting could not be trusted.

E-186: THE SPY INSIDE

May–August 1940

Earlier that spring, before Hitler's invasion of the Low Countries, Ast Hamburg's Major Nikolaus Ritter — a.k.a. DR. RANTZAU — pondered a problem. He knew that when Belgium and Holland were overrun, as soon they would be, it would be the end of Arthur Owens's easy cross-Channel excursions. Yet DER KLEINER — the LITTLE GUY — was irreplaceable. Not only had he been the first to alert the Abwehr to British advances in radar, and to the existence of Britain's coastal radar network, but Ritter could mentally check off many other accomplishments:

> He reported on ship movements, RAF concentrations of aircraft in England and France, the delivery of war materials from the United States, the strengthening of coastal defences, the disposition of balloon barrages, the formation of merchant vessel convoys, the camouflaged locations of fuel dumps. He also gave daily weather reports, often both morning and evening....[1]

Owens had been head and shoulders above all other spies for three good reasons: he was inside British intelligence as a trusted double agent; he was allowed to travel Britain unsupervised; and MI5 accepted in principle that a double agent could be allowed solo visits to the Continent to confer with his German masters. Even having access to a secret transmitter, which Owens may have had, could not match the latter. The trick for Ritter that spring was to find a way for Owens to continue these in-person encounters.

Having meetings at sea was one possibility, and at their April meeting he and Owens discussed the idea, the latter mentioning that he had a Welsh fisherman friend who might be willing to help. They also discussed Owens getting certain "secret papers from aerodromes." A month later, on May 8, A-3504 wirelessed Hamburg: "Have applied for exit permit [for Holland]. Have secret documents. Order of battle RAF. When can we meet?"[2]

Two days later, Hitler launched his attack on France and the Low Countries. A meeting at sea it would be.

MI5 procured the fishing boat and crew, and presumably the RAF documents promised to Ritter. It also planted on Owens a confederate who was to accompany him to the rendezvous. This was a long-time MI5 informer named Sam McCarthy.[3]

For some time previously, Owens had said that DR. RANTZAU had been after him to find and cultivate someone who could replace him in Britain, and who could be brought to Germany for the appropriate training. This presented a tempting prospect to MI5, and Owens was encouraged to find some low-life type who might go for it. Thus it was arranged for McCarthy to happen upon Owens in his pub, posing as a petty criminal willing to do anything for money. Owens was fooled, and over his pints bragged that he was a double agent for the Germans working for MI5. He asked McCarthy if he would like to do so too. The money was very good.

McCarthy promptly reported this to Captain Robertson and it caused a huge flutter. Robertson had to tell his bosses, Liddell and Harker, that Owens appeared to be a double-crosser. There was anxious debate as to whether the rendezvous should be kept. There was talk about sending out an armed trawler or submarine to try to capture DR. RANTZAU, "as was done at Venlo."

In the end, it was decided to ride out the situation and for McCarthy to go along with Owens and keep the meeting with DR. RANTZAU. On the train up to Grimsby with McCarthy on May 19, Owens expanded upon how "rotten" MI5 was, on his contempt for Robertson, and on the advantages of working for the very nice Germans, who by this time were making world headlines by crushing Holland and breaking deep into Belgium and France. He took notes of what they could see from the train. When they arrived, McCarthy slipped away and relayed all this to Robertson by telephone. He was told to stick with it, and the trawler sailed the next morning with the complacent Owens and the now very hostile, probably frightened, McCarthy on board. That night, when an aircraft circled them with a signal light blinking, McCarthy could stand it no longer. He told the captain to darken ship and return to Grimsby, and had Owens locked in a cabin. When Owens was searched he was found to have MI5 secret papers on him along with the authorized RAF documents.

Robertson raced to Grimsby, arriving the following day. Owens squirmed under his close questioning, claiming that he said all those nasty things about him and MI5 because he was testing McCarthy. As for the secret papers — MI5's "IP Club List" — he said he got them from William Rolph, the former MI5 officer who was his partner in a dummy company MI5 had set up for him as cover. He said Rolph had hoped to get £2,000 for them.[4]

This should have been proof enough of Owens's treachery. Two thousand pounds was a great deal of money, and no matter what Rolph might have told him, he ought to have reported the matter to Robertson. The fact that he did not should have been the end of things, then and there; but, no, there was a much deeper problem: Rolph was no ordinary traitor.

In 1916, at the height of the First World War, labour unrest had swept Britain as it had the rest of Europe. It was the inevitable response to the Industrial Revolution and the rise of capitalism, but it was accelerated enormously by the mindless killing of millions of young men in the mud of France and Flanders. The leadership classes — those who led by right of birth or money — had lost enormous credibility among the masses, and in Russia in 1917 this translated into the Bolshevik Revolution and the establishment of the first communist state. Similar unrest stalked the streets and factories of Western Europe, including Britain, where the political and social establishment trembled more in fear of shop stewards than the kaiser. On February 19, 1916, a special counter-subversion group was formed with a nucleus of MI5 officers called the Ministry of Munitions Labour Intelligence (MMLI) department. Its ostensible assignment was to combat enemy-inspired sabotage in the munitions industries, but its actual task was to ferret out and destroy the seeds of revolution.

The MMLI became Britain's first dirty tricks agency of the twentieth century. Its spies and informers spread out among the factories, but instead of seeking German influences they sought to undermine the labour movement by fomenting unrest, promoting violence, and even counselling treason to obtain victims for arrest. When reports of these activities began leaking to the public, MMLI changed its name, becoming the innocuous Parliamentary Military Section 2 (PMS2), but it did not change its tactics. After being caught sponsoring a labour plot to murder the then prime minister, Lloyd George, the ensuing uproar in the House of Commons and in the press resulted in it being dismantled in 1917, with some of its officers being reabsorbed by MI5. Rolph had been a senior member of PMS2.[5]

But PMS2 did not go away. It had begun as an off-shoot of MI5 under Kell's direction, and still had the quiet support of high government officials and many persons of wealth and influence. Its dedicated, decidedly right-wing, and unscrupulous agents were still around, in civilian occupations mostly, and it is certain that Kell used them covertly against the communists in the 1920s and '30s. The IP Club list — the IP likely standing for "Important Persons" — must have been their names, and if it had got to the Nazis, they would have found kindred spirits on it, some of them still in positions of power.[6]

Shortly after being confronted with Owens's accusation, Rolph is said to have been found dead in his flat with his head in the gas stove — a popular method of both suicide and murder in those days. It was just as well. Prosecuting Rolph would have been delicate; the court naturally would have wanted to see what it was he was trying to sell.[7]

It was May 22. What was left of the British army had just been rescued at Dunkirk and the French were on the run. It was decided not to prosecute Owens, even though there was evidence enough to hang him. According to another of Robertson's many notes to file, he was placed under "strict supervision" and warned that if he tried any more tricks, he could go the same way as Rolph.[8]

The immediate problem was what to tell DR. RANTZAU if he had tried to keep the meeting. And he had. The airplane flashing the recognition light did have Major Ritter on board, and after flying around and getting nothing from the black sea below, the German pilot turned for home. When Ritter got back to Hamburg, a wireless message [in English] from A-3504 awaited him. "Sorry. Impossible to leave English coast which [is] under strict watch." A few days later, A-3504 proposed that he and his companion of the failed North Sea rendezvous meet Ritter in Portugal. On May 31, he sent the following message:

> "Getting worried. When is south african coming to help? Safer my man meet you Portugal and bring papers. He will replace me when in Canada…. Shall I try Portugal bringing all dope?"[9]

Owens was first to come, alone, arriving in Lisbon on June 14. Major Ritter awaited him.[10] It had been a long trip for the German. As the fighting was still going on in France, he had had to fly by way of Switzerland, Italy, and Spain to get to Portugal. It gave him lots of time to think.

Ritter decided he could not believe that Owens could have obtained an exit permit and a visa for Portugal on his own, on short notice, just when catastrophe was overtaking France and with Britain likely to be next. He challenged the little Welshman, and Owens broke down. He admitted he had been cornered into telling British intelligence he had been spying for the Germans. Rather than arrest him, they were trying to play him back. But his heart, he insisted, was really with Germany. If Major Ritter wanted, he would be glad to continue to work for him. As proof of his loyalty, he declared he had found someone, a former airman, who was short of money and willing to talk to the Germans.

Owens said he met the man in a pub, morose and loath to talk. When he thawed, he told him how he had been unjustly fired from his technical position with the Air Ministry. He had found a factory job but the pay was not enough. He had a wife and a mistress with a young child. It was the factory job that intrigued Ritter. "Mr. Brown" — Owens dropped his voice as he said the words — had obtained a position in MI5.[11] It took a few seconds for Ritter to digest this. British intelligence! Every spymaster's dream was to land an agent in the enemy's secret service.

After his earlier show of anger and disappointment, Ritter calmed down. He said he was prepared to take Owens at his word. They then parted, back to Hamburg and London respectively. Ritter, however — "with heavy heart" — had decided he would have to strike Owens from his list of reliable agents, even though he would continue to deal with him. He would also have a look at this "Mr. Brown" if Owens ever got him to Portugal.

On June 22, Ast Hamburg sent a new series of spy reports to Berlin, most of them to do with the RAF's order of battle and elements of Britain's air defences. The information, said to have been collected verbally from E-186, an agent of Hamburg's Abt IIIf (counter-espionage section), appeared of great value. It included among other things that the Air Ministry had moved some of its departments out of London into the hotels of Harrogate, a northern spa town, and described in detail the barrage-balloon defences in London. Most precious of all were those messages that gave the head-quarters locations for Fighter and Bomber Command:

> To: Abw I Luft/E Berlin
> Source: E-186 V-mann Ast.Hbg. IIIF
> [Translation]
> In the Stanmore area, northeast of Harrow and 200 to 300 meters northwest of the station at the end of the sub-urban railway line there are a number of barracks of the RAF. This is the location of Southern Bomber Command. All bomber operations outside the country originating in southern England are directed from here. The King is often seen in Stanmore....
> [Translation]
> Fighter Command, previously in Uxbridge, appar-ently has been moved to near High Wycombe in Buckinghamshire....
>
> Back to Abt I Luft Ast.Hbg B.Nr. 1522-23/40[12]

The reports had the locations correct, but switched, although it would have hardly mattered to the Germans. Both would have been recognized by Luftwaffe analysts as prime targets.[13]

The five-day interval between when Owens and Ritter finished their meeting and when the E-186 reports were sent suggests Ritter prepared them himself on his return to Hamburg. The "E" in E-186 stood for *Eingebauter* — literally "built-in" — signifying a spy inside the enemy's intelligence services. This fits with Owens telling Ritter that he had a disaffected former RAF officer working in MI5 who was prepared to turn traitor. It would seem that the E-186 messages were samples Owens had provided of the kind of intelligence he could procure.

Reaction from Berlin was enthusiastic and swift. While the message Ritter would have subsequently sent Owens has not been found, one can get a good impression of what he was asked for by Owens's reply, sent to Berlin in English the next day. As Owens was once again under MI5 control, the words are MI5's:

> To OKW Abw I Luft E
> By hand to Major Brasser
> Message 142 from A-3504 sent 23.6.40 received 24.06
> — 00.02
> [Translation]
> Secret documents safe. Cannot recommend anyone. Can you wait until MacCarthy better? Visa for self week to ten days — probably more.
>
> Back to Abt I Luft Ast.Hbg B.Nr. 1542/40[14]

And later, somewhat plaintively:

> 3504 meldet an 26.6.40
> [Translation]
> Details you require scattered over country. Do my best to locate same. Difficult due to new military area and regulations,
>
> Back to Abt I Luft Ast.Hbg B.Nr. 1560/40

Abw I Luft/E was the Abwehr air espionage section for England at headquarters in Berlin, and Major Brasser was the cover name for its new head, Major Friedrich Busch.

Owens apparently was none too keen to return to Portugal with the documents McCarthy was to bring — presumably the RAF order of battle Owens had promised Ritter at the beginning of May. Or perhaps MI5 did not want to chance sending him alone to Lisbon again. He might not come back. On July 24, the long-suffering, ever-doubtful, but presumably mollified Sam McCarthy — code-named FRANK — arrived in Lisbon. He carried with him a second batch of E-186 intelligence reports and some from Owens.[15]

MI5 was counting on massive German gullibility yet again. Hitler had stunned the world by conquering France in scarcely more than a month, yet in the week prior to McCarthy taking the flying boat from Poole to Lisbon, a defiant British government publicly and contemptuously dismissed Hitler's "final" offer of a negotiated peace. The war would go on, and the invasion preparations that Hitler had already started along France's northern coast would continue. In such circumstances, it should have been impossible for any ordinary person to fly to Portugal on short notice.

Hitler made the peace offer on July 19 in a speech in Berlin that was broadcast around the world. Churchill's reaction was classic: "I do not propose to say anything in reply to Herr Hitler's speech, not being on speaking terms with him." The Foreign Secretary, Lord Halifax, replied for the government.[16]

On his return, McCarthy told a familiar story. The Germans instantly accepted that he was a traitor and were keen to start up sabotage operations in Britain. If he and SNOW could find a suitable spot, the explosives and detonators could by dropped by parachute. A South African agent was waiting in Belgium to come over to help them. The quality of SNOW's information had fallen off of late and DR. RANTZAU hoped he would try harder. McCarthy was given the replacement transmitter SNOW had long demanded, and another questionnaire. He was entered in Hamburg's spy register as agent A-3554.[17]

The transmitter was one of the Abwehr's suitcase models, and MI5 was unfazed by the fact the Germans appeared to have complete confidence he could get it through British Customs.[18] McCarthy also saw no gold tooth in DR. RANTZAU's smile, a defining attribute of Owens's original description of him. Indeed, he gave quite a different picture. According to Robertson:

Frank's description of the Doctor is as follows:
Aged 41, height 5'8", round face, florrid complexion, high cheek bones, clean shaven, fair hair parted on the right side, irregular teeth, no gold visible (this is a distinguishing mark given us by SNOW); has one tooth on the left side of his mouth which protrudes so that it forces his upper lip over the gum when he laughs or talks with emphasis. Speaks with a broad New York accent, swears, is fond of telling filthy stories, and is exceedingly common.[19]

Robertson wrote that he thought this to be the same person, although it is hard to see how he accounted for the discrepancy of the gold tooth, or the mention that RANTZAU behaved like an ugly American. In his memoir after the war, Ritter told of going to Lisbon only once in 1940, and it was in June to meet Owens. It would seem that McCarthy met with Ritter's proxy.

Just at this time, MI5 was bottoming out: staff at all levels were in a state of passive rebellion; Vernon Kell's replacement, Brigadier Jasper Harker, could make no headway with his new chiefs; the influx of thousands of refugees had tipped security processing to Tilt. Many of the experienced officers were ready to quit. Robertson's little double-cross effort was one of the few patches of calm in the rising tide of administrative breakdown. Counting Eschborn, Owens, and now McCarthy, he had three double agents reporting to the Germans — CHARLIE, SNOW, and FRANK (renamed BISCUIT) — plus DRAGONFLY, a developing double agent also with links to Ast Hamburg.

This was a meagre enough showing after ten months of war, but with Churchill in the wings chomping furiously on his cigar and prodding Lord Swinton, at least it was something.

SNOW's wireless messages during July contained a modest amount of disinformation with respect to Britain's invasion defences, combined mainly with accurate daily weather observations for London. There were a few items of general intelligence, however. Among A-3504's weather reports relayed by teletype from Hamburg to Berlin was this:

SECRET
An OKW Abw I Luft/E
3504 meldet an 29.7, 23:30 aus London
[Translation]
SS *Britannia* in Huskinson Dock Liverpool with
American Munitions. *Georgic* Canada Dock.[20]

The SS *Britannia* was a medium-sized passenger ship of the Anchor Line. According to the war ethics of the day, if a passenger vessel was understood to be carrying war materials, it absolved an enemy of moral responsibility for the heavy loss of innocent lives that would come from attacking it. This was general knowledge in 1940, for it was the justification the Germans claimed for sinking the *Lusitania* during the First World War.

Six months later, the *Britannia* was met by the Hamburg-based commerce raider *Thor* off the west coast of Africa. It was sunk by gunfire: 127 crew and 122 passengers perished. Some of those who survived sailed their lifeboats 1,600 miles to the coast of Brazil, an epic of human endurance.

More pertinent, when McCarthy travelled to Lisbon, he had taken along some reports supposedly from Owens. These he delivered, along with his own and those of E-186. One from Owens described bomb damage to Southampton in considerable detail. And then this:

An OKW Abw I Luft/E
3504 meldet an 30.7 aus London uber Lissabon
[Translation]
Part of the administrative staff of the RAF has been quartered in Thames House near Lambeth Bridge. Visible from afar as a big white building.

McCarthy supplied his own version:

Neuer V-Mann von I Luft (3554) meldet bei personlichen Treff in Lissabon 3.8.40
[Translation]
The headquarters for all aircraft production and

Beaverbrook's office are in Thames House near Lambeth
Bridge. Big white building. Not to be missed.

The actual item — according to Robertson — that Commodore Boyle
authorized was this: "Ministry of Aircraft Production is at Thames House,
believe moving to Harrogate. Beaverbrook is the Minister."[21]

The messages were surely an invitation to German bombers if ever
there was one, and how they got past Robertson is a mystery. However,
Hitler had not yet authorized the bombing of inland urban targets.[22] Even
when he did, the Luftwaffe never acted on the messages and Thames House
was spared. McCarthy, of course, could not have foreseen that outcome.

As it so happened, the German secret services, both Nazi and the
Abwehr, had good reason not to want to raze Thames House. It had been
learned from the interrogations of Stephens and Best, the two MI6 men
kidnapped at Venlo, that it was the headquarters of MI5.[23] If this was
true, both the Abwehr and Heydrich's Gestapo could hope to meet their
enemy opposite numbers in the not-too-distant future, a much-preferred
alternative to killing them. The reason? Hitler had decided on invasion.

It was August 1. Thus far, the Luftwaffe's attacks had been limited to
coastal shipping and Britain's southern ports. Churchill, however, had
decreed a fight to the finish, and so it would be. Small craft of all types
were requisitioned by the Germans from along the coasts of the occupied
countries and assembled in the ports and small harbours on the French side
of the Channel. German army planners began calculating the logistics of
the crossing and how a landing force of several divisions could be sustained
while fighting inland toward London. Hitler gave it the name *Unternamen
Seelöwe* — Operation Sealion. It would be the first cross-Channel invasion
of England since William the Conqueror nearly eight hundred years earlier.
First, however, Britain had to be defeated in the air.

Churchill coined the phrase "Battle of Britain," and it came to be
applied to the epic struggle between the young pilots of the RAF and the
Luftwaffe that lasted from the second week of August to the middle of
September. They were evenly matched in energy, zeal, courage, and capability. Their aircraft, especially the fighters, were comparable in armament
and performance, the famous Spitfire perhaps having a slight edge over
the German Bf-109. Britain had an additional edge in that its pilots were

fighting over their own territory, and could be rescued if shot down. And then there was radar, of course. The electronic eyes that could see the German bomber formations assembling over France enabled the defenders to gather enough fighters to make their daylight forays over England costly — too costly in the end.

It is one of the great mysteries of the war. Luftwaffe chief Hermann Göring did open the battle with attacks on the Chain Home radar installations, the radio masts being readily visible from the air. Bunkers had not been provided for the on-site staff, so there were immediate casualties and some stations went blind. Then, for some reason, Göring eased up on the attacks, concentrating on airfields and RAF infrastructure instead. All historians agree it was a decisive mistake. Had he put out the RAF's eyes first, he would have won the battle.

The fighter-to-fighter struggle in the sky over southeast England was at its height when McCarthy arrived back in London on August 20. He had played his part. A-3554 had been established as a spy reporting from the Bristol area, initially on his own, later through A-3504. FRANK was rechristened BISCUIT, soon to become primarily a notional double agent because when A-3504's messages included reports from A-3554, McCarthy was not needed to write them.

McCarthy may have had his own thoughts as to the origin of those Thames House messages. In the days following his return, with the contrails of the enemy criss-crossing the sky over the sunny fields and towns of southeast England, he would get drunk every so often, phone Owens up, and offer to come over and kill him.[24]

NAMES TO THE FLAMES
September–October 1940

In early September 1940, after failing to defeat the RAF over England, Luftwaffe chief Hermann Göring shifted emphasis to bombing cities, and gradually to bombing by night. The British called it the Blitz, and London, Birmingham, Coventry, and other industrial and commercial centres suffered an autumn rain of incendiaries and high explosives.

On November 14, Coventry was devastated by some five-hundred-plus bombers. Birmingham was savagely hit on November 19. On Christmas Eve, 526 died in the fires in Manchester. The bombers were still under orders to go after British war-related industry, as per the 1937 League of Nations resolution that limited bombing to military targets, but as factories were inevitably embedded in urban areas, massive civilian damage and casualties were bound to occur. Public support for the war, however, solidified, and it deeply touched Churchill. His young aide, John Colville, noted in his diary:

> Friday, Sept. 20, 1940
> He [the PM] is becoming less and less benevolent toward
> the Germans — having been much moved by examples
> of their frightfulness in Wandsworth which he has been
> to see: a landmine caused very great devastation there —
> and talks about castrating the lot. He says there will be no

nonsense about a "just peace." I feel sure this is the wrong attitude — not only immoral but unwise....[1]

But the effects of the bombings were indeed frightful. According to some from the Wandsworth district who endured it,

> When a bomb lands you get an outward explosion and then equally as much damage is done when it is drawn in again. Often you found places with walls sucked off. It was as if you were looking into a doll's house with the back off. You could see everything there. The staircase was still there. The beds and all the furniture were still there....
>
> If the bombs dropped in places where a lot of people had been killed they were telling us how many bodies had been picked up. How many limbs they had found — how many heads — horrible things like that....[2]

For Göring, however, cities were more lucrative than airfields. They were large, built-up areas, and when bombs missed their designated military targets, they still were not wasted.

Göring also had some incentive to switch to bombing London by night. On August 12, A-3504 had sent along this:

> 12.8.40 SECRET To OKW-Abw I Luft/E
> Searchlight sites are to be found on top of the Stock Exchange, the Bank of England and Selfridges near Marble Arch.[3]

If this information was true, the bomber pilots needed only to position themselves according to the lights to stand a good chance of landing a dose of high explosive on one of Britain's great monuments — the Parliament at Westminster perhaps (actually hit), or St Paul's Cathedral (buildings destroyed across the street), or Trafalgar Square (cratered, but Nelson's Column remained okay). The loss of a few of these would be a great blow to British morale.

The message cannot be easily explained. It was sent when the air battle over England was primarily by day, and when the German aim was still to defeat the RAF by attrition and by destroying its infrastructure. Attacks on urban areas and widespread night bombing did not get underway until the autumn.

What is also odd is that Robertson continued to have Owens tour the countryside as before, visiting air bases to see what he could see. This may have made sense when Owens was meeting his German controllers on the Continent face-to-face, but it was hardly necessary when contact was limited to wireless.

Nevertheless, even as British and German pilots duelled in the skies over England that desperate summer and fall of 1940, Owens continued to count aircraft at aerodromes:

27.8.40
[Unknown MI5 staffer]

I asked if it was all right for SNOW to go out this after-noon and see if he can get any information about aero-dromes or air raid damage. Captain Robertson said any-thing he could get in this line could be sent over.

Rang Burton and told him SNOW was to go out, suggesting Northolt and other places he could manage. Also told him to try and find what damage had been done last night.

Obtained two items of chicken feed from Major Sin-clair — one about new plane trap formed by shooting wire from guns and the other about new pom-pom gun. Passed this on to Burton, who reported that they had seen 33 Spitfires, 3 Hurricanes, 2 Blenheims, one uniden-tified biplane, all marked YD, and all camouflaged and under cover at Northolt....

As this Northolt news seemed rather a lot of good information, I consulted Major Sinclair, who said he thought I should ring up D of I (Air) and make sure it was all right to send this. I rang up flying officer Baring, and explained that Captain Robertson was away on leave and, in connection with the SNOW case, I wanted to know whether it was all right to pass on the above information which had been observed by our agent from the road.

He consulted the D of I (Air) and returned to the phone to say that under *no* circumstances were we to send over information of this kind, and that if any changes in the original arrangements were contemplated, Captain Robertson or some other officer must go and see the D of I about it. I said I understood that the D of I had told Captain Robertson that anything any ordinarily intelligent person could see from the road was all right to send, but F/O Baring did not seem to think this was the case....[4]

This information was sent anyway, and unmistakeably appears in the Hamburg-Berlin message file, except dated September 18 — nearly three weeks later. The obviously phony "wire trap" information, on the other hand, was forwarded the next day.

In July, when McCarthy went to meet the Germans in Lisbon, he had been asked beforehand by wireless to bring along his national identity card, numbered KRIY 272-2, and his ration book, which happened to be of the pink traveller's type. He was still in Lisbon when Hamburg wirelessed A-3504 for some "specimen names and numbers" for identity cards, which MI5 immediately supplied, having SNOW reply with twenty examples that included the names Wilson, Williams, Williamson, and Burton, the serial-number prefixes CNSO, PNAJ, and BFAB, and the suffixes 318-1, 141-1, and 141-2.[5]

Some six weeks later, in the early-morning darkness of September 6, 1940, Gösta Caroli, a Swedish Nazi who had spied for the Germans in England before the war, landed by parachute in a field near Denton, Northamptonshire. At daylight he was discovered asleep by a farm worker who alerted the local constable. On being arrested, Caroli was found to have brought with him a transmitter, maps, £200 in banknotes, and an identity card with the serial number CNSO 141-1 — an obvious match to one of the serial numbers MI5 had provided.[6]

During his interrogation, Caroli revealed that another parachute spy was to follow, and that they were to rendezvous at a certain pub in Nottingham. Sure enough, two weeks later a man with a Danish passport made out to "Wulf Schmidt" was picked up by police. He was found to possess a British identity card in the name of Williams: PNAJ 272-3. Again the name, letters, and numbers were so close that it could not be coincidence. The connection to Owens was conclusively confirmed by the fact that both spies had on them slips of paper bearing Arthur Owens's name and his current address.[7] Six months earlier, Captain Robertson had berated Owens for not attracting other spies for him to arrest. Now he had two further prizes and the real Arthur Owens had not had to do a thing.

Caroli and Schmidt were certain to be caught. In the weeks immediately before Caroli's arrival, the Germans sent several messages asking Owens to suggest a suitable landing place for a parachute spy, with the promise of others to come in an operation the Germans referred to as *Unternehmen Lena*. The idea, as MI5 understood it, was that Operation Lena was about the Germans sowing a number of spies with wireless sets around England who would then report on British troop movements when the cross-Channel invasion was launched.[8] It was plausible, especially as the RAF had been watching the steady concentration of small craft in the harbours of northern France for much of the summer.

These exchanges with Hamburg seemed to be convincingly backed up by Abwehr wireless traffic intercepted by the Radio Security Service. The Hamburg station was also discovered to be in contact with several outstations (Cherbourg, Brussels, Paris) sending in simple ciphers similar to what the spy ship *Theseus* had been using. Rather than give the traffic to the Government Code & Cipher School, Major Gill and Lieutenant Trevor-Roper again broke the messages themselves. To their great joy, they found they were able to eavesdrop on Abwehr discussions about the *Lena* operation well before the agents were dispatched. MI5, indeed, gave Schmidt the code name TATE even before he arrived in England.[9]

Administrative confusion at MI5 was at its height when these parachute landings occurred. Otherwise, it would have surely occurred to someone that the enemy secret service branches in northern France and Belgium would be unlikely to communicate with each other and Hamburg by wireless when landline teletype was readily available. Indeed, the Abwehr officers could have more easily and securely discussed their *Lena* plans by simply picking up the telephone and talking in simple code.

The MI5 officers involved would also have been well-advised to consult someone with some basic military knowledge. They would have been told mid-September was too close to winter for Hitler to be contemplating conquering England. As a matter of fact, Hitler put the invasion off indefinitely on September 14; Schmidt didn't land until September 19.[10]

Colonel "Tin Eye" Stephens — so-named for the monocle he always wore — led the interrogations of Caroli and Schmidt. He was a forty-year-old former India Army officer with no police or investigative experience, who just two months earlier had been named to head up an MI5 interrogation centre that had been set up in a nineteenth-century mansion and former First World War hospital, Latchmere House, located in south London. They were his first prisoners of any consequence, and he was later to call them "the most spectacular wartime successes of the British counter-espionage service." Both men agreed to change sides. Caroli becoming the double agent SUMMER and Schmidt the double agent TATE.

All shadow of doubt about Owens still lingering in MI5 minds over the North Sea fiasco fell away, and the bomb-damage and ship-sighting reports of A-3504 (Owens/ SNOW) covering Britain's major ports multiplied, supplemented by observations turned in by A-3527 (Eschborn/ CHARLIE) and A-3554 (McCarthy/BISCUIT). Robertson's modest wireless double-agent operation had gone from one transmitter sending for one double agent to three sending for five.[11] This was certain to impress the government heavyweights then eyeing MI5 with sharpened knives.

It all made it very easy for Major Ritter, and he must have been very happy. The identity card scam had buttressed British confidence in Owens and given Ritter two more wireless agents in England whom he knew would be under British control. His adversaries had apparently also accepted in principle the idea that Ast Hamburg, and other Abwehr centres, would chat about their spies by wireless rather than landline, and in ciphers that any novice could break. He must have been pleasantly surprised when the transmitters of Caroli and Schmidt, A-3719 and A-3725, both came on air. The prospect of planting more triple agents on the gullible British was very bright.

By the middle of October, Caroli and Schmidt were in contact with Hamburg. Both men were competent telegraph-key operators and so sent their own messages — Caroli from various places north of London, as though he was a spy on the move; Schmidt always from Barnet, a town northeast of London where the Radio Security Service and MI5's Wireless Branch, presumably with Robertson, had moved to the month before. On November 1, they transmitted their first simultaneous weather observations taken at 5:00 p.m., Caroli's, from near Cambridge, included barometric pressure. On being received by Hamburg, they were forwarded directly to the Luftwaffe's weather service.[12]

MI5 contributed enormously to the German pilots' margin of safety that autumn of 1940 and over the winter. The daily weather reports it sent through SNOW, SUMMER, and TATE always included current conditions, estimates of visibility, cloud cover, and cloud height, and, starting in November, barometric pressure, the latter being a great help to the Luftwaffe's weather service in compiling forecasts.[13] Even a half-day warning as to where it was to be rainy or clear was hugely useful to Luftwaffe planners scheduling what cities to attack, and comforting to nervous U-boat commanders contemplating the dangerous dash across the Bay of Biscay.

Certainly, the Luftwaffe was the best served. In listing the factories and infrastructure damaged and destroyed in the notorious Coventry raid of November 14, A-3504-Owens concluded that monthly production of Spitfires and Hurricanes had been almost cut in half. This could only have been encouragement for Göring's bomber crews, who understood they were supposed to be targeting Britain's war industries rather than randomly bombing.[14]

The British chiefs of staff did not know of these goings-on. They had been asked in September whether they wanted to be closely informed of deception schemes and they said no. It was then left to the director of Air Intelligence, Commodore Boyle, to advise on the offerings of BISCUIT, CHARLIE, SNOW, SUMMER, and TATE.[15] It appears from available MI5 files that neither the current chief of the air staff, Lord Newell, nor his successor, Lord Portal, knew that the Luftwaffe was being given up-to-date weather information. As the Blitz intensified that autumn and winter, the three wireless double agents continued to transmit their observations once or sometimes twice a day.

Captain Robertson and his Wireless Branch boss, Frost, were not supplying this precious intelligence completely on their own. With Kell and his deputy, Holt-Wilson, gone, and with Brigadier Jasper Harker desperately trying to contend with the oars Lord Swinton kept inserting into things, the soft-spoken, former Scotland Yard man, Guy Liddell, was in effect running the show. As solo head of B Division — Mr. Crocker having quit in September — everything pertaining to MI5's double agents theoretically came under his scrutiny, including their weather reports. These he described in his diary as accurate "though limited."[16] Given the detail that was actually in them, especially barometric pressure, it is hard to see what more the Germans could have wanted.

Liddell is of particular interest at this time for another reason.

MI5, it will be recalled, had spent the lion's share of its effort during the 1920s and '30s in counter-subversion work against suspected communists and left-wingers, a legacy of the Bolshevik scare that had gripped Britain's Establishment during the First World War. This had involved intercepting mail and telephone calls, running informers, tailing suspects, and, most important of all, keeping track of people "of interest." This was the task of the Central Registry, the MI5/MI6 secret archive consisting of a card index of names running into the hundreds of thousands backed up by PFs — personal files on individuals — in the tens of thousands. The Central Registry was the main memory of both secret services, but was administered by MI5 and housed in 1940 along with the rest of the Security Service in the former nineteenth-century prison of Wormwood Scrubs.[17]

At the beginning of the Blitz, during the night of September 29, the Registry was swept by flames, apparently hit by a German oil bomb, an incendiary that splashed inflammable fluid when it hit. How it penetrated the roof of Wormwood Scrubs is unknown. No MI5 files have been released that deal with the incident.[18]

Liddell mentions the air attack in his diary:

> I dined with Anthony Blunt and Guy Burgess at the Reform Club. Just as I was going away at 11:30 p.m. a

Molotov breadbasket descended. Three incendiary bombs fell just inside Pall Mall and all sorts of people were rushing about in dressing gowns with bags of sand. When I got into the Mall the whole of St. James Park was lit up as by Roman candles.[19]

The next day's diary entry reads: "When I arrived at the office this morning I found that part of the Registry had been burnt by incendiary bombs and that the card index had been destroyed. Mercifully, we had had it photographed. Some thousand files had also been destroyed."[20]

Anthony Blunt, with whom Liddell dined that evening, was then a thirty-three-year-old Cambridge graduate and art historian who, after the war, was painfully discovered to have been working as a penetration agent for the Soviets. He and Burgess were members of the notorious "Cambridge Five," Englishmen of privilege who were exposed in the 1950s and sixties as having fed the West's most precious secrets to Stalin. The others in the group were Kim Philby, Donald Maclean, and a fifth whose identity is still disputed. Together with Blunt and Burgess, they penetrated MI6, MI5, the Foreign Office, and the Government Code & Cipher School. Their take during the Cold War included secrets pertaining to the atomic bomb and U.S.-U.K. counter-intelligence moves against the Soviets. It was the twentieth century's most spectacular espionage achievement.

Blunt, Burgess, and Maclean had been obvious communists during their student days at Cambridge, Burgess and Maclean noisily so. Philby had been less obvious, but was open about having communist sympathies when serving as a volunteer in the workers' rebellion in Vienna in the mid-1930s. He later covered the Spanish Civil War as a correspondent for the *Times*. The names of all four would have been in the Registry's card index, and there would have been PFs — personal files — on all of them.[21] The fire destroyed the card index that would have led to these dossiers.[22]

For those inclined to conspiracy theories, there are other intriguing facts surrounding this incident:

- In September 1940, most in government saw Stalin as an ally of Hitler and believed that the Soviets were likely soon to come into the war on the side of the Nazis.[23]

- Liddell was then MI5's (and therefore Britain's) counter-espionage chief. How, then, did he come to be chatting amiably over supper at his club with two fairly notorious pre-war Cambridge communists, whose dossiers it would have been his duty to read?
- A PF (personal file) in the Registry could not safely be made to disappear so long as there was a name-card in the index that pointed to it.
- Most of the cards were destroyed.
- The Registry supposedly occupied the glass-roofed former prison laundry which could not be locked.[24]
- Victor Rothschild, a Cambridge scientist personally recruited by Liddell four months earlier, had been assigned the task of having the card-index microfilmed just before the fire, so in a way it was saved.
- The copying, however, was poorly done. Reconstruction of the card index was not completed until June 1941 (when Hitler invaded Russia and Stalin became an ally).[25]
- Once the fire had occurred, it would have been impossible to determine whether specific files and their index cards had been removed before the microfilming.

The card index, however, did exist when Blunt joined MI5 in June. Even allowing for the administrative confusion then gripping the Security Service, it was surely wildly irresponsible for its counter-espionage chief and former Scotland Yard expert on communist subversion not to have personally run Blunt's name through the Registry. How could he possibly not have done so before socializing with him at his club?[26]

It seems he left the vetting to Rothschild, who had introduced him to Blunt in the first place. In a 1943 secret memoir to his Soviet controllers, Blunt recalled being surprised his communist past was not a problem when he entered MI5:

> One thing is, however, mysterious. When I eventually joined MI5 my name was put through the registry in the ordinary way by Rothschild. He told me that the

only records were an intercepted postcard from Maurice Dobbs to *Left Review* suggesting they should print
an article of mine, and mention of my name on a list of
those visiting Russia in 1935.[27]

One would have thought the visit to the Soviet Union alone would have
been enough to disqualify Blunt from the British secret services in 1940,
but, if Blunt is to be believed, Liddell left it to Rothschild to read his file.

Liddell apparently did not read anything on Burgess, either. Blunt's
Cambridge chum had managed to join MI6 (Section D) in January 1939,
having flirted with the secret intelligence service on behalf of Moscow for
two years. There should have been a lot on him, for he had been very open
about his communist activities at university and had also been with Blunt
on the boat trip to Russia in 1935. All the same, MI6 had accepted him,
and that, Liddell could argue, should be good enough for him.

On the other hand, MI5 ran the Central Registry for both services.
Liddell could temporarily launder a file if it went through his office. It
would have been the most natural thing in the world for him to retrieve
a file for Major Vivian at MI6, then simply take out and put back items as
the file came and went. Indeed, it is entirely possible that Liddell referred
Burgess to Vivian in the first place.

And so it was that Blunt and Burgess — both devotees of Stalin —
were dining with Liddell at the Reform Club during that evening of the
"oil bomb." Blunt had just joined MI5; Burgess had been attached to MI6
for over a year. One imagines the two lifting their glasses, red with port,
which both of them liked, in a silent toast to their mutual friends, Kim
Philby and Tomás Harris, both of whom had recently entered MI6 on
Burgess's recommendation. In just a few hours flames would put out of
reach the pre-war pasts of all of them.[28]

For Philby's future, this obliteration was crucial. The Soviet defector
Walter Krivitsky had come over from the United States at the beginning of
the year to submit to questioning by MI5. In describing Soviet espionage,
he mentioned that Russian intelligence had had "a young Englishman
working for it in Spain under cover of a journalist."[29] As there would have
been only a limited number of English journalists covering the Spanish
Civil War, and MI5/MI6 would have routinely had files on every one of

them, Liddell could not have failed to have called up Philby's. The fire guaranteed that no one else would ever do so.

The same might hold for "Tommy" Harris, Blunt's Spanish art dealer friend. Krivitsky mentioned a Soviet agent, "'a well-known painter and perhaps a sculptor' who had purchased planes for the Spanish Republicans." Harris did paint and did deal in looted Spanish art. This could be an allusion to him.[30]

Five months later, Blunt became Liddell's personal aide. This position he developed over the ensuing months into access to the secret files Liddell was dealing with, to what remained of the Registry, to the Abwehr wireless traffic intercepted by the Radio Security Service, to diplomatic decrypts, and to MI5's entire double-cross program. Short of Liddell himself being in direct contact with the Soviets, penetration of MI5 was to be as complete as any Soviet spymaster could have wished.

In January 1941, Blunt passed MI5's final report on the debriefing of Krivitsky to his Soviet controller. Within the month, Krivitsky was discovered dead in a pool of blood in his Washington hotel room, shot through the temple, a .38 calibre pistol in his hand. He had previously told his wife that if ever he was found dead, it would not be suicide.

There were three suicide notes.

BIRMINGHAM IS BURNING

September–November 1940

Major Ritter had heard from Caroli but not yet from Schmidt when he tried the identity-card trick again. At 7:30 a.m. on September 30, a man and woman turned up at the train station of Port Gordon, a tiny coastal town in Scotland. They seemed to be lost, having to ask where they were, and then for advice on what tickets to buy to get to Edinburgh. They were well-dressed, but for the city rather than the country, and the station master noticed that their shoes were wet, and that the man's pants were damp to the knees. The woman had an unfamiliar accent and the man could barely speak English. As they waited on the platform, the station master rang up the local constable.

The constable's name was Grieve, and it is safe to assume that he had lived in the area all his life. The woman claimed she was Danish; the man Belgian. They were refugees who had been in Britain for some time, they said. Constable Grieve asked to see their national identity cards. He would not have had the experience or the eye to spot a reasonably good forgery, but he immediately noticed that the numeral *1* on the man's card was written with a very un-British-like flourish, and that there was no immigration stamp. He asked the pair — probably in that wonderful folksy manner that British constables of the period were famous for — to accompany him to the station. When the man was searched he was found to have nineteen bullets in his pocket and a flashlight marked MADE IN BOHEMIA. His suitcase was forced open and there was the revolver that matched the bullets, and a wireless transmitter.[1]

Meanwhile, a search of the shore near the town turned up an empty rubber dinghy. When inquiries were made down the railway line, a porter at the left-luggage office at Edinburgh station reported that a man had left a wet suitcase in one of the lockers that morning and was to come back for it that evening. Plainclothes constables staked out the area, and when a man appeared and opened the locker, they pounced. He, too, had a revolver in his pocket and at first reached for it, then reconsidered. His suitcase contained another transmitter, maps, and a code disk. His identity card had the number 1 written in the same obviously not-British style. He was arrested.

When the trio were turned over to MI5, it was immediately noted that the serial numbers and names on their identity and ration cards were unmistakably derived from the information supplied earlier by SNOW.[2] The mistakes on the cards were put down to German stupidity.

Had MI5 had a false document section of its own, or had its officers read the First World War memoirs of the American Herbert Yardley or the German spy chief Colonel Nicolai, they would not have supposed it possible that the Abwehr could fail to produce decent forgeries. In fact, every Ast, including Hamburg, had technical specialists, and in Berlin there was a full laboratory for producing all manner of faked papers.[3] MI5 had no similar facilities and, given the intellectual vacuum in science and technology that had existed in the organization for the previous two decades, was not even on the horizon when it came to the theory and practice of faking documents. MI5 saw in the clumsy mistakes what it would have expected of itself.

With the benefit of hindsight, and with the knowledge that Major Ritter was aware at least since June that Owens was under British control,[4] it is possible with some certainty to deduce what was going on. The woman was known as Vera Eriksen, a.k.a. Schalburg, a.k.a. Wedel, and much mystery has long surrounded her. In fact, she was none of the above. After intensive questioning at Latchmere House by Colonel Stephens personally, she admitted that her real name was Vera Starizky, she had been born in Russia, she was Jewish, and she had been a spy since age seventeen. She was twenty-eight, slim and raven-haired, with a finely sculpted face. She spoke Russian, English, French, German, and Danish, and undoubtedly, should she have so chosen, could have achieved summa cum laude in bedroom espionage.

Vera's career had included five years in Paris, where she preyed on the diplomatic community, before finally fleeing her Soviet controller and going over to the Germans. Before the war, she was briefly in England, where she met the Duchess of Chateau-Thierry, and her current assignment was to resume her pre-war contacts, develop relationships with airmen, and report by wireless. At first she had refused, but (so she said) when her husband, a German officer, was killed in a car crash, she accepted the mission in a fit of despondency. She always, she said, intended to turn herself over to the British when she got to London.

It was a superb cover story, and she stuck to it despite a withering grilling by Colonel Stephens. Robertson and Liddell declared themselves convinced, and she would have become yet another wireless double agent, but Stephens would not give up. He seems to have sensed a lie, although his persistence could also have been driven by the novelty of "breaking" a woman. He did not succeed, and Vera was turned over to Klop Ustinov, one of MI5's ablest interrogators. In the end, she was interned for the duration of the war.[5]

It was a near-miss for the British. Vera was the classic penetration agent, and a woman of her brains, beauty, and experience had the potential to wreck havoc if she got loose in British intelligence, or anywhere in the War Office. The two men she had come with apparently were sacrificial Nazis, necessary only because a woman landing by seaplane at night could not be expected to paddle a rubber dinghy to shore on her own. The two, one Dutch and the other Swiss — Karl Drüke and Werner Walti — were more useful to the Germans if they were caught than free, and the mistakes on their identity cards ensured that they would be.

Vera's interrogation ordeal has survived in Britain's National Archives and it is appropriate to note that she made every effort to portray Drüke and Walti as innocent employees of the operation, whose only job was to land her safely. She was prepared to be shot herself to save their lives, but despite her efforts, she was saved while they were not. They were hanged the following August.

Ast Brussels also sent spies to England that same month. They, too, were instantly caught. On September 3, under cover of darkness, two rowboats containing three Dutchmen and a Franco-German were towed across the Channel and released about a mile from shore. All four were keen Nazis and they had been told that they were to hide out with their transmitters for a few days and then report on British troop movements when the German army stormed ashore.

None of these would-be spies had identity papers, only one spoke decent English, all had revolvers, their clothing was German, as was their food — right down to the sausages. And they carried no water. In search of it that morning, one of them was picked up by a coastal patrol; another aroused suspicion because he sought a drink of cider at a local pub before opening time. The other two were netted in the subsequent dragnets.[6]

When the four — Pons, Kieboom, Meier, and Waldberg — were under lock and key at Latchmere House, MI5 invited MI14 to look them over. MI14 was the War Office agency responsible for trying to determine German intentions from the collation of intelligence from all sources. It was headed by the entirely capable Colonel Kenneth Strong, and he talked to the prisoners personally. MI5's Guy Liddell recorded his reaction in his diary: "Strong has a great regard for German efficiency and cannot bring himself to believe that they could have been so stupid, as having sent these men over here without having schooled them properly and worked out plans by which they could be really effective."[7]

They were deliberate sacrifices. There can be no other explanation. They were non-German Nazi zealots and, therefore, to the Abwehr, expendable. Meier had been involved with an organization advocating the merger of Holland with Germany, Waldberg had been a spy in Belgium and France, and Pons and Kieboom belonged to the Dutch Nazi party. The leadership at Ast Brussels, loyal to Canaris and opposed to Hitler, was not going to shed tears if such fodder was caught and condemned to the hangman, as three out of the four were.

The other expeditions that autumn involved a Swede and two Belgians landing by boat on September 23, and three Cubans, a Dane, a Dutchman, and two Frenchmen on November 12. All were badly outfitted and promptly arrested.[8]

Andreas Folmer, the Luxembourger who had so successfully infil-
trated the Belgian Deuxième Bureau, was recruited for one of these trips.
It began for him when the Germans brought him back to Brussels after
Belgium's surrender to denounce and help arrest his former Belgian
secret service colleagues. When this was completed, he was introduced
to a Major Klug who told him his next assignment was to land by sea
in England with two companions to set up a secret pre-invasion radio
transmitter. The three — he, a Belgian, and another Luxembourger —
would pose as refugees and leave by boat from Brest.

After preparations that Folmer found alarmingly careless, the mission began, only immediately to run aground when the boat got stuck
in mud in the harbour. When they tried again a week later, a German
officer in full uniform arrived to oversee their departure, making it
obvious to everyone within sight what was going on. Folmer became
very, very nervous; it would be the kiss of death if any of the watching
Frenchmen was in contact with Britain. Happily for him, the boat's
engine broke down and the trip was aborted once more. Folmer then
sent a polite note to Major Klug saying that the mission was hopelessly
compromised and he wanted no further part in it. To his surprise, he
was suddenly arrested and spent the next nine weeks in a Brussels jail.[9]

The intention of these antics can only be guessed at. Their effect, in
any case, was to contribute to MI5's impression that its Abwehr opponent
was hopelessly incompetent. This lulled it into complacency.

Folmer was doubly lucky. Not only did he miss out on a voyage that
would have put him on the bottom step of the scaffold, but his former boss,
Oscar Reile of the Abwehr's Abt IIIf counter-espionage section, obtained
his release and brought him to Paris. There for the next four years he
worked undercover against the French Resistance with deadly effect.

As for Major Klug, he went on to carry out a similar caper with eight
enthusiastic foreign-born Nazis who were to sabotage Swiss airfields while
pretending to be on a holiday walking tour. Dressed identically in plus-fours
and wearing the same brown shoes, and with capes made from Luftwaffe field
grey, they stood out in the Alps like a parody of the von Trapp family from
The Sound of Music. On being stopped, they had no identity papers, were each
carrying a brand-new Swiss one hundred–franc note, and had in their satchels
their hiking refreshments, a revolver, and explosives. All were imprisoned.[10]

Major Klug — whose name is the German word for "clever" — appears to have been engaged in some gratuitous mischief against the Nazis.

A CONTINENTAL FLOURISH

With the exception of the groups from Ast Brussels, all the spies captured by the British between September 1940 and the following March were linked directly or indirectly to Major Ritter, and had identity papers that were obviously flawed and traceable to the names and numbers provided by BISCUIT and by SNOW.[11] The errors varied, but were always glaring. A 1942 British intelligence report described them as follows:

(I) National Registration Identity Cards are usually forged, and the following typical errors are noticeable:
(a) Address is written in continental instead of English style.
(b) Cards are dated prior to 1.5.40, which is the date by which completion was officially ordered.
(c) The use of initials rather than full Christian names.
(d) Christian names are placed before surnames.
(e) Both halves of the right-hand page of the card have been known to be written in the same hand, whereas in a genuine card they are in different hands.
(2) Ration books are usually forged and there is a preference for Travellers' Ration Books.
(3) In one case a passport was not only falsely filled in, but lacked a visa for this country and the Immigration Officer's stamp.
(4) The numbers of English bank notes frequently run consecutively and consecutive numbers have been found in the possession of different agents.[12]

These are all primitive mistakes that would not have been made by an organization like the Abwehr's documents division, which maintained a library of identity papers from every country in Europe, and which had the capacity to imitate every ink, every type of paper, and every stamp and seal.[13] Moreover, Ritter had lived in the United States for years, and his deputy, Karl Kramer, in Britain. They would have been aware of the differences between English and European writing styles, and never would have allowed a Continental flourish on the numeral *1* of a supposedly British document. They also would have appreciated that if one wanted to get the average policeman in rural Britain to spot a forged document, the errors had to be obvious.[14]

TEMPTING TARGETS

Caroli and Schmidt began sending their messages in mid-September and mid-October 1940 respectively. By then it was obvious to all that the anticipated cross-Channel invasion was not going to happen, at least not that year. The need for them to report on troop movements and ground defences evaporated, although this was never their intended espionage mission anyway. Despite claiming to their British captors that they were the vanguard of invasion, both had been trained, not by the air or army sections of Ast Hamburg, but by Abw I Wi, the section that specialized in economic intelligence.[15]

One can see the reasoning. Canaris did not want Hitler to defeat Britain,[16] so he needed to be able to gauge the state of British civilian morale in the face of the bombings and the ongoing submarine blockade in the North Atlantic. To measure that, the Abwehr required current data on consumer prices, on food and fuel shortages, and on public reaction to the lives lost to the bombings and sinkings. This was how to determine Britain's continued willingness to fight. SNOW, at Hamburg's request, began sending such information in mid-August; this, and the weather observations, became the principal themes of TATE's messages from mid-1941 on,[17] all approved and composed by MI5.

Naturally, Ast Hamburg's agent controllers asked repeatedly for military information, for it fed the illusion that they believed that Owens, Caroli, and Schmidt were at liberty. They also knew that anything provided by these agents would be concocted by the British. What they might not have expected, however, was that they, along with the routine reports on prices and morale, would often be given tactical information that was accurate and valuable. Robertson, backed by Liddell, had got it into his head that his double agents had to send as much high-quality intelligence as possible in order to retain German confidence. The better the information, the reasoning went, the more certain the Germans would be fooled.

First, there were the bomb-damage reports. The long lists of factories destroyed and communications damaged that were wirelessed to Hamburg must have been tremendously encouraging to Göring. The devastation caused by the big raids on London, Liverpool, Coventry, Birmingham, and Manchester were covered in detail.

Second, SNOW and TATE volunteered target identification that seems to have cut very close. The following two messages were received by Abw I Luft/E in Berlin.

> LENA 3725 reports on 17.11.40 at 00.44 hours Number 14 [Translations]
> The Nash and Thompson factory of Tolworth (Surrey) is situated near the Kingston Bypass inside where Hook Road, Ewell Road and the bypass intersect. The factory is closely guarded and camouflaged. No chance of finding out what is made there because people refuse to talk about it.

> 3504 reports on 23.11.40

> The Nash and Thompson factory is 100 yards south of the Kingston Bypass exactly between where Hook Road and Ewell Road cross the Bypass. Gun turrets are made there.[18]

The SNOW message was right. Again, though, Owens was not the author of this message; MI5 was. The company was the principal manufacturer of the multiple-gun, hydraulically operated turrets for British bombers, and for making revolving platforms for radar.

The Luftwaffe followed up with aerial photographs and air attacks, mostly missing the factory but doing a lot of damage to the surrounding town of Surbiton.

It is true that Nash and Thompson was well-known as a manufacturer of aircraft components before the war, and could have been assumed to be a listed target anyway. Perhaps the factory had shifted its production elsewhere. Nevertheless, if MI5 — Robertson, presumably with permission from higher authority — did indeed authorize the transmission of this information, it is hard to understand why they would want to draw the bombers onto this particular target, especially as it was located in a built-up area.

Another SNOW message, delivered just at this time, is even more difficult to explain:

> To: Abw Luft Luft/E
> Message from 3504 on 23.11.40
> [Translation]
> In Egypt no Spitfires; however, some Blenheims. Some machines should be on the way to Egypt. Details difficult to obtain.

This was valuable intelligence. At the time, Hitler was making arrangements to send help to North Africa, where the Italian air force and their obsolete aircraft were being badly shot up by the RAF flying out of Egypt. The German Bf-109 was recognized as outclassing every British fighter except the Spitfire, and planes arrived in Libya in time for the German counterattack that April. About 1,400 British fighters were shot down by Bf-109s before Spitfires were released to the Middle East in mid-1942.[19]

The documents in the MI5 files that would have described how these messages were prepared, and whether Commodore Boyle cleared them, have not been found. Only the German versions of the messages survive, in the records of Nest Bremen that were captured by the British and shared briefly with the U.S. Navy at the end of the war.[20]

What is known, however, is that the questionnaire Caroli had on him when he landed sparked a dispute between MI5 and the director of military intelligence. The Germans wanted Caroli to report on certain land defences in the New Romney area (Kent), which was not information that could be obtained without applying to the intelligence section of the commander-in-chief, Home Forces. This triggered the DMI's attention and his immediate reaction was refusal. He wanted Caroli used to pass over false information, not true.

Again, no contemporary documents that reflect this controversy have been located, so one must rely for details on an unsigned, undated internal MI5 description, obviously written many years later by a participant in the events. Apparently, there was disagreement as to both aim and method: "[T]hese officers were inclined to view the problem from the angle of what they wanted to tell the enemy, rather than from that of what the agent could actually see or learn...." Or, further: "... what additional things he would clearly have to see if he were to purport to see something they wanted to put over...."[21]

Arguing that the threat of invasion made England a "theatre of operations," the DMI tried to talk his fellow directors of intelligence into setting up a special joint committee called the Wireless Section to manage the deceptive information the double agents were to transmit. The unknown author of the MI5 paper commented:

> [I]t is not unamusing that the function of the W-Section was defined as the "collecting, handling and disseminating of F.I. (False Information)": DMI had not yet appreciated that that body would spend far more time "collecting, handling and disseminating" true information in order to build the agents to enable them to put over the false information.

In this regard, MI5 had its champion in Commodore Boyle, the director of Air Intelligence, who "courageously chanced his arm" by approving disclosures pertaining to the other services.[22] He put forward the counter-proposal that the service directors of intelligence themselves form an informal committee — the Wireless Board — which would give authority and a modicum of direction to an operations committee of staff intelligence officers who would actually oversee what information to give the enemy. This became the XX Committee, the Roman numerals for 20 being two Xs.

To keep the purpose and discussions of the Wireless Board "super-secret," it was decided that the directors of intelligence would inform their individual chiefs of staff of what was discussed or decided only verbally, if at all. Minutes would be taken, but only the chairman, General Davidson, would get a copy. There would be no document distribution except under exceptional circumstances.

> Air Commodore Boyle was very insistent that it was essential that the W-Board should not get tied up with formal directives, et cetera; it was obvious to him that it would be necessary to pass items of true information to the enemy, either as buildup of the agents or to maintain their plausibility, and if such matters had to be referred to others, such as the chiefs of staff (who could not expect to familiarize themselves with this art), either permission would be refused or there would be such delay as to have dire results; also, the Twenty Committee and the W-Board would have to do some "odd things" of the kind that it is the job of the directors of intelligence to authorize on their own responsibility.

Masterman, in *The Double-Cross System*, was even more succinct:

> D of I (Air) took the line that knowledge of the double-cross system should be confined to MI5, MI6, and the three Directors of Intelligence, and that risks should be taken to maintain what he felt to be potentially a weapon of great value and that the system should not be allowed to become a plaything of higher authorities who would not use it adequately, and who would also, perhaps, boggle at the responsibilities involved.[23]

It would seem Masterman did not have much faith in Britain's military leaders.

The rules for the XX Committee were about the same: it would meet, discuss, and decide, but written records were to be retained only by MI5 and MI6. The service members of the committee were not to share anything with their superior officers, and any papers they did receive were to be kept to themselves. The committee could give suggestions on what to send the Germans, but the final decision and content of messages would be left to the experts in MI5/MI6, which meant mainly those of MI5. The double-agent case officers would oversee the composing and sending of messages.[24]

The aims of the double-cross program would be as before:

- to limit the expansion of enemy espionage activity by persuading the enemy that it had successful agents in place;
- to derive the enemy's intentions from his questionnaires;
- to use the ciphers given his agents to break into the enemy's general wireless traffic.[25]

As a sop to the DMI, it was proposed that the new committee would also try to stage deceptions whereby German raiders would be lured onto sites where a "hot reception" would await them.

Boyle's proposal was backed up by Liddell, and it prevailed. The Wireless Board came into being without the knowledge of the chiefs of staff and outside any chain of command. It had no authority, no budget, and no presence on paper. It initially comprised the three directors of intelligence, plus Liddell for MI5 and Menzies for MI6. It was to meet only when a member requested a meeting, and was to receive reports from the XX Committee only when the board felt in need of the committee's advice. It was not supposed to give orders, only guidance. It sought to achieve "super-secrecy" by officially not existing.

Liddell and Commodore Boyle were the principal architects of this Mad Hatter's committee of senior intelligence officers who answered to no one, but they had crucial support. MI6 chief Stewart Menzies was included in the discussions at every stage. He was then in the process of overhauling his counter-espionage section — Section V — so that it could directly handle MI5's double agents on their trips abroad. Menzies reported directly to Churchill.

The Wireless Board held its first meeting on January 8, 1941, and it was decided that civilian representation was warranted, with the result being that Sir Findlater Stewart of the Home Defence Executive was secretly approached to join. He was willing to play along, he told the others at the next meeting in February, but he did not see how he could make recommendations or make decisions affecting various government agencies without sometimes having to inform the responsible minister. It was proposed that he share his misgivings with Sir John Anderson, the wartime head of Britain's public service.

Sir John conferred with Churchill. Word came back as follows:

> They both appreciated all the considerations and told Sir Findlater that neither of them could, constitutionally, authorize him to deal with matters which appertained to other Ministries, but obviously there was a job to do and he should get on with it. If there was ever a row about this work Sir Findlater could not claim to have been "authorized" to do what he was about to do, but both Sir John Anderson and the Prime Minister "unofficially approved...."[26]

In other words: the message was, "What you propose to do is breaking the law, but do it anyway."

Sir Findlater Stewart accepted these conditions. The War Office, the Home Office, and the Foreign Office joined the chiefs of staff in the dark.

Caroli, a.k.a. SUMMER, a.k.a. A-3719, did not last long as a double agent. He was used by MI5 as a kind of roving spy, seeing what he could see in the Midlands and making on-the-spot weather observations. Early November found him reporting the weather alternately from Birmingham and from east of Coventry, always in the evenings and always with barometric pressure. His observations complemented those from SNOW (Owens) in London, whose readings were taken in the mornings and, after November 9, also included barometric pressure.

The report Caroli would have made for November 14, the day of the massive Coventry raid, is missing A-3719's Nest Bremen file, which was among the records the British seized from in 1945. The one from Owens on that date is still in his file, but the bottom three-quarters of it has been snipped off, leaving only the date and the Luftwaffe Weather Service address.[27]

According to other messages in his file, Caroli was in London on November 16 and 17, but again "near Birmingham" the evening of the 19th, just before the big raid on that city started. Owens reported that morning that the weather was clear, visibility two miles, cloud cover 90 percent at six thousand feet. Caroli sent at 7:30 p.m. that it was now overcast, visibility was poor, but it was likely to clear.

The raid on Birmingham lasted the night, the bombers coming in waves — about four hundred of them. The effect was devastating. Buildings were destroyed, streets cratered, fires burned everywhere. Worst was the direct hit on the British Small Arms Factory. The night shift had taken to the cellars rather than go to the air raid shelter, and the building came down upon them. Fifty-two out of fifty-three of the buried died before they could be reached. Others were killed, but in ones and twos, here and there. The targets were the factories, but the bombs and incendiaries hit homes as well. Birmingham that night was a second Coventry.

Caroli watched, probably in a field somewhere outside the city where he and his guard had stretched out his aerial. It would have been like looking at a fireworks show from afar: patches of light playing on the cloud bottoms, a mumble of thunder, flashes like lightning, and an orange swath growing on the horizon. It rained the next day, but when it stopped the city was attacked again.

It was MI5's practice at this time to have its double agents actually view what was going to be in their messages, and as Caroli was slated to send in a bomb-damage report, he would have been taken into the city. He would have seen the streets blocked with rubble, the dead being collected, and he certainly would have passed the flattened BSA building where weary rescuers were still digging in the heap of broken concrete and bricks. Caroli subsequently transmitted a very long report that covered the damage, but not the tears. He never sent another weather report.

Caroli was a parson's son, likely attracted to the Nazis by Hitler's promises of a fairer world. He was big and he was resolute. One day in early January, out in the countryside somewhere, he clubbed his guard unconscious, rifled his pockets for £5, tied him up, and took off on a stolen motorcycle towing a "canoe" that he had spotted in a nearby barn. He was headed for the coast. There was a hue and cry and he was caught.

He was returned to detention at Latchmere House. His brief career as the double agent SUMMER was definitely over.[28]

Caroli turned out to be lucky. Churchill had decreed that captured spies that were not otherwise useful should be executed. That would have been Caroli's death warrant, except that his daring and passion for escape — he tried to cut his way through the barbed wire that enclosed Latchmere House — had won him sympathizers among his captors. A legal loophole was found that circumvented the prime minister's order. Caroli survived the war.[29]

A man named Josef Jakobs was not so fortunate. A little more than a week after Caroli had signed off for the final time, Jakobs came down by parachute near Ramsey, Huntingdonshire. He broke his ankle while landing, and the forty-one-year-old German had no choice but to fire his pistol in the air to summon help. During interrogation, he admitted his assignment had been to send weather observations. He also claimed that he had been forced into espionage by the Gestapo after being arrested for helping Jews. In his pocket, he had the address of a Jewish woman he intended to make contact with.

As he was "manifestly unemployable," and because "there was no good reason for him to live," Colonel Stephens, the bitter chief inquisitor at Latchmere House, had the satisfaction of seeing him shot by firing squad at the Tower of London. He was a brave man, Stephens conceded. "His last words directed the 'Tommies' to shoot straight."[30]

CELERY HITS THE JACKPOT

January–July 1941

The five men central to MI5's double-cross program glumly faced one another across the table. It was April 10, 1941. By this time, they normally referred to the double agents only by their code names. SNOW, a.k.a. Owens, had been blown, and with him all but one of the other double agents in wireless contact with Germany. "It was agreed that the Doctor [RANTZAU] knew about our control of agents and probably knew as much about it as SNOW and CELERY," one of them wrote that day. "The fact that he wishes to keep the party alive is a strong argument for closing it down."[1]

It was a terrible blow. The counter-intelligence program that had held such promise, that had reflected so much credit on MI5, appeared wounded beyond recovery. A year before it had been a struggle for MI5 to win recognition for the idea of "turning" captured spies and playing them back to the enemy. Since then, wireless exchanges between Owens and his German contacts had led to the capture of nearly a dozen spies landed by boat and parachute, including two more with transmitters. Ten in all were now sending messages back to Germany under MI5 control. Just recently, two Norwegians who landed by rubber boat in Scotland had been added to the double-agent roster, plus a smooth-talking Yugoslav who at that very moment was in Lisbon duping the German spy chief for Portugal.

Lucky it was, too, that the ciphers provided these spies were simple and apparently widely used. An eloquent appeal from Major Gill of the Radio Security Service had triggered a better effort by the Government Code & Cipher School, and the previous December its cryptographers had broken what appeared to be the main Abwehr hand cipher — i.e., a cipher that can be composed and solved by paper and pencil methods.[2] Early results had indicated it was going to be possible to read what the Germans themselves were saying of the double agents planted on them.

To top it all off, the service directors of intelligence had been sufficiently impressed to agree to the setting up of a committee dominated by MI5 that would independently oversee the information to be fed the Germans. This was the so-called XX Committee. It held its first meeting in a room at Wormwood Scrubs on January 2, 1941. Four months later, it was poised to run down any undiscovered spies through a scheme called Plan *Midas*, whereby the Germans were to be persuaded to make their agent, A-3504 (a.k.a. Owens, a.k.a. SNOW), paymaster to all Abwehr spies in Britain.

All this lovely progress was about to go up in smoke, however. It also opened up the five MI5 officers sitting at the table that day to accusations of amateurism, although it was true that they were amateurs. Guy Liddell, MI5's B Division chief, was a seasoned investigator, but his pre-war experience had all had to do with anti-subversion work rather than counter-espionage against a sophisticated foreign power. His thirty-five-year-old deputy, Dick White, had been a schoolmaster when recruited in 1936, and the sum of his field experience consisted of two years in Germany cultivating people of his own age and social class. Three years his junior, "TAR" Robertson, the officer directly managing the wireless double agents, had spent the 1930s tracking domestic Bolsheviks, not spies.

The remaining two were recent acquisitions: James Marriott, a solicitor from the City (London's financial centre), and J.C. Masterman, a fifty-year-old Oxford academic who had sat out the First World War in comfortable internment in Germany. Masterman had been White's history tutor at Oxford, and within two months of being recruited he was named chairman of the XX Committee. He had no experience whatsoever.[3]

The seeds of destruction were sown in February with a plan to foist another double agent on DR. RANTZAU, by now known to be the Ast

Hamburg spymaster to most of the agents landed in Britain. MI5's air intelligence expert, Walter Dicketts, was selected for the mission and code-named CELERY. He was to pretend to be a veteran airman ready to betray his country because the RAF had refused him a commission. Owens was to introduce him to RANTZAU in Lisbon, Owens going by flying boat and Dicketts following by ship a few days later.[4]

The pair had been in Portugal about a month when the MI6(V) man at the embassy reported to London that Owens had come to see him to declare that the Germans had found him out, and that RANTZAU had accused him outright of working for the British. To salvage what he could, Owens said he had admitted it, but claimed that the British had only caught on to him a few months earlier. RANTZAU had responded by telling him to return to England and pretend nothing had happened.[5] Apparently, the German hoped to turn the tables on MI5.

If it had only been a matter of one double agent blown, it would not have been so bad, but losing SNOW was a catastrophe. SNOW, the five at the table agreed, was disastrously linked to CHARLIE, BISCUIT, GW, SUMMER, TATE, and RAINBOW, as well as the most recent arrival, Dusko Popov, a.k.a. TRICYCLE, and his two fictional sub-agents, BAL-LOON and GELATINE.

Popov was an especially exquisite loss because the Germans had indicated they wanted to send him to Egypt by way of the United States. Altogether, Owens's loss left MI5 with only one double agent of consequence, and he had only just made wireless contact with his German controllers.[6] Robertson's initial reaction was to insist that Owens must be lying. It was all too awful to contemplate.

The situation had been avoidable. MI5 had never seen anything wrong with having CHARLIE, GW, and BISCUIT send their reports through SNOW, but now that SNOW had crashed, it became clear that they must too. Through the *Midas* scheme, SNOW had already made a payment to TATE , so he was blown. TATE had notionally passed on some of the money to RAINBOW, so that finished him. TRICYCLE was compromised because he was just then in Lisbon arranging with the Germans to take the money to pay their agents with him to the United States, where it would be deposited for SNOW to draw on. Doubts about him would lead to doubts about BALLOON and GELATINE.

MI5 had made the most elementary mistake in agent-running: it had put its double agents in contact with one another.[7]

Again, it was a case of MI5 officers failing to inform themselves from the available pre-war espionage literature. Had they read Richard Rowan's *The Story of Secret Service* (1937), they would have learned that during the First World War the Germans were so conscious of the need to isolate their secret agents that in spy school the students were given their own rooms, were identified only by numbers, and were required to wear masks when in sight of each other. The Germans would never have agreed to what was called for by Plan *Midas* unless they knew the spies involved were under British control.

Owens was given a wicked grilling on his return to England, but he stuck to his story. He accused Dicketts of having gone over to the Germans, and also stated that when Dicketts was debriefed he would undoubtedly claim that he, Owens, was working for the Germans and had been all along. This was an echo of Sam McCarthy's accusation some nine months earlier, but the consequences this time were infinitely worse. It meant MI5's entire double-agent operation was fatally compromised.

It was hard to accept. Was Owens telling the truth? Did the Germans really know he had been under British control? Why did they send him back, then? Would they really believe he would pretend he had not been discovered?[8] Owens had flown back to England; when Dicketts followed by ship a week later, he evinced surprise when told of Owens's accusations.

Dicketts had first come to MI5's notice a year earlier, in April 1940, a month before Hitler's invasion of France. He was a stranger out of nowhere who appeared to be shadowing Owens. At first it was thought that he was a German spy, but when detained, Dicketts explained that he had overheard Owens talking suspiciously in a pub, and, being a former air intelligence officer, resolved to investigate. He sidled up to Owens at the bar, and after a time extracted from him that he was a double agent for the British.[9] It was a remarkable coincidence that a former intelligence officer and a present-day double agent should run into each other in one pub out of the thousands in England; MI5 nevertheless accepted it as so.

Dicketts said he was anxious to serve his country in the present war, but an appeal to the director of Air Intelligence, Commodore Boyle, had failed to land him a job. This was easily checked, and when found to be true, MI5 decided to put him to work itself, although not without distaste. There were police files on Dicketts at Scotland Yard and in the United States. He had been something of a con artist, and the Americans wanted him for having fleeced members of the social services bureau in Chattanooga, Tennessee. When it was decided to try to have Owens land another double agent on the Germans through Lisbon, Dicketts was given the mission.[10]

It was the practice then for a double agent returning from abroad to dictate a "chronology" of his experiences to a secretary. This Dicketts did when he got back to London, before he was told of Owens's accusations. It had gone smoothly, he said. His initial meeting with DR. RANTZAU had led to the proposal that he go on to Germany for a more thorough assessment. He was taken to Hamburg, where he was closely questioned by a "German air force type." He passed the test, and after being officially accepted as a spy for the Abwehr, he was taken around the city and also to Berlin to show him how slightly these cities had been damaged by British bombing. He returned to Lisbon after being away three weeks.

Dicketts also described how in setting out for Germany he was driven to the airport near Barcelona by a German embassy employee named Hans Ruser, the nephew of the former Reich minister of economics, Dr. Hjalmar Schacht. Ruser declared himself to be an absolute opponent of the Nazi regime and, as he guided the black Ford V-8 along Spain's narrow roads, sounded Dicketts out as to his willingness while in Germany to meet Dr. Schacht, and a certain "Baron X," who wanted to open covert peace negotiations with Britain. He would do it, Dicketts replied, only if DR. RANTZAU was informed and approved. Ruser agreed.[11]

The meeting with Dr. Schacht and "the Baron" went ahead, and it was proposed that when he returned to England as the Abwehr's newest spy, Dicketts would search British intelligence, and other government circles, for officials who might be amenable to secret peace talks. During subsequent questioning by MI5, he was asked how he was to get the results of these efforts back to Germany. Dicketts appears to have stumbled in answering. He failed to reply convincingly.

Dicketts was pressed more aggressively. It was not Ruser who put him on to the peace party in Germany, Dicketts admitted, but DR. RANTZAU, and it was Dicketts who prompted him to do it.[12]

DR. RANTZAU was not the man he was led to expect, Dicketts explained. At their first meeting, instead of the foul-mouthed type that McCarthy had described, RANTZAU turned out to be like a "very shrewd American business man," who spoke English fluently with a strong American accent and to whom his subordinates accorded considerable deference. Dicketts had had to think fast. This was not a man to be taken in by a flimsy yarn about being an unhappy former airman. Dicketts had a sudden inspiration. He was with British intelligence, he said. He had been sent to Lisbon to sound out German intelligence on the possibility of secret peace talks.

DR. RANTZAU was immediately interested, he said. He questioned him closely, but Dicketts was an experienced liar. RANTZAU said he would send him to Berlin to speak with a higher authority. Ruser only made the suggestion that he also meet Dr. Schacht after he learned about his mission during their drive across Spain.[13]

MI5 accepted this story, and in the ensuing months there was much earnest debate about it. Did the Abwehr's Major Ritter — by now DR. RANTZAU's real name was known — really believe Dicketts was a British intelligence agent? The debate went on and on with the chairman of the XX Committee, J.C. Masterman acting as referee.

It was while Dicketts was in Germany that Owens reported to the MI6 officer at the British embassy that the Germans were on to him. As he absolutely insisted this was so on his return to England, the two MI5 officers who separately questioned him had to take him seriously. It was reluctantly agreed that SNOW, CHARLIE, and BISCUIT had to be shut down. TATE, GW, TRICYCLE, and RAINBOW would be retained for the time being. Owens was taken into close custody. The SNOW wireless operator tapped out A-3504's last message. He was having a nervous breakdown, it said, and could not continue.[14] The leaders of MI5's double-cross program anguished over what to do next.

The big problem was that the Wireless Board and the XX Committee had been specifically set up to oversee the information being sent over to the Germans by Captain Robertson's wireless double agents, principally SNOW, after Caroli's spectacular escape attempt at the beginning of the year. Through January and February, notionally drawing on information supplied by CHARLIE and BISCUIT, SNOW delivered a feast of reports on bomb damage following the big raids on Manchester, Bristol, and Southampton.

TATE also seemed to have retained the Germans' confidence. With the closing down of SNOW, the burden of weather observations and bomb damage reports fell to him. The Germans continued to respond normally to his messages. As this seemed a little too good to be true, it had been decided to put his good standing to the test: he was to urgently ask for money, and to threaten to stop transmitting if he did not get it. The Germans took him seriously, proposing to drop a bundle of pound notes by airplane. When that proved impractical, and he continued to complain, they tried to mollify him by telling him he had been awarded the coveted German military decoration, the Iron Cross.

Next, in a repeat of the tactic that forewarned of the arrivals of Caroli and Schmidt the September before, the Germans wirelessed Schmidt to expect an agent shortly who would be bringing him money and a spare crystal for his transmitter. Another spy then landed by parachute, a twenty-nine-year-old Sudeten German named Karl Richter. The usual errors on his identification papers caused him to be picked up almost immediately, and on being searched he was found to be carrying two wads of money in pounds and dollars. His identity card and ration book were forgeries based on the serial numbers supplied to the Germans by SNOW. A little later, after seventeen hours of interrogation at Camp 020, Richter led his inquisitors to where he had hidden his equipment; it was found to include two radio crystals. Richter was the spy the Germans had advertised.

Richter was one of the millions of small tragedies of the war. He was German, but not by choice or preference — he had acquired citizenship automatically when Hitler annexed western Czechoslovakia. This meant compulsory military service, so he joined the German merchant marine, deserting shortly after the war started only to be nabbed by the Gestapo and put in a concentration camp. After some grim months, he was approached and offered a pardon if he did service as a spy. Yet, despite his lack of real ties to Germany, he responded to his interrogators at Camp 020 bravely, gave details of his mission only grudgingly, and refused offers to switch sides to work under British control. It would cost him his life.

Meanwhile, other attempts to pay Schmidt followed. The Germans finally arranged for him to meet a staff member of the Japanese embassy on a bus, where he would receive the money in a copy of the *Times* the embassy worker was carrying. Despite a glitch in which the pair missed their proper bus and were lost to sight for a while, the rendezvous was successful and Schmidt came back with £200 in "brand new English notes in series."[15] Obviously, as usual, they were counterfeit.

All this tended to reassure XX Committee members and MI5 case officers that the Owens-Dicketts contretemps had not blown MI5's precious double agents after all. But still there was uneasiness.

It was decided to send Dicketts back to Lisbon. The suggestion came from the Wireless Board, apparently at the instigation of Stewart Menzies, the MI6 chief. He would have read the debriefings of Dicketts, and the mention of Dr. Schacht would have caught his eye. Dicketts had returned from Germany via Lisbon with an Abwehr offer to negotiate; the name of Dr. Schacht, famous for having put Germany's finances in order and an outspoken critic of the Nazis, gave weight to the overture. It seems Menzies was now covertly sending him back a response.[16]

Dicketts took the flying boat to Portugal, and when Kramer, the Lisbon KO counter-intelligence officer, heard he was in town he grimly welcomed the news. The report on Hans Ruser's interrogation at Camp 020 after he defected to the Allies in 1943 disclosed the following:

> About May or June, 1941, Dicketts came back again and called on Ruser. At the time Ruser had Mayer-Döhne [the German naval attaché] staying with him. Dicketts and Mayer-Döhne therefore met.
>
> Dicketts told Ruser that he was going to Germany again on a peace mission, and had got a specially arranged escort from the Germans. Ruser told Kramer about this who said: "Yes, and this time he won't get out of Germany." When Ruser went back to Dicketts he rather pointedly advised him not to go to Germany, saying that peace negotiations were rather hopeless just then. Dicketts had secret information from Mayer-Döhne that Germany was about to declare war on Russia. Dicketts immediately took this up and asked Ruser if he meant [because of] Russia but Ruser did not tell him any more.[17]

Dicketts had hit the jackpot; this was news that was as big as it gets for any secret agent. Hitler and Stalin were partners. They had divided Poland between them and a thankful Soviet Union had been freely supplying Germany with the raw materials of war ever since. If Germany attacked Russia, it meant that the invasion of Britain was off for now. Mayer-Döhne had made himself a candidate for the firing squad by giving Dicketts this.

With such a scoop, Dicketts could have returned to Britain, to thanks and praise, then and there. Instead, he ignored Ruser's warning and went on to Germany. It was an act of considerable courage. His "escort" was George Sessler, a twenty-five-year-old former football tough and Abwehr bodyguard. Many years later, Sessler recalled:

> The last evening before our trip to Germany we went out to Estoril and had a good time. We had lobster and went out and sampled Lisbon night life. We met exciting Portuguese girls, had drinks and listened to music. But none of this seemed to impress Dicketts. Although he always smiled pleasantly, one could read in his eyes the question: [I]s this man going to bring me back alive? For the Englishman whom I had met only a few hours earlier I was simply an executioner's assistant.
>
> I remember walking out of a bar and into the night air and him suddenly stopping and saying: "You are very young. I can only rely on the impression you have made on me. But I think you are sincere. George, my life is in your hands!"
>
> I shook his hand and said, "I shall bring you back safely. You can rely on that!"
>
> At the time Dicketts was about forty. He was wearing an English suit. His eyes and his voice betrayed fear when I took him back to his hotel and said goodbye to him at three in the morning.[18]

The pair travelled across Portugal, Spain, and France by train, and Sessler remembered that when they reached Hamburg, Dicketts was questioned behind closed doors by several senior Abwehr officers. Included was Major Ritter, who had been in North Africa but flew back for the meeting.[19]

Whatever Dicketts said, it apparently satisfied his inquisitors. He was allowed to return to Portugal and go on to Britain, arriving in London on June 12. The next day, Menzies sent out an advisory saying that the Germans were likely to invade Russia toward the end of the next month. Churchill ordered the Soviets and President Roosevelt be warned. "From every source at my disposal, including some most trustworthy, it looks as if a vast German onslaught on Russia is imminent," the prime minister told the president.[20]

At least one of these "most trustworthy" sources must have been Dicketts. Until his departure for Portugal, the War Office and the Foreign Office had been at loggerheads over how to interpret the massive movement of German troops and air formations into eastern Europe. Army Intelligence — MI14 — and the Joint Intelligence Committee argued that Russia was to be attacked. The Foreign Office said it was a bluff; it did not make sense for Hitler to take on a new enemy before defeating Britain. Besides, Germany was receiving essential war commodities from Russia and hostilities would interrupt the flow indefinitely. This was logical; Dicketts confirmed that Hitler was not always logical.[21]

This incident also appears to mark the point at which MI6 began deliberately to withhold significant information from MI5. According to the strict division of responsibilities between the two services, when out of England, MI5's double agents reported to and took direction from the MI6(V) officer at the embassy. If Dicketts followed his standing instructions, he would have taken his news immediately to Ralph Jarvis, the MI6(V) officer for Portugal, who would have relayed it to London.

Ordinarily, despite the rule, MI6 would keep MI5 posted on the doings of one of its double agents while abroad. Not this time. Liddell apparently was not told that Dicketts had been tipped off to the attack on Russia, and he definitely did not learn about a second trip to Germany at the time; he only learned of the trip in late 1943, when Ruser defected. Even after the war ended, MI5 was still trying to confirm Ruser's disclosure from prisoner interrogations. Clearly, Dicketts had been ordered to tell his MI5 bosses just so much, and no more.[22]

As for Major Ritter, the hazards of war finally caught up to him. On June 17, the aircraft that was bringing him back to North Africa from the Berlin meeting made a forced landing on the sea near Derna, Libya. Ritter suffered a bad fracture on his upper right arm and was evacuated to hospital in Athens.[23] Five days later, on June 22, Hitler launched Operation Barbarossa. On a front stretching from the Baltic to the Black Sea, 4.5 million German and Axis troops with thousands of panzers lunged east into Russia. Moscow was the goal.

The Russian forces were taken completely by surprise. Stalin had ignored Churchill's warning. Like the mandarins of Britain's Foreign Office, he had assumed Hitler was logical.

MI5 REORGANIZES

Meanwhile, in the spring of 1941, when no one dreamed Hitler would be so foolish as to attack the Soviets, MI5 was finally getting its house in order. The new director-general-to-be, sixty-two-year-old David Petrie, arrived in January and began an exhaustive overhaul. He had been forty years in India, twenty of those with the Department of Criminal Intelligence, and most recently had briefly headed MI6 operations in the Middle East. He was a capable administrator, and when he formally took over in March, he quickly swept up the plethora of special sections and subsections of MI5 into one tightly designed organization. On the negative side, his contact with international espionage during the First World War had been minimal. Most of his career had involved counter-insurgency work in India, mainly against the Sikhs.

Petrie's most dramatic move, at the very beginning of his mandate, was to back transferring the Radio Security Service to MI6, where it was put under the direction of Richard Gambier-Parry, whose secret wireless section had grown substantially in size and sophistication. The Gill/Trevor-Roper team was broken up, the former being abruptly reassigned to a training school and oblivion and the latter taken on at MI6 as head of his own ISOS-traffic analysis section, MI6(Vw), the *w* standing for wireless. Henceforth, MI6 would have sole responsibility for extracting and sharing intelligence from intercepted Abwehr messages — ISOS — and sole responsibility for deciding who outside MI6 should see the decrypts.[24]

It was a surprising thing to do, even though joint direction of the Radio Security Service by the army, Post Office, and MI5 was never a satisfactory arrangement. None of the three had any significant expertise in modern military radio communications, the Royal Navy before the war being the miles-ahead leader through its "Y" service in direction-finding and enemy wireless operator identification. The army (the War Office), on the other hand, began the war with little direction-finding capacity, which was why the RSS was set up based on Post Office fixed receiving stations and civilian "volunteer interceptors." MI5 was not solely at fault for its many failures to observe the basic security procedures appropriate to clandestine wireless operations.

One wonders, however, whether there were deeper reasons behind MI6 taking over the RSS. Both Petrie and Menzies were competent intelligence officers of long experience. It may have been apparent to them that with the destruction of the Central Registry card index, MI5 could never be trusted. The administrative chaos and rapid expansion of the previous year, combined with the loss of more than two decades of dossiers on individuals of interest, mostly communists, guaranteed that there would be little chance of determining whether MI5 had been penetrated, either by the Soviets or the Germans. Up to the middle of June 1941, when Hitler and Stalin were still allies, one was as bad as the other.

MI6 also at this time set up its own counter-espionage registry, exclusive of the Central Registry, and the report prepared by Dicketts on his second trip to Lisbon/Germany went there, as did those pertaining to Dusko Popov, when he was in Portugal and the United States. MI6 also began its own collection of files on the enemy personalities who appeared in the intercepted Abwehr messages.[25]

Taking over the Radio Security Service and distribution of the ISOS product also breathed new life into MI6's counter-espionage section, MI6(V). Headed by Colonel Valentine Vivian, it was actually run by the deputy section head, Felix Cowgill, another former India intelligence officer. He promptly set up his own field officers in the embassies in Portugal and Spain, and sent them those intercepts that might help them identify Abwehr spies about to embark from the two countries. These special Section V officers were to answer to him directly. The existing MI6 heads of station — the passport control officers — were not to have anything to do with ISOS, or even to know about it.[26]

As for MI5, the loss of the Radio Security Service, and Major Gill in particular, cut the remaining lines between its wireless double-agent program and the service's military professionals with at least some expertise in enemy wireless communications. The Wireless Branch was dissolved and Robertson was given his own section — B1A "Special Agents" (the *1* and the *A* placing it in the position of honour at the very top of B Division's counter-espionage roster). While the rearrangement looked fine on paper, the practical effect was to even further isolate Robertson and how he chose to run his wireless double agents from the rest of MI5, and from mainstream British intelligence.

The result was that there was no one to question it when Robertson — now Major Robertson — decided to put a radio technician recently recruited from the BBC in charge of the wireless communications of his double agents. Twenty-five-year-old "Ronnie" Reed was also an amateur ham-radio enthusiast, but that was as far as it went in terms of experience relevant to clandestine wireless operations. Much, much more was needed if MI5 was to stand toe-to-toe against the German army signals personnel backing up Ast Hamburg's Major Ritter.

Meanwhile, MI6(VIII), Gambier-Parry's secret wireless communications section installed near Bletchley Park continued to grow, and grow, and flourish.

MENZIES WANTS TO KNOW

January–August 1941

It was Dusko Popov who made the collapse of the SNOW network in the spring of 1941 so exquisitely awful for the MI5 double-agent managers. He held promise of becoming a super-spy who would earn the Security Service the secret thanks of the nation and a smattering of knighthoods. All this was now in jeopardy.

First code-named SKOOT and then TRICYCLE by the British, and IVAN by the Germans, the twenty-nine-year-old Yugoslav with the easy smile and a knack with women was destined to be one of the more famous spies of the war. His exploits as a double agent became legendary, for he mixed espionage with wining, dining, sex, and the good life on a grand scale. Popov eventually wrote his own story nearly thirty years after the war, the popular *Spy/Counterspy* (1974), which was endorsed as "true" by one of Britain's leading wartime intelligence officers. In the book's introduction, Lieutenant-Commander Ewen Montagu wrote:

> Yet he also had the steel within, the ruthlessness and the cold-blooded courage that enabled him to go back to the German Secret Service Headquarters in Lisbon and Madrid time and again, when it was likely he might be "blown"; it was like putting his head in the lion's mouth.

> Bravely, in cold blood, he risked torture and death to re-establish German confidence in him so that he could make his great contribution to the Allied victory.

And further:

> Having worked with Dusko Popov (then known to me as TRICYCLE) from the time he arrived in war-battered London, I have read with absorbing interest his angle on the exploits of which I knew.... From the start, I fell under the spell of his personality, his sincerity, his gaiety, and his courage. I am sure he will have the same effect on all those who read this book.

There surely could be no better testimonial to his success than such lavish praise from an opponent still deceived after so many years: Popov was, in fact, another one of Major Ritter's triple agents, as later evidence will prove.

The Germans gave warning of Popov's impending arrival in Britain in a way that was to become standard for agents to come. The Government Code & Cipher School had only just broken the "main Abwehr hand cipher" when the following messages were intercepted and deciphered:

> 13.12.40 — Lisbon-Berlin.
> POPOV from Belgrade has reported here. He claims to be employed by ÖLSCHLAEGER and JEBSEN of SCHLOSS (Berlin) for GOLFPLATZ (Great Britain). I request urgent information. POPOV also is in need of money.

> 18.12.40 — Berlin-Lisbon.
> Radio your view as to when our agent POPOV can leave for GOLFPLATZ (Great Britain). His JEBSEN telegram has arrived, but is unintelligible. Refund his expenses.[1]

An MI5 officer awaited Popov when he flew into Whitchurch on December 20, 1940, and for the next ten days he was put through an intensive series of interrogations by various MI5 officers, Major Robertson included, and by Colonel Oreste Pinto, the ace spy catcher of the Dutch government-in-exile. He sailed through it all, for the wireless intercepts confirmed a cover story that had been months in the making.[2]

Popov first came to notice some months earlier when he called on the British embassy in Belgrade to inform officials that he was a lawyer from Dubrovnik and he had been approached to spy for the Germans by a friend from his student days in Germany. The MI6 station officer there encouraged him to develop the contact, so Popov went back to the friend, Johann Jebsen, and indicated his interest. This led to his recruitment by an Abwehr officer named Major Ölschlaeger, who arranged for him to go to England under the cover of a businessman with shipping interests. All this Popov reported to the MI6 officer. The mention of Ölschlaeger and Jebsen in the intercepted messages clinched the truth of his story.[3]

During his vetting on arrival in England, MI5 interrogators did notice one oddity. Popov had been given a surprisingly "primitive" invisible ink, one based on a popular headache remedy called Pyramidon. The secret messages to be written on the letters he was to send to cover addresses in Portugal could be developed by heat, a routine test for secret writing used by all wartime postal censorship agencies. When this observation was put to Popov, he deftly explained that at their last meeting Jebsen had taken away the ink he originally had been given and replaced it with one he said was better, which obviously it was not. This explanation was accepted.[4]

According to what Popov remembered nearly three decades later in *Spy/Counterspy*, Jebsen introduced him not to someone named Ölschlaeger but to a Major Munzinger, "who took orders directly from Canaris." Popov also has Jebsen explaining that he joined the Abwehr because he was an admirer of Dr. Hjalmar Schacht, and Schacht "was on very close terms with Canaris." Jebsen also mentions that he was personally introduced to Canaris by his aide, Colonel Oster, "whose political ideas and philosophy are identical to mine." These statements, if true, put Jebsen firmly on the inside of the army/Abwehr conspiracy against Hitler.[5] Popov implies in his book that he did not know this at the time.

If Popov reported the Schacht-Oster connections during his 1940 interrogations, the significance would have escaped MI5, but not MI6. Because of the Abwehr's secret peace overtures in the fall of 1939, Schacht was known to be a serious opponent of the Nazis, and Oster was known for tipping off the Dutch and the Belgians to Hitler's 1940 invasion plans. This was probably why, after having been cleared by MI5, Popov received an invitation from Stewart Menzies, the head of MI6, to spend the weekend at his brother's stately home in Surrey. There they could talk.

It was quite incredible. Menzies was head of Britain's Secret Intelligence Service. That made him one of the most powerful persons in the country. It put him at Churchill's elbow almost daily, and he was privy to the deepest secrets of the state. Popov was just a lowly Abwehr spy turned double agent. The closest Popov should have got to Menzies was as a name on a piece of paper voyaging across his desk.

They spent a few hours alone in the library of the house. In telling the story, Popov paints a picture of a white-haired and fatherly Menzies, sunk deep in an armchair, eyes on a line of the flames in the fireplace, quietly talking encouragement and advice to the young spy. Then:

> "Now," Menzies paused, put a match to his pipe, apparently collecting his thoughts — "to get to the point, we already have a fair amount of information about many officers in the Abwehr, including Canaris, but I want to know much more about everybody who is intimately connected with Canaris, and also with Dohnányi and Oster. I think you could get that information through Jebsen."
>
> "He'd probably know," I agreed.
>
> "It may be helpful if I explain the reasons behind this request. We know that Canaris, Dohnányi and Oster are not dyed-in-the-wool Nazis. They are what might be termed loyal officers, or patriotic Germans. In 1938 Churchill had a conversation with Canaris. Unofficially — he wasn't in office then. Churchill came to the conclusion that Canaris was a sort of catalyst for the anti-Hitler elements in Germany. That's why I want to know more about the people he attracts. Eventually, I may want to resume the conversation that Churchill initiated. In that event, I must be in a position to evaluate the strength of those around Canaris."

I nodded my understanding. Menzies was contemplating a dialogue with Canaris or those close to him with a view to ousting Hitler.

"I am handling the matter myself," Menzies stressed. "All information you pick up is to come directly to me with no intermediary...."[6]

No solid evidence has ever been found that Canaris and Churchill met before the war, although there is one tantalizing clue. In August 1938, Canaris sent a one-man secret mission to Britain on behalf of the chief of the general staff, General Beck, asking for assurance that Britain would intervene if Hitler carried out his threat to invade Czechoslovakia. "Bring me certain proof that Britain will fight if Czechoslovakia is attacked and I will put an end to this regime," Beck was reported as saying. The emissary was an obscure landowner-politician named Ewald von Kleist-Schmenzin, and he made no progress whatever with the officials of Chamberlain's government. Churchill, however, also received him and was sympathetic, giving him a letter agreeing that a world war would ensue if German troops crossed into Czechoslovakia. As an opposition politician he could do no more than that.[7]

Chances are the officials seen by Kleist-Schmenzin did not know what Canaris looked like. Faking a passport would be nothing to the Abwehr, and Canaris was known to enjoy going around in disguise. With a little hair whitener and a false moustache, Canaris could have been made to look like Kleist-Schmenzin.[8]

Popov said nothing of his meeting with Menzies to anyone. As far as MI5 was concerned, he was simply another turncoat spy whose arrival was especially timely because the XX Committee had only just been set up. The committee's initial membership comprised J.C. Masterman (chairman), Major Robertson, and Flight Lieutenant C.C. Cholmondely for MI5; Felix Cowgill for MI6(V); intelligence officers from the Admiralty, Air Ministry, and Home Forces; and someone from the Home Defence (Security) Executive. Ewen Montagu, then a lieutenant-commander in the naval reserve, represented naval intelligence.

The discussion at the XX Committee's first meeting on January 2 soon turned to how best to use Popov to baffle the Germans.[9]

The war was then in its seventeenth month. MI5 was undergoing a huge and largely uncontrolled expansion that had mixed rigid police-officer types with know-it-all academics and lawyers. Amateurism was rife, evident even in the choice of name for the new committee: the XX Committee (in conversation, the "Twenty Committee"). While it must have seemed terribly clever to whomever thought it up, it would have taken no time at all for an enemy intelligence analyst to notice that the number twenty in Roman numerals is "XX" — a double-cross. Later, there was even a Thirty Committee — XXX — for handling triple agents.

Popov was rushed into service, and was soon provided with some attractive intelligence to take back to his German masters in Lisbon. Before he departed, however, he was given plenty of opportunity to gather other useful intelligence on his own:

> Bill [Popov's case officer] accompanied me frequently on trips I was obliged to make to gather information for the Germans. The XX Committee had decided I should actually do this job myself so the Germans couldn't trip me up when they questioned me. Theoretically the concept was sound. In practice it didn't work all that well.
>
> The hitch was my photographic memory. Not everything I saw could be passed on. A board of experts decided what could be told the Germans. That meant I had to unlearn a good part of what I had seen. I lost more time studying what I had to forget than remembering what I was to report....[10]

The "concept" was not sound at all, but lunatic. It is hard to imagine anything more naive than to allow a freshly turned enemy agent to make observations of value and then solemnly tell him he was not to divulge them when he again came under enemy control. Yet, such was the persuasiveness of the intercepted Abwehr messages that had preceded his arrival.

Indeed, it was 1939 and Arthur Owens all over again, only this time instead of trips to Belgium and Holland to meet DR. RANTZAU, it was trips to Portugal to meet Gustav von Karsthoff, chief of the Abwehr office in Lisbon. Von Karsthoff — so Popov said on his return — was delighted by his offerings and rushed to Berlin with them, bringing back "a Mr. Kramer" (Major Ritter's deputy at Ast Hamburg, Dr. Karl Kramer) bearing a questionnaire that filled nine closely typed pages, forty-six of the fifty-two questions having to do with air intelligence. Popov was told of the plan to send him from England to the United States and then on to Egypt.[11]

It all went so perfectly. Popov, now code-named TRICYCLE, was allowed to extend his travels around Britain — to Coventry, Birmingham, and London — [12] and was again sent back to Lisbon, arriving on March 15. A few days later the Hamburg-Berlin teletype machine clattered out the following from Abt I/Luft:

> A-3570 reports by personal meeting for the period between 14.2 to 15.3.41.
> Subject: New Houses of Parliament
> [Translation]
> The building is between Little Smith Street and Marsham Street, Westminster, and is about 150–200 yards south of Victoria Street towards Westminster Abbey. The building has five floors, is almost new and has an area of about 100 x 80 yards. The upper floors are not used. They are strongly protected by sandbags and steel plates. The outer walls have brick protection 4 feet thick and about 8 feet high. The main entrance is on Little Smith Street and is exactly opposite from sub-station U which is the largest substation of the Westminster Auxiliary (Fire) Service. Winston Churchill's private entrance is on Marsham Street. The King is doing his official business in the same building. I received this information from the deputy chief of the above sub-station at the end of January.[13]

A-3570 did not get it right, but came dangerously close. He was not so much directing the Luftwaffe to where members of Parliament gathered, as to Churchill's underground bunker, which also housed the Cabinet War Room. In the immediate area, but just north of Victoria Street rather than south, it was the brain and nerve centre of the British armed forces, with a roof that was hastily and poorly constructed. A direct hit by a German heavy bomb and the course of the war, and its aftermath, would have been very different.[14]

Was this TRICYCLE? Undoubtedly so. IVAN — Popov's Abwehr code name — was remembered in interrogations after the war as being specifically attached to Abw I/Luft[15] (Abwehr air intelligence), and the coincidence of the spy's reporting period — February 14 to March 15 — corresponds to when Popov was in England between trips to Lisbon. The "by personal meeting" would have had to involve the spy entering Europe through a neutral country, either Sweden or Portugal. Popov, at this stage anyway, was another protegé of Major Ritter.

A-3570's other messages also had to do with air intelligence, but while the information might have appeared genuine to Luftwaffe analysts, most of it was not. The numbers given for aircraft production were not far off the mark, but the elaborate description of the characteristics of Britain's two-man Defiant fighter was useless; it had already been grounded as a failure. There was more material of like type, including one earlier message suggesting that *Lena* parachute spies would not be executed by the British if they were found to be carrying German army identification.[16] Not likely, surely.

All of this suggests MI5 disinformation, although expecting the Germans to believe that a Yugoslav who could barely speak English could have obtained high-grade air intelligence seems to be a bit of a stretch.[17] The message drawing German bombers to Churchill's bunker is another matter. Short of being someone's attempt to kill Churchill, it is likely his mention of "the New Houses of Parliament" was something Popov casually threw in as a result of his case officer showing him around London.

Ironically, the very fact that the message was relayed to Berlin is evidence that it was recognized as false. Canaris had no desire to see Churchill or the king hurt. He would not have wanted it sent on unless Major Ritter thought it was untrue. Fortunately, the Luftwaffe did not act on the information. Its policy still was to target war-related infrastructure, sparing where possible civilian institutions and military and political command centres.

By this time, Canaris had Britain's interests very well looked after. Major Ritter could filter out any really dangerous intelligence that passed through Ast Hamburg, while von Karstoff — also an especially trusted Canaris loyalist — could keep an eye on things at KO Portugal. He was shortly to have the help of another agent especially trusted by Canaris: Paul Fidrmuc, later to be notorious to the Allies as OSTRO.

Fidrmuc was the best. He had been a spy for the Abwehr since 1934, and had operated in Canada, the United States, and Britain before the war. He was sitting in a jail in Denmark awaiting trial for espionage when German troops marched into that country. He was forty-three, sly, well-travelled, and a capable writer in both English and German. He arrived in Lisbon just as Popov made his approach to MI6 in Belgrade.

It may have been coincidence, of course, but if Popov was to operate against England from Lisbon, he needed a case officer. While MI5 might be satisfied to believe that von Karsthoff ran his spies hands-on, it was Abwehr practice — like any espionage organization anywhere — to have staff members of an Ast or KO manage the agents. It would seem Fidrmuc was sent to Lisbon to work in that capacity with Popov.[18]

Indeed, the three men — von Karsthoff, Fidrmuc, and Popov — had much in common. The first two were vintage Austrians, left over from the aftermath of the First World War and the breakup of the former Austro-Hungarian Empire. This had involved the realignment of Austria's borders and the creation of Hungary, Czechoslovakia, and Yugoslavia. Following the breakup, Fidrmuc found himself suddenly a Czech, and von Karsthoff would have been an Italian had he stayed in Trieste after it was chopped off and handed to Italy. No Nazis these two.

Popov, for his part, told the British he was born in Titel, Serbia, but when MI5 tested him on his language proficiency, it was found that along with Serbo-Croat, German, and a smattering of English, he was fluent in French and spoke excellent Italian with a Viennese accent, a considerable achievement for a young man from the Balkan backcountry. The language profile — especially the Viennese accent — better fit a Croat from Dubrovnik, as the Germans understood him to be. If that was the case, then he probably shared the fierce anger of Croatians at being lumped in with the Serbs in the new Yugoslavia, rather than being given independence. That would have made him partial to the Germans, not to the British.[19]

In any case, it was not intended that Popov work through Portugal for long. Major Ritter planned to put his gift for languages to use by getting the British to take him on in Egypt as a double agent attached to the counterespionage agency there — Security and Intelligence Middle East (SIME).[20]

North Africa, up to the beginning of 1941 a backwater of the war, had suddenly burst into view with Indian and English troops under General Archibald Wavell, trouncing three times their number of Italians. Over 115,000 were captured and the rest were thrown back from the threshold of Egypt almost to Tripoli. It was the British army's most brilliant accomplishment of the war.

Mussolini was devastated. The Italian dictator was noted for his bombast, but there was nothing to puff about now. The new Roman legions of the 1940s had been humiliated. Hitler took pity and offered a modest German force to help prop up the Italians. German troops and panzers began landing in Tripoli in January. Then someone on Hitler's staff — maybe Hitler himself — had a very good idea. General Wavell was highly regarded by the Germans. During the interwar years he had been a prominent theorist on the principles of mechanized warfare. He was a tank man, and defeated the Italians by sending his armour around and between and behind them, the parched plains of Libya being perfect for a battle of movement. Against such a commander, one must put a leader of like qualities. Hitler chose General Erwin Rommel.

It was an inspired choice. The fifty-year-old Rommel had once commanded Hitler's personal guard and had made a name for himself during the invasion of France, when his panzer division had been first across the Meuse and had led the dash for the Channel. He had caught Hitler's eye, and to all appearances was a loyal follower of the Führer.

It is testimony to the speed with which Canaris could act that he had Popov aimed on Egypt within weeks of Rommel being named to Africa. If Popov could be properly set up as a double agent for SIME in Cairo, he could fish for intelligence on Rommel as well as on Wavell.

When MI5 switched off SNOW's wireless transmissions on April 13, 1941, Major Ritter was deeply involved in paving the way for Popov in Egypt, and in developing Abwehr espionage capacity in the eastern Mediterranean generally. If dropping Owens meant MI5 was losing confidence in its other double agents, it could affect Popov. Months of planning and preparation could be destroyed just when Rommel had gathered sufficient forces to strike at the British. It was a crucial moment for Major Ritter and undoubtedly the reason why the Germans now proceeded to show tokens of their continuing faith in TATE.

The XX Committee, for its part, must have breathed a collective sigh of relief when Popov returned from his third trip to Portugal at the beginning of May. He told of being congratulated on the excellent intelligence he had been obtaining. He reported no trouble selling Plan *Midas* to von Karsthoff, and his phantom sub-agents, BALLOON and GELATINE, were to be put on the Abwehr payroll. As the FBI was later to observe suspiciously, "von Karsthoff showed very little curiosity about Popov's activities in England, his means of entering or leaving the country, or his sub-agents, but left the impression that he was to manage everything."[21] He was given £300 for BALLOON and GELATINE and US$2,000 for himself.

By the end of May in England, the bombers had largely stopped coming as Hitler switched his Luftwaffe resources to the east for the invasion of the Soviet Union. Britain's scorched and smoking cities were to get a reprieve. Imminent invasion was no longer to be feared. The raison d'être of the Wireless Board, the XX Committee, and Major Robertson's wireless double agents — now reduced to two, TATE and DRAGONFLY — had ceased to be. For the XX Committee especially, finding something new to do was crucial.

The answer was to shift emphasis to general deception. RAINBOW, and the handful of other non-wireless double agents that had been run separately by Major Sinclair, were turned over to Robertson's newly minted B1A section. The XX Committee similarly expanded its mandate to all double agents, although still only in an advisory capacity. Robertson retained actual command. It meant that if he and Masterman were going to make names for themselves in their new roles, Popov, with his rich promise of fooling the Germans in the United States and Egypt, was their best bet.

EXIT MAJOR RITTER

For Major Ritter, June 1941 was a black month, and it got even blacker. Twelve days after breaking his arm when his plane ditched in the Mediterranean, he lost his American triple-cross operation, and with it his job with the Abwehr. His fault had been to assume that what he was getting away with in Britain could be duplicated in the United States. Not so.

William Sebold — TRAMP to the Germans, Harry Sawyer to the Americans — had enjoyed an easy run of it for over a year. His FBI operators at Centerport, New York, had faithfully radioed to Hamburg whatever he gave them, in readable cipher or not, and were sending on his behalf daily weather reports that included barometric pressure that even the FBI acknowledged was useful to German U-boats prowling the Atlantic.

Ritter, however, had over-extended himself. With the FBI looking after the transmitter, he allowed Sebold to become the centre of a small network of spies who sent their information as actual documents smuggled aboard ships bound for Europe. To facilitate this activity, the FBI was enticed into setting Sebold up in a dummy business. Unfortunately, unlike MI5 and Arthur Owens in Britain, the FBI did not leave Sebold to his own devices. When Sebold's spies came calling at his office, it was with the whirring and clicks of FBI cameras behind a two-way mirror on the wall.

It must have seemed low risk at the outset. The United States was not at war, so even if Ritter's agents were eventually arrested, at worst the penalties would only be a few years in jail. And even if the FBI caught on, why should it break up the party when there was no need to? The British had let Owens collect intelligence and obtain it from sub-agents for years without interfering. However, FBI director J. Edgar Hoover had made his reputation and that of the Bureau's by spectacular show trials during Prohibition. The movies and photos were for the press as well as for the courts.

There was indication of what was to come. Earlier in the spring, in a mighty blaze of publicity, the FBI took to the courts with the breakup of the "Joe K" spy ring, a Nazi security service enterprise that went sour when British postal censorship in Bermuda turned up and turned over one of his invisible-ink secret letters. The lucky break of an automobile accident and some good detective work had led to the capture of Kurt Ludwig, a.k.a. Joe Kessler, and his confederates.

On June 29, 1941, the FBI again pounced. In a lightning roundup, twenty-nine agents associated with Sebold were arrested. There were lurid headlines in newspapers across the United States and the world, and fabulous cinema footage of spy-to-spy meetings. It was thrilling stuff and captivated the American public for weeks on end, but it was the last thing

Hitler wanted. Having attacked the largest country in the world just the week before, he did not want to give offence to the most powerful. There was hell to pay in Berlin.[22]

It was tremendously embarrassing to Canaris. A furious Hitler was deaf to any explanations, including that Sebold had been deliberately planted on the FBI. Major Ritter had to take the blame, and the punishment was swift. He was kicked out of the Abwehr, and Abt 1 Luft Hamburg was closed down and its staff dispersed. Ritter wound up in an anti-aircraft unit for the rest of war.[23]

The FBI scoring a double-agent triumph did not bring much cheer to MI5 either. The Bureau was good about it, giving details of its investigation to British Security Coordination, the MI6 office in New York, to pass along to its MI5 colleagues in London.[24] MI5 could claim nothing like it. The minor German agents and sympathizers it had so far arrested had led to no spy rings. All had been individuals, or very small group efforts that had failed at the outset. Yet it was the British who were at war, not the Americans.

MI5's only riposte was to promote its prowess with double agents. Thus Popov — TRICYCLE — slated shortly to pass through the United States on his way to Egypt, was touted to the FBI as a kind of espionage superstar, a deeply cunning professional who had penetrated to the heart of the German secret service apparatus in Portugal and Spain,[25] without giving the Americans any details, or any hint that there were still fears he had been blown by Owens.

Then something really exciting occurred. RAINBOW, a.k.a. George Eibner, the young man who roamed England with a small dance band, and who occasionally exchanged secret-ink letters with the Germans under Major Sinclair's direction, received a letter from Portugal bearing instructions on a piece of film negative posing as a period at the end of a sentence. This was amazing. For more than a year, Eschborn had been struggling at Hamburg's direction to reduce spy-photos to the size of postage stamps. This was new technology light years beyond his best efforts. Major Robertson was hugely impressed.[26]

It wasn't new. To realize this, Robertson had only to read page 214 of Colonel Nicolai's book *The German Secret Service* (London, 1924). Germany's chief spymaster of the First World War wrote:

> Finally the use of photographic reduction in the service
> of espionage deserves mention. It is accomplished by the
> reduction of documents as large as a sheet of typing paper
> to the size of a leaflet a millimetre square. In this way
> agents could receive almost indiscernible instructions
> which they could read with the help of magnifying glass.[27]

But Robertson had not read it; nor had the FBI told its British counterparts that Sebold had arrived in the United States sixteen months earlier
with four microphotographs stuck to the back of his watch. The FBI had
even gone on to make them for him.[28]

At the beginning of August, a few days before he was to leave Lisbon
for the United States, Popov turned in a lengthy note to MI6 that included
the following:

> Very often during recent months the Germans do not
> write any more to their agents in secret ink. They employ
> full stop marks. These are diminutive photographs of let-
> ters reduced to about this size: . It is possible to read
> the whole letter with a microscope. I received six for my
> trip to America. I will show them to J. I am doing what I
> can to arrange for the future correspondence with IVAN
> II with these full stops. The full stops are stuck on the
> interior of the envelope. I have marked on this envelope
> where the full stops have been stuck in my presence....[29]

The "J" stood for Ralph Jarvis, the MI6(V) officer for Portugal. His
boss in London was Felix Cowgill, Menzies's brittle counter-intelligence
deputy. He would be looking forward to Jarvis's report.

Admiral Wilhelm Canaris, chief of the Abwehr, at dinner before the war with Reinhard Heydrich, head of the Nazi security service, the Sicherheitsdienst or SD. Despite the outward appearance of cordiality, Canaris considered Heydrich the most dangerous man in Germany after Hitler and Himmler.

Abwehr document 11.2. 40: Major Ritter reports to Berlin that Arthur Owens, during their February 1940 meeting in Antwerp, claimed to have been given information "from someone known to him in MI5." The note "Ast Hamburg III f hat" following the body of the message indicates that the information was passed over to the Abwehr's counterespionage section, responsible for running penetration agents inside the enemy's intelligence service. The teletype machine is printing *J* for *I*.

Heeres-Fernschreibnetz

-2-

jetzt zwar als Ausbilder zum festen Bodenpersonal, muss aber trotzdem ab und zu wieder Feindflüge machen, weil keine anderen da sind. Erst Ende Januar wurde ich wieder zu einem solchen Feindflug kommandiert. Ich startete gegen zwölf Uhr mittags und kehrte gegen sechs Uhr abends

1.) OKW Abw I Luft/E
    Ast Rhaven
    Ast Kiel
    Nest Bremen

    Betr., England (Belgien, Holland)

    3504 meldet am 11.2. bei einem peroebnl.Treff in Antwerpen :
    Die Piloten der Sabena und der KLM stehen zum
    grossen Teil in Dienst des J.S. Sie berichten
    u.a. regelmässig über ihre Minen-Beobachtungen
    im Kanal. Diese Nachricht habe ich von einem
    mir bekannten MJ.5-Mann.

    Ast Hamburg III f hat.

    Ast Hamburg 403 / 40 I Luft geh.

2.) zurück an Ast I Luft

am III f

NARA

Abwehr document dated 18.9.39: Ast Hamburg passes on to Berlin a report from A-3504 (Arthur Owens) indicating that the British are deploying an ultra shortwave device capable of detecting aircraft at very long range — radar. Abw I Luft/E is the Air Intelligence Section for England at Abwehr headquarters.

Heeres-Fernschreibnetz

1.) OKW Abw I Luft/E
    Nst. Bremen
    Ast Whaven
    Ast Kiel

    3504 meldet am 18.9.39 : Verbindungsingenieur der Fa.
    Blaupkt. nach Philips in Holland erzählt mir folgendes :
    Es ist ein neuer Ultrakurzwellenempfänger gebaut worden,
    der entlang der ganzen Ostküste liegende eingebaut wird.
    Mit diesem können die Ultrakurzwellen, die durch die von
    den Zündkerzen der Flugzeugmotoren auf die Magneten über-
    springenden Funken hervorgerufenen Kurzwellen einwandfrei
    aufgefangen werden. Mit Hilfe des Gerätes kann man mit
    ziemlicher Sicherheit die genaue Entfernung feststellen
    und ebenso Schlüsse auf die Anzahl der Motoren ziehen.
    Die einzige Möglichkeit, die Erzeugung dieser Ultrakurz-
    wellen in den Motoren zu unterbinden oder für den Empfän-
    ger unwirksam zu machen, ist die Anwendung von sog. "sup-
    pressors".

    Ast Hamburg B.Nr. 1257/39 I Luft geh.

2.) zurück an Ast I Luft

NARA

Abwehr document dated 3.8.40: The Luftwaffe is invited to bomb Thames House, a prominent and highly visible building in London said by this A-3504 message to house elements of the RAF staff. German intelligence understood it to contain the headquarters of MI5, but chose not to bomb it.

Owens offers to again meet Major Ritter in Holland, but two days after he sent this message Hitler's invasion of the Low Countries disrupts the plan. Spy and spymaster arrange a North Sea rendezvous instead.

The 1940 pre-invasion spies. Top row: Diaz, Martinez, Meier, Krag. Second row: Jazequel, Kieboom, Waldberg, Pons. Third row: Coll, Eriksen, Hackverria, Van Dam. Bottom row: Walti, Drüke, Robles, Evertsen.

Vera Eriksen a.k.a. von Schalburg offered herself to be shot instead if it would save the lives of her two companions. Werner Walti and Francois Karl Drüke (a.k.a. De Deeker) were executed anyway; she was interned.

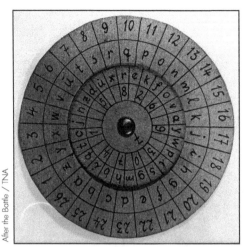

An incriminating possession. A ciphering disk such as this one found on Walti would never have been supplied to a real German spy. Cipher disks are proof of espionage intent, and guaranteed death for those caught with one if the target country executed spies. Britain did, and Walti was.

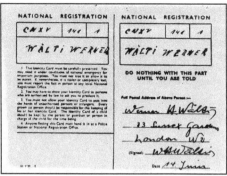

The use of number ones written with a left-handed backstroke (see top of card) is a certain giveaway that the writer is European, not British. This is not a mistake the Abwehr's false documents section would have made. The identity card is also without the appropriate rubber stamps. Walti was sure to be arrested the moment he had to show his papers.

August 1941: Roosevelt and Churchill on the *Prince of Wales* off Newfoundland for their historic "Atlantic Meeting." Behind, left, General George C. Marshall and behind, right, Admiral Harold R. Stark.

Admiral Stark risked losing the entire Pacific Fleet at sea by not keeping Admiral Kimmel, the navy's commander at Pearl Harbor, properly informed of Japanese intentions. Had Kimmel put the fleet to sea just before the surprise attack, it would have been sunk with some fifteen thousand sailors lost.

Huge columns of black smoke billow from the battleships USS *West Virginia* and USS *Tennessee* minutes after being hit by Japanese bombs and torpedoes on December 7, 1941.

Honolulu Star-Bulletin 1st EXTRA

Evening Bulletin, Est. 1882. No. 11287
Hawaiian Star, Vol. XLVIII No. 15249

HONOLULU, TERRITORY OF HAWAII, U. S. A., SUNDAY, DECEMBER 7, 1941

★ PRICE FIVE CENTS

WAR!

(Associated Press by Transpacific Telephone)

SAN FRANCISCO, Dec. 7.—President Roosevelt announced this morning that Japanese planes had attacked Manila and Pearl Harbor.

OAHU BOMBED BY JAPANESE PLANES

SIX KNOWN DEAD, 21 INJURED, AT EMERGENCY HOSPITAL

Attack Made On Island's Defense Areas

By UNITED PRESS

WASHINGTON, Dec. 7.—Text of a White House announcement detailing the attack on the Hawaiian islands is:

"The Japanese attacked Pearl Harbor from the air and all naval and military activities on the island of Oahu, principal American base in the Hawaiian islands."

Oahu was attacked at 7:55 this morning by Japanese planes.

The Rising Sun, emblem of Japan, was seen on plane wing tips.

Wave after wave of bombers streamed through the clouded morning sky from the southwest and flung their missiles on a city resting in peaceful Sabbath calm.

According to an unconfirmed report received at the governor's office, the Japanese announcement shortly after 9 a. m. the fact of the bombardment by an enemy but being previous army and navy had taken immediate measures in defense.

It was also reported that an attempt had been made to bomb the USS Lexington, or that it had been bombed.

CITY IN UPROAR

Within 10 minutes the city was in an uproar. As bombs fell in many parts of the city, and its defense areas the defenders of the islands went into quick action.

Army intelligence officers at Ft. Shafter announced officially shortly after 9 a. m. the fact of the bombardment by an enemy but long previous army and navy had taken immediate measures in defense.

"Oahu is under a sporadic air raid," the announcement said.

"Civilians are ordered to stay off the streets until further notice."

CIVILIANS ORDERED OFF STREETS

The army has ordered that all civilians stay off the streets and highways and not use telephones.

Evidence that the Japanese attack has registered some hits was shown by three billowing pillars of smoke in the Pearl Harbor and Hickam field area.

All navy personnel and civilian defense workers, with the exception of women, have been ordered to duty at Pearl Harbor.

The Pearl Harbor highway was immediately a mass of racing cars.

A trickling stream of injured people began pouring into the city emergency hospital a few minutes after the bombardment started.

Thousands of telephone calls almost swamped the Mutual Telephone Co., which put extra operators on duty.

At The Star-Bulletin office the phone calls deluged the single operator and it was impossible for this newspaper, for sometime, to handle the flood of calls. Here also an emergency operator was called.

HOUR OF ATTACK—7:55 A. M.

An official army report from department headquarters, made public shortly before 11, is that the first attack was at 7:55 a. m.

Witnesses said they saw at least 50 airplanes over Pearl Harbor.

The attack centered in the Pearl Harbor, Army authorities said:

"The rising sun was seen on the wing tips of the airplanes."

Although martial law has not been declared officially, the city of Honolulu was operating under M-Day conditions.

It is reliably reported that enemy objectives under attack were Wheeler field Hickam field, Kaneohe bay and naval air station and Pearl Harbor.

Some enemy planes were reported shot down.

The body of the pilot was seen in a plane burning at Wahiawa.

Oahu appeared to be taking calmly after the first uproar of queries.

ANTIAIRCRAFT GUNS IN ACTION

First indication of the raid came shortly before 8 this morning when antiaircraft guns around Pearl Harbor began sending up a thunderous barrage.

At the same time a vast cloud of black smoke arose from the naval base and also from Hickam field where flames could be seen.

BOMB NEAR GOVERNOR'S MANSION

Shortly before 9:30 a bomb fell near Washington Place, the residence of the governor, Governor Poindexter and Secretary Charles M. Hite were there.

It was reported that the bomb killed an unidentified Chinese man across the street in front of the Schuman Carriage Co., and windows were broken.

C. E. Daniels, a welder, found a fragment of shell or bomb at South and Queen Sts. which he brought into the City Hall. This fragment weighed about a pound.

At 10:05 a. m. today Governor Poindexter telephoned to The Star-Bulletin announcing he has declared a state of emergency for the entire territory.

He announced that Edouard L. Doty, executive secretary of the major disaster council, has been appointed director under the M-Day law's provisions.

Governor Poindexter urged all residents of Honolulu to remain off the street, and the people of the territory to remain calm.

Mr. Doty reported that all major disaster council wardens and medical units were on duty within a half hour of the time the alarm was given.

Workers employed at Pearl Harbor were ordered at 10:10 a. m. not to report at Pearl Harbor.

The mayor's major disaster council was to meet at the city hall at about 10:30 this morning.

At least two Japanese planes were reported at Hawaiian department headquarters to have been shot down.

One of the planes was shot down at Ft. Kamehameha and the other back of the Wa-(Turn to Page 2, Column 5)

Hundreds See City Bombed

Hundreds of Honolulu who hurried to the top of Punchbowl soon after bombs began to fall, saw spread out before them the whole panorama of surprise attack and defense.

Far off over Pearl Harbor the white sky was polkadotted with anti-aircraft smoke.

Sailing away down the navy base were billowing clouds of ugly black smoke. Sometimes a burst of flame reddened the black screen of the smoke.

Out from the silver-colored mouth of the harbor a flotilla of destroyers streamed to sea, smoke pouring from their stacks.
(Turn to Page 2, Column 1)

Names of Dead and Injured

The only emergency hospital reported at 10:30 a list of 6 killed and 21 injured.

The complete list will be secured later. Here is a partial list: Peter Lopes, 16, of 3661 Kaumuamoo St., was reported at 9:30 a. m. to be in serious condition from wounds in the upper abdomen.

Dorothy Oversta, 40, of Kailua, Oahu, is suffering from a mangled thigh, lacerations on the right leg and left arm.

A Portuguese girl, unidentified, 10 years old, died on arrival from injuries wounds.

Another victim who died on arrival was Pogue Logan, 32, of 1881 Kamamalu St., from puncture wounds in the chest.

Cynthia Brandly, 30, Mauuluoa gardens, was released from the hospital after treatment for lacerations.

There were reported killed and one reported killed from the knock that fell at Pearl and School Sts.

Schools Closed

All schools on Oahu, both public and private, will remain closed until further notice, Edward L. Doty, territorial director of civilian defense, announced at 11 a. m. today. This does not apply elsewhere in the territory.

Editorial

HAWAII MEETS THE CRISIS

Honolulu and Hawaii will meet the emergency of war today as Honolulu and Hawaii have met emergencies in the past—coolly, calmly and with immediate and complete support of the officials, officers and troops who are in charge.

Governor Poindexter and the army and navy leaders have called upon the public to remain calm; for civilians who have no essential business on the streets to stay off; and for every man and women to do his duty.

That request, coupled with the measures promptly taken to meet the situation that has suddenly and terribly developed, will be needed.

Hawaii will do its part—as a loyal American territory. In this crisis, every difference of race, creed and color will be submerged in the one desire and determination to play the part that Americans always play in crisis.

BULLETIN

Additional Star-Bulletin extras today will cover the latest developments in this war move.

PART III

RED SUN RISING

July–August 1941

Churchill wanted war between the United States and Germany, and by the summer of 1941 he had a good idea how he might achieve it: Get Roosevelt to provoke the Japanese into attacking America.

At stake was Britain's survival. Hitler's lightning invasion of the Soviet Union in June had diminished the likelihood of a cross-Channel attack and the bombing of British cities had eased, but it all would come back again when Hitler turned his full attention on England once more — perhaps even later that year, considering the rapid collapse of Stalin's armies. Indeed, with the toll German U-boats were taking on British shipping in the Atlantic, Hitler might not even have to invade. The country could starve to death.

The only hope was the United States. Throughout the previous year, President Roosevelt had been sympathetic, but guardedly so. Isolationist feelings ran deep in America, fuelled by the America First Committee and a powerful congressional lobby led by Senator Burton K. Wheeler. With opinion polls saying that 88 percent of Americans opposed joining the war in Europe,[1] and with the prospect of mid-term congressional elections always in mind, Roosevelt had to be sparing and careful in his help to Britain. Germany, meanwhile, was doing everything it could not to cause offence.

That left Japan. If Churchill was to see the United States drawn into the fight with Germany, the war had to go global.[2]

Japan's transition from a closed, quasi-feudal society in the 1850s to a modern military power in barely three generations is one of the social miracles of the modern era. First there was war with China, and then, in 1905, using tactics, weapons, and technology borrowed from Europe, and British-built battleships, it decisively defeated czarist Russia in the struggle for control of Korea. By the late 1930s, it had a huge army, was again engaged in war with China, and had a fully modern fleet, complete with aircraft carriers, the equal to any on the oceans, the Japanese thought, and a match for the Americans and British in everything but numbers.

It was a first-class naval weapon forged by an island nation for exactly the same reason that Britain needed the Royal Navy: to police an empire of colonies and vassal states whose raw materials and commerce would feed the mother country. The problem was, the empire that Japan desired in the Far East was already mainly owned and occupied by the British, and, to a lesser extent, by the French and the Dutch.

The United States, in contrast, was not Japan's natural enemy. Other than the Philippines, it had no significant possessions in the Far East west of the islands of Hawaii, and Hawaii was too far away to be coveted. Besides, Japan's industries relied heavily on the United States for scrap iron, oil, and other commodities, and there was both respect and affection for the Americans for having been first to help open the country to the world.[3]

The French, Dutch, and British, on the other hand, had to be fought sooner or later, and when France and Holland were overrun by Hitler, the Japanese felt that the great opportunity had come. Fending off air attacks at home while engaged in desperate struggles in the Middle East and the North Atlantic, Britain had no significant air or naval forces to spare to defend its possessions in the Far East. Churchill could only hope that when the inevitable clash came, it also somehow pulled in both the United States and Germany.[4]

For a moment Hitler himself seemed to provide an opening. In September 1940, he persuaded Japan into signing the Tripartite Pact, which, among other things, included a clause whereby should Germany, Italy, or Japan be attacked by any nation not already involved in the European War, the other two would come to its aid.[5] Over the next eight months,

Churchill tried to obtain a similar arrangement with the United States, whereby should Britain become embroiled with Japan in defence of its Far East possessions, the Americans would automatically join in. It was a futile hope. Roosevelt made it clear that no president could hope to sell war to Congress in order to save Britain's empire, and only Congress had the constitutional right to declare war.

Then, with Hitler's invasion of the Soviet Union in June 1941, the prospect of Japan advancing on the British seemed to recede. Attacking the Russian behemoth from behind, in Siberia, offered Japan an interim target for its expansionist aims, and one that was handy to its army already in northern China. The world, and especially Britain, waited for Japan to do the obvious.

At the beginning of August, just before the British double agent Dusko Popov was to leave Lisbon for the United States, his German controllers gave him a long list of questions on a series of microdots, many of which dealt with the air and naval defences of Pearl Harbor in Hawaii, home to the U.S. Pacific Fleet.

Only eight months earlier, in one of the most daring and original British exploits of the war, obsolete, canvas-and-glue Fairey Swordfish torpedo bombers launched from the aircraft carrier *Illustrious* made a highly successful surprise attack on the Italian naval base at Taranto, sinking three battleships and doing much other damage. The Japanese had six fleet carriers, each with greater aircraft capacity than the *Illustrious* and better carrier-borne fighters and bombers.

When members of the XX Committee and other officers at MI5 eventually saw the questionnaire, it was plain to them that the Abwehr's help had been sought because the Japanese were considering a similar attack on Pearl Harbor.

The incident of the so-called TRICYCLE questionnaire was first described thirty years later by J.C. Masterman, in his book *The Double-Cross System*, and he excoriated the Americans for having ignored the obvious when Popov turned over the microdots on arrival in New York. "It is therefore surely a fair deduction," he wrote, "that the questionnaire indicated very clearly that in the event of the United States being at war, Pearl Harbor would be the first point to be attacked, and that plans for this attack had reached an advanced state by August, 1941."[6] Two years after Masterman published his book, Popov himself, in *Spy/Counterspy*, depicted an oafish J. Edgar Hoover letting slip from his grasp the opportunity to alert the president and spare America from the "Day of Infamy," the December 7 surprise attack that devastated the U.S. Pacific Fleet, sinking four out of eight battleships and damaging the rest.

Other veterans of wartime British intelligence took up the refrain: "When coupled with the Japanese special interest in the raid on Taranto it seems incredible that Pearl Harbor should not be on the alert for a surprise hit-and-run air raid, *if* Hoover had not failed to pass on what TRICYCLE brought him," said Lieutenant-Commander Ewen Montagu, the Royal Navy's representative on the XX Committee.

MI5's double-agent chief "TAR" Robertson's condemnation was even more severe: "The mistake we made was not to take the Pearl Harbor information out and send it directly to Roosevelt. No one ever dreamed Hoover would be such a bloody fool."[7]

These were harsh words, and they deeply rankled those in the American intelligence services. Hoover was never lovable, but his commitment to the Constitution and to the Office of the President is still legendary. The British portrayed him as venal and stupid.

The FBI, it should be said, was a victim of its own sense of responsibility to maintain the confidences entrusted to it. When, in 1989, retired CIA officer Thomas Troy rose to Hoover's defence in a closely argued article entitled "The British Assault on Hoover: The Tricycle Case," he had to rely on FBI case-file documents that had been heavily redacted, with all references to British intelligence removed. Troy's arguments, though authoritative and logical, were crippled by lack of evidence.[8]

Troy, and an earlier British critic of the MI5's extravagant double-agent claims, David Mure, began with the premise that if the threat implied by Popov's questionnaire was so obvious, why didn't someone in authority in Britain warn the Americans directly? Why leave it exclusively to an agent to deliver information of such importance, and why deliver it to an American civilian agency rather than to the military authorities, or, for that matter, to the U.S. secretaries of state, war, or the navy? Hoover's

British critics simply ignored the question and neither Troy nor Mure could come up with satisfactory theories of their own.[9]

Two years later, when the relevant documents reached the half-century mark, the FBI released them with their content restored, but too late: the wave of interest had passed. However, some twenty-five years later, combined with the declassifying of certain MI5 files in Britain, they permit the piecing together of a truly remarkable story.

It begins with Churchill. He had been an enthusiastic promoter and user of secret intelligence for years, especially during the First World War. He thrilled to tales of espionage and was one of Britain's early champions of code- and cipher-breaking. He certainly would have relished the centuries-old tradition that a nation's spy chief directly serves the head-of-state — monarchs in the Middle Ages, and prime ministers, presidents, and dictators in the twentieth century. This was not something that he was going to miss out on when he became prime minister, and "C" — Stewart Menzies, chief of MI6 — reported to him daily, usually in person.

Menzies gave the code name BONIFACE to his private offerings to Churchill, the term generally covering the intercepted wireless traffic of the enemy deciphered by the Government Code & Cipher School. In 1941, the choicest decrypts were offered first and foremost to the prime minister, and then passed on to the army, navy, and RAF as appropriate. The American equivalent was MAGIC, the code name for deciphered Japanese diplomatic traffic that was broken as a shared task of the U.S. Army's Signals Intelligence Service (SIS) and the U.S. Navy's Combat Communications Section (Op-20-G), both agencies headquartered in Washington, D.C. MAGIC decrypts had an exclusive clientele: the president, the secretaries of state, war, and navy, the army and navy chiefs, and senior service heads and field commanders.

Both BONIFACE and MAGIC covered two superb cryptological accomplishments: the breaking of the Enigma machine ciphers of the German air force (Luftwaffe) by the British and the breaking of the Purple machine cipher of the Japanese by the Americans. The terms also covered decrypts of hand-enciphered messages and codes — Abwehr, German police, and SS wireless traffic with the British; and, with the Americans, the LA, J, PA, and similar diplomatic codes and ciphers of the Japanese. It was the importance of a message, not just the type of encipherment, that determined whether it made the MAGIC or BON-IFACE folders.[10]

Menzies's daily submissions to Churchill could also come from his other sources, including anything MI5's double agents picked up while under MI6's jurisdiction because travelling abroad. If especially valuable, Menzies could withhold such items from MI5 until seen by Churchill. This explains how it happened that when Walter Dicketts was tipped off to the impending German invasion of Russia in June, Churchill got that news first, and everyone else, including MI5, a day or so later. This also appears to have occurred with Popov and the questionnaire about Pearl Harbor.[11]

Before leaving for the United States, Popov secretly met with Ralph Jarvis, his MI6(V) contact in Lisbon, and showed him his microdots plus typed copies of the questions that were on them in both English and German. MI6(V) in London was notified — that is to say, Felix Cowgill — and the reply came back that he should carry on with his mission and give the information to the Americans when he got to New York. Popov left on August 10.[12]

The paper copies of the questionnaire were flown to London immediately, arriving by August 7 at the latest. As the questions indicated German collaboration with Japan at the highest level, the English-language version would have been brought to Menzies's attention immediately, and he would have promptly sent it on to Churchill.[13] What makes this simple deduction of great significance is that Churchill was then on the high seas, aboard the battleship *Prince of Wales*, on his way to meet personally with President Roosevelt.[14]

It was a secret rendezvous, urgently arranged. On July 15, or a day or so after, a twenty-nine-year-old Spaniard had called at the British embassy in Lisbon claiming to be a spy for the Germans who wanted to change sides. His name was Juan Pujol Garcia (later GARBO), and as proof of his mission he produced several "miniature" photographs containing a list of questions the Germans wanted him to try to get answered:

- Does England expect aggression from Japan against British or Dutch possessions in the Far East in the course of 1941?
- What is to be the final objective of such aggression, Hong Kong, Singapore, India, the Dutch East Indies, or Australia?

- What possibilities are considered to defend Hong Kong?
- In what direction is an attack expected in case of war with Japan? Against Singapore, Siam, or the Dutch East Indies?
- How does England expect to resist Japanese aggression? What help is expected from the U.S.A. in case of war with Japan?
- Is England in the condition to dispose of and make available naval forces and arms for use in the Far East?[15]

The implication was grave. It looked like the Germans had been asked by the Japanese to gauge Britain's attitude toward the possibility of Japan attacking British and Dutch colonies in the Far East, rather than going after the Soviets.

It appeared to confirm earlier intelligence. On May 22, a MAGIC decrypt had provided Roosevelt with "proof positive" that Japan was planning the conquest of Southeast Asia and the southwest Pacific. Then, on July 24, another decrypt revealed that Japan had ordered its merchant shipping to withdraw from the Indian Ocean and the southwest Pacific. Such action is a classic prelude to armed conflict on the high seas. The Japanese also had recently obtained permission from Vichy France to set up air bases in French Indochina, giving them control of the sky over Malaya and Singapore. Evidently, Japan was poised to attack Britain in the Far East. Churchill and Roosevelt talked on the transatlantic scrambler telephone that very evening and agreed they had to meet face-to-face.[16]

They had something else on their minds that needed urgent discussion, as well. British scientists had just concluded that a super-bomb based on the heavy element uranium was theoretically possible. This was ominous news, as German scientists had led the world in nuclear physics before the war.[17]

Two weeks later, the White House pretended to the Washington press that Roosevelt was leaving on a yachting holiday, but once over the horizon he boarded the battle cruiser USS *Augusta* to sail for Argentia, the newly constructed U.S. Navy air base overlooking Placentia Bay, Newfoundland. There, on August 9, the two ships and the two leaders met, accompanied by some of their most senior army, navy, and air force chiefs.

Over seventy years later, most contemporary documents that could describe the content of their talks remain under lock and key. Records of their discussions and many of those involving their military staffs, all of which must exist, have never been released. Even Roosevelt's personal account of the meeting has been scissored in half, his description of his four days with Churchill left behind in the vault at the Roosevelt Library.[18] By design, surely, rather than accident, the meeting is known to historians mainly by the press release at its conclusion announcing that the two leaders were resolved that their two countries would respect the right of peoples of all nations to self-determination. This became known as the Atlantic Charter.

More important to Churchill, they also publicly pledged that they were jointly committed to "the final destruction of the Nazi tyranny." This last statement was a stunning victory for the British. It went far beyond anything Roosevelt had so far said about the Nazi regime, and it flew in the face of the virulent anti-war opposition in Congress. Churchill must have done something fairly dramatic to achieve such a result.[19]

The prime minister, so it appears, had played two trump cards. First, wireless messages recently deciphered by the Government Code & Cipher School indicated that the Nazis in Russia were systematically killing innocent civilians by the thousands.[20] Second, he was able to produce a spy questionnaire that showed the Germans were gathering intelligence on the defences of Pearl Harbor, obviously for the Japanese.

Churchill, it should be explained, never allowed himself to be cut off from his daily cocktail of secret intelligence. Before he left on the sea voyage, arrangements were made for him to continue to receive the day's most important German armed forces "telegrams" and "BJs" — "British Japanese" diplomatic decrypts — as selected by Major Morton, Churchill's personal assistant. BONIFACE was dealt with by Menzies, and the hottest items after Churchill sailed on August 4 must have been the decrypts detailing Nazi atrocities in Russia and the novelty of a double agent being given a whole series of microscopic photographs containing questions about the defences of Hawaii. Copies of the decrypts and a copy of the questionnaire would certainly have been among the deliveries of secret papers air-dropped to the *Prince of Wales* every day by weighted bag.[21]

Menzies, of course, could have had the contents of the decrypts and Popov's questionnaire radioed to the *Prince of Wales*, but hard copies with German fingerprints all over them, so to speak, would have been more desirable for the show-and-tell to follow.

Churchill had a flair for the dramatic and, given that no official record has ever been released of these talks with Roosevelt, one can only imagine how he might have made his presentation.

The two leaders normally conferred in the wardroom of the *Augusta*. Churchill would have asked that the room be cleared because he had something of utmost importance to share with the president. Because what he had to say pertained to cryptographic intelligence and to the security of the United States, it is probable that the chiefs of the army and the navy, General George C. Marshall and Admiral Harold R. Stark respectively, would have been asked to remain. It is unlikely there was anyone else present, not even a secretary to take down the conversation.

Churchill would have begun by saying that for some time now the British had been intercepting and decrypting the enciphered wireless messages of German police and SS special forces, which, up to the German attack on Russia in June, had been of small value. Starting in mid-July, however, these messages revealed that the Nazis were carrying out mass executions in the east. As proof, he would have been able to show a July 18 decrypt reporting the execution of 1,153 Jewish "plunderers" in Belorussia, and two others, of August 4, from the SS cavalry brigade reporting the liquidation of some 3,274 partisans and *"judische Bolshevisten"* and another *"90 Bolshevisten und Juden"* shot. Since British claims of German atrocities in Belgium during the First World War had been afterward found to have been pure propaganda, Churchill would have made sure he had on hand the actual decrypts to convince his listeners.[22]

The impact of this information on Roosevelt would have been considerable. The Nazis had certainly demonstrated that they would resort to murder to achieve their political ends, but this was vastly worse. Hitler had said in his book, *Mein Kampf*, that the Germans needed *lebensraum* — "living space" — in the east. Here was proof that he intended to get it, not just by conquest, but by exterminating unwanted elements of the population. To make his point, Churchill probably used rhetoric similar to what he used in an international radio broadcast he gave when back in Britain two weeks later:

> As his armies advance, whole districts are being exterminated. Scores of thousands — literally scores of

thousands — of executions in cold blood are being perpetrated by German police troops upon the Russian patriots who defend their native soil. Since the Mongol invasions of Europe in the sixteenth century there has never been methodical, merciless butchery on such a scale, or approaching such a scale.... We are in the presence of a crime without a name.[23]

By this time the tally in the decrypts was well over ten thousand.

Roosevelt would have been especially sensitive to Churchill's report on the killings. Images of the Japanese army's massacre of thousands of Chinese civilians during the "Rape of Nanking" would have still been vivid in his mind. During his previous term, he had repeatedly warned of a growing danger from Japan and was vindicated when the Japanese seized the Chinese capital in late 1937 and went on a six-week killing spree before the eyes, and cameras, of the resident European community. The photographs and reports were horrific. He would have pictured similar scenes enacted in Russia.[24]

Of all the American presidents, Roosevelt must be rated as one of the most compassionate. He had introduced an array of socialist reforms in the early 1930s in his New Deal program to rescue Americans from the effects of the Great Depression. These included the pioneering Social Security Act, which introduced unemployment and old age benefits for the first time, but his concern for his fellow human beings was not isolationist. In his State of the Union address for 1941, he had passionately expounded to Congress his belief that all mankind was entitled to four basic freedoms: freedom of speech, freedom of worship, freedom from want, and freedom from fear. This is the kind of person who six months later was receiving Churchill's news of Nazi atrocities.

As Roosevelt listened, the prospect of Nazi murderers getting hold of a weapon of unimaginable power may also have figured in his thoughts. Since 1939, after he received a warning letter from the renowned physicist Albert Einstein, Roosevelt had been actively supporting American research aimed at determining whether a super-bomb based on nuclear fission was possible. British scientists now said they believed it was. Even though the prospect was still only theoretical, both leaders must have shuddered at the thought of Hitler getting his hands on such a weapon.[25]

The reason for the meeting, however, was Japan. Undersecretary of State Sumner Wells left one of the few eyewitness accounts of their discussions, a session in which the central theme was the certainty that the Japanese intended soon to seize Britain's Far East possessions. Churchill vigorously sought some guarantee from Roosevelt that this would prompt U.S. intervention. At another session, when neither Wells nor perhaps anyone else was present, Roosevelt probably reminded him that neither Congress nor America at large could be expected to back a declaration of war against Japan to save Britain's empire. It would have been then, perhaps, that Churchill produced a carbon copy of the English-language portion of Popov's Pearl Harbor questionnaire — the German section having been retained in London. It would have been on "onion-skin," a very thin, semi-transparent type of paper used for multiple carbon copies in the days of the typewriter.[26] One can picture it hanging limp, tissue-like, in Roosevelt's hands. Churchill would have watched as he read, the president's expression fading from polite interest to grim realization as he absorbed what it was that the Germans wanted.

HAWAII

Munition dumps and mine depots

Naval units, munition and mine depots on the Island of Kusha. (Pearl Harbour) Where possible drawings or sketches. Naval and munition depots in Lualueai. Exact position. Railway connections. The exact munition ... reserve of the army believed to be in the crater Aliamanu. Information regarding exact position required. Ascertain if the crater Punchbowl at Honolulu is being used as a munition depot. If not, what other military depots are there?

AIR BASES

Lukefield Airdrome. Details if possible with sketches, showing the positions of hangers, workshops, bomb depots and tank fields. Are there any underground tank depots? Exact position of naval air station.

Naval air support base at Kaneohe. Exact details of position, number of hangers, depots and workshops. Equipment.

Army air base at Wicham Field and Wheeler Field. Exact position. Number of hangers, depots and workshops. Are there underground depots?

Bodger Airport. Will this depot be taken over by the Army or the Navy in wartime? What preparations are being made? Number of hangers; are there Possibilities of landing seaplanes here?

Pan American Base. Exact position, sketches. Is the airport identical with Rodgers Airport, or is it a part of it? (A radio station belonging to PA is on the Monapuu Peninsula.)

NAVAL BASE AT PEARL HARBOR
Exact details and sketches of the position of the shipyards, piers, workshops, oil tanks, drydocks and new drydocks believed to be under construction.

Where is the minesweeper depot? How far has work developed in the east and southeast lock? depth of water; number of moorings. Is there a floating dock at Pearl Harbour or is it intended to have one there?

Details regarding new British and American torpedo net defenses. To what extent are these in use? British and American anti-torpedo defense apparatus on warships and other ships. How used at sea? Details of construction....[27]

A curious aspect of this English-language version of the questions is the Canadian word usage and spellings. Canadians, then as now, tend to interchange American and British idioms and spellings: *radio* for *wireless*, *airdromes* for *aerodromes*, *harbour* for *harbor*, (gasoline) *tanks* for *petrol installations*, and so forth. Some textual peculiarities also suggest the translator's first language was not English. As it happens, the veteran Abwehr spy

Paul Fidrmuc was then at KO Portugal; he had lived in Canada before the war working as a freelance magazine writer. This would also account for the tight, newspaper-style composition, and for the typos, which surely would not have been present had the writing been done in Berlin or London.[28]

The document recalled the famous Zimmermann telegram of the First World War. It was proof positive that Japan and Germany were pretending friendship with the United States while secretly plotting against it. The references to sketches, drawings, exact positions, depth of water, and torpedo nets indicated that Pearl Harbor was being mapped out for air attack. Roosevelt could only have concluded that the Japanese were allowing that war with Britain could include war with the United States, and were planning accordingly.[29]

The implied threat to Hawaii would have resonated with the president because of a report submitted earlier in the year by Joseph Grew, the U.S. ambassador in Tokyo. In January he wrote that a number of sources in Japan were saying that in the event of trouble breaking out between the United States and Japan, the Japanese intended to make a surprise mass attack on Pearl Harbor. Although the Office of Naval Intelligence (ONI) dismissed Grew's information, Admiral Stark, chief of naval operations and America's top sailor, took it seriously enough to suggest that the secretary of the navy warn the secretary of war that they should jointly take steps to ensure that a surprise attack could be withstood.[30]

Admiral Stark was aboard the USS *Augusta* along with the two leaders, and when his opinion was sought — as surely it would have been — he would have told Roosevelt that in fact the defences of Pearl Harbor were still weak and its ability to detect an approaching enemy inadequate. As for the Pacific Fleet, provided its aircraft carriers were not lost, the remainder were expendable. Battleships, as Roosevelt himself well knew, had lost their supremacy to air power.[31]

All this would have presented a tempting prospect, one that would not have escaped the two leaders. The Constitution forbade the United States from throwing the first punch when war seemed inevitable. Both Grew's report and the Popov questionnaire indicated that Japan was exploring the possibility of a Taranto-style raid on Pearl Harbor. If Japan could be provoked into carrying out such an attack as a first act of war, the problem of getting America into the war with Germany might be solved.

Roosevelt already had Japan in a squeeze. In July he had frozen the country's assets in the United States in protest over the air bases it was building in French Indochina. This effectively halted all trade between the two countries, denying Japan most of the American oil and scrap iron it needed to run its economy.

As Undersecretary of State Wells looked on, the two leaders now worked out a plan whereby the president would draw the economic noose even tighter, while insisting that Japan withdraw from both Indochina and China. The chances of the Japanese agreeing to quit China were on the underside of nil. Churchill calculated the United States and Britain could be at war with Japan in about three months.[32]

There is separate indication that Churchill thought that war with Japan was fairly certain. Just as the meeting was winding up on August 12, Canada and Australia were sent a secret message from the British government telling them that if war with Japan should be imminent, the BBC would broadcast the code phrase "We hope to include in our programme a talk on the development of air communications in the Far East." If the BBC also gave a date and time, that would be when the hostilities were expected to begin.

Also, in his report on the Atlantic meeting to the War Cabinet on August 19, Churchill said Roosevelt was determined to get into the war, by provocation if necessary. "Everything is to be done to force an incident," the president vowed according to him. The Cabinet minutes recorded this as meaning an incident involving Germany, but Japan, not Germany, had been the principal object of the talks between the two leaders. But then again, no one present would have wanted the truth on the permanent public record, to be gawked at by future generations.[33]

Several days later, on August 27, the following Abwehr wireless message was intercepted, deciphered, and read by the British. It was undoubtedly seen by the Americans, as well:

Berlin to Spain
Following rumour is for further circulation as may be suitable, also for 7580 and 7591. In Japanese naval circles the possibility of a clash with the American and English fleet is looked forward to with utmost calm. It is explained in these circles that even reckoning with

a union of the American fleet with the English, the
strength of the Japanese fleet is today so great that the
ratio of strength would be 2 to 1 in favour of Japan.[34]

The Abwehr office in Madrid was connected to Berlin by telephone,
teletype, and courier. There was no reason for sending such a sensitive
message by wireless in an easy-to-break cipher unless it was intended that
the British and Americans read it.[35]

The SS and German police messages depicting the atrocities in Russia
also appear to have been made available to the British deliberately. When
Churchill's BBC speech on the killings was picked up in Germany, the SS
immediately concluded that the double transposition cipher they were
using was compromised. They demanded another and the armed forces
cipher bureau, OKW/Chi, quickly complied. They were given a double
Playfair system, well-known to professional cryptologists and even easier to break. OKW/Chi was housed next door to Canaris's office on the
Tirpitzuferstrasse and was an agency of OKW's communications chief,
General Erich Fellgiebel. Fellgiebel was an open critic of the Nazis, but
was tolerated by Hitler because of his perceived irreplaceable expertise.[36]

As the summer turned to fall, the decrypts reporting on the killings in
Russia multiplied. They went straight to Churchill, and by diplomatic bag
or secure transatlantic undersea cable on to the United States, and, surely,
to the White House.[37] Meanwhile, the trade embargos, plus the barring of
Japanese ships from the Panama Canal, slashed Japan's import trade by 75
percent, leading to serious shortages in food and fuel.

The Japanese were in a quandary. If Japan did not take up arms soon,
it would be too weak to fight.

WHITHER THE QUESTIONNAIRE?

August 1941

Dusko Popov was not alone that day in early August 1941 when he flew into New York by Dixie Clipper, the giant flying boat on the Lisbon–Bermuda–New York run. As he stepped down into the waiting motor launch, his arm dragged down by a briefcase stuffed with $70,000 in cash, just behind was Hamish Mitchell, a senior MI6 officer.[1] They shared a taxi to the Waldorf-Astoria Hotel.

Mitchell had latched on to Popov when the Clipper made its refuelling stop in Bermuda, sitting beside him for the rest of the trip. His assignment was to use his diplomatic passport to get Popov's briefcase through customs unexamined, but there was more at stake than just the money. Popov was carrying something far more precious: stuck to four telegram forms were close to a dozen microdots containing the questions the Germans wanted answered about the U.S. Pacific Fleet. This was the hard evidence Roosevelt needed if he ever had to prove Germany was complicit in a Japanese plan to attack Pearl Harbor. Popov handed them over to Mitchell in the taxi.[2]

Popov idled alone at the Waldorf for the next two days while the microdots were examined at British Security Coordination (BSC), the New York office of MI6. The wait must have rattled him. When two intelligence officers from the U.S. Army and U.S. Navy called at the hotel on

August 14, carrying out a routine check on persons of possible interest entering America, Popov assumed they were the secret service types he had expected to be waiting to meet him. The first thing he did was ask the army man to help him put his $70,000 — equivalent to $1 million in those days — into the hotel safety deposit box. The assistant manager who arranged matters was a naturalized Italian and Popov blathered on to him about being a British agent pretending to be a German agent, revealing that the money was for his mission. The FBI later called it the "most stupid" thing he could have done.[3]

Back in his hotel room, Popov proceeded to tell the two intelligence officers everything. They must have realized Popov had got it wrong, but they listened anyway. When he reported the incident to the FBI, the army man was careful to stress that the encounter had been entirely an accident. They had sought Popov out, he explained, to collect what information he might have on Yugoslavia, invaded by Hitler's armies in May.

That same afternoon, Charles Ellis, the most senior officer for MI6 in America, turned up at the New York office of Percy Foxworth, chief of the FBI's Special Intelligence Service and principal liaison with BSC, to inform him that the expected British double agent had arrived, was staying at the Waldorf, and that the FBI were welcome to take him over. He had been Britain's "number one agent," Ellis told Foxworth, and with his help the British had been able to "locate all of the radio stations used by the Germans and also to identify a large number of their agents."

This was a huge fib, but it drew Foxworth in, especially as Ellis had brought along samples of his secret ink and copies of his code, his wireless instructions, and a photo-enlargement of a list of questions in English the Germans wanted their spy to get answers to. Foxworth sent the question-naire on to Hoover with the strong recommendation that the FBI take Popov on.[4] If, by any chance, Roosevelt and Churchill did not get Popov's Pearl Harbor questionnaire at their Atlantic meeting, Hoover got it now.

Ellis's boss was William Stephenson — famous after the war as "The Man Called Intrepid" — and he had a direct line to both leaders, via Menzies of MI6 to the prime minister, and to the president via Vincent Astor, the millionaire boyhood chum of Roosevelt who long had been acting as the president's unofficial liaison with British intelligence in the United States. Stephenson was also said to be in direct contact with Churchill.

He would not have missed conveying the explosive questionnaire to both leaders if he had been shown it, and did not think they knew of it. Apparently he was not shown it.[5]

Stephenson, it should be explained, was then nominally in charge of Britain's covert counterattack against Axis activities in the Western Hemisphere. He was a millionaire Canadian in his late forties who had been named to the job personally by Churchill. Within a year, using mainly his own money, he had built up the formidable organization called British Security Coordination — usually just BSC — staffed mostly by Canadians and headquartered in the Rockefeller Centre in New York. However, while he certainly did lead the security and counter-espionage function of BSC, Charles Ellis was the actual MI6 chief for North America.

Until Ellis called on Foxworth, the FBI had understood that Popov was only passing through the United States on his way to Egypt. The Bureau had also been told by the British to expect him on August 12 at La Guardia Airport, but he had landed at nearby North Beach instead. This had led to the mix-up with the army and navy intelligence officers, embarrassing in an organization that prided itself on being methodical. A makeup meeting was swiftly arranged. FBI assistant director Earl Connelley sat down with Popov on August 18, along with Ellis and FBI special agent Charles Lanman. The session lasted three hours.

First of all, Popov reported being interviewed by two army/navy men whom he thought had been sent to meet him. He then described in detail his adventures in Portugal and the instructions he was given for his trip to the United States. He had been told to let the Germans know of his safe arrival by sending an invisible-ink letter. They would in turn reply with a cable, telling him how to get in touch with a fellow agent who would provide him with a transmitter. Popov displayed the torn half of a visiting card he was to show the agent when they met. His cipher was of the transposition type, keywords to be taken from the popular novel *Night and Day*, and his messages, either by letter or by radio, were to be in English or French, although English, wrote Connelley after, presented a "definite difficulty."[6]

> At the time he was working for the British authorities in England, they composed the messages for him in English, which he transmitted. However, in this connection, these

messages were worded in very good English and definitely beyond what Mr. Popov's capabilities are in handling the English language. This same idea will probably have to be pursued here in order that we can simulate the type of diction pursued previously in the messages prepared by the British ...[7]

These were still early days for the FBI as a counter-espionage organization, so Connelley did not automatically assume — as he should have — that Popov must have been blown the moment the Germans received a message from him that was beyond his known English fluency.

When asked about the money in the briefcase, Popov told the FBI that $38,000 of it had come from the British, and that he was to deposit it for them in an American bank; $6,000 was from the Germans to finance his espionage operations, and the remaining $26,000 was his. Connelley had trouble getting his mind around the first item, probably because the FBI had considerable experience with organized crime and good relations with Treasury agents: usually when people launder large sums of their own money it is because it is counterfeit.

Connelley pressed Ellis to elaborate, but the MI6 man was evasive. He would not explain who Hamish Mitchell was either, or why he had accompanied Popov to his hotel. It was Popov, a few days later, who informed the FBI of Plan *Midas* and admitted that the $38,000 actually came from the Germans. He claimed that the idea was to deposit it in the United States, where it would be drawn on by a German spy in Britain whose cheques would be traced by British intelligence. Connelley was appalled. It was, he wrote to Hoover, "the most dangerous thing the British could have done, so far as the safety of Popov [was] concerned."[8]

The actual scheme involved depositing the entire sum, all of it German money, into the account of a fictitious person who would pay the same amount in England to Wulf Schmidt, who then would serve as paymaster to Germany's spies in Britain. MI5 planned to jot down their names when they collected their cash. Connelley would have been even more appalled had he known how silly *Midas* really was.

Ellis again brought with him photo-enlargements of the microdots containing the English-language questionnaire and Popov's wireless transmission instructions. These Connelley attached to his report, not knowing that Hoover had already received the copies Ellis had given Foxworth. The next day, Lanman went around to Popov's hotel and collected what microdots Popov still had, and his other espionage paraphernalia.[9]

There was an additional twist to Connelley's interview with Popov that the FBI man could never have dreamed of. Popov was reciting his story in the presence of the man who was to be his North American spymaster for both the British and the Germans, Captain Charles Howard Ellis. Ellis — known as Dick or "Dickie" to his friends — was at that moment MI6's senior representative in the United States and, apparently, Admiral Canaris's top agent inside British intelligence.

Ellis, it must be said, was surely no Nazi. He was a forty-six-year-old Australian who had been wounded in action four times during the First World War. After joining MI6 in 1921, he spent fourteen years working in Berlin, Vienna, Geneva, and Paris, running White Russian agents against the Soviets. By 1938 he was back in London, running his own espionage service — the 22000 Organization — which then utilized Bill Stephenson's international industrial intelligence network as well as agents in Europe of his own.[10] These included two White Russians who Ellis had run against the Soviets during the 1920s. In 1938–39, he used this same pair to feed information to the Abwehr. His contact was Richard Protze, one of Canaris's most trusted deputies. Protze ran his own espionage agency covering Belgium-Holland and reported directly to the admiral, inviting the conjecture that Ellis was likely acting as liaison between MI6 and anti-Nazi conspirators in the Abwehr.[11]

Connelley gave Popov a cautious thumbs-up. He suggested he should be kept under surveillance and his communications intercepted, but otherwise said he found no reason not to believe him. He confirmed Foxworth's recommendation that the FBI take him on as an American double agent once clearance was obtained from Vincent Astor, then the local security and intelligence chief.

It should be explained that President Roosevelt and Victor Astor were close. Their families had Hudson Valley ties going back to colonial days and Vincent had inherited the family fortune of more than $75 million ($1 billion today) when his father, John Jacob Astor IV, went down with the *Titanic*. He and Roosevelt had played together as boys and as men often partied on Vincent's yacht, where there was food, drink, and gaiety in abundance. In 1938, Roosevelt sent his friend with the yacht on a secret mission to spy out the Japanese military buildup in the Pacific, and that, plus other assignments closer to home, led him to name him, on March 19, 1941, "Area Controller for New York." It was a euphemistic title that made Astor responsible for approving and coordinating the local intelligence-gathering activities of the army and navy, of the FBI, and of the State Department. He was given the naval rank of commander and attached to the Office of Naval Intelligence.

The Astor appointment was specifically aimed at squelching a nasty rivalry that had broken out at the beginning of 1941 between the FBI and the two fledgling New York–based special intelligence units set up by the army and navy. The first was run by a Colonel Frederick Sharp and the second, the navy's Foreign Intelligence Unit, by a civilian industrialist named Wallace B. Phillips, who claimed to have operated his own spy network before the war. Sharp once warned a fellow officer that Astor "stands very close to the great white father so proceed with caution." The navy had the same attitude, and presumably the FBI did as well.[12]

So, when Connelley learned that Popov had been interviewed at the Waldorf by officers attached to Sharp and Phillips, he had to ensure that Astor had no objections before proceeding. This clearance he obtained from Phillips, who reported that Astor had checked out Popov with British Security Coordination and he was deemed to be "O.K." The FBI could have him.[13]

Popov was assigned his official FBI code name. It was nothing nearly as fancy as the "TRICYCLE" of the British: he became ND-63, for "National Defence Informant 63." The German-language microdots and a vial of his secret ink were turned over to the FBI lab in Washington.[14] Hoover, meanwhile, sent a photograph of the microdot-bearing telegram form and a sample microdot enlargement to the White House, noting it was "one of the methods used by the German espionage system in transmitting messages to its agents." The translated sample did not include the questions dealing with Hawaii and this has been seen over the years as evidence that Hoover withheld vital information from the president. It is more likely that he knew Roosevelt had already seen the entire questionnaire, and chose to send an innocuous microdot example through regular channels.[15]

The military significance of the Hawaii questions would have been plain to Hoover, but it was nothing new. He had long been aware of German interest in the Pacific Fleet. The previous November, the FBI had been tipped off by the navy that intercepted and decoded radiograms sent by the Japanese consulate indicated a German couple, Otto and Friedel Kühn, were supplying it with naval intelligence. The FBI's Honolulu office had been watching the pair ever since.[16] Hoover, however, had ceded the counter-espionage lead in Hawaii to the navy. It was better qualified to evaluate the intelligence the Japanese were collecting. A naval power like Japan could be expected to want to keep track of foreign warships in the Pacific; it was properly up to the navy to decide when reasonable interest became alarming.[17]

What made the Hawaii portion of Popov's questionnaire stand out, however, was its repeated request for sketches and the "exact position" of the key installations of Pearl Harbor and the surrounding airfields. Whether this rang any warning bells with Hoover is unknown, but what he thought would have made no difference anyway. The American military services were then fiercely territorial. If Hoover had presumed to comment on the threat implicit in Popov's questionnaire, or had asked questions or given suggestions pertinent to the state of military preparedness in Hawaii, the army and navy brass would have gone through the roof. Hoover had got where he was with his political acumen; it was sufficient that his designated boss, Vincent Astor, knew about the questionnaire. From there, it was up to him to decide what to do with the information it contained.[18]

Hoover had further reason for reticence; like MI5 in England, the FBI was the target of a certain amount of snobbery. There was no shortage of the wealthy — Astor, Stephenson, Phillips — who wanted to dabble in espionage, but they shared no great appetite for police work. The FBI, like Scotland Yard, was first and above all an investigative agency primed to meticulously collect evidence that would stand up in court. It could be dull work, and for some on both sides of the Atlantic, it implied dull people.

So it was that when the British decided the Americans should have an overseas spy service along the lines of MI6, they ignored Hoover and promoted their own choice to start it up, a fifty-year-old First World War army hero and Wall Street lawyer by the name of William Donovan. The president had sent him to Britain on a fact-finding mission the year before, when things looked blackest, and he had come back with the declaration that Britain was "down but not out."

A grateful British government thereafter vigorously sang his praises to the White House, through Stephenson in New York and by emissaries like the director of Naval Intelligence, Rear-Admiral John Godfrey, who visited Washington in the spring. In June 1941, Roosevelt named Donovan "coordinator of information," another spy agency euphemism; his office was shortly to be renamed the Office for Strategic Services, or OSS, the forerunner of the post-war Central Intelligence Agency.

From the British perspective, the beauty of the president opting for Donovan was that he had no background in the black arts of espionage. MI6 could undertake to teach him, with a corresponding expectation of gaining influence over him.

Donovan's appointment became official on July 15. He began with a small office, a few staff, no salary, and direct access to the president's slush fund. Phillips, the wealthy civilian who headed the navy's Foreign Intelligence Unit, and who had received the first reports on Popov at the Waldorf, transferred over to Donovan's organization in late August as its first spy chief, mandated to develop spy networks around the world. Whatever he knew of Popov's Pearl Harbor questionnaire he must have shared with Donovan.[19]

Donovan also needed to establish permanent liaison with British Security Coordination. This task he gave to Allen Dulles, a career diplomat and intelligence aficionado who took up quarters in Room 3603 of the Rockefeller Centre, in the suite of offices occupied by BSC.[20] This put Dulles right down the hall, as it were, from Stephenson, who saw himself as Donovan's mentor and who undertook to give him every assistance.

Having Dulles at the heart of BSC, however, had a more important advantage. Stephenson's organization was connected by undersea transatlantic cable to MI6 in Britain and to the Government Code & Cipher School. It was a secure link, and permitted BSC to send raw wireless traffic collected by listening stations in Canada to GC&CS for processing, and to receive "Most Secret" material in return. To facilitate this, Donovan put his own man in London. On November 20, MI5's counter-espionage chief, Guy Liddell, noted in his diary:

The Director-General asked me to come down and see William Dwight Whitney, who is Bill Donovan's representative over here and will have a small staff working under him. He is to have an office somewhere in Bush House [home of the BBC] which will be for press and propaganda. This will act as cover. His main purpose is to collect as much vital information as he can which has any bearing on the part being played by the United States and the possibility of her entering the war. This information will go direct to Bill Donovan in special cipher for the President.[21]

The connection GC&CS–MI6–Whitney–Donovan was a channel by which Roosevelt could receive British decrypts of the German police and SS reports on the massacres in Russia without any formal record being kept. Because a "special cipher" was used, no one in BSC could see the plain text of this traffic.[22] This direct channel would also have bypassed the army/navy codebreakers, the FBI, and the State Department.

Meanwhile, on August 19, Felix Cowgill of MI6(V) sent the full German-language version of the Popov questionnaire to MI5's Major Robertson. He did not mention there was an English-language version, so MI5 went ahead with its own translation.[23] This translation was reproduced and published for the first time in Masterman's *Double-Cross System*.

On August 28, the XX Committee discussed the questionnaire. The minutes of the meeting make no mention of its Hawaii/Pearl Harbor content.

On September 6, Menzies asked for a meeting of the Wireless Board. Without mentioning Popov specifically, he said he wanted to discuss how to handle the questionnaires of British double agents operating from the United States, proposing that questions relevant to Britain be dealt with by British officials in Washington rather than in London. The board met in Room 206 of the War Office on September 10.[24]

It will be helpful to recall at this point that the Wireless Board was an ad hoc committee of the three service directors of intelligence, plus Menzies of MI6, Liddell of MI5, and Sir Findlater Stewart, representing the civilian authorities. It did not officially exist within the chain of command, its members normally took no paper to or from meetings, only the chairman retained a copy of the minutes, and there was no formal reporting mechanism to the chiefs of staff, the War Office, or the Foreign Office. Each committee member was individually responsible for telling (or not telling) those above him what transpired in the meetings.

Three of the men who were there had definitely seen the whole questionnaire: Menzies, Cowgill, and Robertson.

The discussion turned to Menzies's letter. Members approved his proposal. Cowgill then read out the answers to those parts of Popov's questionnaire that were pertinent to the British. Liddell suggested that Popov had much promise as a double agent in America. Presumably Admiral Godfrey, the director of Naval Intelligence, was told about the information being sought on the Pacific Fleet. It would have been highly improper not to have disclosed that detail. Nevertheless, the minutes taken by Ewen Montagu make no mention of Hawaii or Pearl Harbor.[25]

Nothing went up to the chiefs of staff, or to the War Office, or to the Joint Intelligence Committee, or to the Foreign Office.[26] The British did not forward the Hawaii portion of Popov's questionnaire to the Americans because it never got outside the circle of MI5/MI6, the XX Committee, and the Wireless Board.

On December 17, when the oily water of the devastated Pacific Fleet still lapped the Hawaiian shore, this entry appeared in Liddell's diary:

> TRICYCLE's questionnaire is now in our possession. It shows quite clearly that in August last the Germans were very anxious to get as full particulars as possible about Pearl Harbor.

There is something wrong here. The original copy of the German-language version of the questionnaire had been sent to Major Robertson on August 19, then translated by MI5 and discussed at the XX Committee on August 28. Its implications were debated by the Wireless Board on September 10, with Robertson, Montagu, Menzies, Cowgill, and Liddell present. The German original is still to be found in an MI5 file beside MI5's original translation. There is no way the head of MI5's B Division could honestly suggest that the questionnaire only "came into our possession" after the Pearl Harbor attack.[27]

Liddell's diary was kept in a series of ring binders. It still is. Ring binders make it possible to take pages out and put pages in, anywhere, anytime,
without a trace. The entry for December 17, 1941, cannot be authentic.

But who, then, wrote it? And why?

CALM BEFORE SUNDAY
September–December 1941

Contrary to British accusations during and after the war, the FBI made a sincere effort to run Dusko Popov as a double agent. Within the first week of the FBI taking him over, Charles Ellis was asked to prepare his first invisible-ink letter reporting to the Germans that he had arrived safely.[1] It was probably thought that Ellis had a better chance of composing it in proper Englishman's English, even though he was an Aussie. Popov's ink was ammonium chloride, easily developed by passing a warm iron over the paper.

For some time there was no response. Then, on October 25 and October 30, Popov received a letter and then a cable in open code indicating that he should proceed to Rio de Janeiro. This was in response to a suggestion by the FBI that he propose to meet with German agents in South America to turn over some photographs and notes he had made. So far, no spy in the United States had come forward to collect the questionnaire, and no one had offered to be his radio operator. On the other hand, the FBI had been tracking the activities of German agents in Brazil since the spring through decrypts of their wireless traffic supplied by the small cryptanalysis unit attached to the U.S. Coast Guard and by Canada's Examination Unit.[2]

Next, a lengthy letter arrived from "Mady," Popov's supposed fifteen-year-old girlfriend in Portugal. Much of it seemed innocent chit-chat, but then:

> My dear uncle ... has been travelling abroad, but has returned now. He too sends you a lot of greetings because, as you well know, he is very fond of you. I was very anxious about Dicky, but he is really a nice chap. I got a letter from him some days ago. I would be glad if we could arrange to meet all of us together in some nice place....[3]

When the FBI asked Popov who this "Dicky" might be, he quickly replied that it was "the name of one of the British intelligence officers in London who was acting as a German spy for that organization."[4] And so there was; except another person nicknamed "Dickie" was standing right there at Popov's elbow. One can imagine Charles Ellis's forehead beading with perspiration.

It may have been a threat, of course, but it also may have been an open-code instruction for Ellis to attend a meeting set up by his Abwehr contacts. It is known that Ellis flew to London on November 2.[5] It is not known whether he went on to Portugal.

On November 16, Popov left Miami for Rio. Ten days later, the FBI had the satisfaction of reading the following intercept:

> 24 November 1941 CEL to ALD
> No. 46. IVAN ten thousand deciphered. Receiving his news this evening. Regarding cable via B. Firstly, I can give IVAN apparatus 50 Watt. Secondly, in view of lost mail, shall IVAN send mail here in future? Can give him other cover addresses.
> ALFREDO[6]

There were other similar messages intercepted. The FBI could be forgiven for thinking that Popov's trip to South America was working out just fine.

THE FIRST ATOM BOMB SPY?

The FBI had another German agent in its net late that autumn of 1941. Even as Popov was making arrangements to go to Brazil, another potential double agent was coming the other way.

It began the preceding July, just after the Spaniard, Juan Pujol Garcia, offered his questionnaire to the British in Lisbon and just before Popov set out for the United States with his. An Argentinian named Jorge Mosquera presented himself to the American embassy in Montevideo, Uruguay, to declare that he had been recruited by the German secret service to go to the United States to spy. He had letters of reference from high Nazi officials, three microdot photographs of instructions, the names of individuals he was to contact in New York, and an earnest desire to betray his German masters.

According to his identity papers, he was born in Rosaria, Santa Fe Province, Argentina, in 1895. He said he was the youngest of ten children and that his father had been born in Spain. In 1924 he had moved to Germany where he ran a small import-export business until it was closed down due to the war.[7] He spoke Spanish and German only. No English. He had been recruited by a man named Hans Blum of Ast Hamburg. On hearing all this, the FBI said he could carry on to the United States. Two FBI men were waiting for him when his ship docked in New York. It was November 18.

He was put up in a hotel, placed under blanket surveillance, and questioned intensely. The report on him that went to Hoover ran to forty-eight closely typed pages. The profile that emerged was typical of the double agents already acquired by the British.

As with Popov, and Arthur Owens before him, Mosquera's cipher was of the simple transposition type, full of complications but easy to break. Like them, the keyword was derived from a book, in his case a Spanish one, *Los majos de Càdiz*; and like Owens, he had brought it with him. Also like the others, someone else was needed to operate his transmitter. He had failed the wireless telegraphy course at spy school, he explained.

His invisible ink was phony. Based on zinc and sulphur, it was more complicated than the one given Popov, but still practically useless. The description of how it was to be used filled two pages of the FBI's report, which concluded by noting that only linen paper could be used with it, because the chemical solution reacted with wood pulp. It took no time for the lab to find a developer.

The contacts Mosquera was to make in the United States also turned out to be dead ends. Despite extensive investigation over many months, hidden cameras, microphones, and staged meetings with Mosquera, the persons whose names he had been given proved to be nothing more than naturalized German-Americans with normal sympathy for their homeland. They showed no sign that they were involved in espionage and appeared horrified when Mosquera hinted that he was.

Much, much later, the FBI was to learn that a Spanish-speaking Abwehr spy originally on loan to Franco was "in America" and usually travelled on an Argentinian passport.[8] If this was Mosquera, the connection with the Spanish dictator would have made him one of Canaris's especially trusted agents. At the time, however, the Bureau had no reason to be suspicious. Up to that point, the British had not shared the details of their own experiences in running double agents, and they had given the Americans the false impression that Popov had led to the uncovering of whole networks of spies.

The highlight of Mosquera's recruitment was his microdots. The FBI had seen Popov's only two months earlier; now here was another set, containing an even longer questionnaire — one focused on American aircraft production and new weapons technology. It included some novel items, including questions on poison gas, and this puzzling line: "Deduce artificially the uranium or other alloy which may be substituted therefore as an atom destructor." The awkward English was due to Mosquera having translated the original German into Spanish for the microdots.

When he was asked to elaborate on this item, he reported having a conversation with his Hamburg spymaster (BLUM). The following is taken from a report by Foxworthy to his director in December:

> BLUM further stated to MOSQUERA that he should not limit himself to the instructions on the microphotographs but should give attention to other details, especially details which pertain to experiments performed in the United States relative to the shattering of the atom.

BLUM stated that the German military authorities believed that a great future lies in the developing of high explosives derived through experiments pertaining to the shattering of the atom.

According to BLUM, if any success is gained in the shattering of the atom and high explosives produced as a result thereof, the future high explosive bombs would not have a gross weight in excess of one and one-half pounds. BLUM also stated that the nation which will be victorious in this war will be the one which accomplishes the task of shattering atoms and applying the results thereof.[9]

There is good evidence as to what at this time was prompting the Abwehr's interest in things nuclear. While most of the files at the Abwehr's Asts and branch offices were deliberately burned toward the end of the war, the card index of Nest Bremen survived. The card for R-2232, identified as the spy Hans Dahlhaus, describes him as having submitted a report on U.S. atomic experiments on July 29, 1941, not long after he had returned to Germany from an extended espionage tour of the United States. He had posed as a tobacco salesman and had developed a considerable network of sub-agents.[10]

His report is lost, but one can make a good guess as to some of its content. Up until the fall of 1940, before a publication ban took effect, the scientists working on sustainable nuclear fission published their findings. The March and April 1940 issues of *Physical Review* carried articles that identified the lighter isotope of uranium, U-235, as being most likely to split in an ongoing chain reaction leading to a massive burst of energy and, theoretically, to an explosion of unprecedented magnitude. The problems were how to separate enough of the isotope from natural uranium and how to prove the chain-reaction effect without blowing oneself up. This much was accessible to Dahlhaus even without having an agent inside the relevant scientific circles.[11]

What the FBI made of what BLUM said is not recorded. Uranium was featured in the popular press as a kind of miracle super-fuel, but the concept of releasing energy by splitting atoms in lightning-speed chain reactions leading to colossal explosions had not yet got much beyond a tiny circle of mathematicians and physicists. One would think that the FBI was still well out in the wilderness as to what BLUM was talking about.

Others were not. Roosevelt had been encouraging research on uranium since 1939, and on October 9, 1941, received a briefing on the prospects of developing a uranium super-bomb from his scientific adviser, Dr. Vannevar Bush. He was told of British enthusiasm for U-235, that ten kilograms should be enough to flatten a city if the predicted runaway nuclear chain reaction took place, and the technology to separate that much of the isotope from regular uranium was likely to be hugely expensive. The discussion touched on how little was known of what the Germans might be doing. The president told Bush to do a cost analysis of what it would take in scientific and industrial organization to prove that a U-235 chain reaction was feasible. Roosevelt would then decide what to do next.

In the meantime, strict secrecy would prevail. Knowledge of Bush's assignment would be restricted to the vice-president, Henry Wallace, to the secretary of war, Henry Stimson, to the army chief of staff, General Marshall, and to James R. Conant, chairman of the National Defence Research Council. On November 27, Bush submitted his report.[12]

On December 6, two days after the FBI's report on Mosquera was received by the White House[13] and the day before the Japanese attacked Pearl Harbor, Dr. Bush secretly met with a small group of senior scientists. The president had given the order, he told them. There was to be an all-out effort to determine whether concentrated uranium-235 would produce a nuclear chain reaction fast enough to explode. Money was no object. "If atomic bombs can be made, then we must make them first," Dr. Bush quoted the president as saying.[14]

And so it was. The day before the Japanese dropped the first bombs that opened the war with the United States, the Americans began the process toward the two bombs that would end it — one for Hiroshima, the other for Nagasaki.

WHO'S FOOLING WHOM?

Back in England, remote as if on the dark side of the moon from these happenings in America, MI5 was fussing about its entitlements. By taking over the Radio Security Service earlier in the year, MI6 had acquired an absolute monopoly on the distribution of ISOS (decrypts of Abwehr wireless traffic), and Felix Cowgill had clammed up about anything else to do with TRICYCLE. He was unmoved by requests from the XX Committee and deaf to Major Robertson's plea that he at least give "some small indication" as to how Popov was doing. Liddell had no luck either, Cowgill archly declaring that he was disappointed that his MI5 colleagues did not seem to think he was competent to run a double agent on his own.[15]

There was good reason for MI5 to be anxious. It had sent Popov to the United States with the question still unresolved as to whether Arthur Owens had really confessed to the Germans, which would have blown nearly all of MI5's double agents, including Popov. The folly of notionally linking them together through the payments of Plan *Midas* had sunk in. As one MI5 officer was to write:

> J.H.M. has advanced the theory that if SNOW on his last visit to Lisbon blew his traffic as he said he did, it follows as a natural consequence that the Germans realize TATE and RAINBOW to be under control, and further that they regard TRICYCLE as blown and may also believe that BALLOON and GELATINE are controlled agents. The logical consequence is perfectly clear, if the Germans believe that SNOW's traffic for two and a half months before his visit to Lisbon was controlled by us they must assume since SNOW paid TATE in that period that TATE has been a controlled agent. They must also assume that RAINBOW, who TATE subsequently paid, is also controlled ...[16]

B1A staff and members of the XX Committee had been agonizing over the problem for months, chasing the faint hope that somehow it would turn out that Owens had lied about giving everything away.

In fairness, at the beginning of the summer Robertson had received spectacular confirmation that all of his double agents were okay, including Popov. When SNOW went off the air for good in April, the Germans appeared to accept s A-3504's explanation that he was on the verge of a nervous breakdown, and sent back proposing that A-3725 — Schmidt

— be the Plan *Midas* paymaster instead.[17] Then, when he supposedly received the £20,000 of German money Popov brought to the United States, the only spies the Germans named for him to pay were RAINBOW, the dance-band spy, and MUTT and JEFF, the inept pair of Norwegian saboteurs captured in Scotland earlier in the year. Astoundingly, MI5 took this to mean that there were no other spies in Britain to be paid — in other words, that there were no unknown German spies at large.[18]

This was very wrong. Most of the Abwehr's files, at headquarters in Berlin and in all the Asts, Leitstellen and KOs of Europe, disappeared at the end of the war, probably systematically burned as happened at Ast Hamburg.[19] Nest Bremen was the exception. Some of its records were salvaged, and they show that beginning in August 1943, and speeding up to September 1944, Bremen officials burned the reports of most of their agents in England and the United States. All that is to be learned of the spies Bremen employed against England — eight, at least, in 1943–44 alone — is the code numbers on their file cards. Occasionally a name emerged, but this was only due to the diligence of the U.S. Naval Intelligence officers who combed through the unburnt files matching fragment to fragment.

The destruction at Bremen was done methodically. The agent number and subject matter of each file was recorded before being given to the flames. Thus, one can gather that spies who were German citizens or who took the oath of secrecy were guaranteed postwar anonymity. Important agents recruited in the occupied countries were also protected. A Captain Van der Vliet, for example, codenamed DELPHIN, reported on England from March 1942 to January 1944. His reports were destroyed in August and one can appreciate why. The Allied landings in Normandy had been successful and Holland was about to be liberated. The Dutch authorities would naturally want to seek out for punishment those of their country-men who had worked for the Germans. Allowing Captain Van der Vliet's real name to slip by was an oversight.

Another Dutch spy was codenamed NOLL. The records that remain of him reveal only that he spoke Dutch and English fluently, that he was a recruiter of agents for England, and that he took the oath of secrecy on April 17, 1941. This latter item is significant. The German oath committed one to secrecy until death, so Eghman was undoubtedly an important spy. The date that he took it indicates he was active against England long after the capture of the *Lena* spies and well within the period during which the British claimed there were no genuine enemy agents at large in Britain. Documents destroyed for 1943–44 include those of agents in England numbered 2215, 2220, 2254, 2351, 2596, 2778, and 2866.[20]

And those were only the records obtained from Bremen. Any Abwehr office was entitled to send a spy anywhere if it happened upon a suitable person, coordination being managed by Berlin.

TATE subsequently reported to the Germans that he paid RAIN-BOW and MUTT £500 each, leaving a balance of £19,000, a huge sum. He was then notionally employed as a farm hand, who had days off only on weekends, which gave him an excuse for not spending the rest of the money.[21] This story is so feeble that it is hard to accept that it was put forward in earnest. Meanwhile, RAINBOW was sent instructions on a microdot — the first the British had seen — and received an elaborate questionnaire seeking bomb-target information. MI5 took all this to mean that German faith in B1A's double agents was unshaken.

In November, there was renewed cause for uneasiness. MI6 sent over a report that said that between the time of SNOW's arrival in Lisbon in February and CELERY's arrival by ship a week later — when all the fuss with Owens started — an Abwehr official had boasted that on board the ship was "an agent whom the Germans regarded as a valuable means of planting false information on the British." This could only be CELERY — Walter Dicketts — then posing as an unhappy former RAF intelligence officer prepared to go over to the Germans.[22]

It was a hard chestnut. Dicketts was a veteran of the First World War, and had been recommended by the director of Air Intelligence (Boyle) himself. He had been an MI5 officer for almost a year. Various people in B Division offered various theories. It seemed impossible that he could be actually working for the Germans. If he was, then he was a triple agent. And so on, and on.[23]

It was J.C. Masterman, the XX Committee chairman, who finally put an end to the debate. On November 26, fully eight months after the problem first arose, he prepared a 2,200-word review of the evidence and concluded that the many contradictions could never be resolved because the main witness, Arthur Owens, had all along been working for both sides:

In this regard it is important to remember that we are apt to think of a "double agent" in a way different to that in which the double agent regards himself. We think of a double agent as a man who, though supposed to be an agent of Power A by that power, is in fact working in the interests and under the direction of Power B. But in fact the agent, especially if he started before the war, is often trying to do work for both A and B, and to draw emoluments from both.

This seems to me probably true of SNOW. Perhaps he was 75 percent on our side, but I should need a lot of evidence to convince me that he has not played for both sides. It is always possible that he was paid money under another name and that this money waits for him in America. His later letters to LILY give some warrant for this view, as does his desire to be sent to Canada. We must not exclude the possibility that the DOCTOR [RANTZAU] regards him as a man who has been working at the same time for both sides and who could be bribed or frightened into doing his better work for the Germans.[24]

Painfully convoluted, it nevertheless was a remarkable admission. Even if Owens was working only 25 percent for the Germans, it meant that on all those unsupervised trips to the Continent in 1939–40 he could have been telling the Germans anything at all, including who else was a double agent. MI5's "double-cross system" had been compromised from the beginning, and Masterman acknowledged it. Yet, in his famous book *The Double-Cross System* (1972), he reversed himself and portrayed Owens as working only for the British.

It is not known how widely Masterman's memo was circulated, but Guy Liddell certainly saw it. The subsequent actions — or lack of them — must be seen as his decisions.

First, the slippery Dicketts was cleared of all suspicion and given a £200 honorarium for his good work. He hung around London for the next year and a half, then disappeared.

Second, Masterman actually recommended restarting the SNOW transmitter, which was perfectly possible in that Owens had never sent his own messages and so was not needed. On the other hand, were SNOW to remain shut down while the Germans understood him to be only off-air temporarily, then it would look as though he had been arrested. Liddell opted for shutting it down, which inevitably meant discontinuing CHARLIE (Eschborn) and BISCUIT (McCarthy). They were too closely tied to SNOW not to go.

Third, TRICYCLE, TATE, RAINBOW, BALLOON, GELATINE, MUTT, and GW, and his Spanish sub-agents, PEPPERMINT and CARELESS, were retained, even though the first six were linked to SNOW by Plan *Midas*. TATE (Wulf Schmidt) was additionally and fatally linked to SNOW because of the piece of paper with Arthur Owens's name and address on it that was found on him when he was originally arrested.[25]

In other words, Liddell eliminated the network of double agents who plausibly could have been retained, while keeping those double agents, especially TATE and TRICYCLE (Popov), who the Germans had to know were under British control.

It is an interesting exercise in mental gymnastics to try to fathom Liddell's logic. The Blitz had ended in May, when Hitler shifted the bulk of his air power to the east against the Soviets, so there was no need for Owens's fictitious bomb-damage reports anymore. Evidently, Liddell had read Popov's questionnaire, however, and if he interpreted it as indicating possible war between Japan and the United States, he could have seen it as having momentous potential. There was then much speculation as to whether Japan would attack the Soviets from behind by invading Siberia, or go south against the British and Americans. Popov's Pearl Harbor questionnaire suggested maybe the latter.

Of course, it could simply be that Liddell did not want to have the embarrassment of telling the FBI that Popov was compromised.

When Wulf Schmidt fell ill in November and was hospitalized with a stomach ulcer, MI5 replaced him on the TATE transmitter with a substitute operator who was confident that he could imitate his sending "fist." With Colonel Simpson long gone, and the Radio Security Service split off to MI6, there was no one in MI5 with the wireless expertise to protest this folly. Schmidt was an accomplished telegraphist, sending "clean and fast," and he had been at it for a year.[26] Anyone with signals training in the armed forces would have known the Germans would have had the routine capacity to spot even slight differences in the sending characteristics of their overseas spies. "Ronnie" Reed, however, the twenty-five-year-old former BBC technician was MI5's only "expert."

There was not the slightest chance of getting away with it. Ast Hamburg had grown into one of the most sophisticated wireless-spy centres in the Abwehr. Known as WOHLDORF, it operated from a large mansion on the outskirts of the city under the capable direction of Major Werner Trautmann, a German army signals officer who was up-to-date on the latest wireless technology. He had 120 enlisted men working round the clock listening for the messages of Abwehr agents in Britain, Ireland, Iceland, and the Western Hemisphere, each man assigned to just two spies, whose signals would become as familiar as their voices.

WOHLDORF also boasted a wireless training program for spies run by Richard Wein, who drilled his students on the telegraph key until they obtained a reasonable proficiency. The operators who were to listen for their calls sat in on these sessions. Wein himself trained Owens, and probably Schmidt.

There is simply no question that they would have detected someone was sending for Schmidt. Nevertheless, thirty-five years later Lieutenant-Commander Ewen Montagu was to write about Schmidt: "After some low-level reporting by wireless at the start of his career, he in fact became ill and a[n] MI5 wireless operator successfully imitated his transmission style. As this was not spotted by the Germans ..."[27] How Montagu, as a former intelligence officer, could have made that assumption is perplexing. A competent counter-intelligence opponent should be expected first to play along.

MI5 further threw caution to the wind in the case of Karl Richter, the parachute spy captured the previous May. As the weeks passed, the baleful "Tin-eye" Stephens at Camp 020 maintained the pressure, wringing out information from his prisoner bit by bit. Finally, Richter broke. He blurted out that he had not been sent to spy, but to check up on a wireless agent in England whose messages appeared to be under British control. This had to be Schmidt.[28] It meant Richter's failure to report to Germany because of his arrest had given TATE away in yet another way.

Ironically, Richter's confession might have saved him, for technically his mission had not been one of espionage, but of counter-espionage. The matter was not raised at his trial, but on being convicted, Richter was advised to use it in his appeal. Liddell put MI5's German specialist, Hinchley-Cooke, up to having a heart-to-heart talk with him in his cell. He was persuaded to withhold the argument from his appeal in favour of bringing it forward when he sought clemency from the Home Secretary. Richter adopted the strategy, the Home Secretary chose not to hear him, and he was hanged.[29]

Some of the women in MI5 were a little tearful; Richter was only twenty-nine, and a good-looking and brave young man. One of his interrogators made an eleventh-hour appeal on his behalf, arguing that reports of his execution in the daily papers and on the BBC would raise German suspicions about TATE even further. It did no good. The truth of Richter's mission was "in no way relevant to the normal legal appeal," Liddell wrote in his diary.[30]

Meanwhile, Charles Ellis arrived in London on November 3 for talks with the head of MI6(V), Valentine Vivian, and the following week discussed Popov over lunch with Major Robertson and Guy Liddell. The first two had definitely read the entire Pearl Harbor questionnaire, and with relations between Japan and the United States worsening, they surely would have speculated on the implied threat to the Pacific Fleet. Liddell's diary does not mention them talking about it.[31]

The XX Committee was also debating at this time sending Montagu to Washington to set up a mini-XX Committee to handle any further questionnaires that might be generated by double agents operating from America. Liddell did not much like it, arguing to Colonel Vivian that Montagu was bound to meddle to the detriment of relations between British Security Coordination and the FBI.[32] Montagu was sent out at the beginning of December anyway, arriving in New York on Saturday, December 6.

Montagu then met with Stephenson, the British Security Coordination chief, but it is not known what they talked about. Montagu learned of the attack on Pearl Harbor the next day, from a taxi driver who heard it on the radio and who discounted it as an Orson Welles–type hoax. Montagu knew better.[33]

As for Dusko Popov, he was en route from Rio when the ship's loudspeaker called the passengers to the first-class lounge, where a grim-faced captain awaited them. The Japanese had attacked Pearl Harbor. The United States was at war. More news was to come. At first Popov was overjoyed. He imagined that the Americans had given the Japanese a good thrashing, considering they had been forewarned.

Details of the disaster, in ugly snippets, came in during the day, rippling through the passengers like wind in a field of wheat: Two battleships gone. The *Arizona* blown up. The harbour in flames. The Pacific Fleet crippled.[34]

TORA! TORA! TORA!
September–December 7, 1941

The Japanese attacked at dawn on December 7. Three hundred and fifty aircraft from six aircraft carriers had managed to get within 250 miles of Hawaii unnoticed. Pearl Harbor was taken by surprise, its radar installations improperly manned, its reconnaissance aircraft on the ground, and the ships of the U.S. Pacific Fleet lined up on their moorings like sitting ducks. The score was eight battleships and ten smaller ships sunk or damaged, 188 American aircraft destroyed, mostly on the ground, and over two thousand servicemen and civilians killed or wounded. Japanese losses were trivial: twenty-nine aircraft and fewer than one hundred lives.

The American public was shocked. The newsreel footage of American ships in flames, of American soldiers and sailors running against a backdrop of billowing black smoke, and of Japanese aircraft criss-crossing the sky like hornets, was spectacular. America's war had begun in fine style and there was no resisting when Roosevelt asked Congress to declare it. Yet, even as it did, many politicians were angry. How could this have happened? Pearl Harbor was supposed to be the bastion of U.S. naval might in the Pacific, and yet the Japanese had assaulted it easily and cheaply. The anti-war faction accused Roosevelt of somehow orchestrating the disaster in order to win public support for war. Over seventy years later, the issue of whether the Pearl Harbor debacle was by accident or design still has not been settled.

What makes it one of America's most viral controversies is the evidence that came out after the war that suggested the top brass of the U.S. Army and U.S. Navy knew the Japanese were preparing for war and had their sights on Pearl Harbor. It was revealed that Japanese diplomatic ciphers had been broken on an unprecedented scale, enabling American codebreakers to track nearly every move by Japan toward war. Yet Pearl Harbor was never properly alerted.

Gross negligence was indicated and the secret army and navy inquiries done during the war were severely critical of General Marshall, the U.S. Army chief of staff, and of Admiral Stark, the chief of naval operations.[1] As soon as the war was over, a joint congressional committee was convened to get to the bottom of things, and in 1946 it lowered the finger of blame to the army and navy field commanders at Hawaii.

The navy commander, Admiral Husband E. Kimmel, fought back. He argued that his only response to a possible air attack would have been to put the entire Pacific Fleet to sea, but he did not have fuel reserves or tankers to do that more than once, and if he had done so it could not have been for long. He therefore expected Washington to warn him if Pearl Harbor was seriously threatened.[2] Instead, when relations between Japan and the United States were strained to the breaking point, he was led to believe by navy headquarters in Washington that the Japanese would strike first south, toward Thailand or the Philippines. Nor was he told when it was learned that the Japanese were studying the layout of the ships in Pearl Harbor, or alerted when it was known in Washington that Japan intended to break off relations on December 7, precisely when dawn was just breaking over Hawaii. General Walker C. Short, the army commander, described how army headquarters in Washington had led him to believe that the main danger he had to guard against was sabotage.

It did not matter. The highest authorities in the land had decided both men were to be scapegoats. They were dismissed, accused of dereliction of duty, convicted of errors in judgment, and banished into retirement at less than their proper ranks. In other words, with great cruelty, they were disgraced.

The many books and articles on the subject, some concluding massive mischance, others — the "revisionists" — favouring a Roosevelt-inspired conspiracy, have all tackled the issue through the evidence of the collected decrypts and the often conflicting testimony of those involved. The incident of the TRICYCLE questionnaire has been given scant attention, always because it has been assumed that it began and ended with Hoover's incompetence.

The likelihood that Roosevelt saw the Abwehr's Pearl Harbor questionnaire during his Atlantic meeting with Churchill adds an intriguing new dimension to the controversy. Both leaders had been there with their senior military staffs, and although few details of the conference have ever emerged,[3] certain actions these two men took immediately afterward take on new significance when that possibility is considered.

The first of these acts was to cut off the two Hawaii commanders, Kimmel and Short, from MAGIC, the Japanese diplomatic decrypts that up to that time they had been receiving. The result being that the men most directly responsible for guarding the Pacific Fleet were suddenly blindfolded.[4]

It can be fairly said that no other single action contributed more to the Pearl Harbor disaster. Had Admiral Kimmel and General Short continued to receive MAGIC, they would not have failed to see that the Pacific Fleet at its berth was a likely first target of the Japanese should war break out.

On October 9, nearly two months before the attack, others still on the MAGIC list received the following message sent from Tokyo to the Japanese consul, Nagao Kita, in Honolulu:

> From: Tokyo (Toyoda)
> To: Honolulu
> September 24. 1941
> J-19
>
> Strictly Secret
> Henceforth we would like you to make reports concerning vessels along the following lines insofar as possible.
>
> 1. The waters (of Pearl Harbor) are to be divided into five subareas...
>   Area A. Waters between Ford Island and the Arsenal.
>   Area B. Waters adjacent to the Island south and west of Ford Island.
>   Area C. East Loch.

Area D. Middle Loch.

Area E. West loch and the communicating water routes.

2. With regard to warships and aircraft carriers, we would like to have you report on those at anchor, (these are not so important) tied up at wharves, buoys, and in dock. (Designate types and classes briefly.) If possible, we would like to have you make mention of the fact when two or more vessels are alongside the same wharf.

Army 23260 Trans 10/9/41 (S)[5]

This, like Popov's questionnaire, is so obviously a prescription for air attack that it has become known over the years as the first "bomb-plot" message — *plot* being used here in the sense of plotting targets on a map. It was followed the next day by another message that assigned code letters to the berthing locations of the warships.

29 September 1941

(J19)

Honolulu to Tokyo #178

Re your 3083

(Strictly Secret)

The following codes will be used hereafter to designate the location of vessels.

1. Repair Dock in Navy Yard. (The repair basin referred to in my message to Washington #45): K8.
2. Navy dock in the Navy Yard (The Ten Ten Pier): KT
3. Moorings in the vicinity of Ford Island: FV
4. Alongside in Ford Island: FG. (East and West sides will be differentiated by A and B respectively)

Relayed to Washington, San Francisco.

JD-1: 5730 23313 (D) Navy Trans. 10-10-4: X[6]

Tokyo wanted to know what ships were where *within* the harbour. That could only be for air attack purposes, and it was asked *only* of Pearl Harbor. Admiral Kimmel would have seen it instantly. Yet none of these messages, or others like them, were given to him or to Short.[7]

The postwar congressional inquiry was told that the army did not share these decrypts with General Short because the codes used for army communications were less secure than those of the navy. This is nonsense — for such short messages super-secure, one-time pads could have been used. The Office of Naval Intelligence claimed it did not give the messages to Kimmel because it assumed that the Japanese were merely keeping track of the Pacific Fleet at Pearl Harbor in excessive detail.

What the inquiry did not hear was that the other Pacific command, the Philippines, which was under General Douglas MacArthur and Admiral Thomas Hart, continued to receive MAGIC and did receive the bomb-plot messages. This was described in the 1956 biography of MacArthur by his former chief of staff. General Charles Willoughby:

> We saw some of the intercepts in Manila, on a relay through special channels…. It was known that the Japanese Consul in Honolulu cabled Tokyo reports on general ship movements. In October the daily reports were "sharpened." Tokyo called for specific instead of general reports. In November the *daily* reports were on a grid system of the inner harbor with coordinate locations of American men-of-war.

It was plain to see, Willoughby continued, that "our battleships had become targets."[8]

Also, just after the Atlantic meeting, General Marshall ordered that the written summaries, or "gists," of the incoming decrypts that normally accompanied the army's distribution of the day's MAGIC in Washington be discontinued. The MAGIC recipients affected included the secretaries of state, war, and the navy, the army chief of staff (Marshall), and the chief of naval operations (Stark), as well as the chiefs of army and navy intelligence and war planning. From then on, they received only the raw decrypts. As they were "For Your Eyes Only," each man was required to keep track of their unfolding story by himself.

Consequently, when asked by the congressional inquiry why he missed the "bomb-plot" messages, Marshall was able to reply, "If I am supposed to have final responsibility for the reading of all MAGIC, I would have ceased to be Chief of Staff in practically every other respect.... It was very difficult for me to read MAGIC sufficiently, even as it was."

General Gerow, chief of the General Staff Operations Division, made the same excuse. Both must have been slow readers, however. MAGIC deliveries averaged twenty-six messages a day, the majority of them being fewer than two hundred words.[9]

Admiral Stark also claimed that he never noticed these Honolulu–Tokyo messages, even though they involved the ships and sailors under his ultimate charge. All must have crossed his desk, but apparently neither he nor his director of intelligence gave them any special heed,[10] causing Kimmel's intelligence officer at the time, Lieutenant-Commander Edwin Layton, later to write, "the failure of the office of naval operations to ensure that the bomb plot messages were sent to us at Pearl Harbor was blind stupidity at the least, and gross neglect at best."[11]

The two intelligence officers in Washington responsible for selecting and distributing the decrypted messages were Lieutenant-Commander Alwin Kramer for the navy and Colonel Rufus Bratton for the army — both Japanese linguists. It can be safely assumed they would have been expected — even ordered — to get on the telephone to their higher-ups if they spotted a decrypt of urgent importance in the original Japanese. This did not come out at the inquiries, leaving the impression that Marshall and Stark first knew of the content of any decrypt only after it had been formally translated and sent around. This is highly unlikely.

Of the two officers handling MAGIC, Kramer was the more important, in that he had Admiral Stark and the White House on his daily distribution list. Prior to mid-November, the task of delivering MAGIC to the White House had been shared by the army and navy month over month, the former that fall responsible for July, September, and November, and the latter for August, October, and December. The army, however, alleging security problems, unilaterally cut the White House off from its deliveries; and in October, a navy aide appointed to the White House to receive the day's decrypts filtered them out, passing only summaries to the Oval Office instead. Intentional or not, this gave Roosevelt an iron-clad excuse — should he ever need it — for not knowing about the bomb-plot messages.

In any case, apparently the president did learn that he was not getting the full MAGIC, insisted that from that point on he see the "raw intercepts," and gave the White House delivery job solely to the navy effective November 12.[12]

Upon his return from their Atlantic conference, Roosevelt kept his promise to get even tougher with the Japanese. On August 17 he summoned the Japanese ambassador and warned him that Japan's behaviour in Southeast Asia risked war. The ambassador proposed that the Japanese prime minister, Prince Fumimaro Konoye, meet with the president face-to-face, possibly in Hawaii, to talk out their differences. Roosevelt prevaricated, rudely replying that his schedule was very tight. Meanwhile, Japan struggled with the crippling embargo imposed by the U.S., especially on oil and gas. Japan had oil reserves for only two years, so the country was being pushed into an intolerable position. The government of Prince Konoye fell in October and he was replaced by the former war minister, General Hideki Tojo.[13]

At this same time, the British were breaking much of the same Japanese diplomatic traffic as the Americans — including at least some of the "bomb-plot" messages — and could follow Japan's inexorable drift toward war.[14] Nevertheless, over the objections of his own naval chiefs, on October 25 Churchill sent the *Prince of Wales* and the battle cruiser *Repulse* to Singapore, even though the British then had no appreciable air cover in the Far East and the Japanese in Indochina were in easy torpedo-bombing distance of the Malayan coast.

Historians have long puzzled over Churchill's move. He claimed he intended the ships to serve as a deterrent, but with the recent fatal wounding of Germany's ultra-modern pocket battleship *Bismarck* by obsolete British carrier-launched biplanes, it must have been perfectly obvious what would happen should war bring down onto the ships scores of modern, land-based enemy aircraft. Churchill also uselessly reinforced Hong Kong, acknowledged to be untenable, with two battalions of Canadian troops. If Japan threw down the gauntlet, they, too, were doomed.[15]

COUNTDOWN TO DECEMBER 7

There have been other "countdowns" to December 7 in the many previous accounts of the Pearl Harbor attack, but the following includes new information found in British and Commonwealth archives, and documents lately found in American archives.

November 3: Military Intelligence (MID) in Washington circulated a "reliable" secret-source report that the Japanese director of intelligence and former prime minister of Japan, Koki Hirota, had told the Black Dragon Society in late August that the new Japanese prime minister, Tojo, had ordered general military preparations to be made for an "emergency" with the United States. "War with the United States would best begin in December or in February," Hirota was reported to have said. This information was passed on to the State Department, the U.S. Navy, to all U.S. Army departments, and to the FBI. Apparently, it did not get to Admiral Kimmel or General Short, though.[16]

November 5: The Americans intercepted a message from Tokyo to Japan's ambassador in Washington describing two proposals to be tried on the Americans in an effort to avoid war. The message would have been in the MAGIC package delivered to Secretary of State Cordell Hull, to the chief of naval operations, Admiral Stark, and to the U.S. Army chief of staff, General Marshall. Roosevelt would have only been told about it, as it would be another week before he started receiving the actual decrypts again.

November 10: Against the backdrop of the bombed-out ruin of London's medieval Guildhall, Churchill delivered another speech condemning Nazi atrocities:

> The condition in Europe is terrible to the last degree. Hitler's firing parties are busy in a dozen countries ... and above all else, Russians are being butchered by thousands and by tens of thousands after they have surrendered, while individual and mass executions in all the countries I have mentioned have become part of the regular German routine....
>
> I must say generally that we must regard all these victims of the Nazi executioners, who are labelled Communists or Jews — we must regard them as if they were brave soldiers who die for their country on the field of battle. Nay, in a way, their sacrifice may be more fruitful than that of a soldier who falls with his arms in his hands. A river of blood has flowed and is flowing between the German race and the peoples of all Europe. It is not the hot blood of battle, where good blows are given and returned. It is the cold blood of the executioner and scaffold, which leaves a stain indelible for generations and for centuries.[17]

He went on to warn that the war in Europe threatened to spread to the Far East and, while the Americans were doing their utmost to preserve peace, "should the United States become involved in war with Japan, the British declaration would follow within the hour."

November 13: Roosevelt received an "urgent" report from William Donovan, his newly appointed civilian spy chief: the German chargé d'affaires in Washington, Dr. Hans Thomsen, had said that "if Japan goes to war with the United States, Germany will immediately follow suit." Donovan further quoted Thomsen: "Japan knows that unless the United States agrees to some reasonable terms in the Far East, Japan must face the threat of strangulation.... Japan is therefore forced to strike now."[18]

Donovan's information was crucial. Until that point, war with Japan had not necessarily meant war with Germany. Dr. Thomsen said it now did. The key condition that Roosevelt needed to make losing the Pacific Fleet at Pearl Harbor worthwhile had been met. Even if Japan attacked first, Germany would still join in.

November 18: During talks on the new Japanese proposals with Saburo Kurusu, the special envoy sent out by Tokyo, U.S. Secretary of State Cordell Hull brusquely told him that it was Japan's alliance with Germany and Italy that was the problem: "If Japan had any different ideas on this point, he could tell them [in Tokyo] that they would not get six inches in a thousand years with the U.S. government, who would not have anything to do with the greatest butcher in history."[19]

This was brutal language to use on a foreign diplomat. Hull had read the text of Churchill's speech. To be so sure that the Germans had committed the crimes they were accused of, he must have seen decrypts of the SS and German police traffic dealing with the atrocities. He was too experienced not to have required hard evidence.

Hull then presented the position to Kurusu that Churchill and Roosevelt had worked out together in August. Japan was to abandon its air bases in Indochina and, Hull continued, "In the second place, Japan must withdraw her troops from China. The United States could not find the basis of a general settlement unless this were done." There would be no relaxing of the trade sanctions, either.

This put the Japanese envoy "in a great state" — Hull's words — and he asked that Japan be allowed to retain at least some troops in China, and for the United States to release small quantities of rice and oil exclusively for Japan's civilian population. In exchange, Japan would withdraw entirely from Indochina, Kurusu said. Hull was taken aback. Japan abandoning its air and naval bases in Indochina took away the principal grounds of conflict between their two countries. Hull said he would think about it, which meant he was taking it to the president.[20]

Also on this same day, U.S. Naval Operations (Admiral Stark) unaccountably issued the "North Pacific Vacant Sea Order" whereby all Allied ships were ordered to avoid the Pacific north of Hawaii effective November 25. The six aircraft carriers, two battleships, two cruisers, six destroyers, and eight supply vessels of the Japanese attack force would take up a lot of sea room, and under normal circumstances a chance encounter with another vessel was almost inevitable. The Japanese could sink any ships they came in contact with, of course, but before going down they would likely get off a radio distress message. By all accounts, Admiral Stark should have wanted to see the North Pacific busy with shipping to avoid the possibility of a surprise attack.[21]

November 22: Tokyo showed signs it was getting desperate. According to MAGIC decrypts that Stark, Marshall, Hull, and Roosevelt are supposed to have been reading, the Japanese wanted to avoid war with the United States, but if the talks did not succeed by November 29, "things [were] automatically going to happen."

November 24: Admiral Stark alerted all Pacific commands that the current negotiations with Japan were likely to fail and that a "surprise aggressive movement [could be taken] in any direction including attack on Philippines or Guam." Admiral Kimmel took this to mean that his chief, with whom he was on a first-name basis, believed that the Japanese navy was looking south, not east.

November 25: The North Pacific Vacant Sea Order took effect. The Japanese aircraft carriers were just then leaving their home waters for Hawaii. The empty ocean sparkled before them.

Also on this day, Admiral Stark sent a personal note to Admiral Kimmel in Pearl Harbor describing the tense Japanese-American negotiations behind his warning of the day before. He closed it with, "Neither the President nor Mr. Hull would be surprised over a Japanese surprise attack; that from many angles an attack on the Philippines would be the most embarrassing thing that could happen to us...."[22]

Again he made no mention of Hawaii, even though the evidence is overwhelming that he saw the Pearl Harbor questionnaire either at the Atlantic conference or after Popov delivered it to the FBI, if not by both means. It is also not credible that the chief of naval operations, the top man in the navy and first on the list for MAGIC, did not see the bomb-plot messages targeting the Pacific Fleet.

November 26: Secretary of State Hull dropped all appearances of being conciliatory and returned to his original requirement that Japan break with the Axis powers and withdraw all its troops from China, adding the wholly unreasonable demand — suggested by Churchill — that the Japanese recognize Chiang Kai-shek as China's legitimate leader. This amounted to the wholesale surrender of the Japanese to the Chinese after years of bitter war, so it was bound to be rejected. Stimson, the secretary of war, called it "kicking the whole thing over."[23]

November 27: Admiral Stark issued a formal "war warning," saying that "for all practical purposes" negotiations had broken off and an aggressive move by Japan was expected. "The number and equipment of Japanese troops and the organization of task forces indicates an amphibious expedition against either the Philippines, Thai or Kra peninsula or possibly Borneo." This confirmed Admiral Kimmel's impression that the navy leadership in Washington thought Japan was focused south, not east.[24]

Meanwhile, General MacArthur and Admiral Hart in the Philippines, who were still receiving and reading the Japanese diplomatic decrypts denied Kimmel and Short, were aware that the Japanese had a current, fully developed plan of attack against Hawaii.[25]

Admiral Stark asked Admiral Kimmel to use one of his two aircraft carriers to transfer twenty-five fighter aircraft to the naval bases at Midway and Wake Islands. As this denuded Pearl Harbor's air defence by nearly half, Admiral Kimmel concluded that Admiral Stark — who he understood was in receipt of all intelligence — did not think Hawaii was in any imminent danger. That same day the War Department (Marshall) proposed to replace the marines on Wake and Midway Island with army troops, a lengthy and complicated process that would require Kimmel's other aircraft carrier. Kimmel presumed this was further indication Pearl Harbor was safe for the time being.[26]

With great confidence, he sent both carriers on these routine missions.

Even the Canadians now knew war with Japan was imminent. The work of the little cipher-breaking unit in Ottawa — the Examination Unit — had expanded into low-grade Japanese diplomatic traffic that fall, and it became obvious from the decrypts that the Japanese consulate in Ottawa was primarily interested in military topics, and was especially concerned about the troops Canada was sending to Hong Kong. The British were also providing the Canadian government with daily bulletins on Hull's negotiations with the Japanese, which Canada's prime minister, Mackenzie King, described as being of a "most unyielding character."[27]

November 28: MAGIC decrypts disclosed Tokyo's reaction to Hull's "humiliating" proposals. Japan's ambassadors in Washington were told that relations between the two countries were now "de facto ruptured" but that they were to pretend that the talks were still continuing.[28]

Still that same day, Admiral Stark issued another war warning, which said that the Japanese still might continue negotiations but hostile action was possible. Pacific stations were directed to undertake such reconnaissance "as you deem necessary, but these measures should not be carried out so as to alarm the civilian population or disclose intent." Admiral Kimmel maintained the usual level of reconnaissance.

December 1: The director of naval communications in Washington sent an urgent message to Admiral Hart in the Philippines, with a copy going to Admiral Kimmel, that the Japanese were planning a landing at Kota Bharu on the Malaya Peninsula. That meant the Japanese intended to

attack Singapore, reinforcing Kimmel's impression that the British were the target, not the Americans.[29]

Also, the Americans read a message from Tokyo stressing that the appearance of continued negotiations had to be maintained in order "to prevent the United States from becoming unduly suspicious."

December 2: Churchill received and read a super-secret Tokyo to Berlin decrypt in which the ambassador was told to advise Hitler that a breakdown in talks between Japan and the United States was inevitable and that an "armed collision" leading to "a state of war" with the British and Americans "may happen sooner than expected."[30]

December 3: Army codebreakers released a message of the day before from Tojo, the Japanese prime minister, to the Washington embassy, ordering that its cipher machine and all codes and ciphers save the "PA" and the "LA" codes be destroyed.[31] The destruction by a diplomatic post of its codes and ciphers is universally recognized as a prelude to war.

Canadian aviation pioneer William Seymour met with an official of Canada's Defence Department in the Château Laurier hotel in Ottawa. Seymour had been covertly recruiting American flyers for the air war in England, but now he was told things were about to change:

> Mr. Apedaile informed me that British Military Intelligence had informed Ottawa that it was expected that the Japanese would make a surprise air attack on Pearl Harbor on December 8th, 1941.... Mr. Apedaile then explained to me that if the attack did take place it obviously meant that the United States immediately would be involved in War with Japan, would probably become involved in the War with Germany and Italy, and, therefore, require all the pilots they could train....[32]

In Honolulu, Captain Irving Mayfield, the navy's 14th District intelligence officer, and Lieutenant Colonel George Bicknell of Hawaii Army Intelligence learned from the local navy cryptographic agency, Station HYPO, that Washington had sent Admiral Kimmel an advisory to the effect that Japanese embassies and diplomatic posts in London, Washington, Hong Kong, Singapore, Batavia, and Manila had been ordered to destroy their codes and secret papers. The Honolulu consulate was not included, so Mayfield asked the local FBI's Robert Shivers if they were burning papers there. The FBI had a telephone tap on the consulate. Shivers informed Mayfield they were.[33]

Admiral Kimmel was told, but he did not see it as any different from what was happening elsewhere.

December 4: Lieutenant John Burns, head of the Espionage Bureau of the Honolulu police, was called to the office of FBI agent Shivers, a small man who prided himself on being "deadpan." He was almost in tears. "I'm not telling my men but I'm telling you this. We're going to be attacked before the week is out." Pearl Harbor is going to be hit, he said.[34]

December 5: In England, Victor Cavendish-Bentinck, chairing a subcommittee of Britain's Joint Intelligence Committee, was surprised when told that a Japanese fleet was headed to Hawaii. "Have we informed our transatlantic brethren?" he asked. Yes, he was assured. William Casey, then on Colonel Donovan's staff, confirmed it: "The British had sent word that a Japanese fleet was steaming east toward Hawaii," he remembered.[35]

Still in England, the lead cryptographer for Japanese traffic at the Government Code & Cipher School, confided in his diary, "The All Highest [Churchill] all over himself at the moment for the latest indications re Japan's intentions and rings up at all hours of the day and night...."[36]

December 7–10: In the early hours of the morning of December 7, as the six great Japanese aircraft carriers turned into the wind in the predawn darkness, and as exhaust flames flickered from the engines of the "Kate" torpedo bombers lined up on their decks, General Marshall and Admiral Stark fussed over how they should get word to Hawaii that the latest intelligence indicated Pearl Harbor might be attacked in a couple of hours. Radio? Teletype? Both men turned down picking up the phone.

At 7:55 a.m., Admiral Kimmel was just up for the day when he heard the sound of distant explosions. The navy had been his life for forty-one years. He had begun as a cadet, then served as a gunnery and turret officer, and had sailed around the world during President Theodore Roosevelt's 1907 "white fleet" show of American power. He had spent the First World War on battleships and had witnessed the surrender of the German High Seas Fleet at Rosyth in 1918. An orderly series of commands followed: a squadron of destroyers; the battleship *New York*; a division of heavy cruisers in the Pacific Fleet; and, finally, command of the Pacific Fleet itself. His Hawaii residence was on a hill overlooking the anchorage, and when he stepped outside, he looked down a long green lawn to see black blossoms springing up around, and among, and on, his precious battleships.

Canada was first to declare war on Japan, doing so that very evening. The United States and Britain declared war the following day, on December 8, and Hitler against the United States on December 11.

The Japanese launched coordinated attacks against Hong Kong, Singapore, and the Dutch East Indies, and then the Philippines, just as the Pujol questionnaire had anticipated. On December 8, the Japanese landed virtually unopposed at Kota Bharu, Malaysia, to begin their march down the Kra Peninsula to Singapore. On December 10, the *Prince of Wales* and the *Repulse* were sunk on the open sea by Japanese bombers. The Canadians in Hong Kong held out until Christmas Day, Singapore until mid-February, and the Americans in the Philippines until May.

December 18: Assistant Secretary of State Adolf Berle noted in his diary:

> (Re. PH investigation) Since the Secretary (Hull) as far back as November 27 had been telling the War Cabinet that hostilities might start at any time when the Japanese replied to his last proposals his record is clear. In the evening of the 6th when I came in with the children for a moment, we knew that the forces (Jap) were already started for somewhere, though we did not know where.
>
> All this info was in the hands of the navy — indeed, most of it came from the navy. But there seems to have been no effective orders sent to Pearl Harbor.[37]

None indeed.

POSTSCRIPT, PEARL HARBOR

December 7–31, 1941

It was an oft-told story around the FBI about how Hoover first heard of the Japanese surprise attack. He was in New York that Sunday at a baseball game when the FBI switchboard patched the call from Hawaii through to his private box. Amid the hissing and static came the voice of Special Agent Robert Shivers: "The Japanese are bombing Pearl Harbor. There's no doubt about it — those planes are Japanese. It's war. You may be able to hear the explosions yourself. Listen." Shivers put the phone to the window. Hoover could.[1]

Of all those in leadership positions within the U.S. government and military who had seen Popov's questionnaire, the director of the FBI was probably the only one who was surprised by the surprise. As far as he knew, everyone who needed to know that the Japanese had their sights on Hawaii did know. He had seen to it.

On the other hand, he had not been on the list for MAGIC. None of the decrypted spy messages reporting on the disposition of the warships in Pearl Harbor had crossed his desk. He had no idea that more than a dozen such reports had passed through the hands of army and navy cryptographers over the previous ten weeks, and beneath the eyes of the army and navy chiefs of staff. America's civilian chief of counter-espionage had been kept in the dark in his own field.

Anxious to please, anxious to show that the FBI was on the ball, the next day — December 8 — Hoover sent the president two memos, one outlining the war measures the FBI was taking and the other informing him of a two-hour telephone conversation intercepted by the FBI on December 5 between a Mr. Mori and someone in Tokyo. There had been probing questions about the defences of Pearl Harbor and Hawaii, plus some irrelevant ones that looked to be in open code. The one that sounded most suspicious had asked what flowers were in bloom. "Hibiscus and poinsettia," was the reply.[2]

On December 12, Hoover followed up with another memo that developed the theme. He said the Honolulu special agent in charge (Robert Shivers again) had been convinced the flowers reply indicated a direct and urgent threat to Hawaii, but Navy Intelligence (ONI) had "scoffed" at the suggestion and had failed to refer the matter to higher authority. Although Hoover did not specifically state it, one can see what made Shivers so certain: The hibiscus was the territory's official flower and it normally blooms in February, not December.[3]

Hoover was on the hunt. Someone had messed up, and it was not him. Americans were outraged that the mighty U.S. Pacific Fleet had been caught napping, and that many of their "boys" had been killed. Heads were going to roll, and hungry eyes were already on America's Dick Tracy. No one cared a whisker that the FBI had ceded counter-intelligence leadership for Hawaii to the navy. Hoover well appreciated that occasionally the innocent get the electric chair.

The second half of his memo to Roosevelt was even more accusatory. From Japanese wireless messages intercepted by military authorities in Hawaii and decoded in Washington, the Military Intelligence Division "discovered the messages contained substantially the complete plans for the attack on Pearl Harbor as it was subsequently carried out."

Hoover continued:

> The messages contained a code Japanese word which would be sent by radio to the Japanese fleet as the signal for the attack when the word was repeated three times in succession. Military authorities in Washington sent by Army radio to the Hawaiian Islands the entire plan for

the information of the authorities in Hawaii. On Friday morning, December 5th, the code word previously identified as the signal for the attack was intercepted, which indicated the attack was to be made on Saturday or Sunday, and this information was sent by military radio to the Hawaiian Islands....[4]

Hoover concluded by observing that either "army radio" had failed to get through, or the authorities in Hawaii had failed to act.

The director of the FBI did not disclose it just then, but he had a very solid source. His information came from none other than Colonel John T. Bissell, the army's MID chief of counter-intelligence, the very same officer who had screened answers to parts of Popov's questionnaire earlier in the fall. He let slip to his opposite number in the FBI the following — the writer is actually one of Hoover's deputies:

Col. John T. Bissell today informed G.C. Burton, in the strictest of confidence (and with the statement that if it ever got out that he had disclosed this information he would be fired), that about ten days before the attack on Pearl Harbor a number of Japanese radio intercepts had been obtained in Hawaii. When they were unable to break the code in these intercepts in Hawaii they sent them to Washington where G2 broke them. It was found these radio messages contained substantially the complete plans for the attack on Pearl Harbor as it was actually carried out. The messages also contained a code Japanese word which would be sent out by radio to the Japanese fleet as the signal for the attack, when this word was repeated three times in succession....[5]

Sure enough, the Japanese pilots in their fighters and bombers circling over the black sea north of Hawaii had heard in their earphones "TORA! TORA! TORA!" — Tiger! Tiger! Tiger! — before they turned south and formed up against the red rays of the rising sun.

SAFFORD'S TESTIMONY DECODED

Special Agent Shivers submitted his formal report on the events of December 7 on December 26.[6] In the week before, in the hours he spent picking out the words on his typewriter, he could anytime have walked around the anchorage of the wrecked Pacific Fleet, with the USS *Oklahoma* bottom-up in the oily water, the USS *Arizona* awash to the decks, its upper works a tower of twisted and blackened metal. The air reeked of fuel oil and burned paint.

The report began by asking that it not be shown to the army or navy, a request that Hoover respected since it never was mentioned in any of the subsequent Pearl Harbor inquiries. Shivers then went on to tell how, shortly after the attack, he asked the Honolulu police to raid the Japanese consulate, and how they arrived just in time to save a codebook that the consul general was trying to burn. It was turned over to the navy cryptographers at Station HYPO, the Hawaii branch of Op-20-G. Within a few days, they had used it to decipher some of the messages Consul Kita had sent to Tokyo in the week before the attack. These included some stunning last-minute ships-in-harbour reports.

The HYPO cryptographers normally worked strictly on Japanese navy ciphers. They did not receive diplomatic intercepts and did not have the keys to break that kind of message. However, they happened to have some of Consul Kita's most recent enciphered originals because they had been brought in the Friday before and the day of the attack by the district Naval Intelligence officer, Captain Irving Mayfield. He had managed to persuade one of the local radio-telegraph services, RCA Communications, to secretly hand them over. Ten or so had been easily solved but were of little interest. The rest were in a code-cipher combination that could not be broken. These, on December 9, the codebook unlocked.[7]

This look by the HYPO cryptographers at Japanese espionage activities in their own backyard, as it were, must have been tremendously exciting. The messages clearly set out the Japanese consulate's role in paving the way for the attack, and if they had been available beforehand, the Pacific Fleet could have been ready. In the enthusiasm of the moment, strictly against the navy's rules, the decrypts were shared with Shivers.

The most significant of them, in terms of providing ample warning in ample time, was the so-called "lights message" sent by Kita on December

3. More than four hundred words long after translation, it was apparently prepared by the Abwehr's spy in Honolulu, Otto Kühn, and comprised an elaborate set of procedures for signalling seaward by means of lights at night and visual cues by day. It would seem the idea was to provide Japanese submarines lurking off shore with the latest on the whereabouts of the warships in Pearl Harbor.

#0245 (1) "PA"
From: Kita
To: Foreign Minister, Tokyo
(Secret Military Message No.) (By Chief of Consulate's Code)
To: Chief of Third Section, Naval General Staff
From: FUJI

Re Signals: I wish to simplify communications as follows:
Code:

1. Battle force including scouting force are about to put to sea
2. Several aircraft carriers plan to put to sea
3. All battle force has sailed (1st–3rd dates inc.)
4. Several aircraft carriers have sailed (1st to 3rd)
5. All aircraft carriers have sailed (1st to 3rd)
6. All battle force have sailed (4th–6th)
7. Several aircraft carriers have sailed (4th–6th)
8. All aircraft carriers have sailed (4th–6th)....

The message goes on to explain that 1 through 8 are to be signalled at night on the hour between 7:00 p.m. and 1:00 a.m. by a light in the dormer window of a certain house, or in a certain beach house, or by car headlights on a particular hill. The number of sheets on a clothesline and stars on a sailboat's sail were to do the same during the day.[8]

The "lights message" has been derided by some historians over the years, but the generals sitting on the 1944 Army Pearl Harbor Board took it seriously enough. This was the third in a series of eight investigations into the failures at Pearl Harbor, that began in 1942 and culminated in the 1945–46 hearings of the Joint Committee of Congress investigating the attack. The army probe zeroed in on the lights message: "The period in which the signals were to be given was December 1 to 6. If such information had been available to our armed forces it would have clearly indicated the attack."[9] In other words, if the lights message had got to the decision-makers in Washington or Hawaii promptly, the sirens would have sounded.

It did not happen. The lights message was intercepted and copied the same day it was sent, but did not become available in translation until December 11 — far, far too late. The how and why of this delay is at the centre of determining whether the Americans being surprised at Pearl Harbor on December 7 was by accident or design.

The story accepted by the Joint Committee in its 1946 report runs generally like this. On December 2–3, the Japanese Foreign Ministry in Tokyo sent out circular notices to Japan's diplomatic missions in American- and British-controlled territories ordering them to destroy their high-grade codes and enciphering machines. They were to retain only the low-security LA and PA codes. This became a crucial point because the congressmen accepted testimony that precisely because various Japanese messages indicating war was imminent were in low-grade PA code, they were not deciphered and translated in time. The congressional report, dealing with some specific examples, is worth quoting:

> The messages from Honolulu to Tokyo on December 6 were transmitted in the PA-K2 code system, a relatively insecure Japanese code and one past experience had showed was not ordinarily used for messages which Tokyo considered of the highest importance. The actual content of any message could not of course be known until it could be decoded and translated, and before the attack there was no reason to suspect that the two messages sent from Honolulu to Tokyo on December 6 would prove of unusual interest. It is to be noted, however, that the low-grade PA-K2 was virtually the

only code available to the Honolulu consul after he had
destroyed his major codes pursuant to instructions from
Tokyo on December 2.[10]

The congressmen were basing their conclusion on the testimony of
Captain Laurance Safford, the head of the navy's code- and cipher-breaking section, Op-20-G. When he appeared before the earlier Hewitt inquiry,
he described PA-K2 as an inferior system such that messages encoded in
it were automatically sent to the bottom of the pile when it came to what
intercepts would be processed first.

The messages under discussion were these:

> From: Tokyo (Togo)
> To: Honolulu
> December 6, 1941
> PA-KZ
> #128
>
> Please wire immediately re the latter part of my #123 the
> movements of the fleet subsequent to the fourth.
>
> ARMY 7381 26158 (Japanese) SECRET Trans 12/12/41
> (5)[11]

And the reply:

> From: Honolulu
> To: Tokyo
> December 6, 1941
> #254
>
> 1. On the evening of the 5th, among the battleships that
> entered port were **** and one submarine tender. The
> following ships were observed at anchor on the 6th: Nine
> battleships, 3 light cruisers, 3 submarine tenders, 17
> destroyers, and in addition there were 4 light cruisers, 2

destroyers lying at docks (the heavy cruisers and airplane carriers have all left.)

2. It appears than no air reconnaissance is being conducted by the fleet air arm.

ARMY 25874 JD 7179 Trans 12/8/41 (2-TT)[12]

The Hewitt panel naturally wanted to know how these messages, so clearly indicating an impending air attack, came not to be deciphered immediately. Though rather dry, Captain Safford's replies cover a number of important points.

> **Captain SAFFORD:** We have one more, JD 7381 dated December 6, 1941. This was also an Army translation; so I can only guess at the reason for the delay. It was intercepted at Station 5, Army station, Fort Shafter. It is in the PA-K2 system, which probably had the last or next to the lowest priority in decipherment and translation. The system had been in effect for several years and there was no difficulty in reading messages in it....

> **Captain SAFFORD:** The next is JD serial 7179, dated 6 December 1941, translated December 8, 1941, by the Army. That message was in one of the minor systems, which is known as PA-K2. The notation shows it intercepted at Station 2, San Francisco, and forwarded by teletype.... I believe this message, JD 7179, simply laid in the basket until they got all these other urgent messages over and then it was decrypted and translated as a matter of routine. We had a rigid system of priorities, first by systems and second by the priorities the Japanese assigned their own messages, and a message like this in the normal course of events would only be looked at after the more urgent messages had been caught up to date.[13]

The Shivers report, buried in FBI archives for decades, challenges this testimony. In it, Shivers quoted the Station HYPO translation of the lights message in full and, right at the top, it is numbered "0245 (1) PA," followed by the words: "Secret Military Message No. — By Chief of Consulate's Code." It would appear that the "PA" code Consul Kita retained was not low grade, as Safford claimed, but high grade. It was Kita's code of choice for messages requiring exceptional security.[14]

Once one knows enough to look, there is plenty of evidence in the published records of the 1945–46 Joint Committee Investigating the Pearl Harbor Attack to back up this deduction. First, in a brief appearance before the Hewitt inquiry, America's Albert Einstein of cryptanalysis, William Friedman, had this to say of PA-K2. "That code was a high grade code involving keyed columnar transposition of code text.... It represents what we call a rather good form of enciphered code." He rated it above J-19.[15]

According to other expert testimony, also on the committee record, the PA code was used primarily for messages "classified as 'strictly secret.'"[16]

An example is to be found : "Consul-General Muto San Francisco to Consul Honolulu, 'To be handled with Greatest Secrecy,' 12 Nov. 1941." The preamble to this message identifies it as being in the "PA System" with a "K2 transp. reversed."[17] This is proof that the codebreakers of the army and navy knew long before December 7 — as did the British — that when Kita or Tokyo used the PA code, it was for messages of topmost importance.[18]

To state it plainly, Safford lied when he stated that messages in PA code were not decrypted promptly because PA was seen as a "minor system." It was a high-priority code-cipher combination that the Japanese thought was highly secure, and he knew it.

When it comes down to it, with hindsight, it was never reasonable to think otherwise. That Tokyo on the eve of war would order its overseas missions in soon-to-be enemy territory to destroy all their codes and ciphers except two weak ones just doesn't make sense.

THE *LEXINGTON* HAS LEFT

Special Agent Shivers of the FBI said all the messages reproduced in his report were obtained from Mackay Radio and Telegraph, the British-owned rival to RCA in Honolulu. This suggests Consul Kita used both commercial radio-telegraph services to get his eleventh-hour messages to Tokyo. Hawaii was also linked to the Far East and North America by undersea cable, but the Japanese consulate consistently sent by "radiogram" rather than by "cablegram," meaning by commercial wireless service rather than landline or undersea cable service.[19] To ensure reception reliability, both Mackay and RCA normally sent simultaneously both east and west to wireless relay stations at San Francisco and Manila, the signals then going on to Japan from those locations.

The Americans, with laudable craftiness, opened army wireless listening posts near Manila (Fort Mills) and San Francisco (Station Two) to intercept this traffic, with a listening post in Hawaii itself (Fort Shafter) as backup. This arrangement ensured that the army's Signals Intelligence Service would never miss any Japanese diplomatic messages sent between Honolulu and Tokyo by the commercial radio-telegraph services.[20]

The Japanese were crafty, too. RCA and Mackay had to produce powerful signals to be heard across the Pacific, and the signals of both companies that took the San Francisco route were retransmitted across the North Pacific where the Japanese carrier force was making its approach. This would allow Consul Kita's last-minute intelligence about the warships in Pearl Harbor to be picked up directly by the attackers, and probably accounts for why he did not use undersea cable, and why his last-minute messages had to be given the very best code and cipher security.[21]

As the Japanese carriers neared their aircraft launching point, according to the Shivers report, Mackay Radio sent the following:

December 5, 1941
From: Kita
To: Foreign Minister, Tokyo

1. The three battleships mentioned in your X239 of Friday morning, the 5th entered port. They expect to depart on the 8th.

2. On the same day the LEXINGTON and 5 heavy cruisers departed.
3. The following warships were anchored on the afternoon of the 5th:
    8 battleships
    3 light cruisers
    16 destroyers

Coming in were 4 cruisers of the Honolulu type and 2 destroyers.[22]

This news that the prime prize for the attackers, the fleet aircraft carrier *Lexington*, was no longer in harbour nearly caused the Japanese commander to call off the raid. That three of the battleships were about to leave, however, would have tipped the scales the other way. The Japanese attackers could hardly withdraw and wait. It was now or never.

Shivers concluded from "they expect to depart on the 8th" that there had to be a spy somewhere inside the Pacific Fleet's command. In fact, Admiral Kimmel had no intention of sortieing any part of his force, and, curiously, the army intercept of this message, which became an exhibit before the Joint Congressional Committee, rendered this line as "they had been at sea for eight days."[23]

In any case, the scheme to give the approaching Japanese carriers tactical intelligence on Pearl Harbor right up to the last second, so to speak, was superb, flawed only because the Japanese never dreamed that the Americans would solve their machine ciphers and somehow obtain their most complex hand ciphers and codes.

The first was achieved by inspiration and hard work, the second by burglary. In 1922, a navy intelligence team with help from the FBI and the New York Police Department, broke into the offices of the Japanese consul for New York, opened his safe, and photographed the contents. That was only the first time. The consul's safe, and those of other consulates, continued to be a "never failing source of supply for both 'effective' and 'reserve' diplomatic ciphers and keys" right up to August 1941. These words were set down in a navy paper by Captain Safford, years after his testimony before the various Pearl Harbor inquiries.

They describe the actions that had enabled him truthfully to say that navy cryptographers in Washington were able to read PA-K2 messages within two hours. That reinforced in the minds of his listeners that PA-K2 was low-grade.[24]

The *Lexington*-has-left intercept was in PA-K2. According to Safford, that was why it was not recognized as important, and why it was not decrypted until December 10, five days after it had been received.

Safford was behind another category of misinformation. The following is a finding from the 1944 Hewitt Inquiry:

> On 2 December 1941 the Japanese Consul General at Honolulu received a coded message from Tokyo which stated that in view of the existing situation the presence of ships in port was of utmost importance, that daily reports were to be submitted, and that the reports should advise whether or not there were [barrage] balloons at Pearl Harbor, and whether or not the warships were provided with torpedo nets. This message was intercepted by an Army radio intercept station at Fort Shafter, Hawaii, and was apparently forwarded by mail to the War Department for decryption and translation. The translation supplied by the Army indicates that the message was translated on 30 December.[25]

The message spelled Pearl Harbor as TARGET in capital letters. It was in a well-known code — J-19 — and intercepted early enough that it could have been available to the MAGIC recipients three or four days before the attack. Safford testified, "It was forwarded by air mail and just got lost in the excitement.... That is how I account for this delay, though it is only my supposition."[26]

The problem with Safford's "supposition" is — as he well knew — if a message was picked up in Hawaii, it must also have been picked up in the United States and the Philippines. As noted earlier, the commercial radio-telegraph signals between Tokyo and Honolulu were relayed by receiver-transmitters at San Francisco and Manila, both cities covered by army listening posts. The message was 100 percent likely to be intercepted by the army's Station Two at San Francisco. It then would have been sent to Washington by teletype for deciphering.

Naturally, Fort Shafter also took down the messages when they went from San Francisco to Hawaii, but only to check for any garbles or missing groups occurring on that leg. Its copies of the intercepts could be mailed to Washington because there was no hurry. The Washington codebreakers would already have them.

For messages going the other way, Honolulu to Tokyo, it could be even faster. The RCA and Mackay signals beamed at San Francisco and Manila normally overshot their marks. They could be heard in real time elsewhere in continental United States, and by British listening posts in the Far East and Canada. The copy of the lights message, for example, was obtained from the army intercept station at Fort Hunt, Virginia, just outside Washington, and the Canadian navy's new listening station at Hartlen Point, Halifax, was just a radio skip and a jump farther on. Consul Kita's last-minute reports on Pearl Harbor were fair game for cryptographers around the world, including German and Russian, but thanks to Hartlen Point, especially for the Canadians and British.[27]

THE LAST HOURS REVISITED

December 2–7, 1941

Anyone in official Washington receiving the full file of MAGIC decrypts would have been on tenterhooks after reading on December 2 that Tokyo had ordered its diplomatic posts in Washington, London, Hong Kong, Singapore, Batavia, and Manila to destroy their cipher machines and principal codes. In the sign language of international diplomacy, such an order is semaphore for war. The cities named indicated which countries the Japanese were expecting to fight: Britain, the United States, and Holland.

A Tokyo–Berlin message circulated just the day before revealed that Japan considered that relations with Britain and the United States stood "ruptured" and that "war may come quicker than anyone dreams." Japan's intention, it said, was to refrain from any "direct moves" against Russia. This spelled a surprise attack against the United States and Britain, for sure. Roosevelt and Churchill both definitely saw this message.[1]

This was Tuesday. As Japan's enemies all observed the Sabbath, it would have been a safe bet that the Japanese would launch an attack that Sunday. Before that happened, however, Japan could be expected to reply to Secretary of State Cordell Hull's demand of November 26 that it get out of China and Indochina or suffer the embargo indefinitely.

By Saturday, still no reply. By then, there had been evidence enough that the war would begin with Pearl Harbor, but so far none of the reports of the Honolulu consulate to Tokyo indicating a Taranto-style attack had been passed on. There had been another such intercept that very morning, obviously from one of the consulate's spies. "In my opinion the battleships have no torpedo nets," it said. "I imagine in all probability there is considerable opportunity ... for a surprise attack...."[2]

Nothing could be more definite, and the reason for it not being translated and acted upon is bizarre. Normally, Op-20-G and the Signals Intelligence Service in Washington took turns processing the incoming intercepts, the navy taking the odd days and the army the even. Yet, with war clouds leaden on the horizon, the army gave the staff of its entire code-breaking operation the normal civil-service weekend off — in those days, Saturday afternoon and all day Sunday. This left everything to the navy from noon on, plus all day Sunday. Regardless, the navy's chief translator, Lieutenant Commander Alwin Kramer, gave his own translators the weekend off as well. Anything not translated by noon was going to have to be translated by him or wait until Monday.

Kramer did not work for the navy's communications division. He was actually from the Office of Naval Intelligence and had been assigned to Op-20-G the previous October, his superb command of the Japanese language being seen as helpful to the codebreakers. His job was to evaluate the messages as soon as deciphered, translate the most important himself, and hand-deliver them to the government department heads on the navy's list of MAGIC recipients, with copies going also to the Signals Intelligence Service for distribution to those on the army's list. The three translators under him looked after the rest. He remained under ONI orders throughout the crucial months, weeks, and days leading up to December 7.

This arrangement gave Kramer on-the-spot responsibility that weekend for choosing which decrypts should be seen by the military and political leaders. Since Naval Intelligence was the client department for Op-20-G's code- and cipher-breaking, the handy presence of Kramer explains why Captain Safford could tell the congressional committee that he comfortably went home the afternoon of December 6, even though he was sure from the messages already decrypted that the Japanese would attack the next day. Safford's staff was to watch for the vital messages and decipher them; Kramer was to take it from there.

Kramer's immediate superior was Commander Arthur H. McCollum, chief of ONI's Far East section, which specialized in preparing intelligence appreciations to do with China, Korea, and Japan. The handful of officers on his staff were fluent in the pertinent languages, with McCollum and at least one other speaking and reading Japanese. Kramer reported to McCollum, and McCollum reported to the then director of Naval Intelligence, Captain Theodore Wilkinson. This was a normal chain of command, except that Kramer and his team worked in a room apart from the Far Eastern staff, although in the same building.

When he did his daily rounds, however, Kramer came in direct contact with the White House and the navy's top man, Admiral Stark, chief of naval operations. McCollum was under the impression that Kramer was always showing him what was in his deliveries. He may not have been. This would explain how McCollum could tell the congressional inquiry that he could not remember seeing the bomb-plot messages (Chapter 15) and Wilkinson's hazy recollection of them. They should have been something hard to forget. If they were not lying, perhaps neither man actually saw them.[3]

The fact was, Kramer controlled what his immediate superiors saw, and could do so without them being the wiser. If ordered to withhold translated messages by Admiral Stark, it was his duty to obey, and Stark or the White House could be telephoned before Kramer set out with the day's decrypts. Other than him, only Captain Safford was in a position to see the full file of Japanese diplomatic intercepts handled in the navy building that autumn of 1941.

This could certainly account for the surprising amnesia shown by some of the senior officer recipients of MAGIC when questioned before the various Pearl Harbor inquiries. The messages they could not remember they may not have received.

Because Kramer was to be without translators on December 6 from noon on, he simply ignored the decrypts left over by the army, leaving those dealing with Pearl Harbor unheeded and unread. He still had the December 3rd lights message to contend with, however. It had been intercepted at the army listening post at Fort Hunt on the outskirts of Washington, so it had arrived at the navy building downtown on Wednesday. Being in PA-K2 (which we now know would have been recognized as high priority, not low, and easy to break), it was likely deciphered and delivered to Kramer that same day. He must have read it then, for that was his job.

By Saturday, Kramer had been holding on to the message for a dangerously long time. He had portrayed himself to his staff as being terribly disorganized and a chronic perfectionist, so they were used to decrypts being stalled on his desk. Since the lights message foretold a Japanese air attack the next day, however, it was too hot to keep any longer. That morning he put it into the in-tray of Mrs. Dorothy Edgers, a former schoolteacher who had joined his staff only the week before and whom he knew would be working only until noon. The header, "Secret Military Message ... By Chief of Consulate's Code," had been removed.[4]

Mrs. Edgers, as it happened, was an exceptional Japanese linguist, having lived in Japan and taught Japanese to high-school-level children for two decades before returning to the United States. She saw immediately that the message appeared important and drew it to Kramer's attention. He gave it only a glance and shrugged it off. She went back to her desk, but instead of leaving at 12:30, worked up a rough translation, which she left for Kramer before going home around 3:00 p.m.[5]

Kramer was an intelligence officer of long experience and he had handled MAGIC for months. He was fluent in Japanese. It was his specific task to see to it that the most important decrypts were recognized, translated, and passed on as quickly as possible. With the navy code- and cipher-breakers in a room down the hall, and having read all the previously decrypted Japanese messages leading up to the verge of war, it is just not plausible for him not to have read the lights message as soon as decrypted, or not to have read it before passing it on to Mrs. Edgers. He gave the message no more than a glance when she showed it to him because he already knew what it said.

The lights message sat on his desk the rest of the weekend.[6]

Meanwhile, before it closed up shop, the army sent over a Tokyo–Washington decrypt that told the ambassador that Japan's formal reply to Secretary of State Hull would be coming shortly. It was to be long, with thirteen parts sent first and the fourteenth to follow later. The embassy was to hold on to the completed statement until given a specific time to present it to the United States government, preferably to Hull himself. With his staff translators gone, Kramer could expect to be working on the thirteen parts well into the next day. Then, unexpectedly, when the first part began arriving in mid-afternoon, it was found that the text was in English.[7]

It caused considerable excitement. Op-20-G's cryptographers were not accustomed to unravelling a Japanese encipherment into readable English. Both Captain Safford, head of Op-20-G, and Commander McCollum came in to have a look. The Foreign Office in Tokyo was so determined that nothing in the message be misunderstood that it had translated it itself. The list of grievances it contained and the rejection of Hull's conditions made it obvious to everyone that it amounted to a declaration of war.

McCollum now found out that Kramer had no translators on hand. It seems not to have worried him unduly. Kramer could translate any further decrypts that came in while he waited for the first thirteen parts to be processed. Once these were typed up, he was to deliver them to his usual MAGIC clients immediately, returning to the office to await the promised fourteenth part and the time-of-delivery message. McCollum undertook to come in early the next morning. An off-duty army translator was called in to fill in as needed.

As most government offices in Washington are grouped together within a half mile of the White House, and the army was in a building nearby, it normally took Kramer less than an hour to do his round. At midnight, he telephoned McCollum at home to say that he had made the deliveries, including to the army and the White House, but was unable to find Admiral Stark. He then returned to his office on finding the expected remaining messages had not yet arrived, but instead of camping down to await them, he went home to bed.

Roosevelt read the thirteen parts in his study, along with Harry Hopkins, his trusted aide and confidant. "This means war," he is said to have muttered.[8]

Kramer arrived back at the navy building shortly after 7:30 a.m. on Sunday. Although he was later to claim otherwise, he had been phoned by the officer of the watch during the night and told that two important messages were now available. One was the fourteenth part in English, and the other, a single sentence in Japanese instructing the ambassador to deliver the full fourteen parts to Hull precisely at 1:00 p.m. Kramer, however, instead of going directly to his office, stopped at McCollum's on his way in.[9]

The two chatted about the ramifications of the thirteen parts that Kramer had delivered on his rounds the night before. When the director of Naval Intelligence, Captain Wilkinson, arrived and was told that Admiral Stark had been skipped on the thirteen-part delivery, he said they should make up for it immediately. They put a call in to Stark's office and learned he was on his way in — a surprise, since it was Sunday. Wilkinson and McCollum headed for his office with the thirteen-part message. It was now about 9:00 a.m.[10]

Meanwhile, Kramer went on to his own office, there to find the fourteenth part and the one o'clock messages. Taken together, they indicated unmistakeably that a state of war would exist between Japan and the United States the moment the whole fourteen parts were delivered to Hull.

Kramer put duplicate copies of the fourteenth part of the message into his dispatch pouch and set out for the White House, the State Department, the army building, and Stark's office. He did not take the one o'clock message, apparently because it was still in Japanese. Consisting of only one sentence, he could have scribbled it into English in seconds.

When he got back to Stark's office, McCollum and Wilkinson were still talking with the admiral. Instead of interrupting, he left the fourteenth part of the message with an aide. At 10:20 he was back at his own office. The formal translation of the one o'clock message, done by the army, was on his desk. This, along with some other decrypts, he took on another delivery round that included the White House and the State Department. He retraced his earlier route. McCollum was still in Stark's outer office when he arrived there. Wilkinson had gone. Kramer mentioned the one o'clock message.

There was a time-zone map of the world on the wall. McCollum glanced at it: 1:00 p.m. Washington time would be 7:30 a.m. Hawaii time — dawn.

Captain McCollum became very, very excited. He called Wilkinson back in, and he, too, saw the significance of the time. The Japanese were likely to attack Pearl Harbor in less than three hours. They all but forced their way back into Stark's office. The Pacific Fleet must be warned!

Admiral Stark was unperturbed. The Pacific Fleet was on the alert, he assured them. Wilkinson urged him to pick up the telephone anyway and call Admiral Kimmel direct. He could be on the line in minutes. Stark demurred.

He had a call put in to the White House. The president was unavailable. There was further toing and froing as senior naval staff came in and out of the room. At last Admiral Stark reached General Marshall. The general also nixed using the telephone. The hands of the clock stood toward 11:00.

General Marshall agreed to send the warning on behalf of both of them. It would go to General Short only, and only by commercial radio-telegraph, the slowest means. He should also have sent it over the army and navy radio nets, duplication being the standard practice for an urgent message. He chose not to. His message said:

> Japanese are presenting at one p.m. Eastern Standard Time today what amounts to an ultimatum also they are under orders to destroy their code machine immediately STOP Just what significance the hour set may have we do not know but be on alert accordingly STOP Inform naval authorities of this communication.[11]

When the "flimsy" bearing this warning reached Hawaii's General Short, he crumpled it into a ball and threw it aside.

The bombs and torpedoes had already exploded.

PRISONERS OF DUTY

His details were fuzzy, but the army's chief of counter-intelligence, Colonel Bissell, had been right. The government had known in advance the Japanese were going to attack Pearl Harbor, and it had come from "radio intercepts." However, Kramer, Safford, Stark, and Marshall — evidently with some co-conspirators in the Signals Intelligence Service — had ensured that Hawaii would not be warned.

Why did they do it? Duty comes first to mind. Like soldiers of any of the advanced nations of the twentieth century, they had been trained unflinchingly to follow orders, to obey their commanding officers without question. Under the U.S. Constitution, the head of state, the president, is also commander-in-chief. If Roosevelt told Admiral Stark and General

Marshall, and they in turn told Safford and Kramer that the Pacific Fleet had to be sacrificed in the interests of grand strategy, it would have been their duty to help make it happen. To refuse would have been to disobey orders — unthinkable, except in the most dire of circumstances.

Still, they must have been troubled. Roosevelt, however, had the means to ease their consciences. Throughout September and into December the messages decrypted by the British describing the SS atrocities in Russia had continued to accumulate. Innocent civilians, especially Jews, were being cut down in swaths by the extermination squads. The tally was well into the thousands. The secure transatlantic cable connection between the Government Code & Cipher School and Washington ensured that messages reporting the horrors reached the White House, which could then distribute them to those entitled to MAGIC. That included Safford and Kramer as well as Stark and Marshall.

They all must have deeply believed that withholding the relevant messages from the Hawaii commanders was worth the American lives it was going to cost. Stark, especially, walked the thinnest of tightropes: If at any time in the previous forty-eight hours Admiral Kimmel had got the wind up and had put the fleet to sea, all the battleships would have been sunk in the open ocean, along with most of the attendant warships. Upwards of fifteen thousand sailors' lives would have been lost. It would have been one of the greatest naval defeats in history, for there would have been no losses to speak of on the other side. It is hard to imagine, though, how Stark managed to keep his composure when Wilkinson and McCollum were pressuring him to phone Admiral Kimmel.

After Pearl Harbor, Kramer, Stark and Safford were marginalized for the rest of the war, Kramer to a back desk in Op-20-G with nothing to do, and Stark to England, also to a desk, charting the paper course of the naval build-up for the future Allied landings in Europe. Safford was promptly reassigned to a section dealing with code and cipher security, an enormous demotion. As for the British, it was surely a different story still to be told. The Canadian listening station at Hartlen Point, Nova Scotia, was in direct line from Fort Hunt in Virginia and was linked to Britain and the Government Code & Cipher School by undersea cable. The British could read the same Japanese consular codes and ciphers as the Americans. They had all along been breaking many of the same messages. They certainly saw the Honolulu consulate messages that pointed to an unhealthy Japanese interest in the Pacific Fleet. After more than seventy years, Britain still has not released the pertinent Japanese diplomatic decrypts it definitely has.[12]

And what of Hoover? On December 29, the FBI director was the object of a vicious lashing from a columnist with the *Washington Times-Herald* who claimed that the commission of inquiry that Roosevelt had immediately set up was about to pin the blame for Pearl Harbor on the FBI.

> Long-time Capitol Hill foes of FBI Chief Hoover have been whetting up their snickerness, itching to take a crack at the detective hero as far back as the days of kidnappers and gangsters. Leaders are holding them back with the promise that the report of the Roberts Board of Inquiry will provide the ammunition for an all-out drive to oust Hoover from his seat of tremendous power.[13]

That same day, Roosevelt sent a note to Hoover saying that he still had full confidence in him. This must have come as a great relief. Roosevelt really did have the power to fire him, and Hoover was the object of so much envy and hate that had the president fired him, Hoover was certain the coyotes would be yelping.

Hoover could relax. He had done his duty. He had drawn the president's attention to evidence of major failures on the part of the army and navy. Now, true to his style, he left it to the White House to make the decision on how to proceed — if at all, considering there was a war on. Hoover's job was only to inform, and so he had.

He did not quite let everything go, however. He sent a copy of his December 12 memorandum to Supreme Court Associate Justice Owen J. Roberts, then heading the first of what would be a set of eight inquiries into Pearl Harbor, and urged him to try to get to the bottom of when the alleged messages were sent to Washington, when they were decoded, when the information was sent back to Hawaii, and so forth. Roberts did not follow up.

Hoover was never called to testify at any of the inquiries. That was probably merciful, for it would have disclosed how little he knew, how much he was not told. It would have been embarrassing. He must have had gloomy thoughts as the postwar congressional investigation reeled off the bomb-plot messages and spy report after spy report, all of which someone in high authority deemed him not fit to see. He would surely have connected them to Popov's questionnaire.

Hoover, of course, had to be left out. He was a civilian, not a soldier. He could question or refuse an order from the commander-in-chief. While loyal to the Office of the President, he answered to the Department of Justice. During the gangster days he had earned for himself and the Bureau a stellar reputation for incorruptibility. In short, Hoover could not be counted upon to lie.

STALIN RESCUED

In the summer of 1941, when the Japanese navy's study of the feasibility of attacking Pearl Harbor was well advanced, the ambassador, attachés, and other military advisers at the German embassy in Tokyo enjoyed a privileged relationship with Japan's senior military leadership. They certainly learned that the Japanese had, indeed, noted the lesson of the British raid on Taranto and were considering the possibilities of carrier-launched attacks themselves.[14] Pearl Harbor was a logical target.

This does not mean that Canaris assumed that Japan had already decided that it was going to war with the United States and that there would be a surprise first-strike against the Americans. By the end of July, he knew only that Japan's military and political leadership had pretty well decided that Japan's best prospects lay to the south, toward British and Dutch territories in the Far East. If these could be seized without direct confrontation with the Americans, so much the better.[15] The Japanese navy was only drafting its plans against Pearl Harbor *in case* of war with the United States.

That summer, Russia's ace spy in Tokyo, Richard Sorge, also reported that the Japanese were looking south not north, but Stalin discounted it. It was too good to be true. The Red Army was just then taking a severe beating from the Germans in western Russia; it made more sense for the

Japanese to attack in the east, in Siberia, forcing Stalin into a two-front war. For all Stalin knew, Sorge's intelligence could have been planted on him by the Japanese in a bid to get Soviet troops withdrawn from the east.

It turns out the information *was* planted on Sorge, except not by the Japanese. It was coming from Canaris.

The forty-five-year-old Sorge was one of the truly professional spies of the Second World War. He was born in Russia — his mother was Russian, his father German — and brought up in Germany. He was awarded the Iron Cross for valour during the First World War, but converted to communism while recovering from his wounds in hospital, apparently thanks to the intellectual ministrations of a left-wing nurse. He went on to university, and then to Moscow in the 1920s for training. He was a brilliant linguist, and the Soviets used him in England for a short while, in Germany, in China, and then sent him to Japan in 1933 expressly to set up a spy network. He succeeded admirably, establishing clandestine wireless contact with Moscow and acquiring a number of highly placed informants.

Sorge's cover was that of a journalist for several German newspapers, and he had an office in the German embassy itself. This not only facilitated contact with Japanese officials, but also put him in daily touch with key embassy personnel — the air, army, and naval attachés, and the ambassador. He met the latter over breakfast every morning, and the ambassador was candid to the extent that their conversations often took in the day's secret dispatches from Berlin.[16]

It was through these daily chats that Sorge was able that spring to keep Moscow informed on the build-up of German forces in eastern Europe. Then, on May 5, he came up with a copy of a message to the ambassador from von Ribbentrop, the Nazi foreign minister, advising that "Germany will begin war against the USSR in the middle of June." Since the German Foreign Office enciphered its communications with unbreakable one-time pads, Sorge must have obtained this from the ambassador.

On May 10, Sorge reported that the ambassador and naval attaché were of the opinion that the Japanese would not attack the British in the Far East "as long as Japan continued to receive raw materials from the United States."[17] Canaris would have received this assessment and, considering the denial of essential commodities was the tactic Roosevelt used to provoke Japan, he may have passed it on to Menzies, who in turn gave it to Churchill.

On May 15, Sorge correctly reported that on June 22 the Germans would launch Operation *Barbarossa*, the surprise invasion of the Soviet Union. He even correctly stated the number of divisions to be deployed — 150.[18]

On the face of it, it would appear that the embassy was being incredibly reckless with its secrets. Stalin must have thought so, too, for he rejected the warnings. He is said to have suspected Sorge of being a double agent, and that he was party to a British plot to foster distrust between him and Hitler. When intelligence came in from other sources confirming the massive German build-up in Poland and the east, he chose to believe Hitler's explanation that German troops were concentrating in Eastern Europe so that they could exercise and rearm out of range of British air reconnaissance. Churchill's last-minute alert, thanks to Dicketts, that the Germans were about to invade, merely bolstered Stalin's conviction that it was all deception.[19]

The German ambassador to Tokyo was General Eugen Ott, previously military attaché before getting the top post. As military attachés before the war were chosen by agreement between the Abwehr chief and the chief of the general staff, then Ludwig Beck, it is a safe bet that Ott had the same attitude toward the Nazis as they did. Moreover, the man who replaced him as attaché was Colonel Gerhard Matzky, identified after the war as a member of Canaris's inner circle of conspirators. At the end of 1940, Matzky was recalled to Germany to head up Fremde Heere, the army general staff's intelligence department. His replacement was Colonel Alfred Kretschmer, a forty-seven-year-old veteran of the First World War who had stayed on in the peacetime army and whose service included two years in Fremde Heere. He was also an opponent of the Nazis.

In other words, the German embassy in Tokyo was more an outpost of the German Resistance than an overseas branch of the Foreign Office, its key positions being filled by anti-Nazis loyal to Canaris. With Sorge occupying an office at the embassy, he was an easy way to tip Stalin off to Hitler's plans quickly and safely. Fremde Heere was a key contributor to the planning for Operation *Barbarossa*, so Matzky was the ultimate source of the details Sorge obtained from Kretschmer and Ott. During their breakfast chats, Ott also updated Sorge on what he was gleaning from his Foreign Office masters in Berlin, and from their counterparts in Tokyo.[20] Sorge's great reputation as a spy was based on the intelligence the Abwehr — read Canaris — chose to give him.

At the beginning of October, Sorge reported that Japanese-American talks were in their final stages, and if the Americans refused to lift the various embargos imposed by Roosevelt, Japan would attack British and American possessions in the western Pacific. By now, Stalin was listening. He began moving some of his troops in the east to the Russian front, but the stakes were too high for him to act too boldly. The spectacular collapse of Japanese-American talks in November was still to come.

At this crucial moment, Sorge was arrested. He had fallen in love with one of Japan's most beautiful geishas, and it was his undoing. The hard-nosed spy had taken it in the heart, and even the Japanese who set up the sting were sorry. The curtains were drawn on Stalin's primary window on Tokyo. Stalin, however, had an alternative source.

Approximately a year earlier, Anthony Blunt — son of a parson, related to royalty, distinguished art critic, Cambridge graduate, and Soviet mole — joined MI5. After first serving as a kind of personal secretary to MI5's counter-espionage chief, Guy Liddell, he was given responsibility for a sub-department concerned with tracking the activities in England of the diplomats of neutral nations. This entailed recruiting spies in their embassies, stealing the contents of their wastebaskets, and secretly opening diplomatic bags before they left the country. This latter practice was a First World War trick, and MI6 had been doing it since then. However, when it was described by Herbert Yardley in his book *Secret Service in America*, published in London in 1940 for all to see, MI6 lost interest. It made no objection when MI5, at Blunt's urging, offered to take it over.[21]

According to Blunt's own autobiographical report to the Soviets, he oversaw an operation that involved having agents persuade diplomatic couriers to hand their bags over to port security officials who would put them into a safe while they awaited departure. When they were travelling by air, their flights would be deliberately delayed so that the bags would be turned over for safekeeping. Blunt's people would then be given access to the bags, open and photograph their contents, and then have them carefully resealed so that the couriers would be none the wiser.[22]

Given that all this was first described in Yardley's book *The American Black Chamber* (1931), which went through many printings, including in French and Japanese, before being reissued in 1940, and given that Walter Nicolai covered the same ground in *The German Secret Service* (1924), reprinted in French as *Forces secrets* (1932), it is doubtful that many of the couriers fell for it. The Soviets, on the other hand, had a very great reason to want Blunt to be secretly opening their diplomatic bags. He could freely put into them whatever he wanted, enabling the ever-suspicious Stalin to see for himself what Blunt stole.

On August 14, the same day that Ellis was showing the Pearl Harbor questionnaire to the FBI in New York, Liddell proposed to Petrie that Blunt be nominated to go down to the Government Code & Cipher School periodically to take notes on the most recent BJs — those Japanese diplomatic decrypts of such importance that they were earmarked for Churchill's eyes.[23] Thanks to the generosity of the Americans, with their gift the preceding February of a PURPLE machine and the keys to the PA and J codes, this involved a cornucopia of Japanese consular traffic of the most sensitive and significant sort, intercepted in Britain, Canada, Australia, and Singapore.[24]

It made Stalin a silent third party to the countdown to December 7. Blunt was able to send him, through the Moscow-bound diplomatic pouch, actual copies of the same decrypts of Japanese messages then being read by Churchill. The Soviet leader could also follow Japan's hopeless negotiations with the United States, its growing desperation caused by American-imposed shortages in food, fuel, and raw materials, and its hardening resolve to fight. This was the intelligence he needed if he was to release troops in Siberia for the struggle against the Germans in western Russia. Convinced, he began the transfers in October, and by the end of November, ten new divisions, plus a thousand tanks and a thousand aircraft, were deployed before Moscow.[25]

Of the messages supplied by Blunt, the most critical was that released by the GC&CS on November 25. It was a Tokyo advisory of November 19 to all diplomatic posts abroad that should Japan's access to commercial cable and radio-telegraph services be subject to interruption because Japan was breaking diplomatic relations, the specific "enemy countries" involved would be identified by open-code phrases in the weather reports of Japan's international broadcast-radio service: For Russia, "north wind cloudy"; for Britain, "west wind clear"; for the United States, "east wind rain."[26]

This would have indicated to Stalin that as of the date the message was sent, Japan was still considering the possibility of attacking the Soviet Union. The Japanese had a large army in China, so Siberia was not safe. Stalin could not afford to attack the Germans before Moscow until it was.

Meanwhile, the temperature dropped and snow swept across the plains of the Ukraine. The Russian winter had arrived early and it was to be one of the most severe in living memory. Hitler urged his generals to press on — the spires of the Kremlin were almost within sight — but the fresh troops from the Soviet east now barred the way. On November 27, the German offensive, begun six months earlier with such confidence, stalled, halted. Moscow was a mere thirty-two kilometres farther on.

Next came BJ/35, read by Churchill and, thanks to Blunt, read by Stalin. Available on December 2, it was sent by Prime Minister Tojo to Japan's ambassador in Berlin asking him to tell Hitler that an "armed collision" leading to a state of war with Britain and the United States was to be expected soon, but Japan intended "to refrain from deliberately taking positive action in the North."[27] North wind cloudy was no longer in the forecast.

On December 5, as the Japanese bombers were being readied on their aircraft carriers, the Soviets launched a major attack on the German lines before Moscow. The Germans reeled from the blow. After the huge Russian losses of the preceding months, the attack was totally unexpected. The fighting became desperate — for the Germans.

It was the beginning of the end for Hitler.

PART IV

ULTIMATE SECRETS[1]

September 1939–December 1941

In Berlin, in his office on the Tirpitzuferstrasse, Admiral Canaris had a Japanese woodblock print of a warrior hanging on the wall, a gift from the Japanese ambassador. Canaris had spent six months in Japan as a young man, and must have been impressed by the speed at which this colourful but formal people had advanced militarily. As Abwehr chief, he had seen to it that top-quality officers were sent to Japan as military attachés. For Germany, the benefit of being able to keep abreast of Japan's accomplishments in air and naval developments made this commitment well worth it.

The evidence is ample that Canaris had a direct hand in the Pearl Harbor questionnaire delivered by Dusko Popov that ultimately triggered America's entry into the Second World War.

First, all other considerations aside, the fact that both questionnaires — Dusko Popov's about the Americans and Juan Pujol Garcia's about the British — involved collecting military intelligence for another country meant that they would have required Canaris's approval. It is in the nature of nations that co-operation of that kind with a foreign power is a matter of high policy, requiring consultation with the top leaders concerned, and at least a briefing note to the head of government. There is just no chance that KO Portugal and KO Spain would have sent the two agents on their missions without clearance from a higher authority in Berlin. That meant Canaris.

Further:

- On July 24, the U.S. Navy decrypted a Japanese diplomatic message from "a high authority in Japan" that indicated the Japanese were about to seize British and Dutch colonial possessions in the Far East;
- Admiral Canaris would have seen this message because the German armed forces cipher bureau, OKW/CHI, was then decrypting and reading Japanese diplomatic messages in the same J-19 and PA ciphers as the Americans and British;[2]
- Also on July 24, Churchill spoke openly with Roosevelt about their upcoming shipboard rendezvous over their transatlantic scrambler radio-telephone link. The conversation was picked up and unscrambled by the Nazi radio-telephone intercept service;[3]
- About a week later, MI5's double agent RAINBOW announced he had received a cover letter from his German controller with microdots attached, the first MI5 had seen. An MI5 internal report a year later indicated that RAINBOW, Charles Eibner, had been an agent "planted" on the Security Service by the Germans;
- Within days, Dusko Popov, a.k.a. TRICYCLE, showed his MI6 controller in Lisbon the questionnaire about Pearl Harbor on microdots he said the Germans had given him.

Popov had been scheduled to leave Lisbon for the United States at the end of July but his departure was delayed and his original mission of going on to Egypt was dropped. Place-name errors in his questionnaire suggest it was prepared in haste, and in Lisbon, not Berlin. However, the entire mission was unnecessary because Japan had its own intelligence service and there were thousands of naturalized Japanese living in Hawaii. In addition, the Abwehr also had at least one long-established spy, Otto Kühn, already there.

The evidence is compelling. On learning that Churchill and Roosevelt were about to meet face to face, Canaris rushed to provide Churchill with the means to argue that Japan was contemplating military action against the United States. He could not have predicted where the two leaders would go from there.

Or could he?

THE ANALYSIS

To begin with, there is no argument that German intelligence scored a massive direct hit against British intelligence in 1940 when Arthur Owens turned over details of the coastal radar stations Britain had secretly built. It was decisive information, and Britain could have lost the war had the Luftwaffe properly followed up. Indeed, up until his last cross-Channel trip in April 1940 to see his German controller, Owens was an entirely successful triple agent.

Then came his unmasking by Sam McCarthy during their aborted North Sea rendezvous with Ast Hamburg's Major Ritter. Instead of arresting him for espionage, a few weeks later Captain Robertson sent him again to meet Ritter, this time in Portugal, and this time hopefully really acting for the British. He came bearing the reports of Agent E-186, which, among a number of bomb-target suggestions, included giving away the locations of Fighter Command and Bomber Command. Theoretically, all the Luftwaffe needed to do was smother Stanmore and High Wycombe with high explosive and Britain's air defences would have been reduced to confusion and chaos.

That did not happen. Ritter did send in the E-186 reports, but for some reason that remains obscure, they were not acted upon.

Major Ritter's original intention in 1939 appears to have been to use Owens as a straight spy, who would report by wireless once the war started. But Owens had other ideas, probably because spying for the enemy in wartime Britain was a capital crime. By turning himself in immediately, he minimized the period that he could be accused of working for the enemy and stood a chance of being taken on as a double agent. Getting his wife to denounce him beforehand was probably part of the scheme.

It worked like a charm. Although Ritter understandably did not reveal it when in British custody after the war, the ineptitude of MI5 enabled him to run Owens as a passive and then active triple agent from October 1939 onward. This came about because MI5 had begun the Second World War with little counter-espionage experience relevant to spying by a sophisticated foreign power. This is proved by MI5's evident ignorance of the state of the art as it was to be found in the published spy memoirs of the day. It was also wilfully blind to advances in technology, especially those to do with wireless communications. It was a deficit that could not be made up by relying on the Radio Security Service, itself a largely amateur operation.

The result was, Ritter found himself parrying a British double-agent operation that at first seemed too clumsy to be serious. But it was, and he soon was garnering much useful intelligence by sending Owens back to England with lengthy questionnaires to which the British would have to supply at least some true answers. It was a ploy born of the First World War, when the Germans noticed that the British were prone to giving their spies extensive "inquiry sheets" covering military and economic topics and, in particular, details on the effect of their air raids.[4]

By mid-1940, when it was clear his counter-espionage adversary had little grasp of clandestine wireless operations, Ritter found he could plant double agents on MI5 by allowing the British to intercept wireless messages in easy-to-break ciphers that referred to his spies before they set out for England.

The so-called *Lena* spies, and later TRICYCLE, were all of this type. Consider the following: Only in September did Ritter finally send agents to Britain equipped with wireless sets, ostensibly to hide out until the Germans invaded and then radio back British troop movements. They were a little late for that:

August 13:	Eagle Day. Luftwaffe's maximum effort against RAF fails.
September 3:	Walberg, Meier, Kieboom, and Pons arrive by boat in Britain, ill-trained and ill-equipped (not used, executed).
September 5:	Caroli (SUMMER) lands by parachute (becomes double agent).
September 6:	Attempt to defeat RAF ends.
September 8:	Hitler postpones invasion.[5]
September 14:	Hitler calls off invasion for 1940.

September 15:	London massively bombed. The Blitz begins.
September 19:	Schmidt (TATE) lands by parachute (becomes double agent).
September 30:	Vera Eriksen lands by boat (offer to be double agent rejected).
October 3:	Karl Gross (GOOSE) lands by parachute (temporary double agent).
November ?:	Ter Braak lands by parachute (evades capture).
January 31:	Josef Jakobs lands by parachute (injured on landing).

Canaris, then at Hitler's elbow and aware that the RAF was undefeated, clearly knew the invasion was to be called off even before Caroli was dispatched.[6] This is further evidence, along with the clumsily forged identity papers, that Caroli and the others who followed him were meant to be caught.

A security organization so easily fooled was bound to be victim of multiple penetrations by the enemy, and up to mid-1941, while Hitler and Stalin were still on friendly terms, German and Soviet agents were equally to be feared. Apart from Owens, another for the Germans is definitely known: William Rolph, the source of the super-secret list of right-wingers found on Owens after McCarthy blew the whistle on him. Two for the Soviets were Anthony Blunt, exposed after the war as a member of the notorious Cambridge Five, and Guy Liddell, the B Division chief, who was a Soviet agent-of-influence at the least.

Indeed, the evidence against Liddell is huge. In addition to opening the doors for Burgess, Blunt, and Philby to enter MI5 and MI6, and the access he gave Blunt to his office documents, it is surely not an innocent coincidence that MI5 totally failed to detect Soviet recruitment of young intellectuals at Oxford and Cambridge during the 1930s. As Liddell was then deputy-director of the counter-subversion section, this would have fallen under his mandate. So the failure was largely his. The ultimate fault, however, must lie with whomever in government sanctioned the transfer of Scotland Yard's anti-communist section to MI5 in 1931 after two of its Special Branch investigators were discovered to be working for the Soviets. Liddell was included in that transfer. Basic prudence should have dictated that there might have been a yet undetected third guilty party.[6]

Yet another German agent appears to have been at large. In the second month of the war, when Canaris was conspiring with generals Halder and Beck to overthrow Hitler, Arthur Owens returned from meeting DR. RANTZAU with the warning that the Germans had a spy in the Air Ministry. If this was not something he made up, then it was a direct tipoff from the Abwehr, and if a vast amount of circumstantial evidence counts for anything, Air Commodore Boyle fits the bill. He had been the primary source of intelligence for MI5's double agents both before and after becoming director of Air Intelligence, and by late 1940 was said (by Masterman, at least) to be supplying much of the content of the wireless messages being sent by SNOW, SUMMER, and TATE. Anyone in Hamburg or Berlin then, and anyone now, casually looking at the agent wireless reports being received by Hamburg from A-3504, A-3719, and A-3725. and sent on to Berlin during 1940–41 would conclude that the helpful Commodore Boyle was a spy *par excellence*.

This theory works well if the Germans knew Owens was being supplied with mostly true information, which he apparently was. It also requires either complicity or a considerable lack of intellectual vigour on Robertson's part. Most of the messages prepared for sending to the Germans by wireless that he oversaw, or possibly composed himself, are missing from today's MI5 archives, maybe because they would make Boyle look as guilty as sin.

The German side of the messages are available, however, and if they are examined closely, an alternative picture emerges. The preliminary logic is this: Either the information Boyle approved for sending was good and helped the Germans overall, making him a traitor; or the information was good but did not help the Germans overall, making him a clever counter-intelligence operative. The former is not impossible, but the latter is certainly more likely, since he was a senior civil servant with a long pre-war attachment to the Air Ministry and to its intelligence branch. He also had been runner-up to Stewart Menzies as chief of MI6 when Admiral Sinclair died. He was known and trusted in the highest circles of the governing Establishment.[7]

Considered in this light, Boyle permitting the sending over of current weather information during the Battle of Britain may not have been such a bad move. Allowing that the Luftwaffe would use it to help schedule its raids, Fighter Command could roughly calculate when it could afford to stand down its exhausted fighter pilots for an extra hour or two. The Battle of Britain was that closely fought that a little extra pilot rest could have made a difference.

This theory puts a different slant on some of the other information Boyle released. Did it really matter if the Germans knew the RAF's order of battle, or were told the location of factories that were identified on the pre-war British topographical maps that the Germans already possessed?[8] Was the availability of these maps deception in the first place, conceived and prepared before the war with the intention of moving production elsewhere once it had started?

The information on the RAF airplane repair facilities at St. Athans and elsewhere, which Robertson attributed to Boyle, does not seem so valuable when compared to the Chain Home radar stations or the camouflaged war-production factories, especially as the hangars could be cleared if attacks were expected. Was exaggerating bomb damage to British industry better than minimizing it? Would this deter repeat attacks? Would German pilots get discouraged if they understood their bombing had cut British aircraft production in half yet the Spitfires and Hurricanes kept coming?

If it was Boyle who was behind the messages on the searchlight locations in London, were they falsified in order to throw German bombers off target when night bombing started? Churchill appears to have been at play here. Ladislas Farago, in *The Game of Foxes* — from which his source notes are missing — mentions that during the Blitz the prime minister took a direct hand in choosing what intelligence to feed the Germans, presumably through Boyle and Robertson. Farago wrote:

> Mr. Churchill's somewhat fiendish scheme was to direct the Luftwaffe from strategic areas by giving them bogus intelligence that built up expendable areas as desirable targets. He could be quite callous in selecting the latter. They included certain residential districts. This led to a violent clash between the Prime Minister and Herbert Morrison,

the Cockney statesman, in a heated Cabinet meeting. The Home Secretary, a leader of the Labour party, protested bitterly and vehemently against Churchill's choice of targets, exclaiming: "Who are we to play God?"[9]

There is no reason to disbelieve this anecdote, and it explains why three months into the Blitz it was Boyle who proposed creating the Wireless Board. It capped authority to release target information to MI5's wireless double agents at the directors of intelligence level, and would have enabled Boyle to deal with Captain Robertson without the War Cabinet, the chiefs of staff, the Home Office, or even his own fellow directors of intelligence knowing. The rule that no one was to keep written records would also spare Churchill the inevitable public opprobrium should it be found out — even long after the war — that he had a hand in determining what neighbourhoods, and beyond London, what cities would be bombed.

This may well be one of Britain's outstanding wartime secrets. Most people would not understand anyone wanting the power to decide who gets struck by lightning, but being able to give some direction to German bombers gave Churchill limited ability to save the great monuments of London like St. Paul's Cathedral, the Parliament at Westminster, Tower Bridge, and Buckingham Palace. Their loss would have been a devastating blow to public morale. These were the truly "strategic" targets that, in Churchill's eyes, at least, might have decided the war.

On June 20, 1940, three months before the bombing of England started, the House of Commons sat in secret session to hear from Churchill what he thought was in store for Britain when France surrendered, and what could be expected in the days to come. No record of the debate was kept, but the prime minister's notes for his speech survive:

> … steady continuous bombing probably rising to great intensity occasionally … our bombing incomparably superior, more precise … enemy has great preponderance numbers but their industry is much more concentrated. Utmost importance to preserve morale of people…. This supreme battle depends on the courage of the ordinary man and woman…. All depends on the Battle of Britain.[10]

Churchill had reason to expect German bombers to start attacking British cities. A month earlier, with German panzers bursting out of the Ardennes and the French government in a panic, he had ordered night bombing of the Ruhr. In a note to the French, he explained: "I have examined today with the War Cabinet and all the experts the request which you made to me last night and this morning for further fighter squadrons. We are all agreed that it is better to draw the enemy onto this island by striking at his vitals, and thus aid the common cause."[11]

Over the following weeks, RAF bombers attacked at least ten German cities with high explosive and incendiaries, always at night, and with little hope of actually hitting industrial or war-related targets. Fires were started, houses destroyed, and civilians killed. The aim, according to Churchill's note, was to provoke retaliation, and it is in this context that Arthur Owens's mid-June trip to Lisbon can be viewed. It would explain why Captain Robertson allowed him to go, even though he had been caught red-handed with the William Rolph material. It explains why references to this trip, which are contained in German sources, have been scrubbed from the MI5 records. The reports of E-186 that Owens brought to Major Ritter were intended to tempt Hitler into bombing Britain.

If the E-186 reports dealing with the locations of Bomber and Fighter Command are seen in this way, as bait, it is evident they were chosen judiciously. They were not the real nerve centres of Britain's air defences. This was RAF Uxbridge, the Operations Control Centre for No. 11 Fighter Group covering London and the Southeast. Bomber Command headquarters at High Wycombe could be lost; and so could Fighter Command headquarters at Stanmore, for these served basically planning and administrative purposes. To cripple Uxbridge, even for a day or two, when the war in the air was hot could be disastrous.[12]

This had to be coming from the prime minister. Only he could make the decision to invite German bombers onto so apparently choice a target as Stanmore, probably without mentioning it to Air Marshal Hugh Dowding, who stood to be killed. Fortunately for him, Stanmore and High Wycombe were barely touched by the Luftwaffe during the entire war, and then only by accident. Most important of all, Uxbridge was spared, making the whole episode a serendipitous triumph.[13]

As it so happened, Hitler continued to keep the Luftwaffe on a leash that only reached the docks of Britain's southern ports, hoping instead that with the defeat of France the British would see the uselessness of continuing the fight and come to terms — terms that he was prepared to make generous. Churchill chose to fight on, and in mid-August concentrated attacks on RAF airfields, radar sites, and airplane factories began. When that battle was at its height, with the RAF near the breaking point, Churchill ordered the night-bombing of Berlin. This time Hitler retaliated. On September 15, a mass raid struck London. The RAF was given the vital breather; the ordeal of Britain's cities had begun.

In fairness, bringing the horrors of war directly to the people was not done without feeling. On September 17, in his underground bunker, Churchill was given an ULTRA intercept that indicated unequivocally that the Luftwaffe had given up trying to defeat the RAF and that the threatened cross-Channel invasion was off. Relief and a sense of jubilation pervaded the group gathered around the prime minister. The Germans would continue to bomb, but the main danger had passed. As one who was there remembered:

> There was a very broad smile on Churchill's face as he lit up his massive cigar and suggested we should all take a little fresh air. An air raid was going on at the time but Churchill insisted on going outside the concrete screen at the door. I shall ever remember him in his boiler suit, cigar in his mouth, looking across the park at the now blazing buildings beyond, all the Chiefs of Staff and Menzies and myself behind him. His hands holding his long walking stick, he turned to us and growled, "We will get them for this."[14]

Churchill's vehemence surely derived from the dreadful decision-making position he had put himself in. He was an elected politician and knew full well that many would never understand him inviting German attacks on Britain as a favour to the French, and then putting bricks and stone, palaces and cathedrals, over people's homes. Farago, writing thirty years later in *The Game of Foxes*, could not resist using the pejorative *expendable* to describe the working-class areas of London that inevitably took the brunt of the bombing. Others, especially in the context of socialist Britain during the 1960s and '70s, would have been more severe.

The fact was the choices had to be made or the war was lost. Once the Luftwaffe began bombing London in earnest, it became evident that, despite the city's vast size, it could not handle it all on its own. The city had to be given a respite. Luring the Luftwaffe onto the big cities of the Midlands and onto Bristol and Liverpool was the way to go. Churchill had decided others should share the pain.

Undoubtedly, Clement Atlee, Morrison, and the other MPs in the War Cabinet were glad the responsibility fell to the prime minister. Creating a committee, the Wireless Board, outside the normal reporting channels that took responsibility for giving the Germans information "which might have the consequence of diverting their bombers to other cities and places"[15] was probably quite all right by them. Churchill had taken the added precaution of setting up Sir Findlater Stewart to take the blame should it ever be found out that the government was complicit in the bombing of Coventry, Birmingham, Manchester, and the rest. That might have been all right, too.

The XX Committee was just further cover. Usually presented as a kind of operational subcommittee to the Wireless Board, in fact it had no executive powers. It debated possible action, but could not issue orders. Its service members were junior intelligence officers who were to keep no records and share as little as possible with their bosses. Its chairman — Masterman — was a fifty-year-old Oxford teacher of pre-twentieth-century history with no military or secret service experience, and too erudite apparently to read the open literature on espionage. He had been in MI5 less than two months before being given the XX Committee job. In the context of what was going on, it is impossible not to wonder whether he had been chosen precisely for his stunning lack of qualifications.

Meanwhile, there was Robertson. He ran his double agents through the fall and spring of 1940–41 without benefit of the expertise or knowledge of the army or navy "Y" services, MI6 (VIII), or the Government Code & Cipher School. Scotland Yard had no role. Cowgill of MI6(V) looked on from afar. Liddell left it to him. Because the messages had first to be enciphered, the telegraph operators sending for SNOW and later for

TATE did not necessarily know what information they contained.[16] It was perfect; Boyle could go straight to Robertson. Given the prime minister's penchant for keeping his thumb directly on key military matters, he may even have been behind some of the double agent messages himself.

How else does one account for SNOW's message that told the Germans there were no Spitfires in Egypt? If it drew away some of the deadly FW-190s from the sky above London, it evened the odds a bit in the fight for life between the RAF and the Luftwaffe. Only Churchill, or a real spy, could have been behind that one.

Churchill, Boyle, Robertson — it was a perfect setup because it bypassed everyone else, including the chiefs of staff. It was totally secure because it needed to involve only three people. However, in answering directly to Churchill in an arrangement that circumvented the responsible ministers, it did require that Boyle and Robertson be absolutely reliable and absolutely discreet. Boyle could be depended upon because he was a long-time member of the pre-war intelligence Establishment. Robertson's credentials for Churchill's trust are not so obvious, but trusted he was.

Since Churchill did not become prime minister until May 1940, and Boyle had been supplying Robertson with air intelligence for his wireless agents for some seven months before, the idea of luring enemy bombers away from strategic targets must have been conceived much earlier, probably before the war.

Menzies's predecessor at MI6, Admiral Hugh Sinclair, had recognized as far back as 1930 that air power was likely to be decisive in the next war and, together with Boyle who was then on the intelligence staff of the Air Ministry, recruited and sent to Germany Fred Winterbotham, a thirty-three-year-old former First World War fighter pilot. It was a happy choice. Winterbotham, who had flown with the famous ace Billy Bishop, could talk the language of the skies and easily made a good impression on the Nazis. He was soon running in high political and military circles, supposedly as a junior member of the British air staff. He collected much valuable intelligence on German rearmament and advances in aircraft technology.

It seems Sinclair, finding the government of Stanley Baldwin indifferent to Winterbotham's reports, passed the information to Churchill, then sitting as a backbench MP. He could feel comfortable doing so because Churchill had been a great user of secret intelligence during the First World War and, as a former cabinet minister, was a member of the Privy Council of England. This entitled him to hear state secrets. Churchill turned this information into questions in Parliament, becoming remembered in the 1930s, thanks to Sinclair, as the Cassandra of the upcoming conflict.

The Nazis hoped that what Winterbotham learned would convince Britain that Hitler's plans for Europe were to her advantage. On his first trip to Germany in 1934, Winterbotham was given an audience with the Führer himself, who spoke passionately of the need to defeat communism and of his intention to conquer Russia. This was followed a few days later by Winterbotham having lunch with General Walter Reichenau, who described how an attack on the Soviet Union would be conducted. All of this was given to Winterbotham, evidently on Hitler's order, on the assumption that rational minds in the British government would counsel non-interference.[17]

Winterbotham's subsequent report went to Menzies, Boyle, the Foreign Office, Baldwin, and presumably to Churchill. The effect was the opposite of what Hitler wanted. It convinced Baldwin that another war with Germany was probable and that Britain had better look to its air defences. In 1935, the veteran Conservative MP Philip Cunliffe-Lister was named to the House of Lords — which put him beyond reach of questions in the House of Commons — and became Lord Swinton, the new secretary of state for Air. Britain then embarked on a secret program of air rearmament that included the go-ahead to develop the promising Spitfire fighter design and for "the construction of great shadow factories in the Midlands."[18] The organization of Fighter Command and the development of coastal radar coverage followed. Boyle was an insider to all of this.

When Boyle received the request from Robertson in the first month of the war for permission to send the Germans weather observations, he must have taken the matter up with whoever was still in the loop of Britain's secret air defence preparations. The strategy subsequently adopted by MI5 of feeding its double agents true information to pave the way for false information later was an echo of how, before the war, the Air Ministry under

Lord Swinton had pretended a free exchange of visits and technology with the Luftwaffe while hiding its most novel advances.[19] Hitler was taken in, for he forbade espionage against Britain in 1935, sticking to the ban until 1938.

Indeed, it is not beyond the realm of possibility that Owens was planted on MI5 by MI6 to establish a means of delivering deceptive messages to the Luftwaffe when the bombers started coming. The available evidence fits such a scenario, but, if true, the scheme backfired spectacularly. Owens also delivered hot intelligence to the Germans on his trips across the Channel. It should be noted, too, that Swinton, having left the Air Ministry in 1938, resurfaced in July 1940 when Churchill appointed him chairman of the Security Executive. This put him in overall charge of MI5, and the chaos that ensued when he undertook to reorganize the service during the first months of the Blitz makes it fair to wonder whether the confusion was intentional. It certainly helped hide what was going on between Boyle and Robertson.

One way or another, by the late summer of 1940, Owens was still only one double agent with only one transmitter. If German bombing was to be significantly influenced when the Luftwaffe turned from airfields to urban industry and infrastructure, more wireless double agents reporting the weather were going to be needed. The Luftwaffe was still sticking to the 1938 League of Nations resolution that only allowed the bombing of military targets in built-up areas if they were identifiable. The extra distance to the Midlands and Britain's western ports increased the risk. Churchill could not hope to draw the Luftwaffe off London to other distant cities without it having up-to-date data on local weather conditions, especially visibility. The German bomb aimers were supposed to be able to see what they were doing.

Major Ritter, by extraordinary coincidence, rose to the occasion when he dispatched the *Lena* spies, whose capture was so certain.

The question is: Did the Abwehr somehow know beforehand that Ritter would be playing perfectly into Churchill's strategy. It cannot be answered. Theoretically, Canaris could guess that the British would want to take the pressure off London, but in the end, it was Hitler's decision to expand the bombing campaign. Canaris's proper response would have been to try to provide more and better weather information to the Luftwaffe. It would save airmen's lives.

Experience with Arthur Owens had shown that MI5 was willing to allow a wireless double agent to send the weather. It was just a matter of providing the British with more such agents. The pre-mission wireless chat and poorly forged identity papers ensured that those Ritter did send would be caught. Some were bound to have their transmitters played back under control. Caroli and Schmidt, SUMMER and TATE, were used in just this way, with the bonus that in addition to the weather, they also sent bomb-damage reports. MI5 understood them to be pre-invasion spies in an operation code-named Unternehmen *Lena*. On the other side of the Channel, Ritter had a different name for it: Unternehmen *Isar*.[20]

One might argue that the intelligence triumvirate of Churchill, Menzies, and Boyle could more easily have dealt up front with MI5, but the bottom line was, those in the organization could not be trusted. MI6 could fairly guess that MI5 had been penetrated by the Germans and the Soviets if it considered the Registry fire in September 1940 and the episode involving William Rolph and the secret list of right-wingers he provided to Owens.

The Rolph incident was the trap door for Vernon Kell, MI5's chief since the First World War. Churchill and Menzies would have been familiar with PMS2, the shadowy organization set up by Kell during the First World War to disrupt the Labour Movement. They were insiders themselves of that political era, and would have been aware of PMS2's persistence underground since then, and of its links to right-wing extremists in the upper classes. It would have been possible, then, that Rolph's list included the Nazi-leaning Edward VIII, forced to abdicate in 1936 and banished to the Bahamas with his American paramour, Wallis Simpson. Rolph had been a key player in the early days of PMS2, and the fact that MI5 was still using him, and that he had been caught trying to sell names to the Nazis, was surely reason enough to consider MI5 compromised. Churchill was correct to fire Kell and to send in Lord Swinton to clean house.

Then there was the Registry fire. It would have been a deaf and dumb intelligence officer, surely, who would have not instantly thought *sabotage!* The Registry was beyond comparison the most valuable counter-intelligence asset the British had. Checking names against its index was the most efficient way to keep individuals of known fascist or communist sympathies out of sensitive government or military positions. In time of war, this was vital. The destruction of the Registry card index would have smelled of sabotage to MI6 as strongly as the smoke from the fire.

No documents have been found to show it, but the Security Executive (Swinton) must have ordered an investigation. This could have been done by Scotland Yard, and, if so, certain things would have immediately caught notice. First, the decision to photograph the card index: this obviously created the possibility of illicit copies being made. When it was found after the fire that the copying had been done badly, with many pictures ruined, and the rest of the index in no state to be used for many months, suspicion must have sharpened. Victor Rothschild, who had overseen the copying, would have been looked at very, very carefully.

Inquiries would have soon linked Rothschild with Guy Burgess, and with a particularly suggestive result: The "D" in Section D of MI6 where Burgess worked stood for "destruction." It was the sabotage division of MI6 run by Major Laurence Grand. Further inquiry would have turned up Burgess's communist past, for he had been originally accepted into MI6 by no less than MI6's counter-espionage chief Valentine Vivian, who believed him when he told him he had left his Cambridge communist days behind.[21] As for Burgess himself, making arson look like something else was part of the Section D syllabus.

It was not a smoking gun, but Burgess, in fact, was kicked out of Special Operations Executive (SOE),[22] the successor to Section D, but nothing so direct was done with Rothschild. If the Registry fire *was* sabotage, and Rothschild *was* a suspect, evidence needed to be collected. Moreover, the proper counter-espionage procedure under such circumstances was not to jump too quickly, but to wait and watch. The rapid and uncontrolled expansion of MI5 in 1940 would have made it easy for Scotland Yard or MI6 to insert an undercover agent of their own. This was exactly what Admiral Canaris was doing at the time in Germany. The Abwehr was primarily an overseas espionage agency, but it had informants in the main military and Nazi secret services. MI6 had much reason to be doing the same.

Liddell, however, would have been the prime suspect. He was the one who gave the job of copying the index to a newcomer to MI5 rather than to a trusted staff member. It was a clerical task that surely did not require the oversight of a Cambridge-educated scientist. Some months after Burgess was let go from SOE, Liddell approached the head of MI5's F Division (counter-subversion) with the proposal that its chief, John Curry, take Burgess on. He told Curry that Burgess had been a communist at one time but had "completely abandoned" his past. His "extraordinary knowledge," however, could be useful against Britain's Communist party. Curry did not bite.[23]

It is not known if this attempt to bring Burgess into MI5 got back to MI6, but Liddell would have definitely been under deep suspicion anyway. It would have been remembered that he had been part of the transfer to MI5 of Scotland Yard's remnant anti-communist section in 1931, after it had been found to have been penetrated by the Soviets. In a very small world where nobody could be absolutely sure of anyone's loyalty, this, plus Liddell being seen with Burgess in the Reform Club,[24] would surely have been enough for MI6 to want to deal with MI5 very delicately. Distrust was surely a key factor in MI6 taking over the Radio Security Service, in controlling the distribution of ISOS, and in developing its own Registry. This reorganization was completed by May 1941.

That May also marked the end of the Blitz. The bombers stopped coming. A month later, Boyle transferred to SOE as director of security and intelligence — on the face of it a demotion. Menzies would have pushed for the move. SOE was expanding rapidly, but the destruction of the Registry made it impossible to vet the people being recruited. This was an open invitation to the enemy, both fascist and communist. Boyle was in position to be Menzies's eyes and ears in the new organization.

Meanwhile, with few bombers to deceive, the XX Committee became a sideshow of largely hare-brained deception schemes of little consequence to the war. The same can be said of Robertson's B1A section and the remaining double agents like Williams and Schmidt.[25]

Ever since Ian Colvin's book *Chief of Intelligence* (1951), there has been much talk but little hard evidence to prove that MI6's Stewart Menzies and Canaris had been in contact with each other. The MI5 files reviewed for this book settle the matter: on his two trips to Germany in the spring of 1941, the mysterious Walter Dicketts (CELERY) had been Menzies's emissary.

Consider the following.

Based on documents that survive in the MI5 files, in the early spring of 1940, Owens chanced upon Dicketts in a pub, where, during casual conversation, they mutually discovered their respective careers in secret intelligence, Dicketts for a branch of Air Intelligence during the First World War and Owens for MI5 in the current one. Owens had earlier come upon Sam McCarthy in the same way, and Dicketts, like McCarthy, accepted his offer to join him in working for the Germans.

Like any conscientious secret agent in enemy territory, Owens was constantly trolling for traitors. Both men had presented themselves as disgruntled down-and-outs ready to sell out their country for money — just the types Owens was looking for. He certainly found such a person in William Rolph, who would have been a great catch if Owens had gotten away with it. McCarthy and Dicketts, however, were planted on him, by MI5 in the first instance — as we have seen — but, without MI5 knowing, by MI6 in the second.

According to Robertson's and Liddell's notes from that time, they saw Dicketts merely as a nuisance individual who had cropped up unexpectedly, but whose previous experience "in a branch of Air Intelligence" could be useful in MI5. Due to the fact that the director of air intelligence did not see him as a security risk, and after some discreet inquiries, he was taken on.[27]

At his second-last meeting with Major Ritter in Antwerp before the 1940 invasion of Holland and France, Owens told the German he had acquired an informant in MI5.[26] This was Dicketts.

Walter Arthur Charles Dicketts, however, was no former desk-bound intelligence officer shuffling paper, and never had been. The forty-one-year-old Londoner was a globe-trotting adventurer who had been a teenage spy during the First World War. In 1915, Mansfield Cumming's MI1(c) — the predecessor to MI6 — had arranged for him to be loaned to the French as a messenger boy in the Arsenal in Paris, and he had managed to steal specification drawings for the famed French "75" field gun. His spy career continued until the end of the war, and probably after, when he went off to roam the Far East, followed in the 1920s by a spin around England, France, and the United States as a racing-car driver. He was a compulsive con man, impersonator, and bigamist, who changed identities — and wives — like ties. He took only gin, straight. He was a real-life

James Bond; except that he married the women he made love to, four of them anyway, including a fifteen-year-old.[27]

During his interrogation at Latchmere House in 1943, German embassy employee Hans Ruser recalled that when one day he was about to leave for the airport at Barcelona with the diplomatic bag, the Abwehr counter-espionage officer at Lisbon KO, a Major Kramer, asked that he take an Englishman with him who Canaris "was interested in." During the drive across Spain, Ruser naturally probed his passenger to find out how he had caught the attention of the chief of Germany's secret intelligence service. He pestered him to the point that Dicketts finally told him he was a "leftist" on a peace mission. Then, one evening over drinks, he admitted to being a member of the British Secret Service, later (after sobering up, perhaps) urging Ruser not to tell a soul. This much Dicketts revealed to MI5 upon his return to England in March, minus any mention of Ruser or Canaris. It would appear he was covering himself for his indiscretion.

Ruser further disclosed that he met Dicketts again on the latter's second trip to Lisbon, and that Dicketts was on his way to Germany a second time. This had been withheld from MI5 by MI6, inviting the deduction that Dicketts was on a mission for the latter that the former was not to know about.

One can make an educated guess as to why, in the spring of 1940, MI6 would have wanted to put its own agent on to Owens. The ciphers he said the Germans had given him were too simple to be believable, so there was a game going on somewhere. And was Owens himself legit? MI6 quickly had that answer when Owens recruited Dicketts as a spy. What else was going on could only be determined by having Dicketts get inside MI5 to have a look. That was accomplished, too.

MI6 may have had another incentive for these actions. The kidnapping of Stevens and Best at Venlo had disabled two of MI6's main links to anti-Nazi elements in the German army and Abwehr. If Dicketts could one day go along with Owens on one of his trips to see his German controller, there might be an opportunity to re-establish contact. MI6 would not want MI5 in on that. It had not shared with its sister service the fact that Venlo had been preceded by talks with German army generals at the highest level.

As for Owens, he must have been on top of the world when he was sent to Portugal to meet Ritter in June 1940, just after squirming out of the dangerous situation caused by McCarthy ratting on him. Robertson had accepted that he wasn't a double-crosser, despite the evidence against him over the IP List. Instead of being arrested, he was sent on a mission to Lisbon to explain away the failed North Sea rendezvous, and presumably bearing MI5's usual "chicken feed." As so often before, he also had secret intelligence of his own in the form of spectacular information on Britain's air defences, from a spy inside MI5, no less — Dicketts, a.k.a. E-186. Owens promised Ritter that he would bring this incredible new agent with him on a future visit so that Ritter could size him up himself.[28]

In February 1941, when Owens and Dicketts finally set out for Lisbon, Britain was losing the war. The bombing of British cities was horrendous, and German submarines were crippling British shipping. Despite spreading out the bombing and Churchill's public bravado, the war was not going to last too much longer. Dicketts letting slip to Hans Ruser during their drive across Spain that he was a "British secret service" agent on a peace mission rings true. It also explains why Owens abruptly quit the double-agent business without being able to coherently tell his MI5 bosses why. During Ritter's initial meeting with both agents, he discovered, surely to his shock and horror, that Dicketts was no cheap traitor.

We do not know exactly how he caught on. According to Ritter's 1972 memoir, he had greeted both men with skepticism. Owens got defensive. Then, prodded by Dicketts, he said he had been authorized by MI5 to offer Ritter $200,000 in gold if he would come back to England with them. If true, it gave away absolutely that both Owens and Dicketts were working for the British. It is unlikely that Ritter would at that point have allowed either of them to leave Portugal.[29]

It may be that it was at this point, in Owen's presence, that Dicketts disclosed that he was a member of British secret service on a peace mission. Ritter's immediate show of interest would have shocked Owens. He thought he had been working for the Nazis. Worse, Dicketts might be telling the truth, which meant he was undercover in MI5, and had been all along. Dicketts would therefore know for sure that Owens was a two-time traitor; back in Britain, it might not be jail this time around, but the hangman. When he did return to London, Owens certainly behaved like a frightened man, and did all he could to discredit Dicketts.

There is separate evidence that Stewart Menzies, with or without Churchill's knowledge, was behind this overture to the Abwehr — a month before Owens and Dicketts set out, if Dusko Popov is to be believed.

As MI5's newest double agent, Popov was summoned to meet with Menzies and (partially repeating an earlier quotation) was told by him:

> I want to know much more about everybody who is intimately connected with Canaris, and also with Dohnányi and Oster....
>
> It may be helpful if I explain the reasons behind this request. We know that Canaris, Dohnányi and Oster are not dyed-in-the-wool Nazis. They are what might be termed loyal officers, or patriotic Germans. In 1938 Churchill had a conversation with Canaris. Unofficially — he wasn't in office then. Churchill came to the conclusion that Canaris was a sort of catalyst for the anti-Hitler elements in Germany. That's why I want to know more about the people he attracts. Eventually, I may want to resume the conversation that Churchill initiated. In that event, I must be in a position to evaluate the strength of those around Canaris.
>
> I nodded my understanding. Menzies was contemplating a dialogue with Canaris or those close to him with a view to ousting Hitler.[30]

Popov's anecdote, with his conclusion that a dialogue was being sought with Canaris, was published in 1974 when there was no serious suggestion anywhere that Britain had asked for the Abwehr's help in mid-war.

Indeed, Dicketts identifying himself as being on a mission for the British secret service explains why he was not, to use Masterman's words in *The Double-Cross System*, "painfully executed by the Germans in Germany." Instead, on that first trip to Germany he met with Dr. Schacht, a long-time opponent of the regime, and with the "Baron," Canaris's mentor and closest confidant, and returned safely to England with word that "secret peace talks" were possible. Menzies, remembering the many warnings about Hitler received from the Abwehr and German civilian officials before the war, would have taken this to mean that despite Hitler's successes Canaris and others around him were still hoping to overthrow the Nazis.[31]

Menzies sent Dicketts back to Portugal in May, and he went on to Germany a second time, without MI5 being told of it (then or after). Presumably, he brought with him the British response, though what this was is unknown. It probably touched on the fact that Britain could not hope to carry on alone much longer. If the United States did not soon take up the cause, Britain would have no choice but come to terms with Hitler.

That may have been too awful to contemplate for Churchill, but it was infinitely worse for Canaris and others in the German army opposed to the Nazis. Hitler had just brutally attacked and conquered Yugoslavia. Russia was next. If Britain pulled out of the war, the Nazis would never be budged from power, whether Hitler was dead or alive.

Who apart from Ritter was at this second meeting is unknown, but it may have included Canaris. From March to August, the messages pertaining to his movements that were being intercepted and read by MI6 (but not by MI5) show him to have been skipping from one Abwehr office to another in southeastern Europe in connection with the invasion and occupation of Yugoslavia. The messages for late May and the month of June, however, are missing from the collection, suggesting that they were either sent in a more secure cipher or MI6 has withheld them.[32] Either way, the targeted secrecy indicates Canaris was involved in something of great importance during that period.

We know what that was. During his travels, he took time to visit Madame Szymanska in Berne. He had saved her from the Russians in Poland and had set her up in Switzerland, where she opened up contact with the MI6 office in Geneva. After the war, she told how in conversation he had casually mentioned that Hitler was about to invade Russia. This information she had in turn passed to her MI6 contacts.[33]

What happened seems clear. Britain had sent out a distress call. Canaris had replied through Dicketts and Madame Szymanska with a comforting reply, "Hold on. Help is coming." The reprieve was Operation *Barbarossa*, Hitler's ill-advised invasion of the Soviet Union.

Scarcely three weeks later, on July 15, a Spaniard who could not speak English turned up at the British embassy in Lisbon with a spy's questionnaire indicating that Japan was planning to attack British possessions in the Far East. A few weeks later, Popov was given a similar questionnaire suggesting that Hawaii and the U.S. Pacific Fleet were threatened.

As noted at the beginning, Popov's questionnaire shows signs of having been put together quickly, not in Berlin, but in Lisbon, at KO Portugal. It was a rush job, composed within days of the German intercept services learning that Roosevelt and Churchill were about to meet by ship in the Atlantic.

One must also note that Canaris would have had on his desk decrypts of the SS messages dealing with the exterminations in Russia. They would have been small in number compared to those on the same subject he was getting from the Abwehr field commandos attached to the armies. It must have made sickening reading. Since he had seen to it that the SS messages were in simple ciphers, he could be reasonably certain that Churchill was reading them, too.

Now one must flash back to the beginning of this sequence of events, to the end of January 1941, just before Dicketts set off for Lisbon and then Germany the first time. An informal talk took place between Churchill, a few of those closest to him, and Harry Hopkins, President Roosevelt's principal civilian adviser. Hopkins had come over to England to see how bad things were and to sound out Churchill as to Britain's chances of survival. The real bread and butter of war planning occurred at such meetings, where records were not kept. In this case, one of Churchill's junior secretaries was present. He noted the pith of their conversation in his diary.

They sat after dinner in a circle in the Great Hall at Chequers, with only Churchill standing, leaning on the fireplace mantel. The prime minister declaimed at some length about the need for the United States to get into the war against Germany, while acknowledging there was little appetite for it in the U.S. Congress. Hopkins then had this to say about helping Britain:

> The important element in the situation was the boldness
> of the President, who would lead opinion and not follow
> it, who was convinced that if England lost, America, too,
> would be encircled and beaten. He would use his powers
> if necessary; he would not scruple to interpret existing

laws in the furtherance of his aim.... He did not want war
... but he would not shrink from war.[34]

Hopkins added that if America were to come in, "the incident would be with Japan."

The question then is: Did this somehow get back to Canaris? Did Menzies, on Churchill's order, send Dicketts to Germany in February to sound out the Abwehr chief, and then again in May to deliver the vital intelligence: "Japan, then Germany!"? We will never know.

Canaris was famous, among those who knew him, for his creative solutions to intractable problems. So was Churchill. Menzies of MI6 was not short of imagination either. Maybe, just maybe, Popov's Pearl Harbor questionnaire was an idea born of the three of them.

In any case, giving the president of the United States the excuse and the means to get into a fight with Japan saved Britain and, as a bonus, saved Russia. On December 7, 1941, when Japanese planes dived on the battleships of the Pacific Fleet, the war for the Allies was as good as won.

EPILOGUE

A Rogue Octogenarian

They had mostly died off by 1969, those members of the Wireless Board who knew of the Pearl Harbor questionnaire and of Churchill's attempt to influence the German bombing of England. One of the first to go was Guy Liddell, dead of a heart attack in 1958. Stewart Menzies died in 1968 and with him those MI6 secrets that he never shared. Commodore Boyle was gone, too, and with him his private knowledge of what really had gone on between MI5 and MI6. Left were the younger men who attended those meetings of 1941, meetings that were so secret that the participants were not given the minutes: Ewen Montagu, the recording secretary, and "TAR" Robertson of B1A, both in their late fifties. It was not going to be long before the secrets of the Wireless Board would be secret forever.

Enter John Cecil Masterman, former chairman of the XX Committee. At the time seventy-eight, he could look back over a long but colourless career as an Oxford academic and see that his finest hours were during wartime, when, so he thought, he had carried England's counter-intelligence banner against Hitler's Huns. He decided it was time to tell the world. He proposed to publish the report he submitted at the end of the war.

Reaction from the government was swift and firm: *No!* He was not to seek a publisher. He was still under the Official Secrets Act. *No, no, no.*

Masterman, however, was not prepared to take no for an answer.

The primary objector was Dick White,[1] retired after a postwar career that had included stints as director of both MI5 and MI6, but serving now as a special advisor to the government on intelligence. He had joined MI5 in the late 1930s, served as deputy to Guy Liddell of B Division, and in late 1940 was instrumental in the recruitment of Masterman.

Masterman was given the XX Committee chairmanship at the outset, while White went on to other duties in B-division, none of which required him to attend the meetings of the Wireless Board and the XX Committee, or to be told the details of Dusko Popov's Pearl Harbor questionnaire.

White knew, however, that the "double-cross system" had been a flop. If there was not a postwar internal paper somewhere in the secret service archives saying so, his wartime predecessor as MI6 chief, Stewart Menzies, would have passed along the basic message verbally: MI5 had been inept, amateurish, and definitely penetrated by the Germans and the Soviets. White might have reddened when told how silly it was to have thought that the Abwehr was genuinely using First World War ciphers; that it would allow its spies to communicate with one another; that it did not know how to equip them properly; and so on. On the other hand, perhaps he had known. The wartime documents in which he features indicate a well-travelled, well-informed person with a keen mind.

Masterman was the opposite. In his fifties in the 1940s, he was the quintessential Oxford/Cambridge don. A bachelor, he lived with his mother or in rooms at his club or the university, sealed like a sardine from the rest of the world. He taught modern history, where the choice of courses did not come closer than the 1880s on the theory that present-day events could not be profitably studied until at least a half-century had elapsed. Cricket and all-male dinner parties, where obscure ideas were brandished like rapiers, were his chief recreations, and like many of his type of that era, he had written a detective novel. Otherwise, his contribution to learning was like a mist on the Thames.

He had been brought into MI5 in late 1940 without any background whatsoever in the art of espionage, with little previous interest in contemporary affairs, and with little direct experience with people outside his class.[2] He had ignored warnings that war was imminent while at the University of Freiburg in 1914, and spent the next four years in spartan but comfortable internment at Camp Ruhleben outside Berlin. The life there, amidst other male prisoners of culture and privilege, was not unlike his normal life at Oxford.

In his autobiography, he comes across as a thoroughly artificial person — vain, pleasure-seeking, and self-indulgent. The type was much satirized in the plays and novels of the 1920s and '30s. It is possible that he had been chosen to head the XX Committee for these very qualities; he was not the sort to ever dream that MI6 and the Abwehr might secretly be co-operating.

There is no fool like an old fool, White may have thought as he turned down Masterman's request. He knew his claims in his 1945 report on MI5's double agents were hollow in terms of the "achievements" that Masterman put such stock in. These primarily were the deception operations through 1942 and 1943 that dangled false threats of cross-Channel attacks before the Germans, culminating in using double agents to try to deceive them as to the time and place of the June 6, 1944, Allied invasion of Normandy. White had much reason to doubt the success of any of this.[3]

More delicate were the descriptions in Masterman's "B1A Sectional Report" dealing with luring the Luftwaffe onto residential areas of London and onto the cities of the Midlands. His original report has vanished from MI5's archives, but there is good evidence it covered this topic. MI5's in-house history of the war, John Curry's *The Security Service*, confers on the XX Committee major though undeserved credit (see Chapter 3) for getting the permissions necessary to have MI5's double agents send the Germans daily weather reports and true information, "diverting their bombers to other cities or places."[4] As this had been ongoing, Masterman undoubtedly went into some detail.

The British public knew nothing of any of this and the threatened disclosure could not have come at a worse time. In the late 1960s, left-wing militancy in Britain was on the march in the unions and universities, and there was widespread hostility against the political Establishment, fuelled by the example set by the student protests in the United States against the war in Vietnam. A homegrown example of workers being sacrificed would have been greedily seized upon.[5]

There was also the very human concern that twenty-five years was not a long time for those who had lost their homes and loved ones. No matter how well it could be argued that directing the bombers onto residential areas of London and onto other cities had been necessary, many would still feel a keen sense of betrayal to learn that their own leaders were partially the cause of their personal tragedies.

Masterman persisted, later claiming he was motivated by the desire to use the story of MI5's wartime double-cross triumphs to help restore public confidence in the British secret services, wounded by the recent defection to the Soviet Union of Kim Philby, a senior officer with MI6. This had come on top of the defections of Guy Burgess and Donald Maclean in 1951. White and Whitehall could hardly try to dampen Masterman's tell-all zeal by admitting that MI5 itself had provided ample soil for traitors to grow in.

It was true. The suspicions generated by the Registry fire in 1940 had coalesced once more around Guy Liddell, this time over his possible role in the escape of Burgess and Maclean, to which were added new accusations that Blunt and Liddell had been covert communist fellow-travellers. In the 1950s it was enough to block Liddell's chances of reaching the top in MI5, but in 1964 White received positive confirmation that Blunt and Burgess had been co-conspirators. By then, being dead, Liddell did not matter, but Blunt did. He was art adviser to Her Majesty and a respected veteran of MI5. To avoid the disastrous publicity that would result by arresting him, it was decided — with government approval — to confront him, but to offer to keep his treachery secret in exchange for his detailed confession.[6]

So the answer to Masterman was still *no*, but there was no explaining the real reasons. The Oxford don is not to be admired for the action he then took. He leaked his report to Ladislas Farago, an American author of a number of well-researched books on the Second World War.[7] He was then in the process of writing a comprehensive history of the German secret intelligence service and apparently contacted Masterman in the course of his work.

Farago was to give Masterman considerable credit for his accomplishments. Farago's *The Game of Foxes* (1972) goes on at some length about the messages sent to the Germans by MI5's first double agent, Arthur Owens, in the late summer of 1940. These described the effects of German bombing: "Wimbledon hit … hundreds of houses, railway station and factories destroyed at Morton-Malden … private dwellings damaged at Kenley … Biggin Hill hit … Air Ministry moving soon to Harrogate." And so on. And then:

On the 19th, he began to transmit a series of reports rec-
ommending targets for the raiders. The first directed them
to a munitions plant and aircraft factory at Seighton....

None of these messages was, of course, written by
Owens. He had no part in the collection of the information they contained. All of them were concocted in MI5
where the Double-Cross organization was beginning to
gain its stride under the management of John Cecil Masterman, now a major "specially employed." But if the British themselves produced JOHNNY's reports, what was to
be gained by giving the enemy such detailed, pinpointed
intelligence about his handiwork?

This was the first attempt — feeble as yet — to gain a
measure of control over the Luftwaffe's selection of targets by manipulating the damage reports beamed to the
Germans by double agents.... It was to become highly
effective and was used broadly with a degree of ruthlessness under Mr. Churchill's personal supervision.[8]

Ruthlessness may not be too strong a word if applied to deliberately
drawing German bombers onto factory targets embedded in densely
packed residential areas.

Farago clearly indicates that he was getting his information from
Masterman's *The Double-Cross System*, before it was published, spending
several more paragraphs lauding the XX Committee's "cruel responsibility"
of having to carry the "burden" of giving the Germans true information so
that there would be no suspicion of fakery when the double agents SNOW
and SUMMER sent messages designed to steer the bombers onto targets of
British selection, including Coventry. Masterman could not have bragged
about it better, except that he never did. There were only two mild allusions
to directing German bombers in the book version of *The Double-Cross System* when it came out in 1972. Evidently, much more was in Masterman's
manuscript when Farago saw it, but was deleted before it went to print.[9]

There had been a deal, and here is how we know.

In his preface in *The Double Cross System*, Masterman wrote that the
book was the report on the double-cross work performed by the British,

a report he was asked to write at war's end by MI5 director-general David Petrie, which is consistent with the after-action reports that were asked of all section heads. He said that he started it early in July 1945, and completed it in mid-August. This is a half-truth. All but the first page of Chapter 2 and half of Chapter 3, plus bits and pieces here and there, have been lifted word for word from a lengthy essay in the MI5 "SNOW" files entitled "SNOW, BISCUIT, CHARLIE, CELERY, SUMMER." The last page of this nine-page case summary of some six thousand–plus words is missing, so the author is unknown, but the first page is date-stamped 23 April 1946. Its document number — 1803a — also positions it in the file in that month and year.[10]

Obviously, Masterman did not write this paper. He only joined MI5 in the last two months of the 1939–40 period it covers, and if he had been called back after leaving the service to do the very considerable research needed to write it, he would have surely said so. The most likely author was Major John Gwyer of B1B (Analysis). He is everywhere to be found in the MI5 files, for it was his job to look at as much as he could, see how it connected, and write reports. The two documents in the file on either side of Doc. 1803a are from him. He could only be as accurate as the available information, however, for this particular summary overlooks the trip Owens made to Lisbon in June 1940, and accepts Robertson's incorrect conclusion that it was Ritter that McCarthy saw in Lisbon that July. Otherwise, it largely reflects events as they are to be derived from the pertinent documents that remain in the "SNOW" files.[11]

Clearly, a deal had been struck. It was probably handled by White. In exchange for dropping the bomb-target material, Masterman appears to have been offered a document that more comprehensively tells the story of the 1939–40 double agents, giving him the basis of a book even more attractive to publishers. Masterman agreed, for he certainly would not have got Doc. 1803a otherwise. The question remains: When did this occur?

One must try to puzzle things out from the available hard evidence.

There seems to be no certainty that Farago had access to the "SNOW files" as he claimed. In the first place, it is unlikely anyone then in MI5 would have allowed it, given that he was an uncontrollable foreigner and already a well-known popular writer on wartime espionage. Second, there appears to be nothing about SNOW in *Game of Foxes* that he could not have got from the Abwehr files he discovered or from contact with Masterman.

His description of the other 1939–40 double agents can be traced back to previously published sources, especially Lord Jowitt's *Some Were Spies*, and to his interview with Owens's wartime German controller, Nikolaus Ritter. His research had led him to the captured German records section of the National Archives in Washington, where he stumbled (as did this writer) upon microfilmed documents pertaining to the agents Ast Hamburg had been running in Britain. The Hamburg-to-Berlin message of September 18, 1939, conveying A-3504's report on radar probably convinced him that this A-3504 was a genuine German spy operating in England. By finding and interviewing Ritter in 1969–70, Farago learned his identity — Arthur Owens.[12]

Advance copies of *The Game of Foxes* were released sometime in 1971, and a tentative publishing date of January 14, 1972, was set. These releases mark at least one sure moment when the British authorities learned what was in Farago's book,[13] and they would have been appalled. Not only was there the stuff about controlling German bombing, but by revealing that the secret of radar had been sprung before the Battle of Britain, Farago showed that MI5 had been decisively duped by the Abwehr from the outset. There must have been an instant scramble to get someone to Washington to see what records he had found.

It would have been a rueful awakening. The Abwehr files Farago accessed were from Nebenstelle Bremen, and had been captured by the British army when it entered that city in 1945. They included twenty-two folders containing hundreds of original messages from spies operating in Britain. When eventually they were delivered to London, they vanished into some secret cellar, never again to be seen. However, before being sent away, they had been loaned to the U.S. naval base at Bremen to be sifted through for anything of American interest. The navy microfilmed the lot.[14]

Farago's disclosures about Owens reporting on radar and giving bomb-target information at the behest of MI5 suddenly got infinitely worse. The evidence was in the archives in Washington. It all could be proven.

How White responded can only be guessed at. If the deletions and additions proposed for Masterman's manuscript had not already gone forward, they certainly did so now. Masterman was to claim in his autobiography that he had nothing to do with these revisions — did not even know what they were — but did admit he had lined up Yale University Press as publisher. Masterman's revised *The Double-Cross System* came out within weeks of Farago's *The Game of Foxes*, both without endnotes, unusual for Farago in that his earlier books had been heavily documented.[15] So far so good. The two books would compete with one another and the scholarly community in Britain could be counted upon to rally around one of their own. Masterman's book was devoid even of a bibliography, whereas Farago's went on for eight pages and included the pre-1939 espionage classics of Colonel Walter Nicolai, Henry Landau, and Sir Basil Thomson. Masterman credited only his own ideas, fresh-minted like gold sovereigns entirely from his experiences on the XX Committee. The wonder of it is, with the exception of the sporadic pooh-poohing from the likes of maverick Oxford historian A.P. Taylor and veteran counter-intelligence officer David Mure, *The Double-Cross System* came to be swallowed whole. Farago's book was essentially forgotten; Masterman's became celebrated.

Colonel Nicolai, Germany's spymaster of the First World War, wrote in *The German Secret Service* (1924) that a country at war must first and foremost win the battles for public opinion at home. Britain was at war[16] — the Cold War — and the battles now were about winning or losing world opinion. White was dealing with a rogue octogenarian determined to betray his oath of secrecy for a few rays of sunlight. It is hard not to be sympathetic with how he decided to handle it. The idea of class struggle promoted by the Comintern (Communist International) in the 1920s and '30s still cast its shadow over British workers and students in the 1960s. After Kim Philby's defection, further damage to Britain's image at home and abroad was to be avoided at all costs. Taking advantage of an old man's vainglory[17] by allowing him to publish what was essentially an untrue story was a reasonable tactic under the circumstances.

There was unexpected collateral damage.

When *The Double-Cross System* hit the bookstores, it was found to contain the story of Popov's Pearl Harbor questionnaire. The XX Committee had had little to do with it, but Masterman put it in anyway, along with the veiled accusation that the U.S. government of 1941 had failed to act on a clear warning that the Pacific Fleet was in danger. This played directly into suspicions that had been running for years in and out of Congress that President Roosevelt had sacrificed the Pacific Fleet in order to get into Churchill's war with Germany. This was an especially sensitive issue in the late 1960s, because the United States was in the process of losing the most unpopular war in its history — Vietnam. And it was another president's war.[18]

The Tet Offensive of 1968, when the North Vietnamese attacked the Americans in Hue, was a defeat for them, but a bigger loss for the United States. Support at home for the war collapsed. There were antiwar marches across the land. Draft-dodgers fleeing to Canada became heroes. The "military-industrial complex," the CIA, and the U.S. Armed Forces were vilified by young Americans in their teens and twenties facing compulsory military service. Vietnam had begun as a police action under President John F. Kennedy, but had escalated into a full-scale war involving all the armed services under his successor, Lyndon B. Johnson. It was never formally declared by Congress; it was a White House war.

One can never know how it would have affected the nation if it had been confirmed then that Roosevelt had read Popov's questionnaire, and had allowed the attack on Pearl Harbor to go ahead anyway. The American authorities who knew it was true were not taking any chances. With files bulging with documents that proved Popov's questionnaire did make it to the proper decision-makers, the FBI sat on them and took the blame. J. Edgar Hoover was still head of the Bureau, so the decision was his.

Again, it looks like mischief by Masterman. Because of its importance, White would surely have read the revised version of *The Double-Cross System* before it was cleared for publication. It is hard to believe he would have allowed the two pages about the questionnaire and its printing if he had seen them. But the manuscript was being published in the United States, so Masterman could well have added a few last-minute pages of text. Farago's previous book, *The Broken Seal*, had been about Pearl Harbor, but he had not come up with an item so delicious. Given what we now know of his character, Masterman may have put it in his own book just to show Farago a thing or two.

Hoover died of a heart attack on May 2, 1972. His parting gift to the nation was yielding to whatever damage to his reputation was going to incur because of the Popov questionnaire. It was considerable, mean, and went on for years. He must have given very firm instructions, for the FBI made only token efforts to defend him while holding on to the documents that would have cleared his name. However, the fire lit by Masterman never reached the Oval Office.

Hoover would have been content with that.

APPENDIX
The Historical Context

Throughout much of the eighteenth and nineteenth centuries, Britain and France were the traditional European rivals, going to war against each other over their lucrative colonies in the Americas and Africa and over which of the two would emerge as the dominate power in Western Europe. The German-speaking people of central Europe, though numerous, remained on the sidelines, for they were broken up among a number of smaller countries, the largest being Prussia in the north and Austria in the south, the former taking in much of what is now Poland and the latter some of what is now the Balkans.

Beginning in the late nineteenth century, and led by an inspired Prussian politician, Otto von Bismarck, these various German-speaking fragments moved together to form two large federations, by 1871 becoming Austria in the south and the new Germany in the north. Germany was the more powerful by virtue of Prussia's military traditions and because some of the smaller states it absorbed were long-established centres of industry and commerce. Britain and France were suddenly faced with a new and very competent rival in the competition for colonies, world trade, and overseas resources. An armed clash between the British and French empires and upstart Germany became inevitable.

Whatever the immediate causes of the First World War (1914–18), the larger general cause was the perceived need by Britain and France to blunt Germany's aspirations, both on the Continent and worldwide. It was a war of economic rivalry, pure and simple, and Britain and France achieved their core war aims when the defeated Germany was deprived of its colonies, subjected to reparations that crippled its economy, and saw the territories it occupied with Austria in Eastern Europe returned to the native peoples. An independent Poland, Czechoslovakia, Hungary, and Yugoslavia were thus created.

All this, combined with an economy deeply wounded by the world-wide Great Depression, made the German people easy prey when a fringe political party in the early 1930s promised to restore the economy and regain some of Germany's territorial losses. Hitler had much public support when he moved at the end of the decade to annex part of Czecho-slovakia and conquer Poland.

The new Germany that emerged after 1871 had been quick to embrace new technology. The American Civil War (1861–64) had demonstrated that railways were a hugely effective way to move large armies, and the rifled musket made the Napoleonic tactic of two lines of stand-up soldiers firing at one another mutual suicide. During the Franco-Prussian War (1870–71), the Germans surprised the weary French foot soldiers by arriving for battle by rail, hence well-rested, and by being faster to adapt to the tactics required by the new breech-loading rifles that allowed a man to fire while lying prone.

Forty years later, during the First World War, British and Russian generals demonstrated how little attention they had been paying to these and other advances in weaponry by sending thousands of soldiers directly into the muzzles of German bolt-action rifles and machine guns. They were cut down in swaths, and as the officers were 90 percent derived from the upper classes, this shook the confidence of the people in those they had always assumed to be their betters. In Russia, this led directly to the 1917 Revolution, which saw the execution of the czar, the purging of the aristocracy, and the creation of the first totally socialist state.

To grasp why the new "Union of Soviet Socialist Republics" was so successful in persuading some Britons to turn traitor and become commu-nist spies, one must appreciate the impact on men's minds of the dreadful slaughters that took place during the First World War.

On July 1, 1916, on the first day of the Battle of the Somme, the British took 57,000 casualties because the British commander, General Sir Douglas

Haig, could think of no better tactics than those of Napoleon's a century earlier. Men were called upon to walk toward the German lines until close enough to run in with bayonets fixed. Barbed wire and bullets made short work of them — the final figures for the day being 19,240 dead, 35,493 wounded, and 2,737 missing. (By comparison, on June 6, 1944, when the Allies landed in Normandy, the casualties on Omaha Beach were about two thousand; on Utah about 190, and on the British and Canadian beaches a little less than three thousand. Total for the day, about five thousand.) The final British tally for the whole Battle of the Somme, which lasted by piece-meal attacks until November, was about 419,000, with ninety-five thousand dead, all for a gain of about seven miles on a front of sixteen. These same suicide tactics were repeated time and again throughout the war.

Because Britain organized its field formations according to the villages, towns, and regions the soldiers came from, when an attack went in on a particular day, whole communities or entire villages could lose all or most of their young men all at once. The shock and grief was profound, exacerbated when word trickled through official censorship that battlefield progress was being paid for at the rate of thousands of lives to the mile.

Up until 1914, most European countries were monarchies governed by a ruling class made up mainly of people of inherited privilege. Great Britain, Germany, and Russia were all of this type: king, kaiser, and czar ruling through government leaders either chosen by popular election, heredity, or directly by the monarch. In Britain's case it was a combination of all three: the members of Parliament being elected and the members of the House of Lords and the king's Privy Council there by right of birth and appointment. All three categories, including most MPs, were derived pre-dominantly from the so-called upper class, identified by ancestry, accent, and private boarding school as a child, usually leading to university or military college. According to Nazi calculations at the time, this group comprised about 1 percent of Britain's population but occupied about 80 percent of the positions of power and influence.[1]

The massacres of the First World War, and then the Russian Revolution, caused Britons at every level of society, including some in the upper class, to question the social order they had so long taken for granted. The people had responded to the war cry in 1914 with an outpouring of patriotism. By the end of 1916 it had all gone sour. There was ugly unrest in the factories, then strikes. The execution of Czar Nicholas II and his family in 1918 and the harrying of the Russian aristocrats was an ugly omen of what could happen in England. Then the war ended. Germany, faced with mutiny at home, asked for an end to the fighting. There is no doubt that the "upper class" in Britain breathed a collective sigh of relief. The disillusionment, however, had sunk deep roots.

As good an illustration as any of how sweeping the change of mood was as the First World War came to a close was the fact that the British police, one of the most conservative of institutions, went on strike in 1918 and 1919. Chronic labour unrest became the order of the day, culminating in the General Strike of 1925. The political establishment saw the red hand of the Russian revolutionaries — the Bolsheviks — in it all, and continued to do so through the 1920s and '30s, and into the first years of the Second World War.

THE SECRET SERVICES

Even though espionage goes back to the ancient Romans and was much practised by the kings and city states of the Renaissance, Britain cruised through most of the nineteenth century without feeling the need for a permanent secret intelligence organization. That changed with the emergence of Germany as a rival. In 1909, the Secret Service Bureau was established.

It was a tiny operation, initially manned by only two officers, fifty-year-old Commander Mansfield Cumming from the navy and thirty-six-year-old Captain Vernon Kell from the army. They soon divided the principal tasks between them: Cumming would look after foreign intelligence-gathering by covert means — spying — and Kell would handle counter-espionage. They had no resources to speak of, little money, and only a handful of staff up to the beginning of the First World War. The whole enterprise might have fizzled except for the remarkable intervention of one man who was later to become Britain's most famous politician: Winston Churchill.

Churchill was born into Britain's ruling class in 1874 — an aristocrat of aristocrats — the son of Lord Randolph Churchill, descendent of the dukes of Marlborough. His birthplace was Blenheim Palace, the largest privately owned family home in Britain. He was public-school educated in the usual way for the English nobility (Harrow), and had the usual choices for career: church, state, or military. He chose the military and served for a time in the British army in the Sudan. This got him started as a newspaper war correspondent covering action in the Sudan, India, and in South Africa.

Churchill turned his adventures into books that gained him attention enough to win a seat for the Conservatives in the House of Commons in the election of 1900. Four years later, he switched to the Liberal party and, when it came to power in 1904, he was rewarded with a succession of Cabinet posts. In 1910, when only thirty-six, he became Home Secretary, and in that capacity, in that same year, he gave the Secret Service Bureau sweeping power to covertly open the mails.

It was a major milestone in the history of the secret services in modern times. Hitherto, private letters had been considered inviolate, as were the valises and bags of diplomats entering and leaving a country. It was still an age where gentlemen and nations were expected to stand by their word, and not stoop to low tricks. Churchill injected cynicism into the collection of intelligence, and Germany did not catch on — or catch up — until well into the First World War.

To be sure, it was a simpler time, when most ordinary people of all classes still went to church regularly and assumed that others, including a nation's potential enemies, did likewise, and subscribed to the same Christian principles, even when at war.

COMMUNICATIONS

The technological advance that was to have probably the greatest consequence to the nature of war in the twentieth century was the development by 1900 of wireless communication — radio. After the first transatlantic wireless message was successfully received that year, wireless quickly caught on for ship-to-shore contact and as an alternative to undersea telegraph cables. By the First World War, wireless was in general use by navies and by the foreign services of countries wanting to keep in close touch with distant outposts.

In these early years, the most convenient way to transmit messages was by tapping them out in Morse code, the system of dots and dashes representing the letters of the alphabet that occurs by switching an electrical circuit on and off in short and long pulses, specific combinations representing specific letters. An ordinary wall switch, or a flashlight, can be used to send messages in Morse, but for the wireless the on/off switch was the telegraph key, a small spring-loaded device like a paper stapler that could be operated up and down with one finger. The person transmitting was called a telegraph operator.

Voice radio came later, after the First World War, and by the 1930s had caught on in the same way as television did in the 1950s. Everyone listened to it, for news, music, and programs. It was new, and the Nazis were quick to recognize it as a way to control public opinion. Broadcast radio became a major means of maintaining public morale for all the countries in the Second World War.

Morse code, rather than voice, remained the preferred way to send sensitive messages. The individual letters, rapidly dit-dotted in sequence and usually taken down in groups of five, lent themselves to enciphering, either by jumbling the letters in the message itself or by replacing each letter by another according to a formula agreed upon by sender and receiver. It is the job of the cryptanalyst to figure out that formula from the encrypted text of the messages his wireless listening services have heard and taken down. During the First World War, the British had early and spectacular success against the Germans in this endeavour because code- and cipher-breaking on a large scale was still a novel idea. By the 1930s, however, most major nations were alert to the danger.

What complicates understanding wireless communications of the 1940s, however, is the terminology. The words *code* and *cipher* were often used incorrectly, and interchangeably. Some Japanese diplomatic messages were both encoded and enciphered, "code" being understood to mean using certain numbers or words to mean other words, and sometimes whole phrases, whereas a "cipher" jumbles the letters of a sentence or individually replaces them with other letters or symbols. Morse code, for example, where dots and dashes stand for individual letters, should be Morse cipher.

Also, the early wireless sets were heavy and cumbersome, requiring bulky glass vacuum tubes and other components rather than today's tiny transistors. Batteries were also a problem, due to size, weight, and their short life, as were the required aerials, usually a single wire having to be stretched out some thirty feet or more. A practical, lightweight transmitter/receiver for a lone spy in enemy territory was developed by the British just before the Second World War, but it never came into general use.

SPY VERSUS SPY

Finally, something also needs to be said about the terminology of espionage.

In the English-speaking world, the Americans are the exception with their use of the word *agent* to refer to a person on the staff of a security or intelligence gathering agency — e.g. the *special agent* of the FBI. Everywhere else in the world, *agent* is used as a synonym for *spy*, and this book does, too, except with respect to the FBI. The principle types are:

Spy/Agent:	A person used against a target country to secretly collect sensitive information.
Double agent:	A spy who has been caught by the target country but instead of being imprisoned is forced (usually) to pretend to his original spymaster that he is still free in order to have him send in deceptive reports. The American term is "controlled agent."
Penetration agent:	A spy whose mission is to get inside the secret services of the target country. The British term is "mole."
Triple agent:	A spy whose assignment is to get inside the enemy secret service by offering to be a double agent.

NOTES

Key to acronyms:

CSE   Communications Security Establishment (Canada)

DHH   Directorate of History and Heritage, Canadian Forces (Ottawa)

FBI   Federal Bureau of Investigation (Washington, D.C.)

FDRL   Franklin Delano Roosevelt Library

LAC   Library and Archives Canada (Ottawa)

NARA   National Archives and Records Administration at College Park (Washington, D.C.)

NSA   National Security Agency (Washington, D.C.)

PRO   Public Record Office at Kew (London)*

*   The PRO is now known as The National Achives (TNA). However, because much of the research for this book was done before the name change, PRO is used instead of TNA throughout.

PHH   The multi-volume printed record of the hearings of the Joint Committee on the Investigation of the Pearl Harbor Attack, 1946. It contains the transcripts and findings of the previous hearings and is available in major American reference libraries.

The title of the printed record of the hearings is below:
Pearl Harbor Attack: Hearings Before the Joint Committee on the Investigation of the Pearl Harbor Attack, Pursuant to S. Con. Res. 27, A Concurrent Resolution Authorizing an Investigation of the Attack on Pearl Harbor on December 7, 1941, and Events and Circumstances Relating Thereto. 79th Congress. Congress of the United States. (1946)

INTRODUCTION

1. Ian Colvin, *Chief of Intelligence* (New York: Victor Gollancz, 1951), 218–19.

PROLOGUE

1. Cunningham to Ladd, Memorandum, 27 Jan. 1944, NARA, RG65, IWG Box 126, Doc. 65-37193-144. Strong was a long-time member of British intelligence, having formerly headed MI14 of the War Office, the military intelligence section responsible for Germany. (Not to be confused with General George V. Strong, G-2, in Washington.)
2. Minutes of meeting re CI [Counter-Intelligence]-War Room planning, Feb. 1945; Note on meeting with Lt.-Col. Robertson, 12–25 Jul. 1945: PRO, FO1020/1281.
3. Ayer to FBI Director, 4 Nov. 1944, NARA, RG65, IWG Box 177, 65-54077(1); Hoover to Ayer, 2 Jun. 1945, NARA, RG65, IWG Box 126, f.37193(11).
4. FBI Director to Ayer, 6 Dec. 1944, NARA, RG65, IWG Box 126, f.37193(11).
5. This number comes from "Bibliography of the GIS," 17 Dec. 1945, PRO, KV3/8. Franz Seubert, in 1941 head of Referat 2 of IH West at Abwehr headquarters in Berlin, told American interrogators the number of informers and spies kept on file by the Abwehr's Zentralkartei der V-Leute ran into the "thousands": Cimperman to Director, 29 Jan. 1944, with attached interrogation, NARA, RG65, (230/86/11/07), Box 35, File 100-274818.
6. For the sequence and details of the establishment of these interrogation centres, including the forward interrogation unit at Diest in Belgium, see R.W.G. Stephens, *Camp 020: MI5 and the Nazi Spies* (London: Public Record Office, 2000), 71, 82, 113.
7. Minutes of meeting of CI-War Room, Feb. 1945, PRO, FO1020/1281.
8. For an exhaustive description and assessment of the SD and RSHA, see the sixty-one page U.S. Army interrogation of Dr. Wilhelm Höttl, 9 Jul. 1945, NARA, RG65, IWG Box 61, 65-47826-252-34. Höttl was a senior officer in the RSHA, working first in Amt III and then Amt VI.
9. The 1947 kidnapping by the Soviets of Col. Bernhardi and the attempted kidnapping of Wilhelm Kuebart, both formerly of *Fremde Heere Ost*, is described in CIC Special Agent Charles Hayes to HQ, 970th CIC Det., 7 May 1947, NARA, RG319, Box 472, IRR000391.

10. Richard Gehlen, *The Gehlen Memoirs* (London: Collins, 1972), passim.

11. According to his son-in-law, Col. Manfred Blume, Hamburg IL chief Nikolaus Ritter was deliberately evasive during his Camp 020 interrogation for fear of being tried as a war criminal: Benjamin Fischer, "The Enigma of Major Nikolaus Ritter," *Centre for the Study of Intelligence Bulletin* 11 (Summer 2000): 8–11.

12. John Court Curry, *The Security Service: Its Problems and Organizational Adjustments, 1908-1945* (London: Public Record Office, 1946), 51–52. He saw it as a positive change. It wasn't.
    See also, Thomson's fascinating memoir: Basil Thomson, *My Experience at Scotland Yard* (New York: Doubleday, 1923), 7. He questioned Mata Hari, the most famous of all female spies. Having noted mentally that "time had a little dimmed her charms" because she appeared to be about forty, he let her go like a gentleman: "Madam ... if you will take the advice of one nearly twice your age, give up what you are doing." She did not, and was later shot by the French.

13. Curry, *Security Service*, 228–33. R.W.G. Stephens's "A Digest of Ham" was published as *Camp 020: MI5 and the Nazi Spies* with an introduction by Oliver Hoare in 2000 by the Public Record Office (London). Hereafter it is cited as: Stephens, *Camp 020*.

14. Stephens, *Camp 020*, 117.

15. For instance, Mary Roberts Rinehart, *The Bat* (New York: Grosset & Dunlap, 1926).

16. Oreste Pinto, *The Spycatcher Omnibus* (London: Hodder & Stoughton, 1964), 52.

17. On the need to get confessions, see Stephens, *Camp 020*, 109; and Curry, *Security Service*, 229.

18. Stephens, *Camp 020*, 7. For details on the abuse of prisoners and use of torture at Bad Nenndorf, see article by Ian Cobain, *Guardian*, 17 Dec. 2005.

19. Liddell Diary, 16–22 Feb. 1944, PRO, KV4/193.

20. Stephens, *Camp 020*, passim. See also, Curry, *Security Service*, 228–32.

21. Stephens, *Camp 020*, 281–83. Before the war, Mayer had been a refrigerator salesman.

22. Rudolph to Berlin, 5 Apr. 1942, Canaris W/T intercepts, 26, PRO, KV3/3. Given that the texts of intercepts were withheld from Camp 020 during the war, the interrogators at CSDIC(WEA) may not have known of this message when they questioned Rudolph.

23. Final report on Friedrich Rudolph, 26 Mar. 1946, CSDIC(WEA), NARA, RG65, IWG Box 189, 57039. See also, PRO, KV2/266.

24. First CSDIC(WEA) on Rudolph, 15 Nov. 1945; Correspondence between War Room and CSDIC, 3, 19, and 21 Dec. 1945; and Final report on Rudolph, 2 Apr. 1946; PRO, KV2/266. Numerous documents are missing or withdrawn from this file, one as recently as the year 2000. Stephens would have been the commandant of CSDIC(WEA) at the time.

25. H.J. Giskes, *London Calling North Pole* (London: William Kimber, 1953), 88.

26. Pieter Dourlein, *Inside North Pole: A Secret Agent's Story* (London: William Kimber, 1953).

27. Cimperman to FBI Director, 4 Oct. 1945, enclosing Camp 020 Interim Interrogation Report on Hugo Bleicher (Appendix B), 38, NARA, RG65, IWG Box 184, File 65-56185. The identical report is in NARA, RG319, Box 331, XE003464. There is no "final" report in either place.

28. Abwehr Major Richard Heinrich (HARLEQUIN), captured during 1942 the Anglo-American invasion of North Africa, told an MI6 interrogator that the Germans knew of the impending raid and prepared for it: Testimony of Richard Heinrich, 18 Apr. 1943, PRO KV2/268. When MI6 asked for information on the defences of St. Nazaire, the Germans operating the captured Interallie wireless set recognized the significance of the request and reported it to the Abwehr in Berlin: Erich Borchers, *Abwehr Contre Resistance* (Paris: Amiot-Dumont, 1950), 179. Mathilde Carré alludes to the wireless exchange with London in *I Was 'The Cat'* (London: Souvenir Press, 1960), 139.

29. Both Carré and Borchers refer repeatedly to being in contact with British intelligence through "Room 55" of the War Office. This was MI5's cover address: Curry, *Security Service*, 203, 390. In *Secret War: The Story of SOE, Britain's Wartime Sabotage Organization* (London: Hodder & Stoughton, 1992), 37–40, Nigel West says it was MI6 that was in contact with Interallié without giving a source. I have gone with Curry, Borchers, and Carré.

30. Stephens, *Camp 020*, 92.

31. Peter Day and Andrew Alderson, "Top German's Spy Blunders Helped Britain to Win War," *Sunday Telegraph*, 23 Apr. 2000: n.p. The document on which this article was based was not found when this author looked for it (Jan. 2012) in PRO, KV2/85–87. Day and Alderson wrote the article following the release of one of the earliest batches of MI5 files, so perhaps it was subsequently withdrawn.

32. Stephens, *Camp 020*, 364. Wichmann stuck to his story that he knew little of the day-to-day operation of Ast Hamburg and that what he had known he had forgotten. The only spy he could remember that Hamburg had on file was DER KLEINER — Arthur Owens, also known as SNOW to the British. Otherwise, the Camp 020 interrogators got nothing from him: PRO, KV2/103. One would have thought Schmidt would have made an impression.

33. "The End of the German Intelligence Service," *Interim: British Army of the Rhine Intelligence Review* 8 (24 Sep. 1945) DHH, 581.009(D2). This publication was classified SECRET and was primarily for the edification of British army intelligence officers.

CHAPTER 1

1. Office of Chief of Counsel for Prosecution of Axis Criminality: Interrogation Division, "Interrogation of General Erwin Lahousen," comprising Canaris's Secret Organization (Parts I and II), and Sidelights on the Development of the 20th of July (III), Sep. 1945, PRO, KV2/173. According to a covering letter, the reports were prepared by the Third U.S. Army Interrogation Center.

2. For details of Lahousen's recruitment, see K.H. Abshagen, *Canaris* (London: Hutchinson, 1956), 87–88. Abshagan was Lahousen's trusted deputy and had direct knowledge and experience of his anti-Nazi activities. The MI5 file on him, however, contains information only on his pre-war career as a journalist: PRO, KV2/390. The description of the morning meetings of the Abwehr department heads is from Affidavit of Leopold Buerkner, Nuremberg Trials, 22 Jan. 1946, *www.ess.uwe.ac.uk/genocide/Buerkner.htm.*

3. Abshagan, *Canaris*, 79. He says it was a print of a "demon," which would be the impression of someone unfamiliar with Japanese woodblock art of the Edo period.

4. V/48/F8 to V.F., 15 Dec. 1945, with attached reports of Lahousen, PRO, KV2/173. The reference to Czechoslovakia is from the Lahousen interrogation report (I,1). All subsequent disclosures by Lahousen described in text are from this report unless otherwise noted.

5. "Lahousen," I, 3. The words in parenthesis correct the grammar of the translation.

6. "Lahousen," III, 1. He specifies 80 Tirpitzufer here. See also, Abshagan, *Canaris*, 161–2. The assertion that this plot never existed in Heinz Höhne, *Canaris* (New York: Doubleday, 1979), 377, is negated by Lahousan's testimony. Lahousen used the word *Reichsicherheitshauptamt* for Nazi Security Service but the Nazi secret services had not yet been unified. He meant *Sicherheitsdienst.*

7. "Lahousen," II, 11. The underlined words are as in the document. Lahousen merges the 1941 and 1942/43 missions to Spain that Canaris undertook for Hitler, the first specifically about Gibraltar and the second especially about allowing German troops to cross into Spanish territory. See also, Abshagen, *Canaris*, 212–13. According to the German consul-general in Barcelona at the time, Spanish soldiers would have received a German army crossing into Spain "with open arms." Kempner to Hoover, 13 Jun. 1946 with attached "treatise" of Hans Kroll, NARA, RG65,IWG Box 153, 65-37193. For an examination of this subject, see Leon Papeleux, *L'Admiral Canaris entre Franco et Hitler* (Tournai, Belgium: Casterman, 1977). Note that Lahousen's interrogation was not available to him.

8. "Lahousen," III, 12, 18. The wording in the document is "… and used these 'confidants' for active counter-activity." In the original German, the word was likely *Vertrauensmann*. The use of Jewish "V men" is also reported in Abshagan, *Canaris*, 101, who notes that it was made possible because the

identity of persons recruited for the Abwehr had to be kept secret and so were exempt from screening by the Gestapo. The FBI and MI5/MI6 were aware that some of the spies they had captured were Jewish but this was unlikely to have been known by the U.S. Army intelligence officers who first interrogated Lahousen.

9. "Lahousen," III, 18. Matzky was appointed by General Franz Halder, Chief of the General Staff, who was a dedicated opponent of Hitler and already had been involved in several plans to overthrow the regime.

10. He was then chairman of the CI-War Room, the Allied agency then responsible for distributing the reports from the various interrogation centres.

11. "Lahousen," II, 5; C.J. Masterman, *The Double-Cross System* (New Haven, CT; London: Yale University Press, 1972), 122–23, 131–32; and Curry, *Security Service*, 249. See also, F.H. Hinsley and C.A.G. Simkins, *British Intelligence in the Second World War*, Vol. IV, *Security and Counter-Intelligence* (London: Her Majesty's Stationery Office Books, 1990); and Frank Owen, *The Eddie Chapman Story* (New York: Julian Messner, 1954). There have been several books since 2000 in the same vein. Deceiving British Intelligence for decades as to his importance must have been a career high for the con man.

12. OSS X-2, V/48/F8 to VF, 15 Dec. 1945, PRO, KV2/173, Doc. 2a. This document is marked for the WR-CI, the Counter-Espionage War Room, which means it and the attached reports were seen by Colonel Robertson.

13. "Lahousen," III, 19, PRO, KV2/173 (the typos and capitalizations are as in text). The index of the MI5 file on Canaris lists Helen Alexandre Theotoky in connection with Canaris in 1937 (date partially obscured) with mention of two further reports from her in 1941 — on 16 Jul. 1941 and 25 Oct. 1941. A note on the file (PRO, KV3/8) indicates the actual documents were removed in 1960.

14. F.S. Penny to Director [of FBI], with attachment, 25 Jun. 1944, NARA, IWG Box 210, 65-37193-233.

15. "It appears unlikely that it will ever be possible to determine the degree to which Canaris was merely providing a refuge for kindred spirits or was consciously building an apparatus that in due time could be directed against the regime": Harold Deutsch, *The Conspiracy Against Hitler in the Twilight War* (Minneapolis, MN: University of Minnesota Press, 1968), 62. This is the usual assessment of Canaris's role in the opposition against Hitler. In his public statements afterwards, Lahousen downplayed or avoided disclosing much of what he revealed at his original interrogation.

CHAPTER 2

1. For an excellent overview of the tension between the SA, the SS, and the army, see Robert J. O'Neill, *The German Army and the Nazi Party* (London: Corgi Books, 1968), passim.

2. For an excellent description of how Hitler used a splintered Parliament to obtain absolute power, see William L. Shirer, *The Rise and the Fall of the Third Reich* (New York: Simon and Schuster, 1960), 150–200.

3. Jacques Delarue, *Histoire de la Gestapo* (Paris: Fayard, 1962), 188. This is my translation of his French translation of the original German. The description of the Roehm killings is mainly from this book.

4. Ibid., 206.

5. Nicholas Reynolds, *Treason Was No Crime: Ludwig Beck* (London: William Kimber, 1976), 52–61.

6. Conversation with Admiral Konrad Patzig, ONI Intelligence Report, 23 Feb. 1946, NARA, RG65, IWG Box 177, 66-56830. Patzig was Canaris's immediate predecessor as head of the Abwehr, 1932–34. He was ousted because of his resistance to takeover by the SS.

7. Walter Schellenberg, *The Labryinth: Memoirs of Walter Schellenberg* (New York: Harper & Bros., 1954), 155. Admiral Raeder would have been aware of this relationship when he nominated Canaris.

8. For two excellent contemporary expositions of Hitler's political tactics, see Hjalmar Schacht, *Trial of the Major War Criminals Before the International Military Tribunal*, Vol. VIII, 3 May 1946–15 May 1946 (Nuremberg: International Military Tribunal,1948), n.p (testimony also online by name and date); and Franz von Papen, *Memoirs* (New York: E.P. Dutton & Company, 1955).

9. Franz Liedig, "German Intelligence Branch and 20 July," reprinted in *Interim: British Army of the Rhine Intelligence Review* 14 (Feb. 1946). DHH 581.009(2). The early date of this document and the fact that Liedig had close ties to Canaris that predated him being asked to join the Abwehr, give a great deal of weight to this testimony. It contradicts the assertion that Canaris was "under the führer's spell" until 1937 (Höhne, *Canaris*, 211–18). Of course he had to dissemble and pretend to be an acolyte of the Nazis. How could he do otherwise? His successor, Georg Hansen, did exactly the same thing. Höhne's evidence that he was actually in sympathy with Hitler is not credible.

10. His predecessor, Admiral Konrad Patzig, recalled talking to Canaris toward the end of 1937, when he expressed the opinion that "all of the criminals were on the best route to bring Germany to her knees." When asked why he did not resign and return to the navy, Canaris replied that then the SS would take over the Abwehr and there would be nothing stopping them. He had resolved to "persevere to the bitter end": Patzig, ONI Intelligence Report, 23 Feb. 1946, NARA, RG65, IWG Box 177, 66-56830.

11. The full titles are: *Nachrichtendienst, Presse und Volkstimmung* (Berlin: Mittler, 1920) and *Geheime Machte, Internationale Spionage und ihre Bekampfung im Weltkrieg and Heute* (Leipzig: K.F. Koeler, 1925). The latter was

published initially in English as *The German Secret Service* (London: Stanley Paul, 1924). All are scarce, although *Geheime Macht* has been reprinted.

12. In social psychology today, it is called "enemy imaging." It is characterized by distorted representations of an adversary.

13. William Seltzer, "Population Statistics, the Holocaust, and the Nuremberg Trials," *Population and Development Review* 24, No. 3 (September 1998).

14. "Lahousen," III, 18.

15. See, for example, the following microfilm reels: NARA, RG242, 1360, 1444, 1519, 1529, 1549, et cetera.

16. Ladislad Farago, *The Game of Foxes* (New York: David Mackay, 1972), 161; and David Kahn, *Hitler's Spies: German Military Intelligence in World War II* (New York: Macmillan, 1978), passim.

17. PRO, KV2/266.

18. Interrogation of Erich Pheiffer, NARA, RG319, 27018417/5, IRR Personal, Box 174A — Pheiffer.

19. Order of Battle, GIS Hamburg, 20 Jan. 1946, NARA, RG65, FBI HQ file, IWG Box 133, 65-37193-EBF352, 15; "Names of approx. 400 agents of all nationalities are to hand. Of this figure, roughly 25 per cent have been accounted for," (document of unknown provenance [likely US Navy, ONI]). For a list of the agents themselves, see the card index of agents obtained by ONI and preserved on microfilm at NARA, RG242, T77, Reels 1568–69.

20. Dr. Wilhelm Hoettl, Interrogation Report No. 15, 9 Jul. 1945, 3rd Army Intelligence Center (3 AIC), copy to FBI, NARA, RG65, IWG Box 61, 65-47821-232. This is a sixty-three-page description of Nazi security services by an Austrian insider.

21. Hoettl, 22. Here he is describing the Gestapo chief, SS Obergruppenführer Heinrich Mueller.

22. Abshagan, *Canaris*, 102–04.

23. Curry, *Security Service*, 76, 245–46, and passim.

24. Henry Landau, *Secrets of the White Lady* (New York: Putnam, 1935).

25. For MI6 pre-war cipher usage, see John Whitwell, *British Agent* (London: William Kimber, 1966), 131–32. John Whitwell was the pseudonym for Kenneth Benton, the MI6(V) officer in Madrid from 1941 on. See also, Kenneth Benton, "The ISOS Years: Madrid 1941-3," *Journal of Contemporary History* 30 (1995): n.p. For MI5: Curry, *Security Service*, 369, 375.

26. For details of this transition, see Keith Jeffery, *The Secret History of MI6* (New York: Penguin Press, 2010), 209–11. Notice that Winston Churchill, then the minister for War and Air, had a say in this development.

27. John Bryden, *Best-Kept Secret: Canadian Secret Intelligence in the Second World War* (Toronto: Lester, 1993), 17–18 and passim.

28. Bryden, *Best-Kept Secret*, 18.

29. For the foregoing, see Curry, *Security Service*, 86–113. For an excellent contemporary dramatization of this "mentality," see the Alfred Hitchcock film *Sabotage* (1936).
30. Curry, *Security Service*, 140.
31. Ibid. 99, 124, 142, 375–79. Curry states that there were thirty officers and 103 secretarial and Registry staff to the end of 1938. If this is so, the figure of two "dozen or so" officers engaged in security tasks should be about right.
32. For Colonel Simpson's identity and background, see PRO, WO 201/2864; and Curry, *Security Service*, 177.
33. Curry, *Security Service*, 143–44, 177–78. See also, Dick White on MI5, Jan. 1943, PRO, KV4/170. For twenty-seven operators "twiddling knobs," see Liddell Diary, 2 Oct. 1939.
34. Eric Curwain, "Almost Top Secret," (unpublished monograph, pre-1982) 4–10, 62, 65. Curwain (probably a pseudonym) was recruited by MI6 in 1938 and served throughout the war. This may be the only surviving memoir of someone who worked under Gambier-Parry from the beginning. It is a well-written account. See also, Jeffery, *MI6*, 318–19.

CHAPTER 3

1. PRO, KV2/452.
2. Report, Metropolitan Police, 18 Aug. 1939, PRO, KV2/446, Doc. 295a.
3. Major Vivian, Note to File, 9 Oct. 1936, PRO, KV2/444.
4. Probably Major Otto Pieper of Abt I/Heer, Order of Battle Ast Hamburg, HQ 8 Corp Dist., 20 Jan. 1946, NARA, RG65, IWG Box 133, 65-37193-352.
5. Capt. J. Gwyer, "SNOW" case summary, 10 Aug. 1943, PRO, KV2/451, Doc. 1624a. See also, Gwyer interrogation of SNOW, 10 Apr. 1942, PRO, KV2/451, Doc. 1474c; and Mastermann, *Double-Cross*, 38. For examples of intercepted letters circa 1937 between DR. RANTZAU and JOHNNY, Owen's German code name at the time, see PRO, KV2/445. Their content certainly seems innocuous.
6. Masterman, *Double-Cross*, 39, which is the same as PRO, KV2/451, Doc. 1803a. See also, Gwyer, 10 Aug. 1943, PRO, KV2/451, Doc. 1624a; and Curry, *Security Service*, 124. The suggestion by some writers that MI6 somehow could not get the set to work is nonsense. Radio technology was very well known and Scotland Yard had wireless operators and technicians of its own.
7. For SNOW having another secret address in 1939, see comment on SNOW Junior's disclosures, ca. late 1941, PRO, KV2/451, Doc. 1624(b).
8. Report, Metropolitan Police, 18 Aug 1939, PRO, KV2/446, Doc. 295.
9. Inspector to Superintendent, Scotland Yard, 6 Sep. 1939, PRO, KV2/446, Doc. 302a. Colonel Simpson does not appear in the file again until Oct. 30. He may have been away, for he appears to have been an advisor to MI5 rather than a member of staff. His name also may be among the many documents that

have been removed from this file. For Robertson as head of B3, see Liddell Diary, 6 Sep. 1939.

10. For early messages from Owens, see Va 1002 in England durch afu sender, 28.8.39, NARA, RG242, T-77, Reel 1540. A 29 Aug. message in this file notes the agent number change from "Va 1002" to "3504 I Luft." These documents back up the postwar statements of Major Nikolaus Ritter that Owens transmitted his first messages in August, just before war was declared: Nikolaus Ritter, *Deckname Dr. Rantzau: Die Aufzeichnungen Des Nikolaus Ritter, Offizier Im Geheimen Nachrichtendienst* (Hamburg: Hoffmann and Campe, 1972), 150–51. This is also confirmed by Hinsley and Simkins, *BISWW*, IV, 41.

11. Unattributed (but probably Robertson), Memo to File (title whited out and overwritten as "SNOW"), 1–4, with subsequent page(s) missing, probably 12 Sep. 1939, PRO, KV2/446, Doc. 303a, but also marked Doc. 14A. This indicates it came from another file that had been started at the time. Owens probably just broke a soldered contact.

12. PRO, KV2/446, Doc. 303a. The handwritten "SNOW keying" replaces whited-out text, which actually must have been, "Owens's key," based on a remnant apostrophe, letter counting, and the fact that Owens had not yet been given the SNOW code name. The relevant sentence then becomes: "On Saturday September 9th MEAKIN and I again went to Wandsworth and succeeded in transmitting at 6 o'clock and 7.45 with Owens's key." For the assertion that a prison warder made this first contact, see "Notes written by a former MI5 officer from his personal experience," Hinsley & Simkins, *BISWW*, IV, Appendix 3, 311. The writer is apparently speaking from hearsay. Meakin probably took on the cover "of a warder who knew the Morse code" to hide that he was from the War Office when he and Robertson operated the transmitter, which required an aerial some forty feet long. Contact with Germany from Wandsworth on 11 Sep. is conclusively established by the entry in Liddell Diary, "Sep. 12, a.m." The Nigel West published copy of the diary omits the a.m. and p.m. references for this day — a crucial oversight.

13. Robertson, Note to File, 14 Sep. 1939, PRO, KV2/446, Doc. 304a. The deduction that it was Mr. Meakin again transmitting comes from letter counting the whited-out text at line 2, which establishes that the writer is using the word "Owens," not "SNOW," which means the blank at line 9 should be Lily, Owens's girlfriend, not SNOW. Notice also the use of "had explained" at line 17. If Owens had been present, the simple past tense would have been used. Furthermore, Mr. Meakin is referred to as looking after "the operating side" of the set on 22 Sep. 1939 — Doc. 311a — and a wireless "operator" is mentioned during a transmission session on 26 Sep.

1939 — Doc. 320a. Later case summaries in the available files are missing the paragraphs that would have described Owens's first transmissions, and the "wireless folder" from which extracts from this document were taken, cannot be located.

14. In 1939–40, Ast Hamburg had its own wireless intelligence division, Abt Ii, known as WOHLDORF, and headed by Werner Trautmann. Richard Wein was the W/T instructor and it was he who taught Owens: NARA, RG65, IWG Box 133, 65-37193; and Ritter, *Deckname*, 148–51. Both men were experienced army signals officers and would have certainly noticed any changes in sending "fist." Farago, *Game of Foxes*, 149–50, mentions the German radio operators recognizing Owens's unique Morse sending "fingerprint" when they received his first pre-war messages. Note that no matter whether it was Mr. Meakin or a prison warder sending for Owens, the Germans would have known immediately it was not him.

15. Ritter, *Deckname*, 151.

16. Robertson, Note to File, 14 Sep. 1939, PRO, KV2/446, Doc. 304a. The mission was cleared by Harker and Hinchley-Cook. See also, Dick White on MI5, Jan. 1943, PRO, KV4/170. Maxwell Knight of M section was also consulted. Colonel Simpson does not show up in any of the discussions at this time.

17. PRO, KV2/446, Doc. 304a, 305b. The division of responsibilities between MI5 and MI6 would have required asking MI6 to track Owens's movements on the Continent. For the initiative being Robertson's, see Curry, *Security Service*, 246.

18. "Report on interview with "SNOW," 21 Sep. 1939, PRO, KV2/446, Doc. 309a. ("Owens" has been whited out and "SNOW" overwritten in longhand.) The report mentions that Owen claims he "[a]rrived Friday night...." This, along with Docs. 304a and 305b, is proof that Owens left on 15 Sep. and returned by 20–21 Sep. This puts out of date the Liddell Diary entry of 22 Sep. 1939, which says, "SNOW has been let out of jail and is proceeding to Holland where he is contacting a German agent." He had already returned. (The Nigel West version has 22 Sep. entry under 19 Sep.) The Hamburg–Berlin reports from Owens are dated 18 Sep.: MARA, RG242, T-77, 1540.

19. Curry, *Security Service*, 128.

20. The "/E" stands for England, so the message went directly to the Air Espionage desk for England in Berlin, with a copy to Abw. Ii, the Science and Technology desk: NARA, RG242, T-77, 1540, frame 019.

21. "Er meldete Deutschland die ersten Geheiminformationen über radarstationen, zunächst über deren Existenz überhaupt und dann über die genaue Lage der vier grössten Radarstationen in England": Ritter, *Deckname* 167.

22. Curry, *Security Service*, 143. As an electrical engineer, Owens had regular occasion to visit Philips in Holland (Ritter, *Deckname*, 19), so it is plausible he picked up the information himself.

23. Interview with "SNOW," 21 Sep. 1939, PRO, KV2/446, Doc. 309a; and TAR to Colonel. Vivian (MI6), 23 Sep. 1939, PRO, KV2/446, Doc. 312a. The "600,000 a day" is evidently a response to Owens's mention during his first meeting with DR. RANTZAU that the British had some two hundred thousand troops on the Belgium border ready to strike at Germany by going through Belgium and Holland.

24. PRO, KV2/446, Docs. 311a, 313a, 314a, 316a. See also, "Die erste Wetter-meldung ist irrtumlich ..." Wettermeldung von 3504 aus London/Kingston vom 25.9.39, Ast X, B.Nr. 1285/39: NARA, RG242, T-77, 1540.

25. Owens debriefing, 21 Sep. 1939, PRO, KV2/446, Doc. 309a.

26. PRO, KV2/446, Doc. 492. "Cipher work" was then the responsibility of the female support staff at MI5: Curry, *Security Service*, 375. Liddell tried to get Col. Worledge and Col. Butler to approach the DMI regarding setting up a section for "codes," at the same time making reference to a Miss Dew having an enormous number of obviously encoded intercepts "relative to a man called Schultz": Liddell Diary, 22 Jan. 1940. (Not in Nigel West version.) MI5 used the word code for both codes and ciphers at this time.

27. The "congratulations" cipher is reproduced from PRO, KV2/453 in Michael Smith and Ralph Erskine, eds., *Action This Day* (London; and New York: Bantam Press, 2001), Appendix I, 441–43. For contemporary comment on this type of cipher, see Helen Fouche Gaines, *Elementary Cryptanalysis*, 1939 (Boston: American Photographic Publishing, 1943), 10–11. For examples of SNOW's enciphered messages, see Transmission log, 7 Oct. 1939, PRO, KV2/446. A transposition cipher using a fixed key is about as simple a cipher as one can find. His actual instructions from the Germans involved taking a daily key from a popular novel, a much stronger method: Ritter, *Deckname*, 151–52.

28. Robertson, Note to File, 26 Sep. 1939, PRO KV2/446. He does not indicate whether this permission was conveyed by Boyle, or whether the request did go to the War Cabinet as Boyle said it needed to. It would be helpful to find a document in the Air Ministry files that would corroborate Robertson's statement. Note that Neville Chamberlain was still prime minister at this time, with Churchill in his cabinet as head of the navy.

29. Williams was furnished by "M" — Maxwell Knight — so he was probably an informer that MI5/B2 had been running inside the Welsh nationalist movement. See the "M" reference in Unnamed to B3, 9 Sep. 1939, PRO, KV2/446, Doc. 311a. This document has large deletions.

30. A-3504 reports, 22 Oct. 1939, NARA, T77, Reel 1540. The barrage balloon question is among others on an unnumbered document in longhand: PRO, KV2/446.

31. B3, Note to File, 30 Oct. 1939, PRO, KV2/447, Doc. 382a. Major Sinclair, apparently still in charge of double agents, and Colonel Simpson were also

present for this report from Owens. This is the first reference to Colonel Simpson in the documents after 6 Sep. Presumably he was away during the interval.

32. Nicolai, *German Secret Service*, 214.

33. Eschborn confession, 4–6 Sep. 1939, PRO, KV2/454, Doc. 6a. An example of one of his mini-photographs is Doc. 73a. Other documents in the SNOW files refer to these as "microphotos," but they were nothing like the actual microdots then in use by the Abwehr, which were pencil-point images on camera film, not paper positives. Notice that persuading the British to get CHARLIE to produce mini-photographs gave him the excuse to possess the equipment to make actual microdots. His brother, Erwin, on his way to Canada for internment there, was among those who perished on the *Andora Star*. Charles Eschborn was A-3503 on Major Ritter's agent list.

34. The time when these code names were introduced is determined for Owens by letter-counting the whiteouts on documents in his file over-written with SNOW.

35. PRO, KV2/447: 16 Nov. 1939, Doc. 438a; 14 Jan. 1940, Doc. 563a; 24 Jan. 1940, Doc. 576a; 27 Feb. 1940, Doc. 642a.

36. PRO, KV2/447, Docs. 548b, 584a.

37. Roberts, Note to File, 3 Apr. 1940, PRO, KV2/477, Doc. 718a.

CHAPTER 4

1. Bryden, *Best-Kept Secret*, 14–17 citing documents from the file, LAC, RG24, 12,324, s,4/cipher/4D. See also, Dick White, In-house MI5 Symposium, ca. 1943, PRO, KV4/170.

2. Hugh Trevor-Roper, "Sideways into S.I.S.," in *The Name of Intelligence: Essays in Honor of Walter Pforzheimer*, eds. Hayden Peake and Samuel Halpern (Washington, D.C.: NIBC Press, 1994), 251–257; and E.W.B. Gill, "Interception Work of R.S.S.," 19 Nov. 1940, PRO, WO208/5097.

3. Sometime in 1940, Lt.-Col. Simpson issued a report that noted that an illicit W/T transmitter operating in Britain might not be picked up by MI8(c)'s fixed receiving centres, and, by implication, by any of its volunteer HAM interceptors who were also listening from fixed locations: Curry, *Security Service*, 287–8. The obvious answer was to move the receivers around as the Germans did with their spy ships.

4. NARA, RG242, T-77, 1541, 1569 and Liddell Diary, 21 Sep. 1941. See also, Farago, *Game of Foxes*, 141–46. Farago describes Kaulen's activities in England at some length, taking his information from a report by his Nest Bremen boss, Pheiffer. Kaulen left Britain on 2 Sep., the day before war was declared, joining *Theseus* in Eire. which had a "special Afu transmitter" waiting for him. The ship went directly to Norway .

5. Liddell Diary, 14 Mar. 1940; and Gill, "Interception Work of R.S.S." PRO, WO208/5097.

6. Hinsley and Simkins, *BISWW*, IV, 44; and White, MI5 Symposium, ca. 1943, PRO, KV4/170. See also Chapter 5, Note 9.

7. By 19 May 1940, he was only up to ISOS No. 11: Canaris wireless traffic compilation, PRO, KV3/3.

8. "The Room 40 Compromise," undated, NSA, DOCID 3978516. Apparently an in-house historical examination of the incident.

9. PRO, WO 201/2864.

10. Liddell Diary, 22 Apr. 1940, PRO. See also, Ewen Montagu, *Beyond Top Secret U* (London: Peter Davies, 1977), 34; and Curry, *Security Service*, 178–9.

11. Curwain, "Almost Top Secret," 48–58, 97. The transmitter was a "three-valve" crystal set — "valve" being the British equivalent of "radio tube" in America — comprising two 6L6 tubes in parallel and one 807 for output.

12. Ibid.

13. Indirect evidence of this can be found in the fact that MI6(VIII) was doing traffic analysis — "Y" — for the navy at this time: Jeffery, *MI6*, 340.

14. B3, Note to File, 8 Apr. 1940, PRO. KV2/448. Hinsley & Simkens, *BISWW*, IV, 44, mention that it was thought at the time that SNOW's transmitter could only be picked up "at very close or very long range." This is correct, but it does not mean that the transmitters could not be located. The British Post Office was already using mobile direction-finding (DF) units to pick up local transmissions, and the Germans in Holland and France were to develop the technique to a fine art. For examples of Hamburg's actual instructions to an agent regarding the need to change frequencies to avoid DF, see U.S. Coast Guard decrypts: NARA, CG2-329, 351, 357. The spy could change frequency by changing the crystals in his set.

15. General des Nachrichtentruppe Albert Praun, "German Radio Intelligence," (U.S. trans., 1950), 200–04, NARA, Foreign Militart Studies, P-038. See also, DHH, SCR II, 324. The wholesale capture of SOE agents is well documented in a number of published accounts.

16. Curry, *Security Service*, 180, 287–88.

17. Denniston (GC&CS) to Gill (RSS), 19 Apr. 1940; Robertson to Cowgill, 20 Apr. 1940: PRO, KV2/448. Gill's reaction to the French information is unknown. See also, Liddell Diary, 21 Apr. 1940.

18. Gill was copied on the French report but Robertson was under no obligation to consult him. The RSS was responsible only for interception; action on the results was exclusively up to MI5.

19. B3, Report to File, 8 Apr. 1940, PRO. KV2/448. B3 was Major Robertson.

20. For the foregoing: Ritter, *Deckname*, 150–51.

21. "ROBERTSON, Lt.-Col Thomas Argyll (1909–1994)," Liddell Hart Centre for Military Archives, King's College, London. Robertson's connection with

section B3 is established by a reference to him in Liddell Diary, 6 Sep. 1939. For B3's responsibilities, see Curry, *Security Service*, 161, 177, 287. He mentions that B3 was "under Lt.-Colonel Simpson," but also that he was attached to MI5 in an advisory capacity.

22. Farrago, *Game of Foxes*, 40–48 (He interviewed Ritter); and Benjamin Fischer, "A.k.a. 'Dr. Rantzau: The Enigma of Major Nikolaus Ritter," *Centre for the Study of Intelligence Bulletin* 11 (Summer 2000).

23. "Little is known of SNOW's early career but it is understood that he served in the Royal Flying Corps during the last war. At some date about 1920 SNOW emigrated to Canada where he set up business as an electrical engineer. In 1933 he returned to this country and found employment as an engineer for the Expanded Metal Co.": Gwyer to B1, 10 Aug. 1943, PRO, KV2/454.

24. Robertson, Note to File, 29 Jan. 1940, PRO, KV2/447 Doc. 590a.

25. Liddell Diary, 23 Feb. 1940. PRO. Also mentioned by Curry, *Security Service*, 247. Buss, who had been D of I (Air) from December 1938, was demoted to deputy director of repair and servicing and then retired. He was reinstated as director of intelligence (security) in 1943.

26. PRO, KV2/454, Docs. 66a-b.

27. Robertson, Note re meetings with SNOW, 15 Nov. 1939 and 24 Jan. 1940, PRO, KV2/447, Docs. 438a, 576a.

28. Espionage memoirs of the First World War published in the 1930s make many mentions of the need to keep the identities of spies secret from each other. See: Landau, *All's Fair*, 142; and Richard Rowan, *The Story of the Secret Service* (New York: Doubleday, 1937), 560, 567. It has been a well-established principle for centuries and was the reason each Abwehr office — Ast Hamburg, Ast Kiel, Ast Wilhelmshaven, et cetera — recruited and dispatched its own spies, coordination being effected at Abwehr headquarters in Berlin.

29. Robertson, Note to File, 16 Nov. 1939, PRO, KV2/447, Doc. 438a.

30. Robertson, Note to file, 24 Jan. 1940; PRO, KV2/447, Doc. 576a.

31. A 3504 meldet 4.4.40 bei einen Treff in Antwerpen: "Hauptquartier der 10 und 51 Bomber Squadron in Dishforth. 51 erst seit kurzer Zeit dort. Ausrustung Whitney und Vickers Wellington." NARA, RG242, T77, 1540. This was exactly correct. So he did learn something on his visit to Dishforth. For a cover address for secret letters the British were unaware of: Ritter, *Deckname*, 150. B3 to file, 4 April, 1940; PRO, KV2/477, 722a. Also, Gwyer 10.8.43; KV/451, Doc. 1624(a).

CHAPTER 5

1. Richard Basset, *Hitler's Spy Chief: The Wilhelm Canaris Mystery* (London: Cassell, 2005), 174–5; and Anthony Masters, *The Man Who Was M: The Life of Maxwell Knight* (Oxford: Basil Blackwell, 1984), 76–106.

2. Farago, *Game of Foxes*, 513; and CSDIC interrogation of Major Sandel, 16 Sep. 1945, NARA, RG65, IWG Box 130. For Kuhlenthal as a protegé of Canaris, see HARLEQUIN interrogation, PRO, KV2/275.

3. Traugott Andreas Richard Protze, PRO, KV2/1740-1; Colvin, *Chief of Intelligence*, passim; and Interrogation Report, Oberst Alexander Waag, 22 Aug. 1945, NARA, RG319, Box 242, 68006380. After the fall of France and declaration of war by Italy, Switzerland diminished in importance, for it was landlocked by the Axis and spies could no longer easily come and go.

4. For Busch, the "Nazi" at Eins Luft E, see Lahousen, PRO, KV2/173, Doc. 5a. Busch said he took over as Eins Luft E in Jun. 1940 and remained responsible for receiving espionage reports from England and America until Mar. 1943: Report to Director on Friedrich Busch, 10 Aug. 1945, NARA, RG65, IWG Box 130, 65-37193-307.

5. Ritter, *Deckname*, 19–20; and Farago, *Game of Foxes*, 40–41.

6. Order of Battle, GIS Hamburg, 1946, NARA, RG65, IWG Box 133, 65-37193-EBF352.

7. Interrogation of Georges Delfanne, 8 Mar. 1947, U.S. Army G-2, NARA, RG65, IWG Box 189, 65-57115-5.

8. Bryden, *Best-Kept Secret*, 26, 46, citing documents released by Canada's Communications Security Establishment and in LAC.

9. The Group X (Sebold) messages are found in PRO, HW19/1-6. The files show Strachey began decrypting them in May. See also, Liddell Diary, 13 Sep. 1940 and 9. Jan. 1941. Group 10 in the text is Group X.

10. For the Oslo report, see Hinsley, *BISWW*, I, 99–100, 508–12; and R.V. Jones, *Reflections on Intelligence* (London: Mandarin Paperbacks, 1989), 265–77, 324–77. Both books reproduce the text of the report, so readers can judge for themselves whether Sebold's information was more revealing.

11. Ducase (Sebold, Stein, et cetera), NARA, RG65, WWII, FBI HQ Files, Box 11, "Espionage in World War II," 224.

12. R.V. Jones, *Most Secret War* (London: Hamish Hamilton, 1978), 126, 135–37, 145–50.

13. Bryden, *Deadly Allies*, passim; British chemical and biological research was mainly done in Canada. For the Tizard mission and proximity fuse: ibid., 51.

14. A 3504 meldet 5.4.40 bei einen Treff in Antwerpen, NARA, T-77, 1540. Robertson describes asking Boyle to answer a German request for the "exact location and contents" of RAF maintenance facilities, including those of St Athan's: B3, Note to File, 2 Feb. 1940 and 4 Apr. 1940, PRO, KV2/447, Docs. 643a, 644a, 722a.

15. NARA, T-77, 1540. Nr. 1252/39 is a reference to A-3504's first report on radar.

16. Liddell Diary, 19 May 1940.

CHAPTER 6

1. General Alfred Jodl, Nuremberg testimony, 5 Jun. 1946.
2. Reynolds, *Treason*, 187–90. Beck was undoubtedly getting much of this from Canaris, who was responsible to the army for gathering intelligence on the United States, and who had come to this same conclusion.
3. Deutsch, *Conspiracy*, 115–18. Other authors place Müller's overtures to the Vatican as beginning later, but Deutsch tackles the issue with convincing evidence for September–October.
4. "Summary of Events," from 1939 Foreign Office dossier on the Venlo kidnappings, PRO, FO/371/23107. Marked not to be released until 2015. These are the most authentic of the contemporary documents on the Venlo affair, and the first and only to mention von Rundstedt's direct involvement, contradicting General Halder's claim to the contrary after the war. "Widerscheim" in this file is a misspelling. Note that Canaris is reported to have visited Von Rundstedt to solicit his support for the plot: Abshagen, *Canaris*, 154. Note also that the Liddell Diary entry of 11 Oct. 1939 is out of synch by date and content with the Foreign Office dossier. The entry, indeed, is suspect because it is highly unlikely that Stevens of MI6 would share news of the conspirators' approach with MI5. Klop, moreover, was the surname of the Dutch intelligence agent who was shot during the kidnapping, so it looks like Liddell confused him with "Klop" Ustinov of MI5. The actions involving the BBC appears to be a muddied version of what Best wrote after the war.
5. Erwin Lahousen, Nuremberg testimony, 17 Apr. 1947, PRO, WO 208/4347. Lahousen learned of the order 12 Sep. 1939, during a meeting aboard Hitler's train. See also Abshagen, *Canaris*, 145–46.
6. Summary, PRO, FO/371/23107. According to Best in his memoir, *The Venlo Incident* (London: Hutchinson, 1949), 10, the Germans he met on 21 Oct. were "Captain von Seydlitz and Lieutenant Grosch." The first could be Walther von Seydlitz who took part in anti-Nazi broadcasts after his capture at Stalingrad. The second might be the Abwehr officer mentioned in PRO, KV2/1333.
7. Deutsch, *Conspiracy*, 227–34; and Reynolds, *Treason*, 194–96. Halder invited Camaris to have Hitler assassinated. He angrily declined: Höhne, *Canaris*, 393. For Hitler's tantrums, see Thomas Fuchs, *A Concise Biography of Adolf Hitler* (New York: Berkley Books, 2000), 41. Charlie Chaplin does a hilarious take-off on these tantrums in *The Great Dictator* (1940).
8. Helmuth Greiner, "Direction of German Operations from 1939–1941" (typescript translation), USFET special report 01-SR/43, 17 May 1947, APO 757, U.S. Army, LAC, RG24, 20518, 981SOM(D105-6).
9. On his first trip across the Channel, 15–20 Sep. 1939, Owens told the Germans it was "no secret" in England that British troops were massing along

the Belgian frontier: NARA, RG242, T-77, 1540. For spies in France, see NARA, T-77, 1549, 1569.

10. Greiner, "Direction of German Operations from 1939–1941." Greiner does not specifically mention Canaris but the Abwehr chief was personally responsible for Hitler's briefings. They also normally talked daily, at least by telephone. Note Jodl's mention of the "endless number of reports from Canaris"; Jodl, Nuremberg testimony, 5 Jun. 1946.

11. Mungo Melvin, *Manstein: Hitler's Greatest General* (New York: St. Martin's Press, 2011), 146–47.

12. B.H. Liddell Hart, *The Defence of Britain* (London: Faber and Faber, 1939), 217–19. That Liddell Hart's book influenced the generals is my deduction, but that conclusion really is inescapable, I believe. See also Len Deighton, *Blitzkrieg* (London: Triad/Panther Books, 1985), 173; and Reynolds, *Treason*, 104–06.

13. For the names and brief descriptions of Abwehr spies in the Low Countries and France operated by Nest Bremen in this period see NARA, T-77, 1568-9. Typical of the other Abwehr centres, many of whose records were lost, there will have been many more.

14. See Chapter 2.

15. Henrik Eberle and Matthias Uhl, eds., *The Hitler Book: The Secret Dossier Prepared for Stalin from the Interrogation of Hitler's Personal Aides* (New York: PublicAffairs (Perseus Books), 2005), 49–50. Quotation and previous paragraph translations by Giles MacDonogh.

16. *Deutsche Allgemeine Zeitung*, 22 Nov. 1939, reproduced online by Peter Koblank (2009). This writer is indebted to Koblank for pointing the way to FO371/23107. See *www.venlo-zwischenfall.de*.

17. Summary, PRO, FO/371/23107. Best and Stevens spent the rest of the war in captivity.

18. Walter Schellenberg, the Nazi foreign intelligence chief, told Allied interrogators he believed the SD was behind the Burgerbraukeller bombing in order to enhance its prestige: Information obtained from Schellenberg on the "Venlo" Incident, ca. 1945, PRO, KV2/98. There are also many problems with how Elser was supposed to have carved a hole for a clockwork bomb in a solid wooden post, stage-centre, without being spotted by beer hall customers or Nazi security guards.

19. For the available espionage talent, see the Abwehr card files in NARA, T77, 1549, 1568-9. The most creative was that of a trapeze artist who travelled with a circus touring the front. For the British Army then being devoid of meaningful W/T security, see Curry, *Security Service*, 295–96.

20. U.S. 15th Army, TIC Case No. 865, Final Interrogation Report, Andreas Folmer, 28 Jun. 1945, NARA, RG65, IWG Box 210, 65-56014.

21. "On Jan. 8th Halifax told the Belgian Minister that we had certain information from Italian and other secret sources that the project for the invasion
of Holland and Belgium had not been abandoned and might take place in
Feb. The Belgians apparently had similar …": Liddell Diary, 13 Jan. 1940,
PRO. Two days later, Liddell recorded that the pilot of a downed German
aircraft had papers on him indicating that Belgium and Holland were
targeted. F.H. Hinsley, et al. *British Intelligence in the Second World War*,
Vol. I, *Its Influence on Strategy and Operations* (London: HMSO, 1979),
128, assert that losing these plans was what decided Hitler to go with the
Ardennes as the "main thrust."

22. Major Gill, Interception Work of R.S.S., 19 Nov. 1940, PRO, WO208/5097.
Major Gill asserted that intercepts from Wiesbaden indicated the line of
the "main attack," but he must have meant that these intercepts indicated
that the attack would be through Belgium/Holland/Luxembourg rather
than the Ardennes, for there is no evidence either the British or the French
received intercepted wireless intelligence pointing to the Ardennes.

23. Deutsch, *Conspiracy*, 92–98, 326–41; Abshagen, *Canaris*, 169–78; Liddell
Diary, 5 Apr. 1940; Hinsley, *BISWW*, I, 114–15; J.G. de Beus, *Tomorrow at
Dawn* (W.W. Norton & Company, 1980), passim. Oster was head of Zentrale
at Abwehr headquarters, which was not an operations department. Normal
internal security should have kept the change of plan from him. Alternatively,
Canaris could have ordered him to keep warning Sas. Beck would not have
known about the Ardennes because he was no longer in office.

24. Reynolds, *Treason*, 206.

25. De Beus, *Tomorrow*, 140. For the last-minute warnings reaching the British,
see Liddell Diary, 4–5 Apr., 10 May 1940.

26. This is more plausible than the contention (Höhne, *Canaris*, 415–22) that
the internal Abwehr investigation and the one by the Nazi security service
simply stalled, for no particular reason, even though they had collected
much damning evidence against Oster. In a later partial memoir, Sas wrote:
"Canaris himself saw to it that I was informed." According to Deutsch, getting
directly involved himself would have been an effective way for Canaris to
demonstrate that Oster had been acting on his orders: *Conspiracy*, 326.

27. Curwain, "Almost Top Secret," passim. See also, Jeffery, *MI6*, 314–16, 378–85;
and Nigel West and Oleg Tsarev, *Crown Jewels: The British Secrets at the Heart
of the KGB's Archives* (HarperCollins, 1998), 302–03.

28. Jeffery, *MI6*, 311. There are further allusions to this in Curwain and
Crown Jewels. See also, John Whitwell, *British Agent* (London: William
Kimber, 1966).

29. Whitwell, *British Agent*, 165. The author was without doubt Kenneth Benton,
who in 1941 became the MI6(V) officer in Madrid. Kenneth Benton, "The

ISOS Years Madrid 1941–3," *Journal of Contemporary History* 30, No. 3 (July 1995): 359–410.

30. Louis de Wohl, *The Stars of War and Peace* (London: Rider and Company, 1952). See also, PRO, KV2/2821. The book is fairly rare and far more interesting than de Wohl's MI5 file.

31. De Wohl, *War and Peace*, 27.

32. What he did do, however, was send one of his junior officers around to other astrologers to see how their visions of the heavens compared. Six were checked and six were different: Montagu, *Top Secret U*, 29.

33. Stephen Dorril, *MI6: Fifty Years of Special Operations* (London: Fourth Estate, 2000), 3–4, 189.

34. Winston Churchill, foreword to *I Was A Spy!* by Marthe McKenna (New York: Robert McBride, 1933), 5.

35. Curry, *Security Service*, 128.

36. For MI5's "score" of no spies between Sep. 1939 and the following May, see MI5 monograph, "The German Secret Service," Aug. 1942, Curry, *Security Service*, 430. For the pre-war resident handful, see PRO, KV4/170. Tyler Kent, the American embassy clerk, would not have been included in the calculation. His was a case of a breach in security by an ally rather than espionage.

37. Evidence that Churchill read Nicolai's book can be found in Churchill's 1946 use of the "iron curtain" metaphor to describe how the Soviet Union was shutting itself off from the rest of the world. The metaphor is famous, and its origin has been the subject of much fruitless searching. The term itself refers to a fire-proof drop curtain that was fitted to theatre stages in the days when illumination was by open-flame lamps. The metaphor was known in other languages, but Colonel Nicolai is the only one known to have used it in English before the Second World War. Nicolai wrote: "... the clearer it became that the ring of foes would, in the case of war, shut Germany off from the rest of the world as by an iron curtain"; Nicolai, *German Secret Service*, 59. It was published in German the following year as *Geheime Mächte* (1925). See also: Curry, *Security Service*, 77–78. It would appear from this that MI5 only read Nicolai's first book, *Nachrichtendienst, Presse, und Volkstimmung in Weltkrieg* (1921).

38. Christopher Andrew, *The Defence of the Realm: The Authorized History of MI5* (Toronto: Viking Canada, 2009), 227.

39. This writer has not been able to discover the circumstance of his death.

40. Curry, *Security Service*, 168–74; and David Petrie, "Report on the Security Service," Feb. 1941, PRO, KV4/88.

41. Reynolds, *Treason*, 207.

CHAPTER 7

1. Ritter, *Deckname*, 167.
2. Ritter, *Deckname*, 199; Robertson, Note to File, 4 Apr. 1940, PRO, KV2/447; and NARA, RG272, T-77, 1540.
3. He was obtained from B2, Maxwell Knight's section, where his code name was FRANK. See "Frank," third to last line, B3x, 20 May 1940, PRO, KV2/448, Doc. 853c. See also, reference to Mr. Knight in Doc. 855x in next note.
4. For most of the foregoing, see Robertson, "Note to File, 23 May 1940, PRO, KV2/448, Doc. 855x. This note is some 4,300 words long, but with Rolph's name blanked out. The blanks can be filled in, however, from the mention of "W. N. Rolph" in PRO, KV2/451 Doc. 1803a. Doc. 1803a cannot be entirely trusted, however, because it is at variance with Doc. 855x in several important details, including its suggestion that Owens thought all along that McCarthy was with MI5. In Doc. 855x the whited-out name overwritten in longhand as BISCUIT actually letter-counts as FRANK. See also, Liddell Diary, 22 Apr. 1940.
5. Carl Williams, "The Policing of Political Beliefs in Great Britain, 1914–1918," *www.lse.ac.uk/collections*, citing especially a 1917 letter from J.F. Moylan of the Home Office to William Rolph of MMLI/PMS2 (PRO, HO45/01809/3 425/18). See also, Nicholas Hiley, "Counter-Espionage and Security in Great Britain during the First World War," *English Historical Review* 101, No. 400 (July 1986); Curry, *Security Service*, 72.
6. Robertson. Note to File, 22 May 1940, PRO, KV2/448, Doc. 853x. The connection with PMS2 is definitely established by Robertson mentioning that Rolph was a member.
7. For a discussion of Rolph "gassing himself," Nigel West, *MI5: The True Story of the Most Secret Counterespionage Organization in the World* (New York: Stein &Day, 1982), 4–5. No source is given but the alleged suicide at least is confirmed by Farago, *Game of Foxes*, 218. He does not give his source either. It is odd that Rolph would want to take his own life, since he could be sure MI5 would not want him to stand trial. More likely he was murdered.
8. PRO, KV2/448, Doc. 870c.
9. Ritter, *Deckname*, 200–02; and 3504 messages Nos. 125 and 126 of 31 May, NARA, T77, 1540.
10. Ritter, *Deckname*, 201–16, 242. Because France was just then collapsing and he had to be flown around the country to get to Portugal, his recollection was especially vivid. Meeting confirmed by CDIC interrogation of Julius Bockel, 20 Dec. 1945, PRO, KV2/1333. Also, Ritter originally wrote his memoir in English and extracts from it regarding the meeting with Owens, including the 12–17 Jun. dates, are to be found in Charles Wighton and Günther Peis, *Hitler's Spies and Saboteurs: Based on the German Secret Service Diary of*

General Lahousen (New York: Henry Holt, 1958), 164–70. There is also the message "Friend left fifteenth" at Frame 0335 on Reel T-77/1540 (NARA). From the surrounding messages in this file, it appears that it was an Abwehr security practice not to give names, so this should be Owens. The message "Friend representative wines — Stay one week" of 9 Jun. should also be a reference to Owens, since McCarthy did not go to Portugal until July. There is some scissoring of the message at Frame 0327. Otherwise, there are no documents in the available MI5 "SNOW" files that allude to Owens going to Portugal that spring, although the broken numerical sequence indicates many are missing. It should be noted that the A-3504 weather reports were still being received because Owens's notional wireless operator normally took the observations while he was off spying.

11. Ritter, *Deckname*, 201–02, 211–15. Extracts from the English version of Ritter's memoir, probably written when he was a prisoner of war can also be found in Wighton and Peis, *Hitler's Spies and Saboteurs*, 166–71.

12. NARA, T77, 1539. These messages as copied to Berlin are numbered 1522/40 and 1523/40 respectively "from 22 Juni 1940." This is not the usual format, so it may be that they were prepared on that day but sent to Berlin by courier because of their importance. Because penetration agents were normally run by the Abwehr's counter-espionage sections, Ritter would have had to say E-186 was attached to Abt IIIf.

13. The information was also hot. Bomber Command moved to High Wycombe just that March. Stanmore was in the London Borough of Harrow, with Fighter Command housed in a sixteenth-century building, Bentley Priory. The preamble to one of the Stanmore messages begins with the following identification: "Quelle: engl. Ing. der R.A.F. Bekannter des E 186." That is: "English engineer of the RAF. Contact of E-186."

14. NARA, T-77, 1540. A pencilled note in German directs that McCarthy be changed to "friend" in the typed copy. The "probably more than ten days" suggests that Owens was not any too anxious to make the trip again, or that MI5 did not want to run the risk a second time of him going and not coming back. (This interpretation of the traffic is based on the date the 3504 and E-186 reports were sent to Berlin.)

15. Orphan page extracted from unknown file to MI5 file on Ritter circa Aug. 1940. PRO, KV2/85, Doc. 8Aa. See also, PRO, KV2/451, Doc. 1433B, and the undated SNOW, BISCUIT, CHARLIE, CELERY, SUMMER" case summary which has McCarthy in Lisbon from 24 Jul. to 21 Aug.: PRO, KV2/451, Doc. 1803a. Farago, *Game of Foxes*, 274, also has 24 Jul. Masterman, *Double-Cross*. 44, puts him in Lisbon in Apr. Liddell's diary gives 20 Aug. for his return. He is conclusively identified as V-Mann 3554 reporting from Lisbon on 30 Jul. in NARA, T-77, 1569, and his reports for that week are found on Reel 1540. The second batch of

E-186 messages are those in the group 1884-91/40 and noted as having been sent 29 Jul. 1940: NARA, T77, 1540. These appear to be replies to German queries.

16. John Colville, *Fringes of Power: Downing Street Diaries 1939–1955* (London: Hodder & Stoughton, 1985), 200.

17. PRO, KV2/451, Doc. 1803a.

18. "BISCUIT returned from Lisbon with an up-to-date wireless set in a suitcase and L950": Liddell Diary, 20 Aug. 1940 (NWV). It seems incredible that Liddell accepted that the Germans thought an ordinary British citizen could get through Customs with such an item. For Poole to Lisbon and A-3554: U.S. Navy spy card index, NARA, T77, 1568-9 and actual messages on Reel 1540.

19. Orphan page, undated, PRO, KV2/85, Doc. 8Aa. It appears not to belong in this file.

20. NARA, T-77, Reel 1540. Unless Owens had a secret transmitter somewhere, this message must have been approved by Robertson.

21. Robertson, Note to File, PRO, KV2/448, Doc. 900A. The messages are on NARA, T-77, 1540, under 3504 and 3554.

22. Michael Korda, *With Wings Like Eagles: The Untold Story of the Battle of Britain*, Reprint (Harper Perennial, 2010), 197–98.

23. At the time, the Nazi security service believed that Thames House housed MI5. Today it really is the home of MI5.

24. Unsigned note, 27–28 Aug. 1940, PRO, KV2/448.

CHAPTER 8

1. Colville, *Fringes of Power*, 245.

2. *www.wandsworth.gov.uk/info/200064/local_history_and_heritage/122/wartime_voices/4*.

3. NARA, RG242, T-77, 1540. Note that the Luftwaffe was not yet bombing by night.

4. Single page from what appears to have been a log book or diary, unattributed, 27–28 Aug. 1940, PRO, KV2/448. The messages regarding airplane "traps" (an idea which was obviously unsound) appears in the Hamburg–Berlin file the next day, whereas the information about the Spitfires, Hurricanes, et cetera at Northolt appears in a Hamburg–Berlin message of 18 Sep. 1940, by which time it was out of date. Major Sinclair was the officer actually in charge of double agents at this time: Curry, *Security Service*, 161. Note especially that this message indicates Robertson was allowing messages to be sent without authorization from higher authority. This contradicts Masterman's assurance in *The Double-Cross System* that only approved messages were sent.

5. 1942 SNOW case analysis (pages missing), PRO, KV2/451, Doc. 1433B. SNOW sent several messages with the identity card information beginning with Spruch Nr. 174: NARA, T77, 1540. Note that one is also addressed to IG Berlin, the Abwehr division responsible for faking documents, copy to Abw

I Luft/E in Berlin. Ritter is copied on another while at Ast Brussels. Wilson, Williams, and Burton were the surnames of MI5 officers, the last two then working directly on the SNOW case: PRO, KV2/451, Doc. 1075a.

6. PRO, KV2/451, Doc. 1075a; and Stephens, *Camp 020*, 138–39.

7. Schmidt was also carrying a ration card endorsed with McCarthy's identity card number, KRIY 272-2: PRO, KV2/451, Doc. 1433B. Had Schmidt been a genuine spy legitimately captured, this would have been an example of Ast Hamburg incompetence on a grand scale because it would have led police directly to A-3554. For both Caroli and Schmidt carrying Owens's name and address: OSS file on Ast Hamburg, NARA, RG319, IRR XE010158, Box 6. Had the British officers involved read the pre-war espionage literature, which told how the Germans isolated their spies from each other, they would surely have thought these actions deliberate.

8. Hinsley and Simkins, *BISWW*, IV, 321-27. Aunt Lena was the nickname of Helena Skrodzki, the secretary of Richard Protze, the Abwehr's counter-intelligence chief in Holland-Belgium before the war: Farago, *Game of Foxes*, 101. Both were especially trusted by Canaris, and it was probably Protze that Ritter liaised with when running the *Lena* agents out of Belgium.

9. White, PRO, KV4/170; and Liddell, Diary, 8 Sep. 1940. I was unable to find the Group 1 intercepts he refers to. They are not in HW19/1 which covers the period in question, presumably because HW19 comprises only ISOS decrypts done by Strachey at GC&CS. For Group 1 as Hamburg, see Bob King, "The RSS from 1939 to 1946," *www.zamboodle.demon.co.uk/rss_old/box25his.pdf*; and Trevor-Roper, *Sideways*. The ciphers would have been the simple transposition type for Gill and Roper to break them.

10. Two days after Caroli landed, OKW issued a directive postponing the invasion to 21 Sep., with the go-ahead order to come a minimum of ten days in advance. It was then postponed indefinitely on 14 Sep. See "12 Top Secret Directives" of OKW, U.K. Air Ministry translations, LAC, RG24 981.013(D29). This means both spies were dispatched when Canaris knew that the invasion order was unlikely to be given. See also TATE case summary, 15 Jun. 1942, PRO, KV2/61.

11. PRO, KV2/451, Doc. 1433b; and *Camp 020*, 137–40. Liddell's version of Caroli's landing differs in some details: Liddell Diary, 7 Sep. 1940. Over 90 percent of the content of Caroli's MI5 file — at least three hundred documents — is missing. For the reports of A-3504, and, through him, A-3527 and A-3554, see NARA, T-77, 1540.

12. L-502 Spruch-Nr.17 Ort in der Nahe Cambridge; Wettermeldung von L-503 aus London. For position of 3725 always Barnet, see Message 25, 15.5.41, NARA, T-77, Reel 1540. For Barnet and MI8(c), later Radio Security Service, see Curry, *Security Service*, 289. Lene 502 was Caroli; Lena 503 was Schmidt.

13. SNOW began reporting barometric pressure beginning 13 Nov. 1940 and his messages were thereafter forwarded to the Luftgaukommando XI Wetterdienst: NARA, T-77, 1540. TATE supplied only cloud height and cover at this time, but took over supplying the Germans with barometric pressure when SNOW was dropped by MI5 in Apr. 1941. Ibid., 1541. SUMMER reported barometric pressure from start-up.

14. Von 3504, 25.11.40, NARA, T-77, 1540. This extensive list of damaged and destroyed factories in Coventry is not to be confused with a similar list attributed to TATE and reproduced in Hinsley and Simkins, *BISWW*, IV, Appendix 8, 331–33. A-3504 was reporting on the famous big raid of 14 Nov. 1940; TATE about one that occurred on 8 Apr. 1941 (not 14 Jul.). The difference is that in the first bomb damage intelligence was released with the approval of no higher authority than Robertson or Boyle. In the second, approval was obtained from the Wireless Board and only after a rewrite demanded by Sir Finlater Stewart.

15. For Boyle as the sole director of intelligence officer to vet the information being given the Germans, see, The W-Board, unsigned internal summary, not dated, PRO, KV4/70. See also, Liddell Diary, 10 Sep. 1940.

16. Liddell Diary, 2 Feb. 1941. See also, 16 Sep. 1940. PRO. Masterman, *Double-Cross System*, 66. The non-wireless double agents were being run separately from Robertson's wireless agents so it cannot be assumed that Dick White, Felix Cowgill, and Mr. Frost were aware that the weather was being sent, especially since the reports were being done out of Barnet.

17. Curry, *Security Service*, 56, 77, 375–80. The MI6 "Registry" alluded to in Jeffery, *MI6*, 165, 327, and 626, was, prior to 1941, a small affair of no more than twenty staff. According to Curry, the "full carding" of its names was actually done by the MI5 Registry.

18. For the 29 Sep. date of the fire, see Curry, *Security Service*, 176, and 378; and Andrew, *Authorized History*, 231. The latter states, without giving a source, that the Central Registry was particularly vulnerable because it was housed in the former prison laundry which was glass-roofed. This seems improbable, as the Registry was by far MI5's most valuable asset and there were plenty of empty inmate cells to provide safe and secure storage. The glass roof explanation must be doubted until sourced.

19. Liddell Diary, 24 Sep. 1940 PRO.

20. Liddell Diary, 25 Sep. 1940 (Not in Nigel West Version). This is the wrong date. The statement, "Registry has now moved to Blenheim," of 26 Sep. is also wrong. See Note 19 above.

21. For the notoriety of the first three, and Philby in Vienna, see Phillip Knightly, *Philby: KGB Master Spy* (London: Andre Deutsch, 2003), 32–33, 46–47. Even if MI5 had not picked up on Philby's activities in Vienna, there definitely

would have been a file on him as a journalist, and even more especially so as the Spanish Civil War was seen as a struggle between fascism and communism. Files on journalists, especially those serving overseas, were routinely kept by the security and intelligence services of most advanced countries during this period, and probably still are today.

22. Curry's claim that the fire "… destroyed nearly all" of the files (*Security Service*, 176) is a lot stronger than the remark that it only "badly damaged" the Registry in Andrew, *Authorized History*, 231.

23. This fact makes MI5/MI6 chief Dick White's quoted explanation for how communists got into the secret services at the time ring hollow: "The feeling (was) that anyone who was against the Germans in the war was on the right side": Barrie Penrose and Simon Freeman, *Conspiracy of Silence* (London: Grafton Books, 1986), 248. All the major Soviet penetration agents gained entry into British Intelligence when Stalin and Hitler were close (before Germany's surprise invasion of Russia in Jun. 1941). That qualifies them as latent traitors then.

24. Miranda Carter, *Anthony Blunt: His Lives* (London: Macmillan, 2001), 253; Andrew, *Authorized History*, 231, says (without attribution) the doors were locked.

25. Curry, *Security Service*, 378.

26. Before the fire, it was normal for an MI5 officer to check a newcomer's background through the Registry: Montagu, *Beyond Top Secret U*, 48. Liddell himself acknowledged that "every communist must be regarded as an enemy agent": Liddell Diary, 21 Mar. 1940.

27. West and Tsarev, *Crown Jewels*, 138. Maurice Dobbs was a notorious Cambridge communist and agent-recruiter for the Soviets. There should have been quite a file on him, too.

28. For confirmation that the names and dossiers of Burgess and Maclean were no longer in the Registry: "Blunt had been the only one of the Cambridge Five to attract the pre-war attention of the Security Service": Andrew, *Authorized History*, 268. Obviously, this cannot be so. Recall also that Liddell's diary has the date wrong for this incident (Note 20 above). The diary is in two-ring binders, so pages written later could have been inserted at any time.

29. Knightly, *Philby*, 57, 181, citing David C. Martin, *Wilderness of Mirrors* (New York: HarperCollins, 1980), 56. See also, Andrew, *Authorized History*, 267, n. 26; and Liddell Diary, Jan.–Feb. 1940.

30. Andrew, *Authorized History*, 266.

CHAPTER 9

1. Lord (Earl) Jowitt, *Some Were Spies* (Hodder & Stoughton, 1954), 32–34. He was the prosecutor during their trials so he is an especially reliable source for these details.

2. Gwyer to Robertson, 30 Sep. 1942, PRO, KV2/451, Doc. 1497b. See also, PRO, KV2/451, Doc. 1433B.

3. Fritz Künkele, a pre-war specialist in "criminal chemistry," described his job at I-G in Berlin, 1939–40, as a kind of quality control officer responsible for "[e]xamination and evaluation of counterfeited documents, e.g., exchange of passport photographs, exchange of pages in agents' passports, additional counterfeit visas, and endorsements." He was involved in managing the files that were maintained for the various seals, stamps, and signatures used on foreign documents, including foreign driving licences: Ayer to Director re Künkele, 12 Sep. 1945, NARA, RG65, IWG Box 184, 65-56228. MI5's nearest equivalent was the secret-writing detection facility of Mr. S. W. Collins: Curry, *Secret Service*, 371. Collins was a relic of the First World War: Herbert Yardley, *Secret Service in America*, 1st British Edition (London: Faber & Faber, 1940), 28–42. For German First World War false document capacity: Nicolai, *German Secret Service*, 213.

4. Ritter, *Deckname*, 216.

5. PRO, KV2/14–16, 85.

6. Jowitt, *Some Were Spies*, 18–31; and Stephens, *Camp 020*, passim. Major Sensburg, IH at Ast Brussels, became notorious in the Abwehr for sending untrained and unqualified agents to England and certain death: PRO, KV2/275.

7. Liddell Diary, 8 Sep. 1940.

8. "The officers of Abt I recruited their own agents from Regt 800, PW cages, convicts and from pro-Nazis in occupied territories": USFET interrogation of Ast Brussels Leiter I Major Karl Krazer, 12 Jul. 1945; reprinted in John Mendelsohn, ed., *Covert Warfare* (New York: Garland Publishing, 1989).

9. Interrogation Report on Andeas Folmer, TIC No. 865, 28 Jun. 1945, NARA, RG65, IWG Box 210, 65-56014.

10. Gunter Peis, *Mirror of Deception* (London: Weidenfeld and Nicolson, 1977), 138–39. Peis interviewed one of the unfortunate eight still in prison.

11. Masterman, *Double-Cross*, 49.

12. PRO, KV2/451, Doc. 1433B. Others who were found to have documentation traceable to the information provided by SNOW were: Joseph Jacobs (landed 1 Jan. 1941); Helga Moe and Tor Glad (MUTT and JEFF, 7 Apr. 1941); and Karl Richter. See also, Masterman, *Double-Cross*, 53.

13. Ayer to Director, Interrogation of Fritz Künkele, 12 Sep. 1945, NARA, RG65, IWG Box 184, 65-56228. Künkele worked for Abw I/G in Berlin in the counterfeit documents section.

14. Liddell seems to have suspected this, but did nothing about it. Liddell Diary, 2 Feb. 1941.

15. Interrogation of Major Julius Böckel, CSDIC(WEA), 8 Nov. 1945, PRO, KV2/1333. See also, Interrogation of Dr. Friedrich Praetorius, Oct. 1945, 40, NARA, RG65, IWG Box 169, 65-56466-3.

16. Richard Bassett, *Hitler's Spy Chief* (London: Cassell, 2005), passim. Despite the misleading, this author presents convincing evidence of Canaris's opposition to Hitler.

17. A-1304 first began transmitting such commodity information in August. See his message on food prices and shortages: Hamburg to Berlin, 12 Aug. 1940, NARA, T-77, 1540.

18. NARA, T-77, 1541, 1540. A 1939 Street Directory and a 1940 patent application by co-owner Frazer Nash place Nash and Thompson on Oakcroft Road, off Kingston bypass, midway between the intersections with the bypass of Hook Road and Ewell Road. The Abwehr may have already had this information but because these messages went directly to the Abw I Luft/E desk at Abwehr headquarters in Berlin, and the officer in charge was Major Friedrich Busch, a fervent Nazi, Canaris could not have prevented it from being passed on to the Luftwaffe.

19. Christopher Shores and Hans Ring, *Fighters over the Desert* (London: Neville Spearman, 1969), 217–20, 255. This is an authoritative study of the air battles over the Western Desert from both sides. The authors do not give the losses for the Me 109s but it appears they were disproportionately less than those of their adversaries.

20. U.S. Navy Advanced Base Weser River to British Army of the Rhine, 19 Jan. 1946, re captured German documents, PRO, KV3/207. The Americans borrowed the documents and microfilmed them. They are the core of the NARA, RG242, T77 collection. A search did not turn them up at the National Archives at Kew.

21. The W-Board, unsigned photocopied summary, (not dated, but from a reference to Masterman's *Double-Cross System* it must have been done after 1972, probably by someone who had served on the committee), PRO, KV4/70. The following quotations and descriptions of the Wireless Board are from this document unless otherwise noted.

22. Masterman, *Double-Cross*, 61.

23. Ibid., 62.

24. Curry, *Security Service*, 250.

25. B.2a, Memorandum on the Double Agent system, 27 Dec. 1940, PRO, KV2/63. Section B2 was Maxwell Knight's, and it is either he who wrote this or Major Sinclair, who was in charge of double agents up to about this time. Masterman, *Double-Cross System*, 8–9, plagarizes from this document. Robertson was still B3 at this time: Curry, *Security Service*, 287.

26. W-Board, PRO, KV 4/70. See also, Howard, *BISWW*, V, 7–8. However, Masterman, *Double-Cross*, 61 states, "At a higher level the W. Board was established in September 1940, and it appears from the minutes of the first meeting (30 Sep. 1940) that …" It is clear, looking at the other sources, that this is wrong and very misleading.

27. NARA, T77, 1540. The documents on this reel and others in the series were

photographed by the U.S. Navy in 1945, when the originals were on loan from the British Army, which had captured them at Bremen. This means the scissoring was done by someone on the British side.

28. Liddell Diary, 13 Jan. 1941; and Stephens, *Camp 020*, 138–39.
29. Hinsley and Simkins, *BISWW*, IV, 96–97.
30. Stephens, *Camp 020*, 155–6.

CHAPTER 10

1. J.C. Masterman, Conference notes, 10 Apr. 1941, PRO, KV2/86, Doc. 39a. He identifies those present by their initials — Liddell, Robertson, White, Masterman, and Marriott. This document is marked as being copied sometime in Jul. 1944, from an original in the file PF 66315 CELERY, Vol. 3, serial 124a. This file could not be found at PRO. However, Masterman's Memo to File is reproduced verbatim in Liddell's diary as though Liddell himself wrote it: Liddell Diary, 10 Apr. 1941.
2. Michael Howard, *BISWW*, V, 14, 47.
3. Chapter 19. See also, Andrew, *Authorized History*, 255.
4. PRO, KV2/451, Doc. 1803a. This anonymous postwar after-action report was written in 1946; it is reproduced largely verbatim in Masterman's *Double-Cross System*.
5. MI6 officer (name illegible) to Robertson, 21 Mar. 1941, PRO, KV2/449. MI5's double agents when overseas normally reported to the MI6 officer at the British embassy. See also, Liddell Diary, 22 Mar. 1941.
6. JHM, Extract of memo, ca. Apr. 1941, PRO, KV2/849, Doc. 218b. The "only one" remaining was DRAGONFLY, an English businessman recruited through Ast Hamburg but reporting to the Abwehr in Paris; he made wireless contact on 1 Mar. 1941. See also: PRO, KV2/451, Doc. 1330c.
7. For this list of blown agents, see Partial memo, ca. 1 Apr. 1941, PRO, KV2/449, Doc. 1075a. For an analysis of Midas and its consequences to the named double agents, plus BALLOON and GELATINE, see J.M. Gwyer, memo. 28 Oct. 1941, PRO, KV2/849. For the timing of Midas, see R.G. Fletcher, Dusan Popov, Brief Synopsis of the Case, 15 Jan. 1944, NARA, RG65, WW II FBI HQ Files, Box 11(17), Dusan Popov.
8. Marriott and Gwyer, DR. RANTZAU's meeting with SNOW and CELERY in Lisbon, 17 Nov. 1941, PRO, KV2/451, Doc. 1360b. This is an eleven-page analysis. Note the reference to "Major Ritter's Final Report (Attached)." This is an imagined scenario; it was not based on an actual German report or document.
9. B3 (Robertson), Note to File, 9 Mar. 1940 and 4 Apr. 1940, PRO, KV2/447; Liddell Diary, 7 Apr. 1940; and W-Board meeting re Dicketts, 5 Apr. 1941: PRO, KV2/70.
10. PRO, KV2/674 (as of 2008). See also, "CELERY was a nominee of this office with whom, however, SNOW had sometime before struck up an acquain-

tance": KV2/451, 1803a. This, and subsequent wording, makes it clear he was originally recruited for his air intelligence experience.

11. Chronological report dictated by CELERY, 28 Mar. 1941; KV2/86. This is an "extract" taken 26 Jul. 1944, from an original document in CELERY, Vol. III PF 66315, which was not found in the MI5 files released as of 2008. It was extracted for PF 62876 "VON RANTZAU" by "RB," for an analysis section of B1A/B1B informally operated by Captain Gwyer: Curry, Security Service, 297–99.KV2/86 is the PRO file for Nikolaus Ritter. "Baron X" was Canaris's closest confidant, according to Lahousen: PRO, KV2/173. Ruser could have known this, but not Dicketts.

12. PRO, KV2/86, Doc. 37a. This extract has on it the handwritten notation "by Mr. White," as if to indicate that it was he who did the interrogation. This should be taken cautiously since it might have been added later. Otherwise, none of the extracts in this file indicate who did these interrogations.

13. Ibid. Note that at about this time MI6 stopped using the MI5 Registry as its exclusive library/archives and opened its own "registry." Curry, Security Service, 56–57, 202. The extracts were taken 26 Jul. 1944. PRO, KV2/86. This opens the possibility that the original documents were in an MI6 file, and are still withheld.

14. R.T. Reed, Ruser interrogation, 20 Dec. 1943, PRO, KV2/451, Doc. 1660; and Report on Dr. Friedrich Karl Praetorius, 20 Aug. 1945, 39, NARA, RG65, IWG Box 169, 65-56466-5. CELERY reference to SNOW as the "little man" in these documents shows that he learned that the Germans called him, "DER KLEINER." The Hamburg-Berlin routine weather reports from A-3504 end on 13 Apr., NARA, T-77, 1540. SNOW's "last message" is not in this collection. There are many gaps in the numerical sequence of messages on Reel 1540, probably because Ritter did not normally copy Berlin on his spymaster-to-spy exchanges.

15. Liddell Diary, 23, 25, 27, 29 May, 1941, PRO. Ritter remembered the incident slightly differently in his postwar account: "In the newspaper that Hansen (Schmidt) received was a gift of twenty thousand marks in English pound notes, a part of which admittedly was counterfeit — enough to keep Hansen looked after for the rest of the war": Ritter, Deckname, 241. See also, Masterman, Double-Cross System, 93; Stephens, Camp 020, 164–66; and TATE case summary for B1A, 15 Jun. 1942, PRO, KV2/61, Doc. 306a.

16. Schacht made clear his opposition to Hitler by the personal representations he made to the British before the war. Fest, Plotting Hitler's Death, 74. These Menzies would have been aware of. The 16 May entry in Liddell's diary pertaining to this is suspect. He writes that he urged CELERY be sent back to Lisbon in hopes of persuading Sessler to defect. This is unreasonable. Menzies and the service directors on the Wireless Board

would not have seen it worthwhile to risk a top agent like Dicketts for a 23-year-old German army lieutenant whose job with the Abwehr was body guard and errand-runner. The diary entry is apparently corroborated: THE W-BOARD, undated and unattributed, 10. PRO, KV4/70. Internal evidence on p. 8 indicates it was written after the war, probably in the late 1970s. The author may have consulted Liddell's diary.

17. R.T. Reed, B1A, Report, 12 Dec. 1943, PRO, KV2/451, Doc. 1660a. Letter-counting confirms that blanked-out and overwritten spaces match "Dicketts." "Mayer" is a misspelling in the document. It was Captain Kurt Meyer-Döhne. The attachés were personally approved by Canaris, so he would have released this information under his instructions. JUNIOR has been changed to Ruser to improve readability.

18. Peis, *Mirror of Deception*, 67. For confirmation that Sesslor did accompany Dicketts (CELERY) to Germany, see CSDIC interrogation of Georg Sesslor, ca. 1945, PRO, KV2/528. Since there is proof (Note 14) that Ruser accompanied Dicketts to Germany in February–March, Sessler must be recalling going with him on a subsequent trip.

19. Ibid., 70. Also, PRO, KV2/528. Major Ritter, in Libya at the time, flew back to Berlin on Jun. 5. Saul Kelly, *The Hunt for Zerzura* (London: John Murray, 2003), 173 citing HW19/8 No. 6299-6301. MI5 may not have seen this intercept since Cowgill's clampdown on ISOS was then in force.

20. For Churchill (Eden) to Stalin on 13 Jun.: David E. Murphy, *What Stalin Knew: The Enigma of Barbarossa* (New Haven, CT: and Lonon: Yale University Press, 2005), 148–49. For Churchill to Roosevelt: Foreign Office to Washington, No. 3281, 14 Jun. 1941, PREM3/230/1, PRO. Cited by James Barros and Richard Gregor, *Double Deception: Stalin, Hitler and the Invasion of Russia* (DeKalb, IL: Northern Illinois University Press, 1995), 196.

21. Gregor, *Double Deception*. See also, F. H. Hinsley, BISWW, I, 459–79, especially 472, 476, 479. Hinsley suggests that a decrypt from the Japanese ambassador reporting on Hitler's intentions may have been the clincher. The Czech intelligence service-in-exile also claimed to have been tipped off by its spy in the Abwehr, A-54. Frantisek Moravec, *Master of Spies* (London: Bodley Head, 1975), 204–06.

22. There is no mention of the second trip to Germany in Liddell Diary, while subsequent documents in the MI5 folder on CELERY make it evident MI5 was kept in the dark. The 1943 Camp 020 interrogation of Ruser — (PRO, KV2/451, Doc. 1660a [cited above]) — appears to be MI5's first indication that Dicketts may have made a second trip to Germany, although Ruser could not say that he actually did go. The matter was still in doubt after the war, for Dr. Praetorius, briefly Abt I chief at Ast Hamburg, was asked if he could recall "whether Dicketts came to a second meeting (in Germany)

or whether he failed to come...." Praetorius said he could not remember: CSDIC report on Dr. Friedrich Karl Praetorius, 20 Aug. 1945, 39, NARA, RG65, IWG Box 169, 65-56466-5.

23. Kelly, *Zerzura*, 174, citing PRO, HW19/8, no. 6861. Note that a document in Ritter's MI5 file has him telling the FBI that 17 Jul. was the date of the crash and that he was returning from Africa, not going. The HW19/8 document is proof that it was 17 Jun. and that he was in fact going to Africa: Re. Major Fritz Adolph Ritter, 2 Sep. 1945, PRO, KV2/87. It would be interesting to see whether the original in FBI files has the same mistakes.

24. MI5 Symposium, ca. 1943, PRO, KV4/170. See also, Jeffrey, *MI6*, 359; and Curry, *Security Service*, 179.

25. Curry, *Security Service*, 56, 333. Again, this "registry" is not to be confused with the eight-person registry MI6 started the war with.

26. Benton, "The ISOS Years," passim.

CHAPTER 11

1. Popov, a.k.a. IVAN, collection of intercepts, PRO, KV2/860, Doc. 1040b. The original incoming messages are Nos. 1361, 1422, Group 2, PRO, HW19/2. Group 2 to the end of 1940 covered the Abwehr circuits Oslo, Lisbon, Madrid, and Bordeaux. Distribution of the decrypts was Montagu, Boyle, Denman, Liddell, Robertson, Forster, Vivian, Cowgill, and Gill. That is, for: DNI, DI(Air), MI8, MI5, MI5, MI6, MI6, MI6, and RSS.

2. Summary of the case (SKOOT [Popov's initial British code name]), 4 Jan. 1941, PRO, KV2/845.

3. "Independent reliable evidence shows that, on 18.12.40, the German authorities in Berlin referred to SKOOT as a "Vertrauenmann" then about to leave Lisbon for England. The same source also confirms that SKOOT had wired JEBSEN and had informed the German legation at Lisbon that he was in touch with him and OSSCHLAGER." Hart, Case Summary, B2, 4 Jan. 1941, PRO, KV2/845, Docs. 13b, 14a. "It should be added that SCOOT left an exceedingly favourable impression on us. His manner was absolutely frank, and we all considered without question he was telling the truth. Marriott to B2A, 21 Dec. 1940, PRO, KV2/845, extract from Doc. 2a. See also next note.

4. Memo (partial document), ca. Jan. 1941, PRO, KV2/845, Doc. (no. unreadable). See also, PRO, KV2/846, Doc. 69a. Good recipes for invisible inks were extremely hard to come by and were closely guarded. The Germans did not risk good inks on agents who were likely to be captured. Pyramidon in alcohol, code-named PONAL, was the second-to-last most insecure invisible ink on Abw I/G shelves it was used seldom and only for totally expendable agents: Ayer to Director, interrogation of Fritz Künkele, 12 Sep. 1945, NARA, RG65, IWG Box 184, 65-56228.

5. Dusko Popov, *Spy/Counterspy* (New York: Grosset and Dunlap, 1974), 22–23, 32. The reference to Munzinger is strong evidence the Jebsen anecdote is true, for his name had not yet made much of an appearance in the literature of the German Resistance. He was one of those murdered in early 1945 by the SS for suspected complicity in the 20 Jul. plot. The postwar interrogation of William Kuebart also links Popov to Munzinger through his supposed brother, Ivo (DREADNOUGHT). Schacht's involvement in the attempted coups of 1938 and 1939 was well documented when Popov wrote, but not his connection to Canaris.

6. Popov, *Spy/Counterspy*, 76.

7. Colvin, *Chief of Intelligence*, 59–69; and Peter Hoffmann, *The History of the German Resistance 1933–45* (Cambridge MA: MIT Press, 1977), 60–62. He does a valuable analysis of this incident.

8. The pictures of both men (available on the Internet) in the same profile invite comparison after a little pencil-work. Von Kleist-Schmenzin completed his talks on 19 Aug., so he could have returned soon after rather than the next "Tuesday," as suggested by Vansittart: Hoffmann, *Resistance*, 62 n. 54. It is only on the strength of Vansittart's comment that it has been assumed that he reported to Canaris on 24 Aug.

9. PRO, KV2/63. From internal evidence, this file appears to have been created in the mid-1970s.

10. Popov, *Spy/Counterspy*, 79–80. For proof that he was shown air raid damage, see Minute sheet, Doc. 65a, 14.3.41, PRO, KV2/846. The "board of experts" is presumably the XX Committee.

11. PRO, KV2/845, Doc. 21c and surrounding docs. The Speke airdrome question in the questionnaire connects it to CHARLIE and therefore to I Luft Ast Hamburg.

12. Memorandum to S.I.S. re TRICYCLE, 15 Mar. 1941, PRO, KV2/846, 69a.

13. NARA, T-77, 1540. A-3570 cannot be CELERY/Dicketts because he was in Portugal/Germany at the time. As all other Ast Hamburg 1/Luft spies then in Britain are accounted for, this must be Popov or one that was never discovered. See also below.

14. The proximity of Churchill's bunker to the "New Houses of Parliament" makes it certain the message was not XX Committee deception. German bomb-aiming was not sufficiently accurate that the British could dare place a decoy target that close to one that was real, and of vital importance.

15. During his interrogation at CSDIC after the war, William Kuebart remembered Jebsen being based in Berlin and Popov being attached to Eins Luft: Extracts from Camp 020 Report on Oberstleutnant Wilhelm Kuebart, CSDIC, PRO, KV2/860. Beside the pertinent paragraph someone has written "true."

16. NARA, T-77, 1540. Because of the dates on it, this message appears to have been sent by invisible-ink letter or similar means.

17. For Popov's lack of fluency in English, see Chapter 13.

18. Major Walter Brede said Fidrmuc was especially highly regarded for his regular reports on British aircraft production, beginning Mar. 1941. He was said to receive the information by secret letter from an agent in England: Extract of CSDIC(UK) interrogation of Brede, 9 Aug. 1945. PRO, KV2/197.

19. Unsigned, undated memo, PRO, KV2/846, Doc. 69a; and Wilson, Note to File, 18 Jul. 1942, PRO, KV2/849. For the claim that Popov was from Dubrovnik, see recollection of von Karsthof's secretary in Peis, *Mirror*, 116. Yugoslavia was a creation of the victors of the First World War and when Hitler invaded, Croatians took side with the Germans on the promise of independence.

20. Popov's language abilities suggest that he had been earmarked for North Africa from the outset. With the exception of Spanish Morocco and Egypt, the territories in North Africa were held as colonies of either France or Italy. Ritter was running several straight spies in Egypt at this time: NARA, T-77, 1549.

21. Dusan Popov: Brief Synopsis of the Case, 15 Jan. 1944, NARA, RG65, WWII, FBI HQ Files, Box 11 (17). This was based on information supplied by MI5.

22. The German Foreign Minister, von Ribbentrop, was especially upset: Friedrich Busch interrogation, 5 Sep. 1945, NARA, RG65, IWG, Box 130.

23. For Ritter being dismissed and IL Hamburg disbanded, see Ast Hamburg, NARA, RG65, IWG Box 133, 65-37193-350-2. For Canaris telling Hitler Sebold was planted, see Farago, *Game of Foxes*, 461–62. He presumably got this from his interview with Ritter.

24. But apparently without telling MI5 that Sebold had volunteered himself as a double agent: Hinsley & Simkins, *BISWW*, IV, 131n.

25. P.E. Foxworth, "MEMORANDUM FOR THE DIRECTOR," 7 Jun. 1941, NARA, RG65, FBI HQ File, 65-36994-1.

26. Liddell Diary, 6 Aug., 10 Oct. 1941. For Robertson's reaction: Ibid., 14 Aug. 1941. The reference here is to RAINBOW's microdot rather than to those carried to the United States by Popov, which Robertson learned about no earlier than 19 Aug. See also, Montagu, *Top Secret U*, 72–73.

27. Nicolai, *German Secret Service*, 214. The German version of this memoir says a quarter-millimetre square: Nicolai, *Geheime Mächte*, 147. The book was also published in French as *Forces Secretes* (1932).

28. Dukasic (Sebold, et cetera), NARA, RG65, WWII, FBI HQ Files, Box 11, "Espionage in World War II."

29. CX/####/Y to Robertson, 12 Aug. 1941, with undated attachment attributed to Popov. PRO, KV2/849. The Popov note is a translation because the wording used is beyond Popov's English fluency. Notice the inked insertion: "Tricycle left for New York by yesterday's Clipper" on the covering letter.

This information must be discounted because evidently this note and the unreadable signature were added to the document later by someone not the writer. Other inked additions in the same hand occur on nearby documents and here and there elsewhere in the SNOW files. See also, PRO, Minute Sheet for Doc. 196b.

CHAPTER 12

1. Robert Stinnett, *Day of Deceit* (New York: Free Press, 2000), 33, citing *NYT*, 31 Jan. 1941. Indeed, Americans generally did not see much wrong with Germany dominating Europe and Japan replacing the British Empire in the Far East, so long as the United States had no rivals in the Western Hemisphere.
2. For a good collection of evidence that Churchill wanted to provoke Japan into war in order to get the United States into the fight with Germany, see Richard Lamb, *Churchill as War Leader* (New York: Carroll & Graf, 1991), 147–162.
3. However, during the 1930s there were tensions between Japan and the United States, caused by Japan's aggression in China and also by American racism against Asiatics. See: Henry L. Stimson, *The Far Eastern Crisis* (New York: Harper & Bros., 1936); and James A.B. Scherer, *Japan Defies the World* (New York: Bobbs-Merril, 1938).
4. James Rusbridger and Eric Nave, *Betrayal at Pearl Harbor: How Churchill Lured Roosevelt Into WWII* (New York: Summit Books, 1991), 123. For background to the "inevitable clash," see correspondence involving secretary of state for dominion affairs (UK) and secretary of state for external affairs (Canada), Dec. 1940 to Dec. 1941, regarding actions to be taken in the event of hostile moves by the Japanese: LAC, RG25, 2859, 1698-abcd-40. The same and similar documents can be found in the national archives of Australia and New Zealand.
5. The wording made it exclusively a *defensive* pact. The other two were not required to help if one was an aggressor.
6. Masterman, *Double-Cross*, 80. For a wartime sneer about the FBI's failure to appreciate the significance of Popov's questionnaire, see D.A. Wilson, Memo redouble agents to B1A, 26 Mar. 1943, NARA, RG65, WWII FBI HQ Files, "Dusan Popov." The fact that this British document is in FBI files means the FBI obtained it. It must have deeply soured Hoover's attitude to MI5.
7. Montagu, *Beyond Top Secret U*, 75. For the Robertson quote, see Philip Knightly, *The Second Oldest Profession* (London: Andre Deutsch, 1986), 150. He presumably obtained this from an interview.
8. Thomas Troy, "The British Assault on Hoover: The Tricycle Case," *International Journal of Intelligence and Counterintelligence* 3, No. 2 (1 Jan. 1989).
9. David Mure, *Master of Deception* (London: William Kimber, 1980), 170–77. Mure was a veteran of the security and intelligence services in the Middle

East. His theory was that Soviet influence inside British Intelligence caused the warning to be ignored.

10. Hinsley, *BISWW*, I, 295–6; II, 4; and Rushbridger and Nave, *Betrayal at Pearl Harbor*, 80. For an example of BONIFACE covering SS messages, see Gluck to SS OGruf Martin, 16 Apr. 1945, copy to CSS with the notation "Boniface" on the margin in green ink, a hallmark of the MI6 chief: PRO, HW1/3713. The green ink indicates it was personally handled by Menzies (CSS) and sent on to Churchill. By this time BONIFACE had been largely supplanted by the code-word ULTRA but evidently was still being used by Menzies on decrypts to be directed to the prime minister: PRO, HW1/1-30.

11. See previous chapter.

12. Masterman, *Double-Cross*, 79; and Popov, *Spy/Counterspy*, 149, 153. Leaving "in a few days" and leaving 10 Aug. puts this meeting at 7 Aug. at the latest. It is pertinent to add that the MI6(V) representatives at Lisbon and Madrid operated independently of the MI6 station chiefs. The latter were not allowed to know anything about the management of the double agents: Kenneth Benton, "The ISOS years Madrid 1941–43," *Journal of Contemporary History* 30, No. 3 (July 1995). This accounts for how Philip Johns, the MI6 station chief for Portugal, could declare he knew nothing of TRICYCLE and the microdots.

13. The original German-language copy of the questionnaire is in PRO, KV2/849 after Doc. 204b. Jarvis would obviously have sent the English-language copy to MI6 as well, if for no other reason than that Popov would not have wanted to risk carrying it through customs at the Bermuda stop-over. He had it on microdots anyway.

14. The *Prince of Wales* sailed on 4 Aug., arriving at Placentia Bay on 9 Aug. and staying until 12 Aug.

15. As told by Pujol in Tomás Harris, *GARBO: The Spy Who Saved D-Day* (1945/2000), 11, 51–53, 61. Harris does not specifically say that Pujol managed to get officials at the British embassy in Lisbon to look at the questionnaire, but it seems safe to assume that he did since the PRO description of the GARBO file KV2/40 (photographed in 2006) begins at 15 Jul. 1941, which means the MI6 file on Pujol was first opened then. See also, the file list of start-dates for double agents — July for GARBO — presented to MI5's 1943 internal counter-espionage symposium, PRO, KV4/170.

16. Testimony of Captain A.L.F. Safford, the navy's chief cryptographer, alluding to a "positive proof" decrypt of 22 May and another of 24 Jul. from "a high authority in Japan": Hart Inquiry, 29 Apr. 1944, *PHH*, 25 at 390. The actual decrypts have never surfaced, but Safford saw all MAGIC and the events of 1941 would have been fresh in his mind. He also reported that the president was in daily receipt of his "information" through Lieutenant Commander A.D. Kramer. As the war was still in progress at the time of this

inquiry, witnesses were circumspect with respect to actually mentioning code- and cipher-breaking. The chairman, Admiral Hart, knew what Safford was talking about, however. He had been receiving MAGIC before the outbreak of hostilities. For Churchill on the telephone 25 Jul. with Roosevelt regarding a rendezvous, see Colville, *Fringes*, 419, 421.

17. Richard G. Hewlett and Oscar E. Anderson, *The New World 1939/46: A History of the United States Atomic Energy Commission*, Vol. I (University Park, PA: Pennsylvania State University Press, 1962), 41–45. The National Defence Research Committee received a unanimous report, copy to U.S. Vice-President Henry Wallace, from the British MAUD Committee in mid-July urging that the separation of uranium isotope U-235 for military purposes be proceeded with urgently. For evidence that this likely was a topic of their talks, see Prime Minister to VCAS, 30 Aug. 1941: Winston Churchill, *The Second World War*, Vol. III, *The Grand Alliance* (New York: Houghton, Mifflin, 1950), 814.

18. "Memorandum of trip to meet Winston Churchill," 23 Aug. 1944, FDR Library, Safe Files, Box 1. The chiefs of staff discussions are mainly known from second-hand accounts, rather than documents.

19. Churchill, *Grand Alliance*, 443–44.

20. For these murder messages becoming available as of 21 Jul., see ZIP GPD 292 in special file labelled in longhand, "Executions in Russia 18.7.41 to 13.9.41," PRO, HW16/45. These are excerpted pages on this subject transferred from PRO, HW19. Their existence was first noted in Hinsley, *BISWW*, II, 1981, 669–71. For a more recent overview, see Robert Hanyok, "Eavesdropping on Hell," *www.nsa.gov/publications*.

21. For the categories of intelligence in the package air-dropped to Churchill, see document from PRO/PREM3/485/6 reproduced by Rusbridger and Nave, *Betrayal*, 114. The authors appear correct in defining BJ as specifically meaning British-Japanese. See BJs reproduced in Henry Clausen and Bruce Lee, *Pearl Harbor: Final Judgement* (Cambridge, MA: Da Capo Press, 2001), 353–93. See also, Liddell Diary for BJs, passim. For how the papers got to the ship: Churchill, *Grand Alliance*, 430. The first decrypt mentioning the SS killings in Russia was obtained in July; others followed immediately after he sailed.

22. ZIP/GPD 292/21.7.41; ZIP/GPD 309/6.8.41, PRO, HW16/45. Also found as duplicates in NARA, RG457, HCC, Box 1386. The nine decrypts in Box 1386 dated as having been received 7 Aug. could be the actual set that Churchill showed Roosevelt. The statement in Hanyok, "Eavesdropping," 14 that these particular decrypts were obtained from GCHQ (successor to GC&CS) in the 1980s is not documented. Even if correct, the existence of these decrypts is proof they were seen by Menzies, and therefore by Churchill.

23. Winston S. Churchill, *The War Speeches*, Vol. II, Charles Eade, ed., (London: Cassell, 1952) 59–66. The speech was aired 24 Aug., five days after

Churchill arrived back in London, and the most recent decrypts showed the killings were being done in batches of thousands. He presents it as his report on his meeting with Roosevelt and emphasizes American support for Britain in its struggle with Hitler. He also raises the prospect of the United States being drawn into war with Japan. This is proof Churchill knew the scope and extent of the executions by this date, even though the file — PRO, HW 1/1 — which purports to be a record of his daily ULTRA briefings, suggests that the first such decrypt he saw was dated 28 Aug. 1941. This cannot be true. Hanyok, "Eavesdropping," 39–40, comes to this same conclusion.

24. It is highly likely that Roosevelt saw the sixteen-millimetre film of the atrocities taken by the Episcopal missionary John Magee and shown to both German and American officials, a copy going to Berlin and probably another to Washington. Roosevelt had a relationship with Magee (the latter officiated at Roosevelt's funeral in 1945); and in 1938, *Life* published ten stills that shocked the world. That no actual record has surfaced of Roosevelt being aware of the massacre should be understood in the political context of the United States having ignored calls for sanctions against Japan.

25. Evidence that Roosevelt then told Churchill about the prospect of an atomic bomb can be found in the fact that within a fortnight of returning to England Churchill wrote to his Chiefs of Staff on the subject. Churchill, *Grand Alliance*, 814.

26. See Chapter 13.

27. EXHIBIT C, attachment to Connelley to Director, 19 Aug. 1941, NARA, RG65, FBI HQ file, "Dusan Popov." This, along with EXHIBIT B — Popov's wireless instructions in English — consist of white typing on a black background indicating they could be photographs of the actual microdots, which were tiny bits of negative film. The microdots themselves were photographs of the English-language original, the onion-skin copies of which Jarvis sent to London. The misspellings are on the original.

28. *Dictionary of Canadian English* (Toronto: Gage, 1962). "Oil tanks" for fuel or fuel-oil tanks and "munition dumps" for ammo or ammunition dumps do not conform to normal English, Canadian or American usage. Also, compared to the MI5 and FBI translations, this version has more punch, as one would expect from a journalist, and devotes a greater percentage of the space to Hawaii. The difference becomes obvious when the three versions are read together.

29. Up to this point in time, Roosevelt had seen plenty of intercepted Japanese messages mentioning U.S. warships in ports around the Pacific, or passing through the Panama Canal, but Popov's questionnaire was the first concrete example of Japanese target-intelligence gathering. See the relevant decrypts: *Investigation of the Pearl Harbor Attack: Report of the Joint Committee on the*

Investigation of the Pearl Harbor Attack, Pursuant to S. Con. Res. 27, 79th Congress: A Concurrent Resolution to Investigate the Attack on Pearl Harbor on December 7, 1941, and Events and Circumstances Relating Thereto, and Additional Views of Mr. Keefe, Together with Minority Views of Mr. Ferguson and Mr. Brewster (*PHH*) (Washington, D.C.: United States Government Printing Office, 1946), 12, Exhibits 1–2.

30. Edwin T. Layton, *And I Was There* (Old Saybrook, CT: Konecky & Konecky, 1985), 73. Kimmel received Grew's dispatch along with ONI's disclaimer: Kimmel, *Admiral Kimmel's Story*, Henry Regnery, 1955, 87; and Stinnett, *Day of Deceit*, 30–32.

31. Roosevelt was assistant secretary of the navy in 1920 when Billy Mitchell began his famous campaign to demonstrate that capital ships were helplessly vulnerable to air attack. He proved his point in 1921 by bombing and sinking the target battleship *Ostfriesland*. That lesson, combined with the recent easy crippling of the *Bismarck* by British carrier-launched aircraft, and the destruction of the Italian Fleet at Taranto, would not have been lost on Roosevelt, or on Stark.

32. For a discussion of the "now worked out a plan," see George Morgenstern, *Pearl Harbor: The Story of the Secret War* (New York: Devin-Adair, 1947), 117–21, 138, 147, who cites testimony of Undersecretary of State Sumner Wells, who was present at the Atlantic Meeting. Morgenstern is an especially valuable commentator on the Pearl Harbor controversy.

33. Dominions Office (UK) to Government of Australia (copy to Canada), 12 Aug. 1941, LAC, RG25, 2859, 1698-A-40. It would be fascinating to find out whether and on what day this message was actually sent. The answer does not seem to be in the Canadian archives but it might be in those of Australia, South Africa, or New Zealand. For Churchill's quote, see War Cabinet documents, Vol. XI, 1941, PRO, CAB65/19.

34. No. 9710, Group XIII/11, Berlin to Spain, RSS 238/27/8/41, PRO, HW19/12. The numbers 7580 and 7591 refer to Abwehr agents operating in France, presumably Vichy France, where the Americans would have had diplomatic representation.

35. The teletype line Madrid–Paris–Berlin was in operation until 1943, when it was disrupted by bombing: Interrogation of embassy radio operator, F. Baechle, 16 Aug, 1945, NARA, RG457, (190,07,01) Box 773. For the Canadians being able to intercept Madrid–Berlin, see MI8 to Defensor, 28 Aug. 1941; LAC, RG24, 12341, 4/int/2/2. It must have been in a simple hand cipher, likely of the transposition type, because GC&CS had not yet broken the Abwehr Enigma machine. This is proved by an analysis of the postwar collected Canaris wireless traffic where one finds on page 4 in the entry 17.12.41, No. 847, the parenthetical (ISK 546) standing for an

earlier Enigma message. Other messages for July–August are numbered between 8 and 10,000 and, as they are obviously not in the ISK series, must be ISOS. The breakthrough on Abwehr Enigma appears to have occurred at the end of November.

36. For the Government Code and Cipher School noticing the change, see PRO, HW3/155. For OKW/Chi being responsible creating and overseeing German military ciphers: CSDIC, Interim Report Trautmann and Schlott-mann, 10 Oct. 1945, NARA, RG65, IWG Box 133, 65-37193-333. OKW/Chi was headquartered at 80 Tirpitzufer Strasse, next to the Abwehr's offices. It was here that the explosives and small arms were hidden for the aborted Abwehr-inspired coup of 1939: "Lahousen," III, PRO, KV2/173. OKW/Chi is short for OKW/Chiffre.

37. The German Police decrypts in NARA, RG457, HCC, Box 1586 are dupli-cates from the British set check-marked on the distribution list as the "for file" copies.

CHAPTER 13

1. Mitchell, an "English businessman," had been the security officer with the Brit-ish Purchasing Commission in 1940 before transferring over to British Security Coordination: Montgomey Hyde, *Room 3604* (New York: Dell, 1964), 78–79. As MI5 did not have an overseas security function, this means that he would have been an MI6 officer. Popov, *Spy/Counterspy*, 154, incorrectly remembered it being BSC's John Pepper who took the briefcase through customs.

2. Col. Sharp, MID, to Assistant Chief of Staff, G-2, 15 Aug. 1941, NARA, RG65, FBI HQ file "Dusan M. Popov." FBI documents cited in this chap-ter are from this file unless otherwise noted. Sharp wrote that Popov was reported to have given Mitchell a package while they shared the taxi and Ellis subsequently produced copies of some of the microdots at a meeting with the FBI on 14 Aug., so they can be assumed to have been in that package. See Note 4 below.

3. Connelley to Director, 20 Aug. 1941; and C.H.C. to Foxworth, 21 Aug. 1941. This action by Popov must have caused the army/navy officers to wonder how he managed to get the cash through customs, leading them to back-check his arrival and discover the details about Mitchell: Sharp to G-2, 15 Aug. 1941.

4. Foxworth, MEMORANDUM FOR THE DIRECTOR, 14 Aug. 1941. Hand-written notations on this document indicate that it was specifically drawn to Hoover's attention, and its attachment — a "questionnaire" — was forwarded to Hoover on 16 Aug., indicating the earliest that the FBI director would have seen it. It would have been a photographed or typed copy of the English-language version that was on two of the microdots Popov was carrying. Popov had done none of the things Ellis claimed of him.

5. There is moderately strong evidence for this deduction. The secret "BSC History" that Stephenson had compiled in 1945, and which only finally became available in the 1990s, makes only bare mention of Popov and says nothing of Pearl Harbor or his questionnaire, which Stephenson surely would not have missed including had he known of it: Nigel West, introduction to, *The Secret History of British Intelligence in the Americas, 1940–45*, by William Stephenson (New York: Fromm International, 1999), 388–93. There is no mention in Montgomery Hyde, *Room 3604*, either. Indeed, Stephenson disclaimed the Popov/Pearl Harbor story that author William Stevenson wrote into his controversial autobiography of him, *A Man Called Intrepid* (1976): See Bill Macdonald, *The True Intrepid: Sir William Stephenson and the Unknown Agents* (Surrey, BC: Timberholme, 1998), 148–50. Also, strangely, Ellis is referred to in the documents as "STOTT's assistant," rather than Stephenson's, but STOTT is a code name derived from Ellis's personal past. Stephenson is never mentioned by name.

6. Connelley to Hoover, PERSONAL AND CONFIDENTIAL, 20 Aug. 1941. This was a follow-up to his report of 19 Aug. and appears to have been done for the record, after Connelley and Hoover talked on the telephone.

7. Connelley to Director, 19 Aug. 1941. It is curious that he used the verb "transmit," for up to the time he left for the United States, Popov's communication with Portugal had been by personal visit or secret-ink letter. Ellis must have shown Connelley the text of some of these letters.

8. Ibid., 6. See also, Carson to Foxworth, 21 Aug., and 23 Aug. 1941. Popov may have been instructed to say the thirty-eight thousand dollars was British money because it would have been subject to seizure under the recent law freezing Axis assets in the United States. It was an outright lie, however, to say that the spy was to draw directly from the account in the United States, and cashed cheques were to be traced. The actual scheme involved an equivalent amount being paid in England to a British double agent. Popov hid this fact, although the FBI eventually sorted out the truth: "A Brief Synopsis of the case," Dusan M. Popov, 15 Jan. 1944, NARA, RG65, WWII, FBI HQ Files, Box 11(17). The sum in British funds was twenty thousand pounds: Liddell Diary, 3, 25 Aug. 1941.

9. Connelley to Director, 19 Aug. 1941, Exhibit C and Exhibit D. These are white on black, presumably because they are photographs taken by a camera mounted on a microscope, a not uncommon piece of scientific equipment at the time. The FBI lab was soon to develop an apparatus for making direct enlargements and positive prints. Popov's transmission frequencies were to be 13400 and 6950 kcs, requiring an aerial of twenty-five metres.

10. Jeffrey, *MI6*, 194–5, 316.

366 · FIGHTING TO LOSE

11. Peter Wright, *Spycatcher* (Toronto: Stoddart, 1987), 325–30. See also, H.A.R. Philby to Miss Paine, 25 Nov. 1946, with attachments and other documents pertaining to the interrogation of Richard Traugott Protze, PRO, KV2/1740. Protze disclosed that a Captain Ellis had handed over "extensive information about the organization of the English Secret Services." It appears to have been a slip because he then said Ellis was a Russian and the information was only partly believed. Protze probably played a part in the Abwehr's secret peace overtures to Stephens and Best in 1939 that led to the Venlo incident. It was in his territory. See Chapter 6.

12. Thomas Troy, *Wild Bill and Intrepid* (New Haven, CT: and London: Yale UP, 1996), 98–108. See also, Joseph E. Persico, *Roosevelt's Secret War: FDR and World War II Espionage* (New York: Random House, 2001).

13. Connelley to Director, 20 Aug. 1941. Hoover was *required* to go through Astor on intelligence matters involving the army and navy: James Strodes, *Allen Dulles: Master of Spies* (Washington, D.C.: Regnery Publishing, 1999), 204.

14. Laboratory Report re Dusan Popov, 3 Sep. 1941, Lanman, "Synopsis of the Facts," 17 Sep. 1941. The lab only reported on eight microdots, even though Lanman collected eleven from Popov. The omitted three were the two comprising the English-language "Exhibit C" and Popov's wireless transmitting instructions, "Exhibit B." As these were in English, Lanman apparently saw no reason to send them to the lab. See also, "Brief Synopsis of the Case," 15 Jan. 1944 (above).

15. John Bratzel and Leslie Rout, "Pearl Harbor, Microdots, and J. Edgar Hoover," *American Historical Review*, 87, No. 5 (December 1982). The illustrated text shows that Hoover sent Photo #2 from Q1 of the FBI lab report. These were the general queries of the questionnaire, beginning with "All information regarding the American air defense ..." and ending with the paragraph on Canada's air training plan: FBI Laboratory Report, 3 Sep. 1941. The particular example may also have been chosen simply because it was the first item in the report.

16. Shivers to Hoover, Report, 26 Dec. 1941, NARA, RG65, FBI WWII HQ file, "Julius Kuehn."

17. Robert B. Stinnett, *Day of Deceit: The Truth about FDR and Pearl Harbor* (New York: Free Press, 2000), 85–86. Hoover's rationale is inferred by the present writer, not by Stinnett. The issue of normal/acceptable espionage came up at various times during the post-attack Pearl Harbor inquiries.

18. Hoover also long prided himself on simply laying out the facts in his reports to higher authorities, leaving it to his political or military clients to draw what inferences they would: Richard Powers, *Secrecy and Power: The Life of J. Edgar Hoover* (New York: Free Press, 1987), 238.

19. Phillips did not last long as Donovan's spy chief. He left Donovan's employment shortly after the Pearl Harbor attack on 7 Dec. It is not known under what circumstances.

20. Strodes, *Allen Dulles*, 203.

21. Liddell Diary, 20 Nov. 1941. Churchill could also send messages directly to Roosevelt by this means.

22. The collection of British-supplied German Police Decrypts for 1941 found in the U.S. National Archives at College Park surely got to the United States by this route. See NARA, RG457, HCC, Box 1386. The Americans were not intercepting and decrypting this traffic at this time.

23. Cowgill to Robertson, 19 Aug. 1941, PRO, KV2/849, Doc. 204b; and Luke to Cowgill, 22 Aug. 1941 Doc. 206a. The texts of the two questionnaires are next in the file, the German-language one being a carbon copy on onion-skin paper, suggesting that the English version on the microdots had been on onion skin, as well. Cowgill could not turn this over to MI5 because it was either in Roosevelt's possession or still on the *Prince of Wales*.

24. PRO, KV4/64.

25. Ibid. An internal reference to Masterman's *Double-Cross System* makes it certain that the W-Board summary in KV4/70 and probably the minutes were written after 1972, probably by Ewan Montagu from memory or personal notes.

26. This assertion is based on the assumption that if after nearly seventy years no one has found mention of the Pearl Harbor questionnaire in the wartime archives of these bodies, they were not informed. Note that the Wireless Board and XX Committee understood that the "junior" Joint Intelligence Committee in Washington was only to deal with questions dealing with Britain and the Commonwealth.

27. According to his diary, Liddell was on leave the week of 19 Aug. when Cowgill sent MI5 the questionnaire, which theoretically would give him an excuse if his 17 Dec. statement were ever challenged. However, surely he would have read his files on his return and surely the questionnaire would have been at the top in his in-basket. In any case, he was at the Wireless Board meeting.

CHAPTER 14

1. "His first communication in secret writing containing the information requested by the Germans was sent on August 22, 1941. Further communications were sent on September 15, 16, October 7, 8, 9, and 10, 1941, containing information prepared by the Army and Navy in response to questions contained in Popov's questionnaire…." Brief Synopsis of the Case, 1/15/44 collected in "Espionage (World War II)"; NARA, RG65, WW II, FBI HQ file, Box 11(17), Dusan Popov.

2. Effective 17 Jun. 1941, Coast Guard decrypts were distributed to MID, ONI, State Department, and FBI. NARA, RG457, SRH-270. For background on

Canada's code- and cipher-breaking agency that started up in Ottawa that spring, see Bryden, *Best-Kept Secret*, passim.

3. FBI, Memorandum re TRICYCLE, 5 Oct. 1943, PRO, KV2/854, 662B. It is not clear whether this is a translation of Portuguese into Englishmen's English, or whether Mady was a fifteen-year-old English-language prodigy. "Uncle" could well be Canaris. Notice the use of "chap," a middle- to upper-class British word. For the lower classes, the word "bloke" would have been used instead. Apparently obtained from FBI files.

4. Popov appears to have been alluding to "Dickie" Metcalf, a.k.a. BALLOON.

5. "I went over to see Valentine Vivian and found him with Dick Ellis who had just flown over from New York...." Liddell Diary, 3 Nov. 1941; PRO.

6. Quoted in Caffery to Berle re CEL espionage ring, 5 Sept. 1942; NARA, RG457, SRIC.

7. Foxworth to Director, 16 Dec. 1941. See: Max Fritz Ernst Rudloff with aliases (ND 98), NARA, RG65, WWII FBI HQ File: 65-37233-4.

8. A source inside Spain reports that there is "now in America" a Spanish-speaking German spy close to Franco who travels on an Argentinian passport. Siscoe to Hoover, 14 Aug. 1944; IWG Box 153, 65-37193-237(1). FBI reaction to this news cannot be determined because Hoover's messages in the Mosquera file after that date are heavily redacted.

9. "Synopsis of Facts," 4 Dec. 1944, 22. See: Max Fritz Ernst Rudloff, NARA, RG65, WWII FBI HQ File, 65-37233 (above).

10. NARA, RG242, T-77, 1569, card 1549. See also, Farago, *Game of Foxes*, 648–49, who states categrically that Canaris saw the report, but without citing his sources. They must have existed, however, because the quotation he attributes to von Roeder echoes the information asked for in Popov's March questionnaire (which Farago would not have seen).

11. Hewlett and Anderson, *The New World*, 13–25.

12. Bush to Conant, 9 Oct. 1941; Records of the Office of Scientific Research and Development, U. S. Atomic Energy Commission. Hewlett and Anderson, *The New World*, 45–46, 611.

13. "Synopsis of Facts," 4 Dec. 1944, 22, See: Max Fritz Ernst Rudloff, NARA, RG65, WWII FBI HQ File, 65-37233 (above). According to the cover sheet to this report, at least five copies were made and considering the novelty and importance of the content, especially the reference to microdots, one must have been sent to the White House, to the attention of the vice-president, Henry Wallace, if not directly to Roosevelt.

14. Arthur H. Compton, *Atomic Quest* (Oxford University Press, 1956), 61–64.

15. Robertson to Cowgill, 17 Sept. 1941. PRO, KV2/849. Liddell Diary, 14 Aug., 15 Nov. 1941.

16. Gwyer to B1A, 10 Oct. 1941; PRO, KV2/849. JHM was Marriott, the lawyer.

17. Liddell Diary, 3 Aug. 1941, PRO.
18. Masterman, *Double-Cross*, 3, 59, 85. Curry, *Security Service*, 252. MI5 took the proof to be the intercepted Abwehr wireless traffic (ISOS) that dealt with its double agents.
19. "Order of Battle GIS (Hamburg)," prepared for GSI(b) HQ 8 Corps. Dis., 20 Jan. 1946, 1; NARA, FBI HQ file, IWG Box 133, file 65-37193-EBF352.
20. NARA, T-77, 1529. Index file cards on A-2057 DELPHIN and F-2368 NOLL; NARA, T-77, 1549. The "F" before a number indicates someone whose job it was to find and recruit spies.
21. B1A TATE case summary, 15 June 1942; PRO, KV2/61, Doc. 300a. Only a handful remain of the hundreds of documents that were once in this file. Also see: KV2/1333.
22. Memo by Gwyer and Marriott, 17 Nov. 1941; PRO, KV2/451, 1360b.
23. See, for example, "Major Ritter's Final Report of the SNOW Case (Translation) — Berlin 31/7/1941"; PRO, KV2/451, Doc. 1360b, undated and unattributed but probably an attachment to Gwyer and Marriott, 17 Nov. 1941. This peculiar document is a fictitious scenario in which the MI5 officers who wrote it imagine how Major Ritter might have come to the conclusion that CHARLIE, GW, and TATE might not be compromised despite SNOW's confession and the fact that Karl Richter had never reported back on his mission to contact TATE. It is useful in that it confirms that MI5 did not know Dicketts went to Germany a second time, and that Owens did not operate the SNOW transmitter.
24. Masterman, "Note on Memorandum, 'Dr. Rantzau's meeting with SNOW and CELERY in Lisbon,'" 26 Nov. 1941; PRO, KV2/451, Doc. 1368b. It is in reply to the scenario analysis described in the previous note.
25. See Chapter 8, note 7.
26. "… during TATE's illness in Nov. 1941 his transmitter was operated by one of our own men who had learnt successfully to imitate TATE's style; since that date, although TATE continued to draft the messages in his own words and assist in encoding, he has never been allowed actually to operate himself." B1A/ JV memo "TATE," 21/8/42. See also: R.T. Reed, "TATE," 12 Nov. 1941. Both in KV2/61–62.
27. Montagu, *Beyond Top Secret U*, 69.
28. Stephens, *Camp 020*, 166.
29. Ibid., 164–66. See also Liddell Diary, 7 Nov. 1941, PRO. We only have Liddell's word for it that Hinchley-Cooke did the persuading.
30. For the man who would have saved him: Captain R. Short, Note to File, 29 Nov. 1941, PRO, KV2/61. In his diary Liddell argued the opposite and attributed to Lord Swinton the position that a reprieve would be "detrimental to B1A." Liddell Diary, 7 Nov. 1941.

31. Liddell Diary, 3, 15 Nov. 1941.

32. Liddell Diary, 1 Oct. 1941, PRO.

33. Montagu, *Top Secret U*, 78.

34. Popov, *Spy/Counterspy*, 190–91.

CHAPTER 15

1. The Army Pearl Harbor Board and the Naval Court of Inquiry, both of which reported in early 1944, are the most honest sources of what happened for they were non-partisan politically and their questions were well-informed and well-aimed. The Naval Court found so severely against Admiral Stark — that "he failed to display the sound judgement expected of him" — that, had it been made public, the president would have had to fire him. *PHH*, 39 at 329.

2. Kimmel, *Kimmel's Story*, 28–29; and Layton, *And I Was There*, 115. Likewise, a shortage of aircraft and aircrew precluded continuous, around-the-compass air reconnaisance out to the potential strike distance. Kimmel sensibly husbanded these resources on the expectation that ONI would warn him of an approaching threat. Ibid., 75, citing *PHH*.

3. The chief of the army and later the air force, General Henry "Hap" Arnold, felt that the discussions he was involved in were only "window dressing" to some "epoch-making" secret accord between the president and the prime minister: Layton, *And I Was There*, 133, citing Arnold's wartime diary held by the Library of Congress.

4. Roberta Wohlstetter, *Pearl Harbor: Warning and Decision*, (Redwood City, CA: Stanford UP, 1962) 176–82. Wohlstetter notes conflicting testimony at the hearings into the Pearl Harbor attack, but provides proof that withholding MAGIC from the two commanders did, indeed, begin in Aug. and is skeptical that it had anything to do with security concerns that arose the previous May. As it would have had to have been a decision of both General Marshall and Admiral Stark, and they were aboard the USS *Augusta* by at least 4 Aug., and 2–3 Aug. was a weekend, it seems safe to conclude that they made the move after the conclusion of the Atlantic meeting on 12 Aug. See also, Layton, *And I Was There*, 91, 119, 137. He confirms Kimmel was cut off from all MAGIC after July.

5. *PHH*, 12, at 261. The (S) means it was intercepted at the navy's Station SAIL at Seattle and forwarded to Washington. It, and the reply (following note) were also intercepted by Station CAST in the Philippines, Station Two at San Francisco, and Station Seven at Fort Hunt outside Washington: Stinnett, *Deceit*, 102–05. It was also taken down by the army at Fort Shafter, Hawaii: Rusbridger and Nave, *Betrayal*, 130–31.

6. Stinnett, *Deceit*, 104.

7. Compare the testimony reported in the Joint Committee Report on the Pearl

Harbor Attack, 1946, (*PHH*) with the observations made in the attached minority report and the views of Frank B. Keefe. Later, Kimmel wrote: "These Japanese instructions and reports pointed to an attack by Japan on ships in Pearl Harbor. The information sought and obtained, with such painstaking detail, had no other conceivable usefulness from a military viewpoint": Kimmel, *Kimmel's Story*, 87. This is obvious even to a lay person. See also, Stinnett, *Day of Deceit*, 105; and Toland, *Infamy*, 58–60. Of the many decrypts of Japanese messages reporting on American warships in harbour in the Pacific, only those involving Pearl Harbor dealt with the berthing positions: *PHH*, passim.

8. Charles Willoughby, *MacArthur 1941–1951* (London: William Heinemann, 1956), 22, quoting a staff report of the period. The "grid system" is an allusion to the coded map-reference message mentioned above. Notice how he stresses that these reports were made "daily," which suggests there were more bomb-plot messages than reported to the inquiries. "Cable" was common usage for telegram. Also from Willoughby: "As Pearl Harbor approached we got many of the intercepts of that period; there was a considerable time lag as they all came via Washington; we set up our own plant during the war and eventually cut the decoding time of all the local items." Confirmed by Stinnett, *Day of Deceit*, 112. See also: Edward Drea, *MacArthur's ULTRA: Codebreaking and the War Against Japan, 1942–1945* (Lawrence, KS: University Press of Kansas, 1992), 11, citing several NARA, RG457 files.

9. Colonel Rufus Bratton, in charge of distributing the army decrypts, testified that he received the order from Marshall on or after Aug. 5: *PHH*, 9, at 4584. As by that date Marshall was aboard the *Augusta*, he must have issued the order immediately on his return to Washington. For the navy, see the testimony of Captain Alwin Kramer. *PHH*, 33, at 849.

10. Wohlstetter, *Pearl Harbor*, 176–80. Also, Kramer, *PHH*, 33, at 849. MAGIC decrypts were separately produced by both army and navy code breakers, pooled, and distributed by safe hand to a shared list of recipients, the army normally looking after those in the war and state departments and the navy, the navy and the White House. For the figure of "26 a day," see *PHH*, 33, at 915. MAGIC summaries were resumed in Mar., 1942.

11. Layton, *And I Was There*, 167.

12. Clausen and Lee, *Pearl Harbor: Final Judgement*, 46; and Stinnett, *Deceit*, 169. Built-in "deniability" is a common ploy of elected leaders expecting to have to answer awkward questions. Roosevelt began receiving "raw intercepts" again on Nov. 12.

13. Timothy Wilford, *Pearl Harbor Redefined* (Lanham, MD: University Press of America, 2001), 8, citing Minoru Nomura, "Japan's Plans for World War II," *Revue Internationale d'Histoire Militaire*, 38 (1978): 210–17. Japan was 90 percent dependant on American oil.

14. The Government Code and Cipher School then had the capacity to break
PURPLE and the Consular J-codes, including J......19: Rushridger and Nave,
Betrayal, 136. Ian Pfennigwerth, *A Man of Intelligence: The Life of Captain
Theodore Nave* (Kenthurst, NSW, Austalia: Rosenberg, 2006), 175–6, men-
tions the Australians breaking the J-19 "Winds Message" of Nov. 19 and
Tokyo's code-destruct orders on information supplied by Far East Combined
Bureau, Britain's regional cryptanalysis agency based in Singapore. Proof
that the British were reading the same codes is the selection of decrypts
Henry Clausen obtained from GC&CS in 1944 and reproduced in Clausen
and Lee, *Pearl Harbor: Final Judgement,* 353–93. Also note that the British
had wireless listening stations that could pick up signals sent by Mackay
Radio and RCA in Honolulu, most notably Hartland Point in Nova Scotia
(see Chapter 17). For example: Canadian Examination Unit decrypt, D-180:
KITA to Foreign Minister, Tokio, Rec'd Oct. 28, 1941 (Author's possession).

15. The South African prime minister, Jan Smuts, recognized the ships were
being endangered. When they put in at Capetown, he cabled Churchill: "If
the Japanese really are nippy there is an opening here for a first-class disaster." Notice also that Churchill throughout the previous year had steadfastly
refused to send to the Far East any tanks or modern aircraft and he knew
that the Japanese were likely in possession of captured British documents
indicating that Britain's chiefs of staff considered Singapore impossible to
defend: Richard Lamb, *Churchill as War Leader* (New York: Carroll & Graf,
1993), 151; and Rusbridger and Nave, *Betrayal,* 97–104.

16. "Information received from the Orient," MID to ONI, FBI, etc., 3 Nov., 1941,
NARA, RG65, IWG Box 229, 65-9748-17. The document is only marked
CONFIDENTIAL, which suggests it was sent out routinely. I could find no
reference to it in the Pearl Harbor histories I consulted.

17. Speech at Mansion House, 10 Nov. 1941. Eade, ed., *War Speeches of the Rt.
Hon. Winston Churchill,* Vol. II.

18. Persico, *Roosevelt's Secret War,* 141, citing William Donovan to Roosevelt,
13 Nov. 1941, in PSF, Roosevelt Library. This was a great find because one of
the strongest and longest-running arguments against Roosevelt luring Japan
into war to help Britain has been that he could not have counted on Hitler
coming in on Japan's side. Apparently, he could.

19. Secretary of State for Dominion Affairs (UK) to Secretary of State for External
Affairs (Canada), "For your Prime Minister," Most Secret, 20 Nov. 1941, LAC,
RG25, Box 5742, 28-C(s). This is a summary of Hull's personal description of
his meeting with Kurusu given to "His Majesty's Minister" on Nov. 18.

20. Ibid. The same message was sent to Australia and New Zealand.

21. Wilford, *Pearl Harbor Redefined,* 11, citing OPNAV to CINPAC, no. 181705,
18 Nov. 1941, in "The Role of Radio Intelligence...", NARA, RG457, SRH,

190/36/9/2 Entry 9002, Box 9. The Vacant Sea Order is also covered in Stinnett, *Day of Deceit*, 144–46, who cites the testimony of Rear-Admiral Richmond Turner of the navy's war plans division (a primary recipient of MAGIC) before the 1944 Navy Hart inquiry: "We were prepared to divert (ship) traffic when we believed war was imminent. We sent the traffic down by the Torres Strait, so that the track of the Japanese task force would be clear of any traffic."

22. *PHH*, 39 at 314.

23. Wohlstetter, *Pearl Harbor* 242-46. Hull and Roosevelt knew the Japanese could not accept recognizing Chiang-Kai'shek because it would have been a huge loss of face both nationally and in the Far East. For the idea of Japan recognizing the Chinese leader emanating from Churchill, see Lamb, *Churchill*, 157, citing PRO FO 371/35957.

24. The minority report of the Joint Congressional Committee *Investigation of the Pearl Harbor Attack* (*PHH*) was highly critical of this "war warning" as being so ambiguous as not to be meaningful. The Naval Court of Inquiry found that Admiral Kimmel was entirely justified in thinking the Japanese were looking to the Far East rather than to Hawaii, based on the information he received from Washington. *PHH*, 39 at 314-15.

25. "… our battleships had suddenly become 'targets.'" Wiloughby, *MacArthur*, 22.

26. Wilford, *Pearl Harbor Redefined*, 12, from *PHH*, 17, at 2479; and Kimmel, *Kimmel's Story*, 46-7.

27. Bryden, *Best-Kept*, 91, citing documents obtained from the Canada's Communications Security Establishment (author's possession). See Notes 19–20 above. Mackenzie King Diary, 1 Dec. 1941, LAC.

28. Tokyo to Washington, 28 Nov. 1941, army decrypt trans. *PHH*, Hewitt Inquiry, 37, at 684.

29. Safford testimony, Hart Inquiry, Day 32. Kota Bharu was defended only by a brigade. Had the British commander at Singapore received this intelligence, he could easily have got enough troops up Kota Bharu to repel the invasion. The Japanese were only landing less than a division, and by means primitive in comparison to the amphibious landings later conducted by the Allies.

30. Reproduced in Clausen and Lee, *Pearl Harbor: Final Judgement*, 360.

31. Tokyo to Washington, 2 Dec. 1941, army trans. 12-3-41, Clausen and Lee, *Pearl Harbor: Final Judgement*, 339.

32. Wilford, *Pearl Harbor Redefined*, 99, citing from Seymour's papers held in the St. Catharines Museum, St. Catharines, Ontario, Canada. Seymour was a distinguished Canadian, so his testimony must be considered reliable, and it is backed up by a statement from the wartime Canadian bureaucrat who got Canada started on code and cipher-breaking, Lester B. Pearson, later Canada's prime minister: Ibid., 101, citing a letter from Pearson to Seymour,

Jan. 31, 1972. Joseph Apedaile was attached to the British Commonwealth Air Training Plan.

33. OpNav to CINCAF, CINCAP, COM 14, COM 16, 3 Dec. 1941, Exhibit 8, Hart Inquiry; and Clausen and Lee, *Pearl Harbor: Final Judgement*, 69, 96.

34. John Toland, *Infamy: Pearl Harbor and Its Aftermath* (New York: Doubleday, 1982), 302 citing oral history tape recording done by the University of Hawaii.

35. Private letter to author quoted in Constantine FitzGibbon, *Secret Intelligence in the Twentieth Century*, (London: Hart-Davis, 1976), 255. There is no reason not to accept his assertion, especially as it is backed up by William Casey in *The Secret War against Hitler* (New York: Berkley, 1989), 7. As America's CIA chief during the Cold War, Casey must be considered a reliable witness.

36. Christopher Andrew, "Churchill and Intelligence," in *Leaders and Intelligence*, ed. Michael Handel (London: Frank Cass, 1989), 189.

37. Adolf Berle, Diary, 18 Dec. 1941, FDRL.

CHAPTER 16

1. Don Whitehead, *The FBI Story* (New York: Random House, 1956), 182. The game was between the Washington Redskins and the Philadelphia Eagles.

2. Richard Gid Powers, *Secrecy and Power: The Life of J. Edgar Hoover* (New York: Free Press, 1987), 240. See also, *PHH*, Hewitt Inquiry, III, at 451–2, There was initially some confusion about who took the call. Apparently, it was actually Mr. Mori's wife.

3. Ibid. The Americans received confirmation after the war that the Japanese were using a flower code to indicate the state of things in Pearl Harbor. The Operations Order of the task force gave "The cherry blossoms are all in their glory" as the code phrase for no warships in Pearl Harbor: *PHH*, Hewitt Inquiry.

4. Hoover to Early, 12 Dec. 1941, Steve Early papers, FDRL. Reproduced in Thomas Kimmel Jr. and J. A. Williams, "Why Did the Attack on Pearl Harbor Occur? An Intelligence Failure? FBI Director J. Edgar Hoover Thought He Knew," *Intelligencer*, 17, No. 1 (2009).

5. Ibid., citing D.M. Ladd to Director, 12.11.41, from "Pearl Harbor documents from Mr. Hoover's and Mr. Nichols Official files." After the war Japanese airmen revealed that the final signal that launched the raid was the thrice repeated: "Tora, Tora, Tora!" for "Tiger, Tiger, Tiger!"

6. Shivers to Director, 26 Dec. 1941, NARA, RG65, WWII FBI HQ file "Julius Kuehn" (hereafter: "Shivers Report") See also, Whitehead, *FBI Story*, 190–93. This author must have been allowed to see the Shivers report for his account matches it closely.

7. *PHH*, 37, Hewitt Inquiry, Exhibit 40 (Mayfield Report), at 912-13. Farnsley Woodward with J.J. Rochefort; *PHH*, 36, at 319–24, and 350–52. Their testimony should be read with *PHH*, 37, Hewitt Inquiry, Exhibits 55–56,

at 982–3. Kahn, *Codebreakers*, 45 and Stinnett, *Deceit*, 112 say HYPO did have the PA code, having got it from a Registered Intelligence Publications circular, but the content of the circular in question has never been released. Also note Stinnett's assumption that HYPO was reading PA-K2 because its chief, Joseph Rochefort, testified that HYPO could read most of the "simple stuff": *Deceit*, 107. Even the Canadians could read the housekeeping LA code, but PA-K2 was not simple. See Note 15 below.

8. Shivers Report, Note 6 above; Mayfield Report, Note 7 above, 912. Also accurately reproduced in Whitehead, *FBI Story*, 190–91. Note that, according to Farnsley Woodward, the "lights message" in Exhibit 56 is not the HYPO version of Exhibit 40. It is the Op-20-G translation with deletions done in Washington.

9. *PHH*, 39, Army Board Report, at 100.

10. *PHH*, 1, at 231. The specific reference is to messages of 6 Dec. but it has been taken to apply to all Honolulu–Tokyo messages in PA-K2, including the lights message. Layton, *And I Was There*, 283.

11. *PHH*, 37, Hewitt Inquiry, at 701. This is not the copy referred to as being in Exhibit 13 when Safford commented on it. That is missing. The (5) in the lower right-hand corner indicates it was intercepted at Fort Shafter in Hawaii and therefore mailed to Washington. But Fort Shafter was only backup. The message would have been intercepted at any of the intercept stations in the continental United States and forwarded to the Washington code breakers the same day.

12. *PHH*, 37, Hewitt Inquiry, Exhibit 13, at 669.

13. *PHH*, 36, Hewitt Inquiry, Safford Report, at 66–7. One of the "urgent" messages he alludes to was the thirteen-part message that came in that day conveying Japan's implied declaration of war. But it was sent in English. There was little other traffic. See next chapter.

14. Shivers Report, Note 6 above. The HYPO version of the message with this preamble is reproduced incidentally (probably accidentally) in *PHH*, Hewitt Inquiry, Exhibit 40. The version provided to the Joint Congressional Committee, however, is without the preamble. *PHH*, Exhibit 2.

15. *PHH*, 36, Hewitt Inquiry, Friedman, at 310–11.

16. *PHH*, 37, Hewitt Inquiry, Exhibit 56A, at 995–6. The description here applies to the transposition rules for "WA and WO (PA)" codes. It follows then that the analysis in Kahn, *Codebreakers*, 18–19. of the 4 Dec. message, "At 1 o'clock on the 4th a light cruiser of the Honolulu class hastily departed," would appear to be that of a message in LA code, not PA. Considering the innocuous content of the message, this is not surprising.

17. *PHH*, 37, Hewitt Inquiry, at 1010–11. See also the preceding message of 13 Nov., also in PA. The content is highly revealing, and therefore must have been considered highly sensitive.

18. While members of the Joint Committee investigating the Pearl Harbor attack heard that the PA Code had been around for years, examples in the official record before 2 Dec. 1941, are rare. A comparison of American and British intercepts of the Japanese messages collected for the Clausen investigation shows that "PA=Chief of Consulate's Code=Chef de Mission Cypher=In Government Code=CA." The famous Tokyo to Washington 1 o'clock message is headed "Purple (Urgent-Very Important) #907, To be handled in Government Code." As all codes had been destroyed except PA and LA, this must refer to PA. See especially the message reproduced in Clausen & Lee, *Pearl Harbor: Final Judgement*, 313–93.

19. The point needs to be made because of the ubiquitous references in the literature to Kita's messages being "cables." The Japanese normally alternated month over month between the two services, MacKay the odd months and RCA the even: *PHH*, 36, at 331.

20. Stinnett, *Deceit*, 192. Interestingly, this made it unnecessary to get copies of Kita's radiograms from RCA, according to the arrangement said to have been initiated by Roosevelt through RCA president David Sarnoff. For the same bomb-plot messages being intercepted in the Philippines (Station CAST/Fort Mills) and in the United States (San Francisco–Fort Hunt), see Stinnett, *Deceit*, 100, 103. This is proof that RCA/Mackay sometimes sent the same messages by both routes.

21. Not to belabour the point, but there is not a chance in the world Kita would have sent such messages in a weak code. He would be putting the entire surprise attack operation at risk.

22. Shivers Report.

23. *PHH*, 2, at 672; and *PHH*, 37, Hewitt Inquiry, Exhibit 57, at 998. The latter shows that the message had been intercepted by Station Two, San Francisco. Note that Captain Mayfield's report to the Hart Inquiry uses the Shivers version.

24. L.F. Safford, "A Brief History of Communications Intelligence in the United States," (1952), NARA, SRH-149. His ONI colleague Alwin Kramer may have been the source of this information. Apparently he participated in a "black bag" operation against the office of the Japanese consul in New York earlier in the year. Layton, *And I Was There*, 284. Also: Robert Hanyok and David Mowry, *West Wind Clear: Cryptography and the Winds Message Controversy* (Washington, D.C.: National Security Agency, 2011), 21–24.

25. *PHH*, 37, Hewitt Inquiry, at 486; and *PHH*, R1, at 229. I have substituted "barrage" for "observation" balloon because it is clear that is what was meant: *PHH*, 37, Hewitt Inquiry, at 01. Barrage balloons were the tethered blimp-like balloons used by the British over London and elsewhere during the Blitz. They were intended to deter low-flying aircraft.

26. *PHH*, 36, Hewitt Inquiry, Safford, at 66.

27. Fort Hunt normally intercepted the Tokyo–Washington diplomatic traffic but was also on the geodesic line Honolulu–San Francisco–Fort Hunt–Hartland Point (Halifax). For the Canadians intercepting Kita traffic at this time: Examination Unit decrypt D-180, KITA to Foreign Minister, Tokio, 22 Oct. 1941; CSE Archives (author's possession). This was probably obtained from Hartlan Point which was then assigned to German clandestine and Japanese diplomatic traffic. Bryden, *Best-Kept Secret*, 45, citing, LAC, RG12, 2158. Hartland Point was connected by landline and undersea cable to Ottawa and to the Government Code and Cipher School in Britain. Since the Canadian code breakers were then only able to handle the low-grade LA code, the higher grade messages would have been forwarded to GC&CS. For proof the British were reading messages in Purple, J-19 and PA, compare British messages reproduced in Clausen and Lee, *Pearl Harbor: Final Judgement*, 353–93 with American versions.

CHAPTER 17

1. Tokyo to Berlin, 30 Nov. 1941, JD-6943, ARMY, translated 1 Dec.; *PHH*, 37, Hewitt Inquiry, Exhibit 18, at 664. For Churchill seeing the British translation of the same message, see Note 27 below. The message makes a mockery of the time and energy invested by the various inquiries in trying to determine whether there had been a "winds execute" message in open code on Japanese broadcast radio indicating what countries Japan was intending to fight. On 1 Dec. Roosevelt knew the answer, as did Safford and Kramer, who definitely would have seen this message. The "winds" controversy appears to have been instigated by Safford to divert attention away from this and other more revealing messages.

2. *PHH*, 37, Hewitt Inquiry, at 999.

3. *PHH*, 4, 1746–47; *PHH*, 7, 3390-91.

4. *PHH*, 37, Hewitt Inquiry, at 983; and Chapter 16, Note 8. Notice the use of the word "attic" instead of "dormer" as used by the HYPO/Shivers version. Notice also his statement that Kramer's dilly-dallying "slowed up the whole process" of translating and making MAGIC available: Layton, *And I Was There*, 284. This is hidden in the evidence presented at the Pearl Harbor inquiries because the messages submitted showed only time of translation, not decryption. British code-breaking agencies showed time of decryption.

5. Layton, *And I Was There*, 281–83. Notice he writes that Kramer did not give the lights message the attention it warranted because it was in "a low-grade consular cipher." From Chapter 16 we know it was high-grade.

6. Because it arrived on an odd day, when it was the navy's turn to decipher incoming intercepts, it can be assumed the army's Signals Intelligence Service was unaware of it at that point.

7. PHH, 37, Hewitt Inquiry, Tokyo to Washington, 6 Dec. 1941, Army 7149, at 694.

8. Layton, *And I Was There*, 290.

9. The officer of the watch that began at 7 a.m. testified that the fourteenth part and the army translation of the one o'clock message were ready by 7:15, but Kramer did not come in until nine o'clock: *PHH*, 33, Naval Court, Alfred Pering, at 802–4. He also said Kramer had been phoned at home about the messages during the night, as certainly he would have been since the one o'clock message was sent in PURPLE and in "Government code," a method reserved for the most urgent and most important messages. The middle watch officer, F.M. Brotherhood, was more circumspect, but did testify that at the end of his shift he left for Kramer "those dispatches which were supposed to be delivered to him." These must have included the fourteenth part, which was in English, and a copy of the one o'clock message in Japanese, because Brotherhood said the "original" was sent to the army for translation: *PHH*, 33, at 839–44. Kramer claimed he had not been phoned and that he came in at 7:30: *PHH, 33*, at 858–61.

10. Arthur A. McCollum, "Unheeded Warnings," in Paul Stillwell, *Air Raid: Pearl Harbor! Recollections of a Day of Infamy* (Annapolis, MD: Naval Institute Press, 1981), 85–87. McCollum's recollections back up Pering's statement that Kramer did not arrive in his own office until nine o'clock. See also *PHH*, 36 at 24-27.

11. *PHH, 39*, Army Board Report, at 93–5.

12. See the selection of decrypts, including some BJs, collected from the Government Code and Cipher School in 1944 and reproduced in Clausen and Lee, *Pearl Harbor: Final Judgement*, 353–93. Wartime cryptogapher Eric Nave, who was with the Australian section of the British Far East Combined Bureau, reported personally breaking a J-19 message in Nov. 1941, and states that the code was then well-known to the Government Code and Cipher School: Rusbridger and Nave, *Betrayal*, 25, 136. These claims are backed up by Ian Pfennigwerth, *A Man of Intelligence*, 174–75, citing documents in Australia's National Archives.

13. Powers, *Secrecy*, 243.

14. The proof of this assertion is Popov's questionnaire itself. However, Jebsen's description in *Spy/Counterspy*, 142–44, of hosting a fact-finding visit of Japanese army and navy officers to Taranto in April appears also to be true.

15. Evidence obtained from Richard Sorge by the Japanese after his arrest and made available to the House Committee on Un-American Activities, Hearings on the American Aspects of the Richard Sorge Spy Case 82 Congress(9, 22, 23 Aug. 1951). Sorge said he obtained this from the German Ambassador who, in this case, was a Canaris protegé.

16. "Herr Sorge sass mit zu Tisch," *Der Speigel*, 3 March 1951.

17. H.C. on Un-Amercan Activities, Sorge Case; and David E. Murphy, *What Stalin Knew: The Enigma of Barbarossa* (New Haven, CT; and London: Yale UP, 2005), 86–86.

18. Murphy, *What Stalin Knew*, 87.

19. Ibid.

20. H.C. on Un-American Activities, Sorge Case, Testimony of Mitsusada Yoshikawa, (1946) He was the Japanese prosecutor who interrogated Sorge after his arrest.

21. West and Tsarev, *Crown Jewels*, 140; and Yuri Modin, *My Five Cambridge Friends* (New York: Farrar Straus Giroux, 1994), 92. See also, Curry, *Security Service*, 259–60. Note the deletion on p. 260, which undoubtedly refers to intercepting diplomatic bags. Herbert Yardley, *Secret Service In America* (London: Faber & Faber, 1940), 49–50, went into detail about how to open diplomatic mail, photograph its contents, and then reseal everything without leaving traces, so the practice was hardly a secret anymore.

22. West and Tsarev, *Crown Jewels*, 140; and Carter, *Anthony Blunt*, 274, citing an interview with Desmond Bristow. There was nothing new in what Blunt was doing. See next paragraph.

23. Liddell Diary, 14 Aug. 1941, and passim. See also, Curry, *Security Service*, 260, which specifically mentions BJs. A 1942 Soviet assessment of Blunt's work during Oct.–Nov. 1941 reported him as having supplied data on the deployment of Japanese troops and being responsible for the liaison between MI5 and GC&CS and the "distribution of diplomatic decrypts": West and Tsarev, *Crown Jewels*, 145–46.

24. For examples of British intercepts of pre-Pearl Harbor Japanese diplomatic traffic that was copied to MI5 — that is, for Blunt — see Clausen & Lee, *Pearl Harbor: Final Judgement*, 353–77. Up to this writing, only isolated Japanese decrypts from this period have been released at the PRO, so this collection, which Clausen obtained from GC&CS in 1944, is extremely valuable for what it can reveal of how closely Churchill could follow for himself the Japanese-American trajectories to war.

25. "Reinforced by the Siberian divisions which Stalin had risked moving from the Far East on the basis of reports, including Philby's, it beat the Germans back.... " Genrikh Borovik, *The Philby Files* (New York: Little, Brown, 1994), 195. As head of the Iberian desk, Philby was not then in a position to supply much intelligence useful to Stalin's decision, so the other "reports" must have included Blunt's. Stalin, who was chronically suspicious, would have needed to see at least some actual carbon copies of the decrypts to be convinced. See examples reproduced on the inside cover of *Crown Jewels*.

26. Clausen and Lee, *Pearl Harbor: Final Judgement*, 354. There are two typos: No. 2363 should be 2353 and No. 09127 should be 098127. I have rendered

"communications" as "commercial cable and radio-telegraph services" for clarity, since that is definitely what was meant. British and American companies overwhelmingly dominated cable and radio-telegraph communications worldwide, and a clash with either the U.S. or Britain would see these services terminated instantly. There was another version of this "winds" message decrypted and released at the same time.

27. "Foreign Minister Tokyo to Ambassador Berlin, 30th November, 1941 (In Chef de Mission Cypher recyphered on machine)," Clausen and Lee, *Pearl Harbor: Final Judgement*, 360–61. The American version — Tokyo to Berlin, 30 Nov. 1941 (Purple CA) — was available to Roosevelt the day before: *PHH*, 37, Hewitt Inquiry, Exhibit 18, at 664. It is more muted in tone, but the message is the same. The fact that the British version was marked BJ means it was definitely read by Churchill. The two leaders would surely have discussed it during their next transatlantic scrambler telephone conversation.

CHAPTER 16

1. Endnotes are not provided for incidents described and sourced in earlier chapters.

2. "European Axis Signals Intelligence in World War II as Revealed by TICOM Investigations," prepared by chief, Army Security Agency, 1 May 1946. Short title: TICOM Report, NSA, DOCID 3560861. Found online. The Germans had not broken PURPLE, however.

3. Colville, *Fringes*, 419; and Liddell Diary, 6 Aug. 1941. See also, Joseph P. Lash, *Roosevelt and Churchill, 1939–1941* (New York: W.W. Norton & Company, 1978), 393, and the allusion to "leakage" in Churchill, *Grand Alliance*, 430.

4. Nicolai, *German Secret Service*, 208. It was not a healthy practice. Spies caught with such documents would be shot.

5. OKW issued a directive postponing the invasion to 21 Sep., with the go-ahead order to come a minimum of ten days in advance. It was then postponed indefinitely on 14 Sep. See "12 Top Secret Directives" of OKW, U.K. Air Ministry translations, LAC, RG24, 981.013(D29). This means both spies were dispatched when Canaris knew that the invasion order was unlikely to be given.

6. Andrew, *Authorized History*, 129–30, 158–59. It could, of course, have been simply a matter of purging Scotland Yard by dumping the infected part onto MI5.

7. Jeffery, *MI6*, 328–30. The very fact that his name was put forward to be considered by Hankey, Wilson, Cadogan, et cetera, gives him this stature. The governing Establishment centred on members of the Privy Council. (See Appendix.)

8. And they did have them. A set of topographical maps of major British cities belonging to OKH were captured by the Canadians. For the originals: LAC,

RG24, 20440. This file also contains ground photographs of potential air targets collected by German spies before the war.

9. Farago, *Game of Foxes*, 280 Farago sourced his other books extensively and used primary documents. The complete lack of endnotes in *Game of Foxes* suggests they existed in a draft manuscript but were dropped prior to publication.

10. Churchill, *War Speeches*, I, 210–14.

11. Churchill to Paul Reynaud, 16 May 1940. War Cabinet minutes, 15 May, TNA, CAB 65/13/9.

12. Indeed, in response to a German questionnaire Robertson submitted to him, Boyle specifically said that the Group locations of Fighter Command were not to be disclosed: Robertson, Note to File, 24 Jul. 1940, PRO, KV2/448, Doc. 900a. He did approve directing the Luftwaffe's attention to Harrogate, however, which is certainly a case of sending the bombers onto an innocent target.

13. The operations room at Uxbridge was completed just before the war, and built sixty feet underground. RAF Stanmore Park was in the London borough of Harrow with Fighter Command itself housed in nearby Bentley Priory.

14. Frederick Winterbotham, *The Ultra Spy: An Autobiography* (London: Macmillan, 1989), 208. Winterbotham is the "I" in this description.

15. Curry, *Security Service*, 247. This is the only direct reference to diverting German bombers on to cities of British choice that this writer found in available documents of the period. It apparently escaped the MI5 censor's scissors.

16. This would apply especially during 1940 and early 1941 when Robertson was still B3 and Arthur Owens's case officer.

17. Winterbotham, *Ultra Spy*, 128, 136–40.

18. Winterbotham, *Ultra Spy*, 153, and passim. In the Westminster parliamentary system, government department heads (ministers) normally sit in the House of Commons, where they are theoretically required to truthfully answer the questions put to them by Opposition MPs during the daily Question Period. The upper chamber — the House of Lords, the Senate of Canada, et cetera, — does not have the same onus of truth because the members are not elected. (Author's opinion.)

19. Winterbotham, *Ultra Spy*, 158–59, 164–66. Churchill had been in this loop before the war, which might explain why he did not object to releasing the weather information in 1939, although then the head of the Royal Navy.

20. Message 174 from 3504, 8 Aug. 1940; NARA, T-77, Reel 1540, Frame 419. Notice "Betrifft Identity Cards" followed by "Bezug ISAR."

21. Both frequented the Reform Club, which catered to political "progressives," so an investigator could easily have linked them there. According to Russian sources, Burgess claimed Grand had once given him the task of planting misinformation on Rothschild, designed to disrupt efforts to secure Palestine as a homeland for Jews, which, if true, Grand would certainly have remembered: John Costello and Oleg Tsarev, *Deadly Illusions* (New York: Crown Publishers, 1993), 239–40, citing a letter from Burgess in his NKVD file.

22. Kim Philby, *My Silent War* (London: MacGibbon & Kee, 1968), 12.

23. Andrew, *Authorized History*, 270–72.

24. The entry for 24 Sep. in his diary, where he mentions dining at the Reform Club with Burgess to 11:30 p.m. the evening of the Registry fire, establishes an alibi for Burgess, except that Liddell got the date wrong! See Chapter 7, Note 21.

25. See Hesketh, *Fortitude*, passim.

26. NARA, RG2 42, T-77, I540, Frame 0282.

27. PRO, KV2/674. This is MI5's CELERY "folder," which when examined in 2008, contained little more than some biographical material and copies of CELERY's correspondence with Robertson and Commodore Boyle. Dicketts's real name had been removed from all documents and on one the name had been cut out with a razor blade. See also, "Ripples in Time," *Straits Times*, 24 Oct. 1930; and "Charming Crook," *Milwaukee Sentinal*, 13 Nov. 1949. For straight gin, see PRO, KV2/451, Doc. 1658z.

28. Ritter, *Deckname*, 213–15.

29. Ritter, *Deckname*, 242–52. He places the meeting in Oct. 1940, but this does not properly fit into the sequence of his descriptions of the other 1940 spies. For evidence it was February: Hamburg to OKW, 27 Feb. 1941; 3504, meldet bei einem Treff in Lissabon am 17.2.41; and regarding the latest FLAK guns being developed in Britain, NARA, T-77, Reel 1540. There was one report a day taken from Owens between 15–20 Feb. and all were sent on 27 Feb. The message numbers in the lower right corner are consecutive. This proves the meeting took place and Ritter then returned to Hamburg to file his reports.

30. Popov, *Spy/Counterspy*, 76.

31. Deutsch, *Conspiracy*, 149–66; and Hoffman, *German Resistance*, 60–61. See also, Chapter 6.

32. PRO, KV3/3.

33. Postwar interview with Madame Szymanska, Colvin, *Chief of Intelligence*, 91–2, 138. The available intercepted movement messages have him in Vienna in April, and Salonic, Athens, and Sofia to late May, PRO, KV3/3. For Szymanska being used by Canaris as a contact with MI6, see Lahousen, III,1. Also, Jefferys, *MI6*, 380–82. He suggests she was an agent developed by MI6 but the facts are she was *provided to* MI6.

34. Colville, *Fringes*, 346–47. This particular item is especially valuable because accounts of the informal meetings of the Allied decision-makers by independent observers are rare, but one can be sure these informal sessions were where much of the real work was done. Colville was a minor staffer in Churchill's entourage who happened to be in the room. He kept a diary, which is preserved in longhand.

CHAPTER 19 — EPILOGUE

1. John Campbell, "A Retrospective on John Masterman's *The Double-Cross System*," *International Journal of Intelligence and CounterIntelligence* 18 (2005): passim; and C.J. Masterman, *On the Chariot Wheel: An Autobiography* (Oxford: Oxford University Press, 1975), 348–55. This is a valuable social document for the insight it gives into Britain's privileged class of the 1930s.
2. Masterman, *Chariot Wheel*, 176 and passim.
3. Apart from anything White knew from his own secret sources, he had at hand the postwar, after-action report of Roger Hesketh dealing with deception operations in 1944. Thorough and honest, the case it makes for the success of Plan *Bodyguard* and *Fortitude* is very weak, and Hesketh dismisses earlier efforts like Plan *Starkey*. It was released by MI5 in the late 1990s. See Roger Hesketh, *Fortitude: The D-Day Deception Plan* (New York: Overlook Press, 2000). One must ignore the claims in the "Introduction" and read the book.
4. Curry, *Security Service*, 247. He mentions that details can be obtained from the "B1A sectional report." Because it was a directorate that included the XX Committee, this was probably the "history" Masterman wrote, co-opting it to his own credit. The permission to report the weather had actually been obtained in 1939. See Chapter 3.
5. This writer was an overseas post-graduate student at Leeds University 1966–68. Student militancy was very strong, but to a Canadian looking on, the demonstrations seemed to have more show than depth. The protest marches were huge, however, and certainly would have worried the authorities.
6. Tom Bower, *The Perfect English Spy: Sir Dick White and the Secret War 1935–90* (London: William Heinemann, 1995), passim. Blunt and Liddell were exposed by the accusations of Michael Straight and Goronwy Rees.
7. Farago listed Masterman's *The Double-Cross System in the Second World War* in the Unpublished Documents section of the "Bibliography" of *The Game of Foxes* (662). Note the slight variation from the actual title of Masterman's book and the fact that Farago finished his in 1971. See Note 14 below.
8. Farago, *Game of Foxes*, 269. The messages he describes are all to be found in NARA, T77, 1540.
9. Farago, *Game of Foxes*, 175, 270–71, 662. In addition to his reference to Masterman's book-to-be in his "Bibliography," Farago's designation of Masterman

as the "official historian" of double-cross is further evidence that Farago had a preview of his work. The "two allusions" refer to the giving of the location of an aircraft factory and the attempt to draw air attacks onto aerodromes, an ineffectual strategy adopted for TATE after establishment of the Wireless Board: See Masterman, *Double-Cross*, 11, 83.

10. PRO, KV2/451, Doc. 1803a. It is bracketed in the file by "Extract from Ritter's final interrogation report," 16 Jan. 1946, Doc. 1802b; and Gwyer to Major Vesey, 15 May 1946, Doc. 1804a. Apparently Owens and Caroli were still in custody when Doc. 1803a was written.

11. PRO, KV2/451, Doc. 1803a. Some mistakes: McCarthy was planted on Owens (Chapter 18) and the first meeting at sea was set for 21 May 1940. See Spruch nr 115 von 3504, NARA, T-77, 1540.

12. Farago, *Game of Foxes*, 159.

13. Farago, *Game of Foxes* (New York: David Mackay, Advance Reading Copy — tentative publishing date, 14 Jan. 1972).

14. CO U.S. Naval Advanced Base Weser River to CO British Army of the Rhine, 19 Jan. 1946, with attachments, PRO, KV3/207. Bremen was in the British occupation zone, so liaison had to be with the U.S. Navy presence in the port. Note Farago's description of finding the microfilms in a U.S. Navy footlocker at NARA: Farago, *Game of Foxes*, xi.

15. Campbell, "A Retrospective," *IJIC*: 326. He bases his statement that the two books came out "within weeks" of each other on a collection of newspaper reviews.

16. Anyone who doubts the seriousness of the "war" in the 1960s in the inner sanctums of Western governments should be reminded that the Cuban Missile Crisis took place in 1962, and brought the world within a hair's breadth of nuclear conflagration.

17. White used the term. See Campbell, "A Retrospective," *IJIC*: 320–53.

18. For how the Pearl Harbor controversy played into disillusionment with the war in Vietnam, see Frank Paul Mintz, *Revisionism and the Origins of Pearl Harbor* (Lanham, MD: University Press of America, 1985), 69–77.

APPENDIX: THE HISTORICAL CONTEXT

1. Schellenberg, *Invasion 1940*, 26.

SELECT BIBLIOGRAPHY

PRIMARY SOURCES

DHH   Directorate of History and Heritage — Ottawa

LAC   Library and Archives Canada — Ottawa: Record Groups 24 20518; RG 25 2859, 5742

NARA   National Archives and Records Administration (NARA) — Washington: Record Group 65, IWG and FBI WWII HQ files; RG 165; RG 242, T-77, reels 1529-1569; RG 319, IRR and XE files; RG 457, HCC, SRH, SRIC; RG 65, FBI WWII HQ files

NSA   National Security Agency — Washington

PHA   *Investigation of the Pearl Harbor Attack: Report of the Joint Committee on the Investigation of the Pearl Harbor Attack, Pursuant of S. Con. Res. 27, 79th Congress, A Concurrent Resolution to Investigate the Attack on Pearl Harbor on December 7, 1941, and Events and Circumstances Relating Thereto, and Additional Views of Mr. Keefe, Together with Minority Views of Mr. Ferguson and Mr. Brewster.* 39 vols. Washington, D.C.: United States Government Printing Office, 1946.

PRO   The National Archives (TNA) a.k.a. the Public Record Office — London: Record Groups CAB, KV2, KV3, KV4, FO, WO

SECONDARY SOURCES

Abshagen, K.H. *Canaris*. London: Hutchinson, 1956.

Andrew, Christopher. "Churchill and Intelligence." In *Leaders and Intelligence*, ed. Michael Handel. London: Routledge, 1989.

————. *The Defence of the Realm: The Authorized History of MI5*. Toronto: Viking, 2009.

————. *Her Majesty's Secret Service: The Making of the British Intelligence Community*. London: Hodder & Stoughton, 1986.

Barros, James, and Richard Gregor. *Double Deception: Stalin, Hitler and the Invasion of Russia*. DeKalb, IL: Northern Illinois University Press, 1995.

Basset, Richard. *Hitler's Spy Chief: The Wilhelm Canaris Mystery*. London: Cassell, 2005.

Bazna, Elyesa. *I Was Cicero*. London: Andre Deutsch, 1962.

Benton, Kenneth. "The ISOS Years: Madrid 1941–3." *Journal of Contemporary History* 30, No. 3 (July 1995): 359–410.

Best, S. Payne. *The Venlo Incident*. London: Hutchinson, 1949.

Birch, Frank. *The Official History of British Sigint, 1914–1945*. Vol. I. Pt.1. Milton Keynes, UK: The Military Press, 2004.

Bleicher, Hugo. *Colonel Henri's Story*. London: William Kimber, 1954.

Borchers, Major E. *Abwehr Contre Résistance*. Paris: Amiot-Dumont, 1949.

Borovik, Genrikh. *The Philby Files*. Toronto: Little Brown and Company, 1994.

Bower, Tom. *The Perfect English Spy: Sir Dick White and the Secret War, 1935–90*. London: William Heineman, 1995.

Bratzel, John F., and Leslie B. Rout, Jr. "Pearl Harbor, Microdots, and J. Edgar Hoover." *American Historical Review* 87, No. 5 (December 1982): 1342–1351.

Bryden, John. *Best-Kept Secret: Canadian Secret Intelligence in the Second World War*. Toronto: Lester, 1993.

Budiansky, Stephen. *Battle of Wits: The Complete Story of Codebreaking in World War II*. New York: Simon & Schuster, 2000.

Bywater, Hector C., and H.C. Ferraby. *Strange Intelligence: Memoirs of Naval Secret Service*. London: Constable & Company, 1931.

Campbell, John. "A Retrospective on John Masterman's *The Double-Cross System*." *International Journal of Intelligence and CounterIntelligence* 18 (2005): 320–353.

Carré, Mathilde-Lily. *I Was "The Cat."* London: Souvenir Press, 1960.

Carter, Miranda. *Anthony Blunt: His Lives*. London: Macmillan, 2001.

Cave Brown, Anthony. *Wild Bill Donovan: The Last Hero*. New York: Times Books, 1982.

Churchill, Winston. Introduction to *I Was A Spy!* by Marthe McKenna. New York: Robert McBride & Co., 1933.

―――. *The Second World War.* 6 vols. Boston: Houghton, Mifflin, 1950–1953.

Clausen, Henry, and Bruce Lee. *Pearl Harbor: Final Judgement.* 1992. Cambridge, MA: Da Capo Press, 2001.

Colville, John. *Fringes of Power: Downing Street Diaries, 1939–1955.* London: Hodder & Stoughton, 1985.

Colvin, Ian. *Chief of Intelligence.* London: Victor Gollancz, 1951.

Compton, Arthur H. *Atomic Quest.* Oxford: Oxford University Press, 1956.

Costello, John, and Oleg Tsarev. *Deadly Illusions.* New York: Crown Publishers, 1993.

Curry, John Court. *The Security Service 1908–1945: The Official History.* 1946. London: Public Record Office, 1999.

Curwain, Eric. "Almost Top Secret." Unpublished monograph. Pre 1982.

Deighton, Len. *Blitzkrieg.* London: Triad/Panther Books, 1985.

Delarue, Jacques. *Histoire de la Gestapo.* Paris: Fayard, 1962.

Deutsch, Harold. *The Conspiracy Against Hitler in the Twilight War.* Minneapolis, MN: University of Minnesota Press, 1968.

De Wohl, Louis. *The Stars of War and Peace.* London: Rider and Company, 1952.

Donat, Robert, and Madeleine Carroll. *The 39 Steps.* Film. Directed by Alfred Hitchcock. London: Gaumont-British Pictures, 1935

Dorril, Stephen. *MI6: Fifty Years of Special Operations.* London: Fourth Estate, 2000.

Dourlein, Pieter. *Inside North Pole: A Secret Agent's Story.* London: William Kimber, 1953.

Drea, Edward. *MacArthur's ULTRA: Codebreaking and the War against Japan, 1942–1945.* Lawrence, KS: University Press of Kansas, 1992.

Eade, Charles, ed. *The War Speeches of the Rt. Hon. Winston S. Churchill.* Vol. II. London: Cassell & Company, 1952.

Eberle, Henrik, and Matthias Uhl, eds. *The Hitler Book: The Secret Dossier Prepared for Stalin from the Interrogations of Hitler's Personal Aides.* New York: PublicAffairs, 2005.

Elliot, Geoffrey. *Gentleman Spymaster: How Lt.-Col. Tommy "Tar" Robertson Double-Crossed the Nazis.* London: Methuen, 2011.

"The End of the German Intelligence Service." *Interim: British Army of the Rhine Intelligence Review* VIII (24 Sept. 1945).

Ewing, Alfred W. *The Man of Room 40: The Life of Sir Alfred Ewing.* London: Hutchinson & Co., 1937.

Farago, Ladilas. *The Broken Seal: The Story of "Operation Magic" and the Pearl Harbor Disaster.* New York: Random House, 1967.

―――. *The Game of the Foxes.* New York: David McKay, 1972.

Fischer, Benjamin. "A.k.a. 'Dr. Rantzau': The Enigma of Major Nikolaus Ritter." *Centre for the Study of Intelligence Bulletin* 11 (Summer 2000): 8–11.

FitzGibbon, Constantine. *Secret Intelligence in the Twentieth Century.* London: Hart-Davis, 1976.

Fleming, Peter. *Operation Sea Lion: The Projected German Invasion of England in 1940*. New York: Simon & Schuster, 1957.

Fouche Gaines, Helen. *Elementary Cryptanalysis*. Boston: American Photographic Publishing, 1943. (1939)

Fuchs, Thomas. *A Concise Biography of Hitler*. New York: Berkley Books, 2000.

Garbo, Greta, and Lionel Barrymore. *Mata Hari*. Film. Directed by George Fitzmaurice. Hollywood, CA: MGM, 1931.

GARBO: The Spy Who Saved D-Day. 1945. Toronto: Dundurn, 2000, as part of the Secret History Files series, with an introduction by Mark Seaman.

Giskes, H.J. *London Calling North Pole*. London: William Kimber, 1953.

Grunberger, Richard. *The 12-Year Reich: A Social History of Nazi Germany*. New York: Ballantine, 1972.

Hanyok, Robert. "Eavesdropping on Hell." *www.nsa.gov/publications*.

Hanyok, Robert, and David Mowry. *West Wind Clear: Cryptography and the Winds Message Controversy*. Washington, D.C.: National Security Agency, 2011.

Hayward, James. *Double Agent Snow: The True Story of Arthur Owens, Hitler's Chief Spy in England*. London: Simon & Schuster, 2013.

Hesketh, Roger. *Fortitude: The D-Day Deception Plan*. 1948. New York: Overlook Press, 2000.

Hewlett, Richard G., and Oscar E. Anderson, Jr. *The New World 1939–1946*. Vol. I, *A History of the United States Atomic Energy Commission*. University Park, PA: Pennsylvania State University Press, 1962.

Hiley, Nicholas. "Counter-Espionage and Security in Great Britain during the First World War." *English Historical Review* 101 No. 400 (1986): 635–70.

Hinsley, F.H. et al. *British Intelligence in the Second World War*. Vol I, *Its Influence on Strategy and Operations*. London: HMSO, 1979.

Hinsley, F.H., and C.A.G. Simkins. *British Intelligence in the Second World War*. Vol. IV: *Security and Counter Intelligence*. London: HMSO, 1990.

Hoffmann, Peter. *The History of the German Resistance, 1933–45*. Cambridge, MA: MIT Press, 1977.

Höhne, Heinz. *Canaris*. New York: Doubleday, 1979.

Howard, Michael. *British Intelligence in the Second World War*. Vol. V, *Strategic Deception*. London: HMSO, 1990.

Hyde, Montgomery. *Room 3604*. 1962. New York: Dell, 1964.

James, Admiral Sir William. *The Codebreakers of Room 40*. New York: St Martin's Press, 1956.

Jeffery, Keith. *The Secret History of MI6*. New York: Penguin Press, 2010.

Jones, R.V. *Most Secret War*. London: Hamish Hamilton Ltd., 1978.

———. *Reflections on Intelligence*. London: Mandarin Paperback, 1989.

Jowitt, The Earl. *Some Were Spies*. London: Hodder & Stoughton, 1954.

Kahn, David. *The Codebreakers: The Story of Secret Writing*. 1967. New York: New American Library, 1973.

———. *Hitler's Spies: German Military Intelligence in World War II*. New York: Macmillan, 1978.

Kimmel, Husband E. *Admiral Kimmel's Story*. Chicago: Henry Regnery, 1955.

Kimmel, Thomas Jr., and J.A. Williams. "Why Did the Attack on Pearl Harbor Occur? An Intelligence Failure? FBI Director J. Edgar Hoover Thought He Knew." *Intelligencer* 17, No. 1 (Winter-Spring 2009): 53–59.

Knightly, Phillip. *Philby: KGB Master Spy*. London: Andre Deutsch, 1988.

Korda, Michael. *With Wings Like Eagles: The Untold Story of the Battle of Britain*. New York: HarperCollins, 2009.

Lamb, Richard. *Churchill as War Leader*. New York: Carroll & Graf, 1991.

Landau, Henry. *All's Fair: The Story of the British Secret Service*. New York: G.P. Putnam's Sons, 1934.

———. *Secrets of the White Lady*. New York: G.P. Putnam's Sons, 1935.

Lash, Joseph P. *Roosevelt and Churchill 1939–1941: The Partnership that Saved the West*. New York: W. W. Norton & Company, 1978.

Layton, Edwin T. *And I Was There*. Old Saybrook, CT: Koneck & Kinecky, 1985.

Liddell Hart, B.H. *The Defence of Britain*. London: Faber and Faber, 1939.

Lockhart, R.H. Bruce. *British Agent*. New York: G.P. Putnam's Sons, 1933.

Macdonald, Bill. *The True Intrepid*. Surrey, BC: Timberholme, 1998.

Mackenzie, Compton. *Greek Memories*. London: Chatto and Windus, 1939.

Masterman, J.C. *On the Chariot Wheel: An Autobiography*. Oxford: Oxford University Press, 1975.

———. *The Double-Cross System in the War of 1939 to 1945*. New Haven, CT; and London: Yale University Press, 1972.

Masters, Anthony. *The Man Who Was M: The Life of Maxwell Knight*. Oxford: Basil Blackwell, 1984.

May, Ernest. *Strange Victory: Hitler's conquest of France*. New York: Hill & Wang, 2000.

Mendelsohn, John., ed. *Covert Warfare*. New York: Garland Publishing, 1989.

McCollum, Arthur A. "Unheeded Warnings." In *Air Raid! Pearl Harbor: Recollections of a Day of Infamy*, ed., Paul Stillwell. Annapolis, MD: Naval Institute Press, 1981.

Miller, Russell. *Codename Tricycle*. London: Secker & Warberg, 2004.

Mintz, Frank Paul. *Revisionism and the Origins of Pearl Harbor*. Lanham, MD: University Press of America, 1985.

Modin, Yuri. *My Five Cambridge Friends*. New York: Farrar Straus Giroux, 1994.

Montagu, Ewen. *Beyond Top Secret U*. London: Peter Davies, 1977.

———. *The Man who Never Was*. New York: J.P. Lippencott, 1954.

Moravec, Frantisek. Introduction to *Master of Spies*, by C.J. Masterman. London: The Bodley Head, 1975.

Moreland, Nigel. *Science in Crime Detection*. London: Robert Hale, 1958.

Morgenstern, George. *Pearl Harbor: The Story of the Secret War*. New York: Devin-Adair Company, 1947.

Mungo, Melvin. *Manstein: Hitler's Greatest General*. New York: St. Martin's Press, 2011.

Mure, David. *Master of Deception*. London: William Kimber, 1980.

Murphy, David E. *What Stalin Knew: The Enigma of Barbarossa*. New Haven, CT; and London: Yale University Press, 2005.

Nicolai, Walter. *Geheime Machte; Internationale Spionage un ihre Bekampfung im Weltkrieg and Heute*. Leipzig: K.F. Köhler, 1925.

————. *The German Secret Service*. London: Stanley Paul, 1924.

O'Neill, Robert J. *The German Army and the Nazi Party*. London: Corgi Books, 1968.

Owen, Frank. *The Eddie Chapman Story*. New York: Julian Messner, 1954.

Paine, Lauran. *German Military Intelligence in World War II: The Abwehr*. New York: Stein and Day, 1984.

Papeleux, Leon. *L'Admiral Canaris entre Franco et Hitler*. Paris: Casterman, 1977.

Papen, Franz von. *Memoires*. New York: E.P. Dutton & Company, 1955.

Peis, Gunter. *Mirror of Deception*. London: Weidenfeld and Nicolson, 1977.

Penrose, Barrie, and Simon Freeman. *Conspiracy of Silence*. London: Grafton Books, 1986.

Persico, Josephe (sic). *Roosevelt's Secret War: FDR and World War II Espionage*. New York: Random House, 2001.

Pfennigwerth, Ian. *A Man of Intelligence: The Life of Captain Theodore Nave*. New South Wales: Rosenberg, 2006.

Philby, Kim. *My Silent War*. London: MacGibbon & Kee, 1968.

Pinto, Oreste. *The Spycatcher Omnibus*. London: Hodder & Stoughton, 1964.

Popov, Dusko. *Spy/Counterspy*. New York: Grosset and Dunlap, 1974.

Powers, Richard. *Secrecy and Power: The Life of J. Edgar Hoover*. New York: The Free Press, 1987.

Putlitz, Wolfgang zu. *The Putlitz Dossier*. London: Allan Wingate, 1957.

Reile, Oscar. *L'Abwehr: le Contre-Espionage Allemand en France de 1935 a 1945*. Paris: Editions France-Empire, 1962.

————. *Geheime Westfront: Die Abwehr, 1935–1945*. N.p.: Welsermühl, 1962.

Reynolds, Nicholas. *Treason Was No Crime: Ludwig Beck*. London: William Kimber, 1976.

Ritter, Nikolaus. *Deckname Dr. Rantzau*. Hamburg: Hoffmann and Campe, 1972.

Roberts Rinehart, Mary. *The Bat*. New York: Grosset & Dunlap, 1926.

Rowan, Richard, *The Story of the Secret Service*. New York: Doubleday, 1937.

Rushbringer, James, and Eric Nave. *Betrayal at Pearl Harbor*. New York: Summit Books, 1991.

Schellenberg, Walter. *Invasion 1940: The Nazi Invaion Plan for Britain*, with an introduction by John Erickson. London: St. Ermin's Press, 2000.

Scherer, James A.B. *Japan Defies the World.* Indianapolis, IN: Bobbs-Merril, 1938.

Seltzer, William. "Population Statistics, the Holocaust, and the Nuremberg Trials." *Population and Development Review* 24 No. 3 (September 1998): 511–52.

Shirer, William L. *The Rise and the Fall of the Third Reich.* New York: Simon & Schuster, 1960.

Sidney, Sylvia, and Oskar Homolka. *Sabotage.* Film. Directed by Alfred Hitchcock. London: General Film Distributors, 1936.

Smith. Michael, and Ralph Erskine, eds. *Action This Day.* London; and New York: Bantam Press, 2001.

Stephens, R.W.G. *Camp 020: MI5 and the Nazi Spies.* 1946. New edition, with an introduction by Oliver Hoare. London: Public Record Office, 2000.

Stephenson, William, ed. *The Secret History of British Intelligence in the Americas, 1940–45.* Introduction by Nigel West. New York: Fromm International, 1999.

Stevenson, William. *A Man Called Intrepid.* London: Macmillan, 1976.

Stimson, Henry L. *The Far Eastern Crisis.* New York: Harper & Bros., 1936.

Stinnett, Robert. *Day of Deceit: The Truth about FDR and Pearl Harbor.* New York: The Free Press, 2000.

Strodes, James. *Allen Dulles: Master of Spies.* Washington: Regnery Publishing, 1999.

Thomson, Basil. *My Experience at Scotland Yard.* New York: Doubleday, Page & Company, 1923.

Toland, John. *Infamy: Pearl Harbor and Its Aftermath.* New York: Doubleday, 1982.

Trevor-Roper, Hugh. "Sideways into S.I.S." In *The Name of Intelligence: Essays in Honor of Walter Pforzheimer,* eds. Hayden Peake and Samuel Halpern. Washington, D.C.: NIBC Press, 1994.

Troy, Thomas. "The British Assault on Hoover: The Tricycle Case," *International Journal of Intelligence and Counterintelligence* 3, No. 2 (1 January 1989):169–209.

———. *Wild Bill and Intrepid.* New Haven, CT; and London: Yale University Press, 1996.

West, Nigel, and Oleg Tsarev. *Crown Jewels: The British Secrets at the Heart of the KGB's Archives.* London: HarperCollins, 1998.

Whitehead, Don. *The FBI Story.* New York: Random House, 1956.

Whitwell, John [pseud. for Kenneth Benton]. *British Agent.* London: William Kimber, 1966.

Wighton, Charles, and Gunter Peis. *Hitler's Spies and Saboteurs.* New York: Henry Holt and Company, 1958.

Wilford, Timothy. *Pearl Harbor Redefined.* Lanham, MD: University Press of America, 2001

Williams, Carl. "The Policing of Political Beliefs in Great Britain, 1914–1918." London: London School of Economics, Centre for Philosophy of Natural and Social Science, [2002?].

Willoughby, Charles. *MacArthur 1941–1951*. London: William Heinemann, 1956.

Winterbotham, F[rederick].W. *Secret and Personal*. London: William Kimber, 1969.

———. *The Ultra Spy*. London: Macmillan, 1989.

Wohlstetter, Roberta. *Pearl Harbor: Warning and Decision*. Redwood City, CA: Stanford University Press, 1962.

Wright, Peter. *Spycatcher: The Candid Autobiography of a Senior Intelligence Officer*. Toronto: Stoddart, 1987.

Yardley, Herbert. *The American Black Chamber*. Indianapolis, IN: Bobbs-Merril, 1931.

———. *Secret Service in America*. London: Faber & Faber, 1941.

INDEX

ABOUT THE AUTHOR

A noted Canadian journalist and politician, John Bryden is also a respected military historian. His *Deadly Allies* tells the story of Canada's role in the development of chemical and biological weapons during the Second World War, and *Best Kept Secret* deals with Canada's involvement in wartime code and cipher breaking.